Physics 1

Controlled Assessment

Exam Help

Reference

Published by CGP

Editors:
Katie Braid, Charlotte Burrows, Mary Falkner, Christopher Lindle, Matteo Orsini Jones, Rachael Rogers, Camilla Simson, Hayley Thompson, Megan Tyler, Rachel Ward, Karen Wells, Charlotte Whiteley, Sarah Williams.

Contributors:
Mike Bossart, Gemma Hallam, Adrian Schmit.

From original material by Paddy Gannon.

ISBN: 978 1 84762 223 5

With thanks to Janet Cruse-Sawyer, Jane Ellingham, Ian Francis, Jamie Sinclair and Glenn Rogers for the proofreading.
With thanks to Laura Jakubowski for the copyright research.

Groovy website: www.cgpbooks.co.uk
Printed by Elanders Ltd, Newcastle upon Tyne.
Jolly bits of clipart from CorelDRAW®

How to use this book

Learning Objectives
- These tell you exactly what you need to learn, or be able to do, for the exam.
- There's a specification reference at the bottom that links to the AQA A specification.

Examples
These are here to help you understand the theory.

Tips and Exam Tips
- There are tips throughout the book to help you understand the theory.
- There are also exam tips to help you with answering exam questions.

Learning Objectives:
- Know that crude oil is a mixture of lots of different compounds.
- Know that the substances in a mixture are not chemically bonded to each other.
- Know that most of the compounds in crude oil are hydrocarbons.
- Know that the properties of substances are not changed when the substance is in a mixture.
- Know that mixtures can be separated using physical methods such as distillation.
- Understand how fractional distillation is used to separate crude oil into fractions.

Specification Reference C1.4.1, C1.4.2

1. Fractional Distillation of Crude Oil

Crude oil is a fossil fuel that is formed deep underground from the remains of plants and animals. Loads of useful products can be made from crude oil using a technique called fractional distillation.

What is crude oil?
Crude oil is a **mixture** of many different compounds. A mixture consists of two (or more) elements or compounds that aren't chemically bonded to each other. Most of the compounds in crude oil are **hydrocarbon** molecules. Hydrocarbons are basically fuels such as petrol and diesel. They're made of only carbon and hydrogen.

Properties of mixtures
There are no chemical bonds between the different parts of a mixture, so the different hydrocarbon molecules in crude oil aren't chemically bonded to one another. This means that they all keep their original properties, such as their boiling points (the temperature at which they turn from a liquid into a gas). The properties of a mixture are just a mixture of the properties of the separate parts.

Separating mixtures
Because the substances in a mixture all keep their original properties, the parts of a mixture can be separated out by physical methods.

Example

Crude oil can be split up into its separate fractions by fractional distillation. Each fraction contains molecules with a similar number of carbon atoms to each other.

Figure 1: A fractionating column.

Fractional distillation
Crude oil can be split into separate groups of hydrocarbons using a technique called fractional distillation. The crude oil is pumped into piece of equipment known as a fractionating column, which works continuously (it doesn't get switched off). This fractionating column has a temperature gradient running through it — it's hottest at the bottom and coldest at the top.

164   Chemistry 1.4   Crude Oil and Fuels

Exam Tip
You could also be asked to interpret data on rooting powders in the exam.

2. Rooting powders
Plant cuttings won't always grow in soil. If you add rooting powder, which contains the plant hormone auxin, they'll produce roots rapidly and start growing as new plants. This helps growers to produce lots of clones of a really good plant very quickly.

Figure 9: A gardener using rooting powder when planting cuttings.

Practice Questions — Fact Recall

Q1 What is gravitropism?

Q2 What effect does auxin have on cell elongation in a plant root?

Q3 Explain how plant roots grow in response to moisture in the soil.

Practice Questions — Application

Q1 A scientist conducted an experiment to study phototropism in cress seedlings. 12 cress seeds were planted in Petri dish A and left directly under a light source. Another 12 cress seeds were planted in Petri dish B and provided with a light source placed to one side. The growth of the seeds after two weeks is shown in the diagram:

light source

cress seedlings

A   B

Tip: Don't forget to refer to the experiment in your answer to Q1 a). Don't just talk about what you know about auxin.

a) Describe how the distribution of auxin in the shoots of the cress seedlings will differ between Petri dish A and Petri dish B.

b) i) Other than the position of the light source, the scientist tried to keep the conditions in both Petri dishes the same. Explain why she did this.

ii) Give two conditions that the scientist needed to keep the same during the experiment.

Q2 Dan grows plants for a garden centre. He is trying to work out the best rooting powder to use for his cuttings. From the same type of plant, he grows 50 cuttings in rooting powder A, 50 in rooting powder B and 50 without rooting powder. He grows all the cuttings under the same conditions. His results are shown in the table.

		Powder A	Powder B	No powder
Average increase in root length (mm)	After 1 week	8	10	6
	After 2 weeks	17	19	14
	After 3 weeks	24	28	20

a) From these results, what can you conclude about which rooting powder is the best to use? Explain your answer.

b) Explain why Dan grew some cuttings without rooting powder.

Practice Questions
- There are a lot of facts to learn for GCSE Science — fact recall questions test that you know them.
- Annoyingly, the examiners also expect you to be able to apply your knowledge to new situations — application questions give you plenty of practice at doing this.
- All the answers are in the back of the book.

How Science Works
- How Science Works is a big part of GCSE science. There's a whole section on it at the front of the book.
- How Science Works is also covered throughout the book wherever you see this symbol.

HOW SCIENCE WORKS

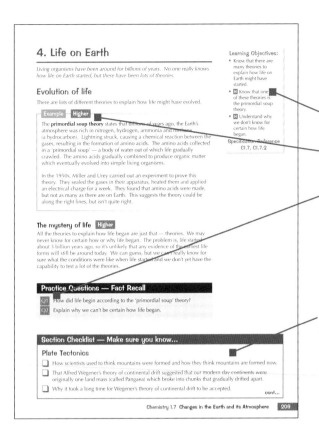

Higher Exam Material

- Some of the material in this book will only come up in the exam if you're sitting the higher exam papers.

- This material is clearly marked with boxes that look like this:

- If you're sitting the foundation papers, you don't need to learn it.

Section Checklist

Each section has a checklist at the end with boxes that let you tick off what you've learnt.

Glossary

There's a glossary at the back of the book full of all the definitions you need to know for the exam, plus loads of other useful words.

Exam-style Questions

- Practising exam-style questions is really important — there are some testing you on material from every section.

- They're the same style as the ones you'll get in the real exams.

- All the answers are in the back of the book, along with a mark scheme to show you how you get the marks.

- Higher-only questions are marked like this: **1** (b)

Controlled Assessment and Exam Help

There are sections at the back of the book stuffed full of things to help you with the controlled assessment and the exams.

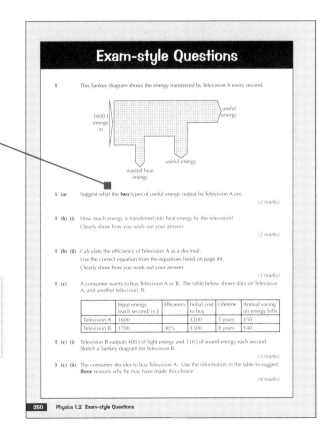

1. The Scientific Process

Science is all about finding things out and learning things about the world we live in. This topic is all about the scientific process — how a scientist's initial idea turns into a theory that is accepted by the wider scientific community.

Hypotheses

Scientists try to explain things. Everything. They start by observing something they don't understand — it could be anything, e.g. planets in the sky, a person suffering from an illness, what matter is made of... anything.

Then, they come up with a **hypothesis** — a possible explanation for what they've observed. The next step is to test whether the hypothesis might be right or not — this involves gathering evidence (i.e. data from investigations).

The scientist uses the hypothesis to make a **prediction** — a statement based on the hypothesis that can be tested. They then carry out an investigation. If data from experiments or studies backs up the prediction, you're one step closer to figuring out if the hypothesis is true.

Testing a hypothesis

Other scientists will use the hypothesis to make their own predictions, and carry out their own experiments or studies. They'll also try to reproduce the original investigations to check the results. And if all the experiments in the world back up the hypothesis, then scientists start to think it's true.

However, if a scientist somewhere in the world does an experiment that doesn't fit with the hypothesis (and other scientists can reproduce these results), then the hypothesis is in trouble. When this happens, scientists have to come up with a new hypothesis (maybe a modification of the old hypothesis, or maybe a completely new one).

Accepting a hypothesis

If pretty much every scientist in the world believes a hypothesis to be true because experiments back it up, then it usually goes in the textbooks for students to learn. Accepted hypotheses are often referred to as **theories**.

Our currently accepted theories are the ones that have survived this 'trial by evidence' — they've been tested many, many times over the years and survived (while the less good ones have been ditched). However... they never, never become hard and fast, totally indisputable fact. You can never know... it'd only take one odd, totally inexplicable result, and the hypothesising and testing would start all over again.

Learning Objectives:

- Know what a hypothesis and a prediction are and understand their roles in developing scientific ideas.
- Understand that scientists try to explain observations using evidence collected in investigations.
- Understand the importance of carrying out fair tests and collecting repeatable, reproducible and valid results.
- Understand why some decisions relating to science are not just based on scientific evidence but take other factors into account.

**Specification Reference
How Science Works**

Tip: Investigations include lab experiments and studies.

Tip: Sometimes it can take a really long time for a hypothesis to be accepted. Have a peek at the story of Alfred Wegener's theory of continental drift on pages 199-201 for a perfect example of this.

Example

Over time scientists have come up with different hypotheses about the structure of the atom.

 About 100 years ago we thought atoms looked like this.

 Then we thought they looked like this.

 And then we thought they looked like this.

Figure 1: *A scientist doing a laboratory experiment.*

Collecting evidence

If a hypothesis is going to get accepted, there needs to be good evidence for it. The way evidence is gathered can have a big effect on how trustworthy it is.

Results from experiments in laboratories are great. A lab is the easiest place to control variables so that they're all kept constant (except for the one you're investigating). This makes it easier to carry out a **fair test**. For things that you can't investigate in the lab (e.g. climate) you conduct scientific studies. As many of the variables as possible are controlled, to make it a fair test.

Old wives' tales, rumours, hearsay, "what someone said", and so on, should be taken with a pinch of salt. Without any evidence they're not scientific — they're just opinions.

Sample size

Data based on small samples isn't as good as data based on large samples. A sample should be representative of the whole population (i.e. it should share as many of the various characteristics in the population as possible) — a small sample can't do that as well.

The bigger the sample size the better, but scientists have to be realistic when choosing how big.

Example

If you were studying the health effects of adding chlorine to drinking water it'd be great to study everyone in the UK (a huge sample), but it'd take ages and cost a bomb. Studying a thousand people would be more realistic.

Quality of evidence

You can have confidence in the results if they can be repeated (during the same experiment) and other scientists can reproduce them too (in other experiments). If the results aren't **repeatable** or **reproducible**, you can't believe them.

> **Example**
>
> In 1989, two scientists claimed that they'd produced 'cold fusion' (the energy source of the Sun but without the big temperatures). It was huge news — if true, it would have meant free energy for the world forever. However, other scientists just couldn't reproduce the results, so they couldn't be believed. And until they are, 'cold fusion' isn't going to be accepted as fact.

Figure 2: *Stanley Pons and Martin Fleischmann — the scientists who allegedly discovered cold fusion.*

If results are repeatable and reproducible, they're said to be **reliable**.

Getting valid evidence

Evidence also needs to be **valid**. Valid means that the data answers the original question.

> **Example**
>
> **Do power lines cause cancer?**
>
> Some studies have found that children who live near overhead power lines are more likely to develop cancer. What they'd actually found was a **correlation** (relationship) between the variables "presence of power lines" and "incidence of cancer". They found that as one changed, so did the other.
>
> But this evidence is not enough to say that the power lines cause cancer, as other explanations might be possible. For example, power lines are often near busy roads, so the areas tested could contain different levels of pollution from traffic. So these studies don't show a definite link and so don't answer the original question.

Tip: See page 13 for more on correlation.

Communicating results

Once evidence is collected it can be shared with other people. It's important that the evidence isn't presented in a **biased** way. This can sometimes happen when people want to make a point, e.g. they overemphasise a relationship in the data. (Sometimes without knowing they're doing it.) And there are all sorts of reasons why people might want to do this.

> **Examples**
>
> - They want to keep the organisation or company that's funding the research happy. (If the results aren't what they'd like they might not give them any more money to fund further research.)
>
> - Governments might want to persuade voters, other governments, journalists, etc.

- Companies might want to 'big up' their products. Or make impressive safety claims.

- Environmental campaigners might want to persuade people to behave differently.

There's also a risk that if an investigation is done by a team of highly-regarded scientists it'll be taken more seriously than evidence from less well known scientists. But having experience, authority or a fancy qualification doesn't necessarily mean the evidence is good — the only way to tell is to look at the evidence scientifically (e.g. is it repeatable, valid, etc.).

Issues created by science

Scientific knowledge is increased by doing experiments. And this knowledge leads to scientific developments, e.g. new technologies or new advice. These developments can create issues though. For example, particular scientific developments might be ignored if they could create political issues, or emphasised if they help a particular cause.

Tip: See page 171 for more on global warming.

> **Example**
>
> Some governments were pretty slow to accept the fact that human activities are causing global warming, despite all the evidence. This is because accepting it means they've got to do something about it, which costs money and could hurt their economy. This could lose them a lot of votes.

Scientific developments can cause a whole host of other issues too.

Figure 3: Dolly the sheep — the first mammal to be cloned. A great scientific advance but some people think that cloning animals is morally wrong.

> **Examples**
>
> - **Economic issues:** Society can't always afford to do things scientists recommend (e.g. investing heavily in alternative energy sources) without cutting back elsewhere.
>
> - **Social issues:** Decisions based on scientific evidence affect people — e.g. should fossil fuels be taxed more highly (to invest in alternative energy)? Should alcohol be banned (to prevent health problems)? Would the effect on people's lifestyles be acceptable?
>
> - **Environmental issues:** Chemical fertilisers may help us produce more food — but they also cause environmental problems.
>
> - **Ethical issues:** There are a lot of things that scientific developments have made possible, but should we do them? E.g. clone humans, develop better nuclear weapons.

2. Limitations of Science

Science has taught us an awful lot about the world we live in and how things work — but science doesn't have the answer for everything.

Questions science hasn't answered yet

We don't understand everything. And we never will. We'll find out more, for sure — as more hypotheses are suggested, and more experiments are done. But there'll always be stuff we don't know.

> **Examples**
>
> - Today we don't know as much as we'd like about the impacts of global warming. How much will sea level rise? And to what extent will weather patterns change?
> - We also don't know anywhere near as much as we'd like about the Universe. Are there other life forms out there? And what is the Universe made of?

These are complicated questions. At the moment scientists don't all agree on the answers because there isn't enough repeatable, reproducible and valid evidence. But eventually, we probably will be able to answer these questions once and for all. All we need is more evidence. But by then there'll be loads of new questions to answer.

Questions science can't answer

There are some questions that all the experiments in the world won't help us answer — the "should we be doing this at all?" type questions.

> **Example**
>
> Think about new drugs which can be taken to boost your 'brain power'. Some people think they're good. Or at least no worse than taking vitamins or eating oily fish. They could let you keep thinking for longer, or improve your memory. It's thought that new drugs could allow people to think in ways that are beyond the powers of normal brains — in effect, to become geniuses.
>
> Other people say they're bad. Taking them would give you an unfair advantage in exams, say. And perhaps people would be pressured into taking them so that they could work more effectively, and for longer hours.

The question of whether something is morally or ethically right or wrong can't be answered by more experiments — there is no "right" or "wrong" answer. The best we can do is get a consensus from society — a judgement that most people are more or less happy to live by. Science can provide more information to help people make this judgement, and the judgement might change over time. But in the end it's up to people and their conscience.

Learning Objectives:
- Know that there are some things that haven't yet been explained by science because we don't have enough good evidence.
- Understand why some questions can't ever be answered by science alone.

Specification Reference
How Science Works

Figure 1: *The night sky. We can use high powered telescopes to observe the Universe but we still have little idea what it's made from or how it was formed.*

Tip: It's important that scientists don't get wrapped up in whether they <u>can</u> do something, before stopping to think about whether they <u>should</u> do it. Some experiments have to be approved by ethics councils before scientists are allowed to carry them out.

3. Designing Investigations

To be a good scientist you need to know how to design a good experiment. That's what this topic is all about — how to make your experiment safe and how to make sure you get good quality results.

Making predictions from a hypothesis

Scientists observe things and come up with hypotheses to explain them (see page 1). To figure out whether a **hypothesis** might be correct or not you need to do an investigation to gather some evidence. The evidence will help support or disprove the hypothesis.

The first step is to use the hypothesis to come up with a **prediction** — a statement about what you think will happen that you can test.

Tip: Sometimes the words 'hypothesis' and 'prediction' are used interchangeably.

Example

If your hypothesis is "eating a diet containing a large amount of saturated fat causes a high blood cholesterol level", then your prediction might be "people who eat large amounts of saturated fats will have a high level of cholesterol in their blood".

Tip: See page 3 for more on valid evidence.

Investigations are used to see if there are patterns or relationships between two variables. For example, to see if there's a pattern or relationship between the variables 'amount of saturated fats eaten' and 'blood cholesterol level'. The investigation has to be a **fair test** to make sure the evidence is **valid**.

Ensuring it's a fair test

Tip: A variable is just something in the experiment that can change.

In a lab experiment you usually change one variable and measure how it affects the other variable. To make it a fair test everything else that could affect the results should stay the same (otherwise you can't tell if the thing you're changing is causing the results or not — the data won't be valid).

Example

You might change only the temperature of a chemical reaction and measure how this affects the rate of reaction. You need to keep the concentration of the reactants the same, otherwise you won't know if any change in the rate of reaction is caused by the change in temperature, or a difference in reactant concentration.

Figure 1: *Students measuring the rate of a chemical reaction.*

The variable you change is called the **independent variable**. The variable you measure is called the **dependent variable**. The variables that you keep the same are called **control variables**.

Example

In the rate of reaction example above, temperature is the independent variable, the rate of the reaction is the dependent variable and the concentration of reactants and volume of reactants are control variables.

Control experiments and control groups

To make sure no other factors are affecting the results, you also have to include a **control experiment** — an experiment that's kept under the same conditions as the rest of the investigation, but doesn't have anything done to it.

Example

You investigate antibiotic resistance in bacteria by growing cultures of bacteria on agar plates, then adding paper discs soaked in antibiotic.

If the bacteria are resistant to the antibiotic they will continue to grow. If they aren't resistant a clear patch will appear around the disc where they have died or haven't grown.

A disc that isn't soaked in antibiotic is included to act as a control. This makes sure any result is down to the antibiotic, not the presence of a paper disc.

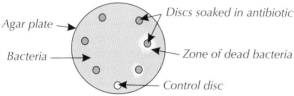

Figure 2: An investigation into antibiotic resistance.

It's important that a study is a fair test, just like a lab experiment. It's a lot trickier to control the variables in a study than it is in a lab experiment though. Sometimes you can't control them all, but you can use a **control group** to help. This is a group of whatever you're studying (people, plants, lemmings, etc.) that's kept under the same conditions as the group in the experiment, but doesn't have anything done to it.

Tip: A study is an investigation that doesn't take place in a lab.

Example

If you're studying the effect of pesticides on crop growth, pesticide is applied to one field but not to another field (the control field). Both fields are planted with the same crop, and are in the same area (so they get the same weather conditions).

The control field is there to try and account for variables like the weather, which don't stay the same all the time, but could affect the results.

Tip: A pesticide is a chemical that can be used to kill insects.

Figure 3: Crops being sprayed with pesticides.

Trial runs

It's a good idea to do a **trial run** (a quick version of your experiment) before you do the proper experiment. Trial runs are used to figure out the range (the upper and lower limit) of variable values used in the proper experiment. If you don't get a change in the dependent variable at the lower values in the trial run, you might narrow the range in the proper experiment. But if you still get a big change at the upper values you might increase the range.

> **Example**
>
> For a rate of reaction experiment, you might do a trial run with a temperature range of 10-50 °C. If there was no reaction at the lower end (e.g. 10-20 °C), you might narrow the range to 20-50 °C for the proper experiment.

Tip: If you don't have time to do a trial run, you could always look at the data other people have got doing a similar experiment and use a range and interval values similar to theirs.

Trial runs can also be used to figure out the intervals (gaps) between the values too. The intervals can't be too small (otherwise the experiment would take ages), or too big (otherwise you might miss something).

> **Example**
>
> If using 1 °C intervals doesn't give you much change in the rate of reaction each time, you might decide to use 5 °C intervals, e.g 20, 25, 30, 35, 40, 45, 50 °C.

Trial runs can also help you figure out whether or not your experiment is repeatable.

Tip: Consistently repeating the results is crucial for checking that your results are repeatable.

> **Example**
>
> If you repeat it three times and the results are all similar, the experiment is repeatable.

Ensuring your experiment is safe

To make sure your experiment is safe you must identify all the **hazards**. A hazard is something that can potentially cause harm. Hazards include:

Tip: You can find out about potential hazards by looking in textbooks, doing some internet research, or asking your teacher.

- Microorganisms: e.g. some bacteria can make you ill.
- Chemicals: e.g. sulfuric acid can burn your skin and alcohols catch fire easily.
- Fire: e.g. an unattended Bunsen burner is a fire hazard.
- Electricity: e.g. faulty electrical equipment could give you a shock.

Scientists need to manage the risk of hazards by doing things to reduce them.

Figure 4: *Scientists wearing safety goggles to protect their eyes during an experiment.*

> **Examples**
>
> - If you're working with sulfuric acid, always wear gloves and safety goggles. This will reduce the risk of the acid coming into contact with your skin and eyes.
> - If you're using a Bunsen burner, stand it on a heatproof mat. This will reduce the risk of starting a fire.

4. Collecting Data

Once you've designed your experiment, you need to get on and do it. Here's a guide to making sure the results you collect are good.

Getting good quality results

When you do an experiment you want your results to be **repeatable**, **reproducible** and as **accurate** and **precise** as possible.

To check repeatability you need to repeat the readings — you should repeat each reading at least three times. To make sure your results are reproducible you can cross check them by taking a second set of readings with another instrument (or a different observer). Checking your results match with secondary sources, e.g. other studies, also increases the reliability of your data.

Your data also needs to be accurate. Really accurate results are those that are really close to the true answer. Collecting lots of data and calculating a mean will improve the accuracy of your results. Your data also needs to be precise. Precise results are ones where the data is all really close to the mean (i.e. not spread out).

Learning Objectives:
- Know how to collect good quality data, taking repeatability, reproducibility, accuracy, precision and equipment selection and use into account.
- Understand what random errors, systematic errors and anomalous results are.

Specification Reference How Science Works

Tip: For more on the mean see page 11.

Tip: Sometimes, you can work out what result you should get at the end of an experiment (the theoretical result) by doing a bit of maths. If your experiment is accurate there shouldn't be much difference between the theoretical results and the result you actually get.

Example

Look at the data in this table. Data set 1 is more precise than data set 2 because all the data in set 1 is really close to the mean, whereas the data in set 2 is more spread out.

Repeat	Data set 1	Data set 2
1	12	11
2	14	17
3	13	14
Mean	13	14

Choosing the right equipment

When doing an experiment, you need to make sure you're using the right equipment for the job. The measuring equipment you use has to be sensitive enough to measure the changes you're looking for.

Example

If you need to measure changes of 1 ml you need to use a measuring cylinder that can measure in 1 ml steps — it'd be no good trying with one that only measures 10 ml steps, it wouldn't be sensitive enough.

The smallest change a measuring instrument can detect is called its **resolution**. For example, some mass balances have a resolution of 1 g, some have a resolution of 0.1 g, and some are even more sensitive.

Figure 1: *Different types of measuring cylinder and glassware — make sure you choose the right one before you start an experiment.*

Figure 2: A mass balance that has been set to zero.

Also, equipment needs to be calibrated so that your data is more accurate.

> **Example**
>
> Mass balances need to be set to zero before you start weighing things.

Errors

Random errors

The results of your experiment will always vary a bit because of **random errors** — tiny differences caused by things like human errors in measuring. You can reduce their effect by taking many readings and calculating the mean.

Systematic errors

If the same error is made every time, it's called a **systematic error**.

> **Example**
>
> If you measured from the very end of your ruler instead of from the 0 cm mark every time, all your measurements would be a bit small.

Just to make things more complicated, if a systematic error is caused by using equipment that isn't zeroed properly it's called a **zero error**. You can compensate for some systematic and zero errors if you know about them though.

> **Example**
>
> If a mass balance always reads 1 gram before you put anything on it, all your measurements will be 1 gram too heavy. This is a zero error. You can compensate for this by subtracting 1 gram from all your results.

Anomalous results

Sometimes you get a result that doesn't seem to fit in with the rest at all. These results are called **anomalous results** (or outliers).

> **Example**
>
> Look at the data in this table. The entry that has been circled is an anomalous result because it's much larger than any of the other data values.
>
> | Experiment | A | B | C | D | E | F |
> |---|---|---|---|---|---|---|
> | Rate of reaction (cm³/s) | 10.5 | 11.2 | 10.8 | 85.4 | 10.6 | 11.1 |

You should investigate anomalous results and try to work out what happened. If you can work out what happened (e.g. you measured something totally wrong) you can ignore them when processing your results.

5. Processing and Presenting Data

Once you've collected some data, you might need to process it, and then you'll need to present it in a way that you can make sense of.

Learning Objectives:
- Know why data is often organised into tables and understand the limitations of using tables to organise data.
- Be able to calculate ranges and means.
- Be able to select and draw an appropriate graph to display the data collected in an investigation.

Specification Reference
How Science Works

Organising data

It's really important that your data is organised. Tables are dead useful for organising data. When you draw a table use a ruler, make sure each column has a heading (including the units) and keep it neat and tidy.

Annoyingly, tables are about as useful as a chocolate teapot for showing patterns or relationships in data. You need to use some kind of graph for that.

Processing your data

When you've done repeats of an experiment you should always calculate the **mean** (average). To do this add together all the data values and divide by the total number of values in the sample.

You might also need to calculate the **range** (how spread out the data is). To do this find the largest number and subtract the smallest number from it.

Tip: You should ignore anomalous results when calculating the mean and the range.

Example

Look at the data in this table. The mean and range of the data has been calculated for each test tube.

Test tube	Repeat (g) 1	Repeat (g) 2	Repeat (g) 3	Mean (g)	Range (g)
A	28	37	32	(28 + 37 + 32) ÷ 3 = 32.3	37 − 28 = 9
B	47	51	60	(47 + 51 + 60) ÷ 3 = 52.7	60 − 47 = 13
C	68	72	70	(68 + 72 + 70) ÷ 3 = 70.0	72 − 68 = 4

Plotting your data on a graph

One of the best ways to present your data after you've processed it is to plot your results on a graph. There are lots of different types of graph you can use. The type of graph you use depends on the type of data you've collected.

Bar charts

If either the independent or dependent variable is **categoric** you should use a bar chart to display the data.

Tip: Categoric data is data that comes in distinct categories, for example, blood type, type of fuel, metals.

You also use a bar chart if one of the variables is **discrete** (the data can be counted in chunks, where there's no in-between value, e.g. number of people is discrete because you can't have half a person).

There are some golden rules you need to follow for drawing bar charts:

Tip: These golden rules will make sure that your bar chart is clear, easy to read and easy to understand if someone else looks at it.

- Draw it nice and big (covering at least half of the graph paper).
- Leave a gap between different categories.
- Label both axes and remember to include the units.
- If you've got more than one set of data include a key.
- Give your graph a title explaining what it is showing.

Have a look at Figure 1 for an example of a pretty decent bar chart.

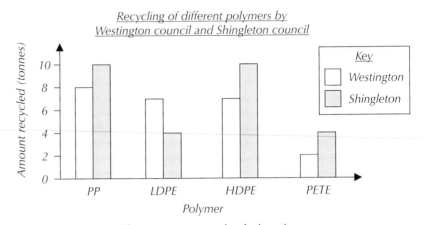

Figure 1: An example of a bar chart.

Line Graphs

If the independent and the dependent variable are **continuous** (numerical data that can have any value within a range, e.g. length, volume, temperature) you should use a line graph to display the data. Here are the golden rules for drawing line graphs:

Exam Tip
You could be asked to draw a bar chart or a line graph in your exam. If so, make sure you follow the golden rules or you could end up losing marks.

- Draw it nice and big (covering at least half of the graph paper).
- Put the independent variable (the thing you change) on the x-axis (the horizontal one).
- Put the dependent variable (the thing you measure) on the y-axis (the vertical one).
- Label both axes and remember to include the units.
- To plot the points, use a sharp pencil and make a neat little cross.
- Don't join the dots up. You need to draw a line of best fit (or a curve of best fit if your points make a curve). When drawing a line (or curve), try to draw the line through or as near to as many points as possible, ignoring anomalous results.
- If you've got more than one set of data include a key.
- Give your graph a title explaining what it is showing.

See Figure 2 for an example of a pretty good line graph.

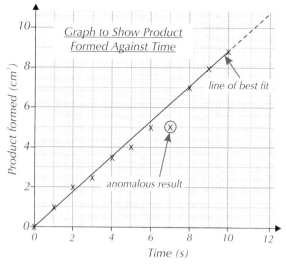

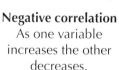

Figure 2: *An example of a line graph.*

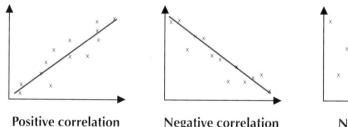

Tip: If you're not in an exam, you can use a computer to plot your line graph and draw your line of best fit for you.

Scatter graphs

Scatter graphs are very similar to line graphs but they often don't have a line of best fit drawn on them. Like line graphs, scatter graphs can be used if the independent and dependent variables are continuous.

Tip: Scatter graphs can also be called scattergrams or scatterplots.

Correlations

Line graphs and scatter graphs are used to show the relationship between two variables (just like other graphs). Data can show three different types of **correlation** (relationship):

Positive correlation
As one variable increases the other increases.

Negative correlation
As one variable increases the other decreases.

No correlation
There's no relationship between the two variables.

Tip: If all of the points are very close to the line of best fit then it's said to be a strong correlation. If there is a general trend but all the points are quite far away from the line of best fit it's a weak correlation.

You also need to be able to describe the following relationships on line graphs.

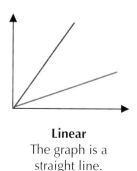

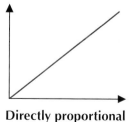

Linear
The graph is a straight line.

Directly proportional
The graph is a straight line where both variables increase (or decrease) in the same ratio.

Tip: On this graph the lines show positive linear relationships, but you can get linear relationships that show negative correlation too.

Learning Objectives:
- Be able to draw conclusions based on the data available.
- Understand the difference between correlation and causation, and the possible reasons for correlation.
- Be able to evaluate investigations.

Specification Reference
How Science Works

6. Drawing Conclusions

So... you've planned an amazing experiment, you've done the experiment, collected some data and have processed and presented your data in a sensible way. Now it's time to figure out what your data actually tells you.

How to draw conclusions

Drawing conclusions might seem pretty straightforward — you just look at your data and say what pattern or relationship you see between the dependent and independent variables.

But you've got to be really careful that your conclusion matches the data you've got and doesn't go any further. You also need to be able to use your results to justify your conclusion (i.e. back up your conclusion with some specific data).

Example

This table shows the rate of a reaction in the presence of two different catalysts.

The conclusion of this experiment would be that catalyst B makes the reaction go faster than catalyst A.

Catalyst	Rate of reaction (cm³/s)
A	13.5
B	19.5
No catalyst	5.5

The justification for this conclusion is that the rate of the reaction was 6 cm³/s faster using catalyst B compared with catalyst A.

You can't conclude that catalyst B increases the rate of any other reaction more than catalyst A — the results might be completely different.

Correlation and causation

Tip: Causation just means one thing is causing another.

If two things are correlated (i.e. there's a relationship between them) it doesn't necessarily mean that a change in one variable is causing the change in the other — this is really important, don't forget it. There are three possible reasons for a correlation:

Tip: Lots of things are correlated without being directly related. E.g. the level of carbon dioxide (CO_2) in the atmosphere and the amount of obesity have both increased over the last 100 years, but that doesn't mean increased atmospheric CO_2 is causing people to become obese.

1. Chance

Even though it might seem a bit weird, it's possible that two things show a correlation in a study purely because of chance.

Example

One study might find a correlation between the number of people with breathing problems and the distance they live from a cement factory. But other scientists don't get a correlation when they investigate it — the results of the first study are just a fluke.

2. They're linked by a third variable

A lot of the time it may look as if a change in one variable is causing a change in the other, but it isn't — a third variable links the two things.

Example

There's a correlation between water temperature and shark attacks. This obviously isn't because warmer water makes sharks crazy. Instead, they're linked by a third variable — the number of people swimming (more people swim when the water's hotter, and with more people in the water you get more shark attacks).

3. Causation

Sometimes a change in one variable does cause a change in the other.

Example

There's a correlation between smoking and lung cancer. This is because chemicals in tobacco smoke cause lung cancer.

You can only conclude that a correlation is due to cause when you've controlled all the variables that could, just could, be affecting the result. (For the smoking example above this would include things like age and exposure to other things that cause cancer).

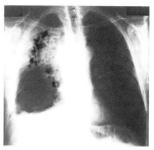

Figure 1: *A coloured chest X-ray of a smoker who has lung cancer.*

Evaluation

This is the final part of an investigation. Here you need to evaluate (assess) the following things about your experiment and the data you gathered.

- **Repeatability**: Did you take enough repeat readings of the measurements? Would you do more repeats if you were to do the experiment again? Do you think you'd get similar data if you did the experiment again?

- **Reproducibility**: Have you compared your results with other people's results? Were your results similar? Could other scientists gain data showing the same relationships that are shown in your data?

- **Validity**: Does your data answer the question you set out to investigate?

Once you've thought about these points you can decide how much confidence you have in your conclusion. For example, if your results are repeatable, reproducible and valid and they back up your conclusion then you can have a high degree of confidence in your conclusion.

Learning Objectives:

- Understand the importance of a balanced diet.
- Know what carbohydrates, fats and proteins are used for by the body.
- Understand why the body needs small amounts of vitamins and mineral ions.
- Understand what is meant by the term 'metabolic rate'.
- Understand why metabolic rate varies between different people.
- Know that exercising increases the amount of energy you use.

Specification Reference B1.1.1

1. Diet and Metabolic Rate

Your diet is important. It's where you get your energy from, as well as the nutrients your body needs to stay healthy.

The importance of a balanced diet

For good health, your diet must provide the energy you need (but not more) — see page 19. But that's not all. There are five important **nutrients** — carbohydrates, proteins, fats, vitamins and mineral ions. Each nutrient has different uses in the body — so you need to have the right balance of these too (see Figure 1). You need:

- enough carbohydrates to release energy,
- enough fats to keep warm and release energy,
- enough protein for growth, cell repair and cell replacement,
- tiny amounts of various vitamins and mineral ions to keep your skin, bones, blood and everything else generally healthy.

You also need enough fibre to keep everything moving smoothly through your digestive system.

Some sources of the main nutrients are shown in Figure 2.

Figure 1: This food wheel shows what the relative proportions of different foods should be in a healthy diet.

Nutrient	Sources
Carbohydrates	Pasta, rice
Fats	Butter, oily fish
Protein	Meat, fish
Vitamins	Various, e.g. vitamin C is found in oranges. Vitamin D is in eggs.
Minerals	Various, e.g. calcium is found in milk. Iron is found in red meat.

Figure 2: Table showing sources of the main nutrients.

Varying energy needs

You need energy to fuel the chemical reactions in the body that keep you alive. These reactions are called your **metabolism**, and the speed at which they occur is your **metabolic rate**. There are slight variations in the resting metabolic rate of different people — take a look at the examples on the next page.

- Muscle needs more energy than fatty tissue, which means (all other things being equal) people with a higher proportion of muscle to fat in their bodies will have a higher metabolic rate.

- Physically bigger people are likely to have a higher metabolic rate than smaller people — the bigger you are, the more energy your body needs to be supplied with (because you have more cells).

- Men tend to have a slightly higher rate than women — they're slightly bigger and have a larger proportion of muscle. Other genetic factors may also have some effect.

- Regular exercise can boost your resting metabolic rate because it builds muscle.

Tip: Your resting metabolic rate is your metabolic rate when you're at rest (not doing very much).

Figure 3: The more muscle you have, the higher your metabolic rate.

Exercise and energy needs

When you exercise, you obviously need more energy — so your metabolic rate goes up during exercise and stays high for some time after you finish (particularly if the exercise is strenuous).

So people who have more active jobs need more energy on a daily basis — builders require more energy per day than office workers, for instance. Different activities need different amounts of energy — see Figure 4.

Activity	Average Amount of Energy Burned (kJ/min)
Sleeping	4.5
Watching TV	7
Cycling (5 mph)	21
Jogging (5 mph)	40
Climbing stairs	77
Swimming	35
Rowing	58
Slow walking	14

Tip: A kJ (kilojoule) is a unit of energy.

Figure 4: A table showing the average number of kilojoules burned per minute during different activities.

This means your activity level affects the amount of energy your diet should contain. If you do little exercise, you're going to need less energy, so less fat and carbohydrate in your diet, than if you're constantly on the go.

Practice Questions — Fact Recall

Q1 What does the body need carbohydrates for?

Q2 Why does the body need vitamins and mineral ions?

Q3 What is meant by the term 'metabolic rate'?

Q4 True or false? Everybody's metabolic rate is exactly the same.

Q5 Explain how your activity level affects the amount of energy you use.

Practice Questions — Application

Q1 Meat is a major source of protein. Explain why people who don't eat meat should still make sure they get enough protein in their diet.

Q2 Joe is a professional rower. He spends 35 hours a week in training. Paula is a graphic designer. She spends 40 hours a week in the office, but likes to go cycling at weekends.

   a) Who would you expect to have the higher resting metabolic rate, Joe or Paula? Give a reason for your answer.

   b) Who would you expect to have a higher energy intake? Explain your answer.

Q3 On an expedition across the Antarctic, a man dragging a sledge behind him can expect to burn between 6000 and 7000 calories a day. A man working inside one of the Antarctic research stations burns about 2750 calories per day.

   a) Suggest why the man dragging the sledge burns so many more calories than the man in the research station.

   b) Suggest two nutrients that someone on this type of expedition is likely to need in large amounts. Explain your answer.

Tip: Calories are a measure of the energy in food — see p. 21.

2. Factors Affecting Health

Our health can be affected by what we eat. But it can also be affected by things like how much we exercise and factors we inherit from our parents.

An unbalanced diet

People whose diet is badly out of balance are said to be **malnourished**. Malnourished people can be fat or thin, or unhealthy in other ways.

The effects of eating too much

Excess carbohydrate or fat in the diet can lead to **obesity**. Obesity is a common disorder in developed countries (e.g. the UK) — it's defined as being 20% (or more) over the maximum recommended body mass. Hormonal problems can lead to obesity, though the usual cause is a bad diet, overeating and a lack of exercise.

Health problems that can arise as a result of obesity include: arthritis (inflammation of the joints), **type 2 diabetes** (inability to control blood sugar level), high blood pressure and heart disease. It's also a risk factor for some kinds of cancer.

Eating too much can also lead to other health problems. Too much saturated fat in your diet can increase your blood cholesterol level (see next page). Eating too much salt can cause high blood pressure and heart problems.

The effects of eating too little

Some people suffer from lack of food, particularly in developing countries (e.g. Ethiopia). The effects of this type of malnourishment vary depending on what foods are missing from the diet. But problems commonly include slow growth (in children), fatigue, poor resistance to infection, and irregular periods in women. A lack of vitamins or minerals in the diet can cause **deficiency diseases**.

Examples

- A lack of vitamin C can cause scurvy, a deficiency disease that causes problems with the skin, joints and gums (see Figure 1).

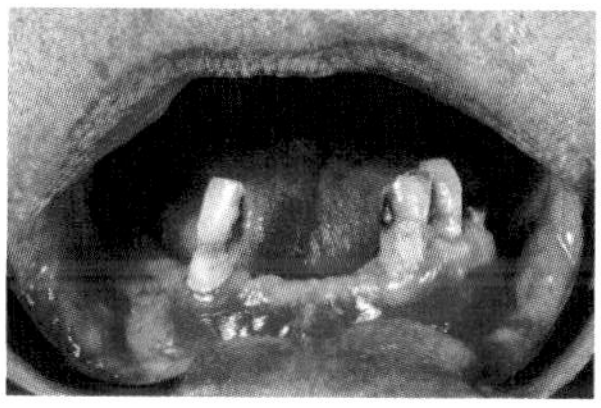

Figure 1: Scurvy can cause the gums to swell and the teeth to fall out.

- A lack of iron (a mineral) can cause iron deficiency anaemia, a deficiency disease that affects the red blood cells, making you feel tired and weak.

Learning Objectives:

- Understand that by not eating a balanced diet, you can become malnourished.
- Understand that malnourished people can be overweight or underweight.
- Understand that an unbalanced diet can cause health problems such as type 2 diabetes and deficiency diseases.
- Understand how exercise helps to keep you healthy.
- Understand that inherited factors can affect your metabolic rate, as well as your health (e.g. your blood cholesterol level).

Specification Reference B1.1.1

Tip: Malnourishment is different from starvation, which is not getting enough food of any sort. And remember, you can also become malnourished by eating too much — it just means that your diet is badly out of balance.

Exam Tip
You don't need to learn the effects of any specific deficiency diseases for the exam — these examples are just to help your understanding.

A lack of exercise

Exercise is important for good health as well as diet — people who exercise regularly are usually healthier than those who don't. Exercise increases the amount of energy used by the body and decreases the amount stored as fat. It also builds muscle so it helps to boost your metabolic rate (see pages 16-17). So people who exercise are less likely to suffer from health problems such as obesity.

However, sometimes people can be fit but not healthy — e.g. you can be physically fit and slim, but malnourished at the same time because your diet isn't balanced.

Inherited factors

It's not just about what you eat and how much exercise you do — your health can depend on inherited factors too.

Tip: Your thyroid gland is in your neck. It makes hormones (see page 47) that regulate your metabolic rate.

Some people may inherit factors that affect their metabolic rate, e.g. some inherited factors cause an underactive thyroid gland, which can lower the metabolic rate and cause obesity.

Tip: Coronary heart disease can result in things like angina (chest pain) and heart attacks.

Other people may inherit factors that affect their **blood cholesterol level**. Cholesterol is a fatty substance that's essential for good health — it's found in every cell in the body. But you don't want too much of it because a high cholesterol level in the blood has been linked to an increased risk of various problems, including coronary heart disease. Some inherited factors increase blood cholesterol level, which increases the risk of heart disease.

> **Example**
>
> The liver is really important in controlling the amount of cholesterol in the body. It makes new cholesterol and removes any that isn't used from the blood so that it can be eliminated from the body. The amount the liver makes depends partly on inherited factors.

Practice Questions — Fact Recall

Q1 What does it mean if someone is malnourished?

Q2 How can an unbalanced diet lead to obesity?

Q3 Give one health problem that can be caused by obesity.

Q4 True or false? A lack of certain minerals in the diet can lead to deficiency diseases.

Q5 Explain why people who exercise on a regular basis are usually healthier than those who don't.

Q6 Give two ways in which inherited factors can affect health.

3. Evaluating Food, Lifestyle and Diet

Learning Objectives:
- Be able to evaluate information about food and health.
- Be able to evaluate information about how lifestyle affects health and disease.
- Understand that to lose weight, you need to take in less energy than you use up.
- Be able to evaluate claims made about slimming products.

Specification Reference
B1.1, B1.1.1

This topic is all about using your scientific knowledge to evaluate information about (yep, you've guessed it) food, lifestyle and diet. Don't panic though, I'll explain everything over the next three pages...

Evaluating information on food

In the exam, you may get asked to evaluate information about how food affects health.

Here are some of the things that might make you classify a food as being unhealthy:

- A high saturated fat content — eating too much saturated fat can raise your blood cholesterol level (see previous page).

- A high sodium or salt content — eating too much salt (usually in the form of sodium) can lead to health problems such as high blood pressure.

- A high energy content — the energy in food is usually measured in kilojoules (kJ) or calories. Eating too many high energy foods could lead to obesity.

On the other hand, a food that is low in calories but high in protein, fibre or important vitamins and minerals may be considered fairly healthy.

Tip: A high energy food isn't necessarily bad for you — but if you take in more energy than you use up, you could end up becoming overweight.

Example

Look at the two food labels shown below. Which food is healthier? Explain your answer.

A

NUTRITIONAL INFORMATION	
	per serving
Energy	388 kJ
Protein	6 g
Carbohydrate	14 g
of which sugars	6 g
Fat	4.2 g
of which saturates	2.2 g
Fibre	3.5 g
Calcium	200 mg
Sodium	250 mg

B

NUTRITIONAL INFORMATION	
	per serving
Energy	305 kJ
Protein	3 g
Carbohydrate	9 g
of which sugars	8 g
Fat	2.1 g
of which saturates	0.5 g
Fibre	3 g
Calcium	500 mg
Sodium	125 mg

Looking at the two food labels above, food A has a higher protein content than food B, but it also has a higher energy content, a much higher saturated fat content and double the sodium content of food B. Food B also provides more calcium than food A. So food B is the healthier food.

Exam Tip
The information you get in the exam could also be in the form of a table, chart or graph.

Figure 1: This food label shows levels of sugar, fat and salt as a percentage of an adult's guideline daily amount.

Evaluating information on lifestyle

You might also get asked to evaluate information about how lifestyle affects health. Your lifestyle includes what you eat and what you do.

Example

A person who eats too much fat or carbohydrate and doesn't do much exercise will increase their risk of obesity. This means they'll also increase their risk of developing the health problems associated with obesity — like type 2 diabetes and heart disease (see p. 19).

Remember, you'll need to use your knowledge of how diet and exercise affect health to answer exam questions — make sure all the facts on pages 16-20 are well lodged in your memory.

Evaluating slimming claims

There are loads of slimming products (e.g. diet pills, slimming milkshakes) and slimming programmes (e.g. the Atkins Diet™) around — and they all claim they'll help you lose weight. But it can be difficult to know whether or not they actually work. In the exam, you could be asked to evaluate a claim made about a slimming product. If so, it's a good idea to look out for these things:

Is the report a scientific study, published in a reputable journal?

Before results are published in a scientific journal, they're reviewed by other scientists (in a process called peer review) to make sure they were obtained in a scientific way. This doesn't guarantee that the results are correct, just that they seem reasonable to the experts.

Tip: A reputable journal is one with a good reputation. Reputable scientific journals include Nature, Science, and the British Medical Journal.

Was it written by a qualified person, not connected with the people selling it?

Someone who works for the company that makes the slimming product might present their results in a **biased** way to make the product sound better than it really is (see page 3). Results from an independent study are less likely to be biased.

Tip: In this case, an independent study is one which is carried out by scientists with no connection to the product or who don't stand to gain from it.

Was the sample of people asked/tested large enough?

Large samples are generally better than small samples as they're more representative of the population as a whole (see page 2).

Example

A common way to promote a new diet is to say, "Celebrity A has lost x pounds using it". But effectiveness in one person doesn't mean much. Only a large survey can tell if a diet is more or less effective than just eating less and exercising more — and these aren't done often.

Have there been other studies which found similar results?

Results that can be reproduced by other scientists are more likely to be believable (see page 3).

Misleading slimming claims

Really, all you need to do to lose weight is to take in less energy than you use. So diets and slimming products will only work if you...

- eat less fat or carbohydrate (so that you take in less energy), or

- do more exercise (so that you use more energy).

So some claims may be true but a little misleading.

> **Example**
>
> Low-fat bars might be low in fat, but eating them without changing the rest of your diet doesn't necessarily mean you'll lose weight — you could still be taking in too much energy.

Practice Questions — Application

Q1 Two food labels are shown below. Both labels use a "traffic light" system to show the levels of fat, salt and sugar present in the food. Red means "high", orange means "medium" and green means "low".

Food A   Food B

a) i) Which food has the highest level of fat?

ii) Why might a food that is high in fat be considered unhealthy?

b) The maximum recommended daily salt intake for an adult is 6 g. What percentage of this intake would you get from Food B?

c) Which of the two foods shown above is healthiest? Give a reason for your answer.

Q2 The manufacturers of a slimming milkshake make the following claim:

HOW SCIENCE WORKS

"8 out of 10 people lose weight using our milkshake".

The claim is based on the results of a trial carried out by the manufacturers. The trial involved 20 women, all of whom drank the same slimming milkshake for one month. 16 women said they lost weight. No other data was collected and the women weren't independently weighed.

Do you think the manufacturers have enough evidence to make their claim? Give two reasons for your answer.

- Know what a
  pathogen is.
- Know the two main
  types of pathogen:
  bacteria and viruses.
- Know that pathogens
  can reproduce quickly
  once inside the body.
- Know how bacteria
  and viruses make you
  feel ill.
- Know that the body
  has different ways
  of defending itself
  against pathogens.
- Know how white
  blood cells help to
  defend the body
  against pathogens.
- Know that antibodies
  are specific to a
  particular type of
  pathogen.
- Understand how
  the production of
  antibodies leads to
  immunity.

Specification Reference
B1.1.2

4. Fighting Disease

*Part of being healthy means being free from disease.
But that's easier said than done...*

Pathogens

Microorganisms that enter the body and cause disease are called **pathogens**.
Pathogens cause **infectious diseases** — diseases that can easily spread.
There are two main types of pathogen — bacteria and viruses.

Bacteria

Bacteria are very small living cells (about 1/100th the size of your body cells),
which can reproduce rapidly inside your body. They make you feel ill by
doing two things:

- producing **toxins** (poisons)
- damaging your cells

--- **Example** ---

Vibrio cholerae — these bacteria cause cholera (a nasty diarrhoeal disease).
They make you feel ill by releasing a toxin into the small intestines.

Viruses

Viruses are not cells. They're tiny, about 1/100th the size of a bacterium.
They replicate themselves by invading your cells and using the cells'
machinery to produce many copies of themselves. The cell will usually then
burst, releasing all the new viruses (see Figure 1). This cell damage is what
makes you feel ill.

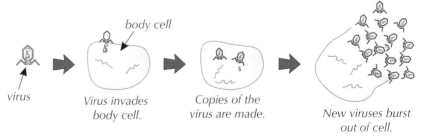

body cell

virus — *Virus invades body cell.* — *Copies of the virus are made.* — *New viruses burst out of cell.*

Figure 1: *A virus replicating in a human cell.*

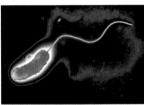
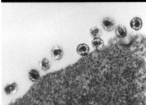

Figure 2: *A Vibrio
cholerae bacterium (top).
HIV particles (blue)
infecting a white blood cell
(bottom).*

--- **Example** ---

HIV — this virus infects and destroys cells that normally help to defend the
body against disease (like white blood cells, see next page). This makes
HIV sufferers more likely to get ill from infection by other pathogens.

Your body's defences

In order to cause disease, pathogens first need to enter the body.
Luckily your body has a few ways to stop them doing just that, including:

1. The skin

Your skin stops a lot of nasties getting inside your body. If you cut yourself though, pathogens can get into your bloodstream through the wound. To try and prevent this from happening, small fragments of cells (called platelets) help blood clot quickly to seal wounds. If the blood contains low numbers of platelets then it will clot more slowly.

2. Mucus in the respiratory tract

Your respiratory tract (breathing pipework) is lined with sticky mucus. This traps pathogens that are in the air and stops them from reaching the lungs. Tiny hairs in the respiratory tract beat to move the mucus away from the lungs, back towards the mouth.

Figure 3: *Bacteria (yellow) sticking to mucus (blue) on microscopic hairs in the nose.*

The immune system

If something does make it through your defences, your immune system kicks in. The most important part is the **white blood cells**. They travel around in your blood and crawl into every part of you, constantly patrolling for pathogens. When they come across an invading pathogen they have three lines of attack:

1. Consuming them

White blood cells can **engulf** pathogens and digest them (see Figure 4).

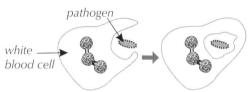

Figure 4: *A white blood cell engulfing a pathogen.*

2. Producing antitoxins

These counteract toxins produced by the invading bacteria.

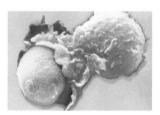

Figure 5: *A white blood cell (blue/pink) engulfing a pathogen (yellow/green). Seen under a microscope.*

3. Producing antibodies

Every invading cell has unique molecules (called **antigens**) on its surface. When your white blood cells come across a foreign antigen (i.e. one they don't recognise), they will start to produce proteins called **antibodies**. The antibodies then lock onto the foreign antigens and kill the invading pathogens (see Figure 6).

Exam Tip
Don't be tempted to write 'white blood cells engulf disease' in the exam — white blood cells engulf <u>pathogens</u> (which cause disease).

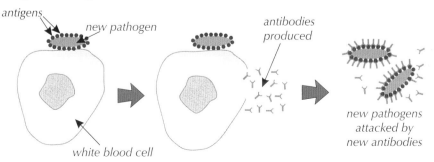

Figure 6: *Diagram showing the production of antibodies.*

The antibodies produced are specific to that type of antigen — they won't lock on to any others. Antibodies are then produced rapidly and carried around the body to kill all similar bacteria or viruses (i.e. ones with the same antigens).

If the person is infected with the same pathogen again the white blood cells will rapidly produce the antibodies to kill it — the person is naturally **immune** to that pathogen and won't get ill.

Example

Say you're infected with the mumps virus. When your white blood cells come across the foreign antigens on the surface of the virus, they'll start to produce the antibodies to destroy it. Eventually they'll produce enough antibodies to overcome the infection — but, in the meantime, you'll feel ill.

If you ever get infected with the mumps virus again though, your white blood cells will 'remember' and rapidly produce the antibodies to destroy it — so you shouldn't get sick again. You're immune to mumps.

Practice Questions — Fact Recall

Q1 Name two types of pathogen and explain how each one makes you feel ill.

Q2 Give three ways in which white blood cells help to defend the body against disease.

Q3 What does it mean if a person is immune to a particular pathogen?

Practice Questions — Application

Q1 As a child, John suffered from measles. Measles are caused by a virus.

   a) Explain why John is unlikely to get ill with measles again.

   b) German measles are caused by a different virus, which John has never had before. Explain why John could still become ill from German measles.

Q2 *Clostridium tetani* is the bacterium that causes tetanus. It usually enters the body through deep cuts.

   a) Suggest two ways in which *Clostridium tetani* bacteria may make you feel ill.

   b) Suggest one way in which the body tries to prevent *Clostridium tetani* from entering the bloodstream.

5. Fighting Disease — Vaccination

Vaccinations have changed the way we fight disease.
We don't always have to deal with the problem once it's happened —
we can prevent it happening in the first place.

What are vaccinations?

When you're infected with a new microorganism, it takes your white blood cells a few days to learn how to deal with it. But by that time, you can be pretty ill. Vaccinations can stop you feeling ill in the first place.

Vaccinations involve injecting small amounts of dead or inactive microorganisms. These carry antigens, which cause your white blood cells to produce antibodies to attack them — even though the microorganism is harmless (since it's dead or inactive).

> **Example**
>
> The **MMR vaccine** is given to children. It contains weakened versions of the viruses that cause measles, mumps and rubella (German measles) all in one vaccine.

If live microorganisms of the same type then appear at a later date, the white blood cells can rapidly mass-produce antibodies to kill off the pathogen. The vaccinated person is now immune to that pathogen and won't get ill (see Figure 1).

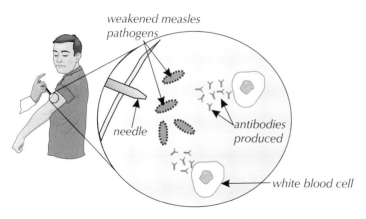

weakened measles pathogens

needle

antibodies produced

white blood cell

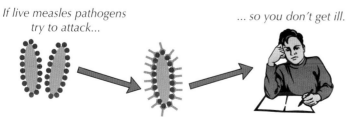

If live measles pathogens try to attack...

... so you don't get ill.

... they are quickly recognised and attacked by antibodies...

***Figure 1:** A diagram to show how vaccination works.*

Learning Objectives:

- Understand how vaccinations work.
- Know what the MMR vaccine is used for.
- Understand that if enough people are immune to a particular pathogen, the spread of the pathogen is reduced.
- Be able to evaluate the pros and cons of vaccinations.

Specification Reference B1.1.2

Exam Tip
You need to learn this example for your exam.

Tip: The 'weakened' viruses in the MMR vaccine are still alive, but aren't able to cause disease.

Tip: Remember, antibodies are specific to a particular type of pathogen (see p. 26). So a vaccination against the typhoid virus will only protect you against typhoid — it won't make you immune to anything else.

Tip: Some vaccinations "wear off" over time. So booster injections may need to be given to increase levels of antibodies again.

Vaccinations — pros and cons

You need to be able to weigh up the pros and cons of vaccinations.

Exam Tip
In the exam, you might get asked to 'evaluate' the pros and cons of vaccinations. This means giving a balanced account of both the advantages and the disadvantages, before trying to come up with an overall judgement.

Pros

- Vaccines have helped control lots of infectious diseases that were once common in the UK (e.g. polio, measles, whooping cough, rubella, mumps, tetanus...). Smallpox no longer occurs at all, and polio infections have fallen by 99%.

- Big outbreaks of disease — called **epidemics** — can be prevented if a large percentage of the population is vaccinated. That way, even the people who aren't vaccinated are unlikely to catch the disease because there are fewer people able to pass it on. But if a significant number of people aren't vaccinated, the disease can spread quickly through them and lots of people will be ill at the same time.

Cons

- Vaccines don't always work — sometimes they don't give you immunity.

- You can sometimes have a bad reaction to a vaccine (e.g. swelling, or maybe something more serious like a fever or seizures). But bad reactions are very rare.

Figure 2: *A baby being given the MMR vaccine.*

Balancing the risks

Deciding whether to have a vaccination means balancing risks — the risk of catching the disease if you don't have a vaccine, against the risk of having a bad reaction if you do. As always, you need to look at the evidence.

> **Example**
>
> If you get measles (the disease), there's about a 1 in 15 chance that you'll get complications (e.g. pneumonia) — and about 1 in 500 people who get measles actually die. However, the number of people who have a problem with the vaccine is more like 1 in 1 000 000.

Practice Question — Application

Q1 Whooping cough is a severe cough that can cause serious breathing difficulties in young babies.

In 2012, the US state of Washington declared a whooping cough epidemic. The Department of Health encouraged all adults to get booster vaccinations against the disease, to help protect babies who were too young to receive the vaccination.

a) What is a 'whooping cough epidemic'?

b) Suggest how a whooping cough vaccination might work.

c) Explain how a large-scale vaccination of adults could help to protect babies who haven't been vaccinated.

6. Fighting Disease — Drugs

There aren't vaccinations against every pathogen (not just yet, anyway) so you're still going to get ill sometimes. And that's when drugs come in...

Different types of drugs

Painkillers (e.g. aspirin) are drugs that relieve pain. However, they don't actually tackle the cause of the disease, they just help to reduce the symptoms. Other drugs do a similar kind of thing — reduce the symptoms without tackling the underlying cause. For example, lots of "cold remedies" don't actually cure colds — they have no effect on the cold virus itself.

Antibiotics (e.g. **penicillin**) work differently — they actually kill (or prevent the growth of) the bacteria causing the problem without killing your own body cells. Different antibiotics kill different types of bacteria, so it's important to be treated with the right one.

But antibiotics don't destroy viruses (e.g. flu or cold viruses). Viruses reproduce using your own body cells, which makes it very difficult to develop drugs that destroy just the virus without killing the body's cells.

Antibiotic resistance

Bacteria can **mutate** — in other words, their genetic material can change. Sometimes the mutations cause them to be resistant to (not killed by) an antibiotic. Resistant strains ('types') of bacteria like **MRSA** (see below) have increased as a result of a process known as **natural selection**.

> **Examples**
>
> - MRSA (methicillin-resistant *Staphylococcus aureus*) causes serious wound infections and is resistant to the powerful antibiotic, methicillin.
>
> - Some strains of the bacteria that cause TB (a lung disease) are now resistant to several of the antibiotics that would normally be used to fight them.

How antibiotic resistance develops `Higher`

If you have an infection, some of the bacteria might be resistant to antibiotics. This means that when you treat the infection, only the non-resistant strains of bacteria will be killed. The individual resistant bacteria will survive and reproduce, and the population of the resistant strain will increase (see Figure 1, next page). This is an example of natural selection. The resistant strain could cause a serious infection that can't be treated by antibiotics (like MRSA).

Learning Objectives:

- Understand that some drugs reduce the symptoms of a disease, but don't destroy the pathogens.

- Understand that antibiotics (e.g. penicillin) are drugs used to kill bacteria.

- Understand that different antibiotics kill different bacteria and that antibiotics have no effect on viruses.

- Understand why it's hard to produce drugs to kill viruses.

- Understand that bacteria can mutate and that this can lead to the development of antibiotic-resistant strains, e.g. MRSA, by natural selection.

- **H** Understand in more detail how populations of antibiotic-resistant bacteria develop.

- Understand that by avoiding over-use of antibiotics, we can slow down the spread of antibiotic resistance.

- **H** Understand why antibiotics are now usually only used to treat more serious infections.

Specification Reference B1.1.2

Tip: There's more on natural selection on pages 110-111.

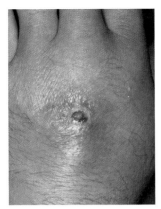

Figure 2: *A wound infected with MRSA.*

Figure 1: H *How antibiotic resistance develops.*

Labels in Figure 1: resistant bacterium; Treatment with antibiotic; non-resistant bacterium; Only resistant bacteria survive; Population of resistant bacteria increases due to natural selection.

Slowing down the development of antibiotic resistance

To prevent antibiotic resistance spreading, it's important not to over-use antibiotics.

> **Example** — **Higher**
>
> Doctors now try to avoid over-prescribing antibiotics. So you won't get them for a sore throat, only for something more serious.

Practice Questions — Fact Recall

Q1 True or false?
Painkillers can be used to tackle the cause of an infection.

Q2 What is an antibiotic? Give one example.

Q3 Why is it important to be treated with the right antibiotic for a particular infection?

Q4 Explain why it can be difficult to develop drugs that kill viruses.

Q5 a) Name a strain of bacteria that has developed antibiotic resistance.

b) By what process have resistant strains of bacteria increased?

Q6 Why is it important not to over-use antibiotics?

Practice Questions — Application

Q1 Chloe is suffering from the flu, which is caused by a virus.

a) Explain why Chloe's doctor will not prescribe her antibiotics.

b) Chloe's doctor recommends a flu remedy. Suggest why the flu remedy will not help to clear Chloe's infection any quicker.

Q2 James has a mild bacterial infection. James' doctor tells him it will clear up on its own and does not prescribe him antibiotics. Suggest why James' doctor did this.

Q3 Many strains of the bacteria *Streptococcus pneumoniae* are now resistant to the antibiotic penicillin. Describe how populations of penicillin-resistant *Streptococcus pneumoniae* may have increased.

7. Fighting Disease — Investigating Antibiotic Action

Scientists developing new antibiotics or disinfectants need to be able to test whether or not they actually work. That means setting up bacterial cultures...

Culturing microorganisms

You can test the action of antibiotics or disinfectants by growing **cultures** of microorganisms in the lab. Microorganisms are grown (cultured) on a "culture medium". This is usually agar jelly containing the carbohydrates, minerals, proteins and vitamins the microorganisms need to grow. Here's how to test the action of antibiotics:

- Agar jelly is heated to kill any unwanted microorganisms. The hot agar jelly is then poured into shallow round plastic dishes called Petri dishes.

- When the jelly's cooled and set, inoculating loops (wire loops) are used to transfer microorganisms to the culture medium. The microorganisms then multiply.

- Paper discs are soaked in different types of antibiotics and placed on the jelly. Antibiotic-resistant bacteria will continue to grow around them but non-resistant strains will die (see Figures 1 and 2).

- A paper disc not soaked in antibiotic can be included as a control — this should show that any results are down to the antibiotic, not the disc itself.

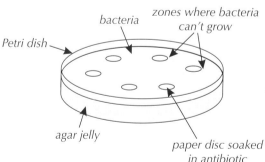

Figure 1: *Diagram to show how antibiotic action can be investigated in the lab.*

Avoiding contamination

The Petri dishes, culture medium and inoculating loops must be **sterilised** before use, e.g. the inoculating loops are passed through a flame. If equipment isn't sterilised, unwanted microorganisms in the culture medium will grow and affect the result.

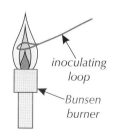

The Petri dish must also have a lid to stop any microorganisms in the air contaminating the culture. The lid should also be taped on.

Learning Objectives:
- Know that bacteria can be cultured in the lab to investigate the action of antibiotics and disinfectants.
- Know how to prevent contamination of bacterial cultures.
- Understand why bacterial cultures are kept at 25 °C in schools, but at higher temperatures in industry.

Specification Reference B1.1.2

Tip: You can test the action of disinfectants in exactly the same way as antibiotics — just soak the paper discs in disinfectants instead.

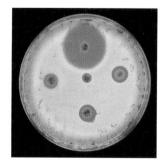

Figure 2: *Antibiotic discs on a bacterial culture. You can see clear zones around the discs where the bacteria can't grow.*

Tip: You can sterilise equipment in a machine called an autoclave — it basically steams equipment at high pressure. Your school might have an autoclave.

Incubation temperatures

In the lab at school, cultures of microorganisms are kept at about 25 °C because harmful pathogens aren't likely to grow at this temperature. In industrial conditions, cultures are incubated at higher temperatures so that they can grow a lot faster.

Practice Question — Application

Q1 Giles is investigating the action of different antibiotics against a strain of bacteria. He cultures the bacteria on a dish containing agar jelly.

a) Giles transfers the bacteria to the jelly using a sterile inoculating loop.

i) How could Giles have sterilised the loop?

ii) Why did Giles need to sterilise the inoculating loop?

Once Giles has transferred the bacteria to the dish, he places 6 paper discs, each soaked in a different antibiotic, onto the jelly. He then tapes a lid on the dish and leaves it for a few days.

His results are shown in the diagram below.

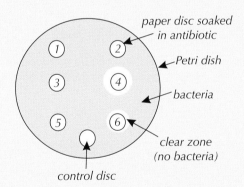

paper disc soaked in antibiotic

Petri dish

bacteria

clear zone (no bacteria)

control disc

b) i) Which antibiotics were the bacteria resistant to? Explain your answer.

ii) Which antibiotic was most effective against the bacteria? Explain your answer.

iii) Give one variable Giles should have controlled in order to make this a fair test.

HOW SCIENCE WORKS

c) Explain why Giles put a lid on the Petri dish before leaving it overnight?

d) Giles was working in a school laboratory. Explain why his cultures had to be kept at 25 °C.

Tip: There's more on variables and fair tests in the How Science Works section at the start of this book. See page 6.

8. Fighting Disease — Past & Future

The way we deal with diseases now is very different to a hundred years ago. And it's changing all the time...

The work of Semmelweis

Ignaz Semmelweis was a doctor who worked in Vienna General Hospital (in Austria) in the 1840s. While he was there, he saw that women were dying in huge numbers after childbirth from a disease called puerperal fever.

He believed that doctors were spreading the disease on their unwashed hands. By telling doctors entering his ward to wash their hands in an antiseptic solution, he cut the death rate from 12% to 2%.

The antiseptic solution killed bacteria on doctors' hands, though Semmelweis didn't know this (the existence of bacteria and their part in causing disease wasn't discovered for another 20 years). So Semmelweis couldn't prove why his idea worked, and his methods were dropped when he left the hospital (allowing death rates to rise once again — d'oh).

Nowadays we know that basic hygiene is essential in controlling disease (though recent reports have found that a lack of it in some modern hospitals has helped the disease MRSA spread). In fact, a better understanding of things like immunity and how antibiotics work has changed the way we treat disease too.

The spread of antibiotic resistance

For the last few decades, we've been able to deal with bacterial infections pretty easily using antibiotics. As a result of this, the death rate from infectious bacterial diseases has fallen dramatically.

> **Example**
>
> During the First World War, nearly 20% of US soldiers who caught pneumonia (a bacterial infection) died as a result. During World War II, this figure dropped to less than 1% thanks to treatment with penicillin.

But bacteria evolve antibiotic resistance, e.g MRSA bacteria are already resistant to certain antibiotics. And over-use of antibiotics has made this problem worse — by increasing the likelihood of people being infected by antibiotic-resistant strains (see pages 29-30). As a result, bacteria that are resistant to most known antibiotics ('superbugs') are becoming more common.

People who become infected with these bacteria can't easily get rid of them (because antibiotics don't work) and may pass on the infection to others. So antibiotic resistance is a big problem and it's encouraged drug companies to work on developing new antibiotics that are effective against these resistant strains.

Learning Objectives:

- Understand how Semmelweis reduced deaths through hand-washing and how this affects infection control in hospitals today.
- Understand why the way we treat disease has changed over time.
- Understand that antibiotics have reduced deaths from bacterial diseases.
- Understand why antibiotic resistance is increasing and that new antibiotics need to be developed as a result.
- Understand how mutations in bacteria and viruses could lead to epidemics and pandemics — and be able to evaluate the consequences.

Specification Reference B1.1.2

Figure 1: *Photograph of the doctor, Ignaz Semmelweis.*

New and emerging dangers

We face new and scary dangers from pathogens all the time...

Bacteria

As you know, bacteria can mutate to produce new strains (see page 29). A new strain could be antibiotic-resistant, so current treatments would no longer clear an infection. Or a new strain could be one that we've not encountered before, so no-one would be immune to it. This means a new strain of bacteria could spread rapidly in a population of people and could even cause an **epidemic** — a big outbreak of disease.

Tip: TB is a very serious lung disease caused by a bacterial infection.

> **Example**
>
> Multi-drug-resistant TB (also known as MDR-TB) is a form of TB that has developed resistance to multiple antibiotics, making it hard to treat. Scientists in China have reported an MDR-TB epidemic there — over one hundred thousand Chinese people develop MDR-TB each year and a third of all new TB cases in China are antibiotic-resistant.

Viruses

Viruses also tend to mutate often. This makes it hard to develop vaccines against them because the changes to their DNA can lead to them having different antigens. There'd be a real problem if a virus evolved so that it was both deadly and very infectious. (Flu viruses, for example, evolve quickly so this is quite possible.)

Tip: White blood cells recognise pathogens by their antigens (see p. 25) — so even if you've been vaccinated against a virus, if its antigens change, your white blood cells won't recognise it and you won't be immune.

If this happened, precautions could be taken to stop the virus spreading in the first place (though this is hard nowadays — millions of people travel by plane every day). And vaccines and antiviral drugs could be developed (though these take time to mass produce). But in the worst-case scenario, a flu **pandemic** (when a disease spreads all over the world) could kill billions of people.

> **Example**
>
> Between 1918 and 1920, a mutated strain of the H1N1 flu virus caused a pandemic that is thought to have killed up to 50 million people.

Practice Questions — Fact Recall

Q1 What did the doctor Ignaz Semmelweis discover in relation to infectious disease?

Q2 How have antibiotics affected death rates from infectious diseases?

Q3 Explain why drug companies are trying to develop new antibiotics.

Practice Question — Application

Q1 In 2009, a mutated version of the H1N1 virus appeared, causing a flu pandemic. Suggest how the appearance of the mutated virus might have led to the pandemic.

Section Checklist — Make sure you know...

Diet and Metabolic Rate

- [ ] That for good health, you need a balanced diet — this provides the energy you need (but not more), as well as the right balance of nutrients.
- [ ] That carbohydrates and fats are needed by the body to provide energy and that proteins are needed for growth, cell repair and cell replacement.
- [ ] That the body needs tiny amounts of vitamins and mineral ions to keep healthy.
- [ ] That your metabolic rate is the speed at which the chemical reactions in your body occur.
- [ ] How things like muscle mass and exercise habits affect resting metabolic rate.
- [ ] That the more exercise you do, the more energy you use.

Factors Affecting Health

- [ ] That you can become malnourished by eating an unbalanced diet and that malnourished people can be underweight or overweight.
- [ ] That an unbalanced diet can lead to obesity, which increases your risk of type 2 diabetes.
- [ ] That an unbalanced diet can result in a lack of vitamins or minerals, which can cause deficiency diseases.
- [ ] That exercise keeps you healthy by increasing the amount of energy used by the body and decreasing the amount stored as fat.
- [ ] That inherited factors can affect your metabolic rate, overall health and blood cholesterol level.

Evaluating Food, Lifestyle and Diet

- [ ] How to evaluate information about how food and lifestyle affect health, and how lifestyle affects disease.
- [ ] That to lose weight you need to take in less energy than you use up, so you need to eat less or exercise more.
- [ ] How to evaluate claims made about slimming products.

Fighting Disease

- [ ] That pathogens are microorganisms that enter the body and cause disease, e.g. bacteria and viruses.
- [ ] That bacteria make you feel ill by producing toxins and causing cell damage, and that viruses make you feel ill through cell damage.
- [ ] How the body defends itself against pathogen entry (e.g. through the skin and respiratory tract).
- [ ] How white blood cells help to defend the body against pathogens — by engulfing pathogens, producing antitoxins and producing antibodies.
- [ ] That antibodies only lock onto and kill specific pathogens.
- [ ] How the production of antibodies leads to immunity — if you're infected with a pathogen for a second time, white blood cells will rapidly produce antibodies to kill it and you won't get ill. **cont...**

Fighting Disease — Vaccination

☐ How vaccinations work — dead or inactive pathogens are used to trigger the production of antibodies by white blood cells.

☐ That the MMR vaccine is given to children to protect them against measles, mumps and rubella.

☐ That if enough people are immune to a particular pathogen, it can reduce the spread of the pathogen, preventing an epidemic.

☐ The pros and cons of vaccinations and how to evaluate them.

Fighting Disease — Drugs

☐ That drugs (such as painkillers) reduce the symptoms of a disease, but don't kill pathogens.

☐ That antibiotics (such as penicillin) are drugs that kill the bacteria which cause infectious diseases.

☐ That antibiotics are specific, so it's important to be treated with the right one.

☐ That antibiotics don't destroy viruses.

☐ That viruses reproduce inside body cells, making it difficult to develop drugs against them.

☐ That bacteria can mutate, leading to the development of antibiotic resistance by natural selection and that MRSA is an example of a strain of antibiotic-resistant bacteria.

☐ 🄷 How populations of antibiotic-resistant bacteria develop — when you treat an infection, only resistant bacteria will survive and reproduce, increasing the population of the resistant strain.

☐ That to prevent antibiotic resistance spreading, it's important not to over-use antibiotics.

☐ 🄷 That doctors won't usually prescribe antibiotics for a mild infection, e.g. a sore throat.

Fighting Disease — Investigating Antibiotic Action

☐ That the effectiveness of antibiotics and disinfectants can be tested by growing cultures in the lab.

☐ How to prevent the contamination of bacterial cultures — by passing inoculating loops through a flame to sterilise them, by sterilising Petri dishes and culture media, and by taping lids onto Petri dishes.

☐ Why bacterial cultures are kept at 25 °C in schools, but at higher temperatures in industry.

Fighting Disease — Past & Future

☐ How Semmelweis reduced deaths from infectious disease through hand-washing and how this still applies in modern hospitals.

☐ That increased understanding of immunity and antibiotic action has changed how we treat disease.

☐ That antibiotics have reduced deaths from bacterial diseases such as pneumonia.

☐ Why antibiotic resistance in bacteria is increasing (e.g. the over-use of antibiotics).

☐ That new antibiotics are being developed as a result of increasing antibiotic resistance.

☐ How mutations in bacteria and viruses could lead to epidemics and pandemics.

☐ What the consequences of these epidemics and pandemics might be and how to evaluate them.

Exam-style Questions

1   The Body Mass Index (BMI) can be used to determine
whether people are overweight or underweight.

1 (a)   The formula given below can be used to calculate BMI.
The table shows how BMI can be used to classify people's weight.

$$BMI = \frac{body\ mass\ (in\ kg)}{height^2\ (in\ m)}$$

BMI	Weight Description
below 18.5	underweight
18.5 - 24.9	normal
25 - 29.9	overweight
30 - 40	moderately obese
above 40	severely obese

1 (a) (i)   Kate is 1.56 m tall. She weighs 64 kg. Use the formula to calculate Kate's BMI.

(1 mark)

1 (a) (ii)   According to the table, what is Kate's weight description?

(1 mark)

1 (b)   An excess of carbohydrate or fat in the diet can cause weight gain.
What are both carbohydrate and fat needed for by the body?

(1 mark)

1 (c)   Explain how exercise can help you to lose weight.

(2 marks)

2   Robin is going on holiday. His doctor advises him to get a vaccination against the
hepatitis A virus. The virus causes a type of liver disease.

2 (a)   Suggest how the hepatitis A virus makes you feel ill.

(1 mark)

2 (b) (i)   The vaccination should make Robin immune to hepatitis A.
Suggest how it will work.

(4 marks)

2 (b) (ii)   The vaccination against hepatitis A will not make Robin immune
to the hepatitis B virus. Explain why.

(2 marks)

2 (c)   There are currently no drugs available which will cure hepatitis A.

Suggest why scientists may have had difficulty developing
a drug that will get rid of a hepatitis A infection.

(2 marks)

3   The graph below shows the number of measles cases reported each year worldwide, along with the estimated vaccine coverage.

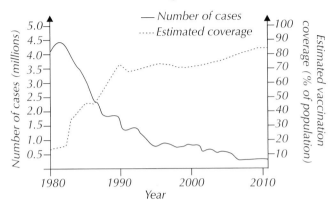

3 (a)   Measles is caused by a pathogen. What is a pathogen?

(1 mark)

3 (b)   Describe the trends shown in the graph.
Use data from the graph to support your answer.

(4 marks)

3 (c)   Evaluate how far this data supports the case for vaccinating
people against measles.

(3 marks)

4   A doctor needs to find out which antibiotics will treat a patient's infection,
so she sends a sample of bacteria taken from the patient to be cultured in the lab.

A lab technician fills a Petri dish with agar jelly. When this has set, he transfers the
bacterial sample to the dish using an inoculating loop.

4 (a)   Describe **two** steps the lab technician should take during this process to avoid
contamination of the bacterial culture.

(2 marks)

Once the lab technician has transferred
the bacteria, he places 5 different
paper discs, each soaked in a different
antibiotic, onto the agar. He also puts
one paper disc that hasn't been soaked
in antibiotic onto the agar. He leaves
the Petri dish overnight. The diagram
shows the dish a few days later.

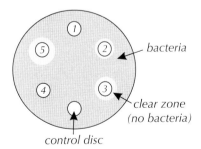

4 (b)   From these results, which antibiotic (1-5) is the best one to use to treat the patient's
infection? Explain your answer.

(2 marks)

4 (c)   The bacteria that caused the infection are resistant to some of the antibiotics tested.
Explain how the bacteria may have developed resistance to these antibiotics.

(5 marks)

1. The Nervous System

First up in this section, an overview of the nervous system...

What is the nervous system?

Your nervous system is what allows you to respond to changes in your environment. It also allows you to coordinate your actions. The nervous system is made up of all the **neurones** (nerve cells) in your body — there's more on these on the next page.

Stimuli and receptors

A change in your environment that you might need to respond to is called a **stimulus** (the plural is 'stimuli'). A stimulus can be light, sound, touch, pressure, pain, chemical, or a change in position or temperature.

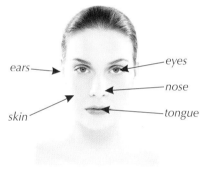

ears — *eyes*

nose

skin — *tongue*

Figure 1: *The five sense organs.*

Stimuli are detected by groups of cells called **receptors**. They change stimulus energy (e.g. light energy) into electrical impulses.

Many receptors are found in **sense organs**. You have five different sense organs — eyes, ears, nose, tongue and skin (see Figure 1). They all contain different receptors.

Learning Objectives:

- Know that the nervous system allows humans to respond to their environment and coordinate actions.
- Know that changes in the environment (stimuli) are detected by receptor cells.
- Know that light is detected by receptor cells in our eyes, and how these receptor cells have the same structure as most other animal cells.
- Know the types of stimuli receptors in our ears, nose, tongue and skin detect.
- Know that information from receptors travels via neurones to the brain, where a response is coordinated.
- Know that muscles and glands are effectors.
- Know how muscles and glands respond to nervous impulses.

Specification Reference B1.2.1

The sense organs and their receptors

- **Eyes** — contain light receptors which are sensitive to light. Like most animal cells, light receptors have a structure called a **nucleus**, which contains their genetic material (see page 96). They're also filled with a jelly-like substance called **cytoplasm** and are surrounded by a **cell membrane** (see Figure 2).

- **Ears** — contain sound receptors which are sensitive to sound. They also contain "balance" receptors which are sensitive to changes in position.

- **Nose** — contains smell receptors which are sensitive to chemical stimuli.

- **Tongue** — contains taste receptors which are sensitive to chemical stimuli. The taste receptors can detect bitter, salt, sweet and sour, plus the taste of savoury things like monosodium glutamate (MSG).

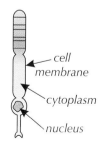

cell membrane

cytoplasm

nucleus

Figure 2: *A light receptor cell.*

Tip: Nerve impulses are electrical signals that pass along neurones. They carry information around the body at a very high speed.

- **Skin** — contains receptors that are sensitive to touch, pressure, pain and temperature change.

The central nervous system (CNS)

The central nervous system (CNS) is where all the information from the receptors is sent, and where reflexes (see p. 43) and actions are coordinated.

The central nervous system consists of the brain and spinal cord only (see Figure 3). Neurones transmit information as electrical impulses to and from the CNS. This happens very quickly.

Effectors

'Instructions' from the CNS are sent along neurones to **effectors**. Effectors are **muscles** or **glands** which respond to nervous impulses and bring about a response to a stimulus. Muscles and glands respond to nervous impulses in different ways:

- Muscles contract.

- Glands secrete chemical substances called hormones (see page 47).

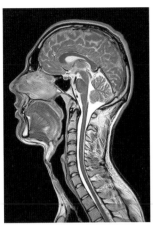

Figure 3: *Scan of the head and neck. The brain and upper spinal cord can be seen in orange/red.*

Different types of neurone

Different types of neurone are involved in the transfer of information to and from the CNS:

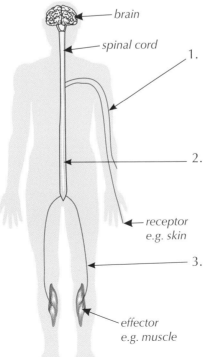

brain

spinal cord

1. **Sensory neurones**
   The nerve cells that carry signals as electrical impulses from the receptors in the sense organs to the central nervous system.

2. **Relay neurones**
   The nerve cells that carry signals from sensory neurones to motor neurones. They are found in the central nervous system.

receptor
e.g. skin

3. **Motor neurones**
   The nerve cells that carry signals from the central nervous system to the effectors.

effector
e.g. muscle

The transmission of information to and from the CNS is summarised in Figure 4:

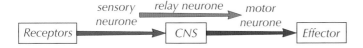

Figure 4: *Flow diagram showing the transmission of information to and from the CNS.*

Practice Questions — Fact Recall

Q1   What is a stimulus?

Q2   What are cells called that detect stimuli?

Q3   The diagram on the right is a light receptor cell.
      What is the object labelled X?

Q4   Which two sense organs are sensitive to chemical stimuli?

Q5   Which type of effector secretes hormones?

Q6   A sensory neurone is a type of neurone.
      Name two other types of neurone.

Practice Questions — Application

Q1   A dog hears a cat moving in the garden, so runs towards it.

   a) i) What is the stimulus in this situation?

      ii) What detects the stimulus in this situation?

      iii) What name is given to the type of neurone that transmits
          information about the stimulus to the central nervous system?

   The dog's brain sends an impulse to the dog's muscles which
   act as an effector.

   b) i) What type of neurone transmits information from the central
          nervous system to an effector?

      ii) How do the dog's muscles respond to the nerve impulse?

Q2   Complete the table to show how each stimulus is detected.

Stimulus	Sense Organ	Receptors Sensitive To
A loud bang		
A moving object		
Walking on a slanted floor		
Touching a hot object		
An unpleasant smell		
Standing on a pin		

Exam Tip
Make sure you know
which type of neurone
transfers information
to which place in the
nervous system — it's
easy to get the different
types of neurones
confused and they often
come up in exams.

Learning Objectives:

- Know that synapses are connections between neurones.

- Understand that chemicals are released at the synapses, which allows information to be transferred from one neurone to the next.

- Know that reflexes are fast, automatic responses to stimuli.

- Know that sensory neurones, relay neurones and motor neurones are all involved in reflexes.

- Know the order of events in a simple reflex action and understand the roles of receptors, effectors, sensory neurones, relay neurones, motor neurones and synapses.

Specification Reference
B1.2.1

2. Synapses and Reflexes

Reflexes are rapid responses to stimuli that happen without you having to think about them — they're automatic. The neurones involved in a reflex aren't all joined together though — they have gaps between them called synapses.

Synapses

The connection between two neurones is called a synapse. The nerve signal is transferred by chemicals which diffuse (move) across the gap. These chemicals then set off a new electrical signal in the next neurone. This is shown in Figure 1.

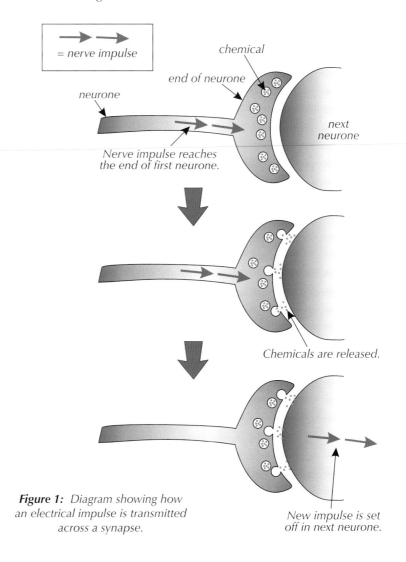

Figure 1: *Diagram showing how an electrical impulse is transmitted across a synapse.*

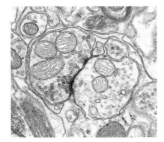

Figure 2: *A synapse viewed under a microscope. The neurones are shown in green. The red dots contain the chemicals that diffuse between the neurones.*

Neurones deliver information really quickly because the signal is transmitted by electrical impulses. Synapses slow down the transmission of a nervous impulse because the diffusion of chemicals across the gap takes time (it's still pretty fast though).

Reflexes

Reflexes are fast, automatic responses to certain stimuli. They bypass your conscious brain completely when a quick response is essential — your body just gets on with things. Reflexes can reduce your chance of being injured, although they have other roles as well.

Tip: 'Automatic' means done without thinking.

Examples

- If someone shines a bright light in your eyes, your pupils automatically get smaller. This means that less light gets into your eyes, which stops them getting damaged.

- Adrenaline is a hormone (see p. 47), which gets your body ready for action. If you get a shock, your body releases adrenaline automatically — it doesn't wait for you to decide that you're shocked.

- The knee-jerk reflex helps maintain posture and balance. Doctors test this reflex by tapping just below the knee with a small hammer. This stimulates pressure receptors, making a muscle in the upper leg contract, which causes the lower leg to rise up.

Figure 3: *The knee-jerk reflex. Doctors often use this test to see if a patient's reflexes are working properly.*

Reflex arcs

The passage of information in a reflex (from receptor to effector) is called a reflex arc. The neurones in reflex arcs go through the spinal cord or through an unconscious part of the brain. Here are the main stages in a reflex arc:

1. When a stimulus is detected by receptors, impulses are sent along a sensory neurone to the CNS.

2. When the impulses reach a synapse between the sensory neurone and a relay neurone, they trigger chemicals to be released (see previous page). These chemicals cause impulses to be sent along the relay neurone.

3. When the impulses reach a synapse between the relay neurone and a motor neurone, the same thing happens. Chemicals are released and cause impulses to be sent along the motor neurone.

4. The impulses then travel along the motor neurone to the effector.

5. If the effector is a muscle, it will respond to the impulse by contracting. If it's a gland, it will secrete a hormone.

Because you don't have to think about the response (which takes time) a reflex is quicker than normal responses. Figure 4 summarises a reflex arc:

Tip: Flick back to page 40 for more on sensory, relay and motor neurones.

Tip: Remember, electrical impulses pass between the different neurones via diffusion of chemicals at the synapse. They don't just jump between the neurones.

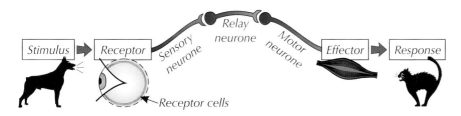

Figure 4: *Block diagram of a reflex arc.*

Example

If a bee stings a person's finger, the reflex response is that the hand moves away from the source of pain. Here's the pathway taken by this reflex arc:

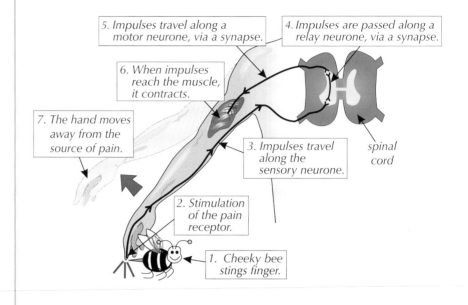

5. Impulses travel along a motor neurone, via a synapse.

4. Impulses are passed along a relay neurone, via a synapse.

6. When impulses reach the muscle, it contracts.

7. The hand moves away from the source of pain.

3. Impulses travel along the sensory neurone.

spinal cord

2. Stimulation of the pain receptor.

1. Cheeky bee stings finger.

Practice Questions — Fact Recall

Q1 a) What is the connection between two neurones called?

b) How do nerve impulses travel between two neurones?

Q2 What is a reflex?

Q3 Do reflex arcs travel through conscious parts of the brain?

Q4 What neurone comes after the sensory neurone in a reflex arc?

Q5 If the effector in a reflex arc is a gland, what will the response of that reflex arc be?

Practice Question — Application

David steps on a drawing pin and immediately pulls his foot up off the pin.

Q1 a) What is the stimulus in this response?

b) What is the effector in this response? How does it respond?

c) Complete the pathway taken by this reflex arc.

Stimulus → Receptor → Sensory neurone...

3. Homeostasis

The internal conditions in the body must be kept constant — it stops cell damage that could happen if we didn't keep on top of things. Luckily there are some clever systems in place to keep everything plodding along steadily.

What is homeostasis?

To keep all your cells working properly, certain things must be kept at the right level — not too high, and not too low. Homeostasis is the way in which this happens. The posh way of saying it is that "homeostasis is the maintenance of a constant internal environment".

Bodily levels that need to be controlled include:

Examples

- Temperature
- Ion content of the body
- Water content of the body
- Blood glucose content

There's a bit more on each of these examples in the rest of this topic.

Learning Objectives:

- Know that the internal conditions in the body must be carefully controlled.
- Know why body temperature must be controlled.
- Know that the ion content of the body is controlled and that ions leave the body via the skin in sweat and via the kidneys in urine.
- Know that the water content of the body is controlled and how water leaves the body via the lungs, the skin and the kidneys.
- Know why the blood glucose level needs carefully regulating.

Specification Reference
B1.2.2

Controlling body temperature

All of your metabolic reactions (the chemical reactions that go on inside your body to keep you alive) are controlled by proteins called **enzymes**. The enzymes within the human body work best at about 37 °C — and so this is the temperature your body tries to maintain.

A part of the brain acts as your own personal thermostat. It's sensitive to the blood temperature in the brain, and it receives messages from receptors in the skin that provide information about skin temperature.

Body temperature needs to be controlled to within a few degrees. If it becomes too high or too low it can be very dangerous.

Controlling ion content

Ions (e.g. sodium, Na^+) are taken into the body in food, then absorbed into the blood. If the food contains too much of any kind of ion then the excess ions need to be removed. E.g. a salty meal will contain far too much Na^+.

Some ions are lost in sweat (which tastes salty, you'll have noticed). The kidneys (see Figure 1) will remove the excess from the blood — this is then got rid of in urine.

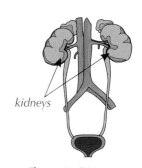

kidneys

Figure 1: *Diagram of the kidneys*

Controlling water content

There's also a need for the body to constantly balance the water coming in against the water going out. Water is taken into the body as food and drink and is lost from the body in these ways:

Tip: Some water is also lost in faeces. Lovely.

- through the skin as sweat.
- via the lungs in breath.
- via the kidneys as urine.

The balance between sweat and urine can depend on what you're doing, or what the weather's like...

Examples

- On a cold day, or when you're not exercising, you don't sweat much, so you'll produce more urine, which will be pale (since the waste carried in the urine is more diluted).

- On a hot day, or when you're exercising, you sweat a lot, and so you will produce less urine, but this will be more concentrated (and hence a deeper colour). You will also lose more water through your breath when you exercise because you breathe faster.

Figure 2: During exercise water is lost through sweating, and this has to be replaced.

Tip: For more on metabolism, have a look back at page 16.

Controlling blood glucose

Eating foods containing carbohydrate puts glucose (a sugar) into the blood from the gut. The normal **metabolism** of cells removes glucose from the blood. But if you do a lot of vigorous exercise, then much more glucose is removed.

That's because glucose is used by your cells as an energy source. A hormone called **insulin** helps to maintain the right level of glucose in your blood, so your cells get a constant supply of energy.

Practice Questions — Fact Recall

Q1   What is homeostasis?

Q2   Why must body temperature be kept constant?

Q3   Give two ways in which ions are lost from the body.

Q4   Give three ways in which water is lost from the body.

Q5   Name a hormone involved in the regulation of the blood glucose level.

Q6   Why must the blood glucose level be carefully controlled?

4. Hormones

Along with the nervous system, hormones allow us to react to changes in the environment and in our bodies in order to keep everything ticking over nicely.

What are hormones?

Hormones are chemicals released directly into the blood to regulate bodily processes. They are carried in the **blood plasma** (the liquid part of the blood) to other parts of the body, but only affect particular cells (called **target cells**) in particular places. Hormones control things in organs and cells that need constant adjustment.

Examples

- Follicle stimulating hormone (FSH), luteinising hormone (LH) and oestrogen are hormones involved in the regulation of the menstrual cycle (see pages 49-51).

- Insulin is a hormone that helps control the glucose content of the blood.

Make sure you learn this definition:

> Hormones are chemical messengers which travel in the blood to activate target cells.

Glands

Hormones are produced in (and secreted by) various **glands**.

Examples

1. The **pituitary gland** — this produces many important hormones including FSH and LH.

2. The **ovaries** (females only). The ovaries produce oestrogen.

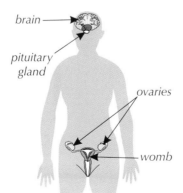

brain
pituitary gland
ovaries
womb

Figure 1: *Diagram showing the location of the pituitary and ovaries in the body.*

As hormones are carried in the blood, they tend to travel around the body relatively slowly (compared to nervous impulses anyway). They also tend to have relatively long-lasting effects.

Learning Objectives:

- Know that hormones are chemical substances which control many functions in organs and cells.
- Know that hormones are carried in the blood to their target organs.
- Know that glands secrete hormones.
- Know that the pituitary gland secretes follicle stimulating hormone (FSH) and the ovaries secrete oestrogen.

Specification Reference B1.2.2

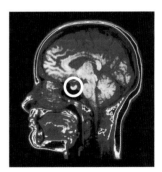

Figure 2: *Scan of the brain. The pituitary gland (green structure) is circled in white.*

Exam Tip
The pituitary gland and the ovaries are the two examples of glands that you need to learn for the exam. There are loads more glands in the body though, each doing its own thing.

Comparing nerves and hormones

Hormones and nerves do similar jobs in the body, but with a few differences. These are summarised in Figure 3.

Nerves	Hormones
Fast action	Slower action
Act for a short time	Act for a long time
Acts on a very precise area	Acts in a more general way

Figure 3: *Table summarising the differences between nerves and hormones.*

If you're not sure whether a response is nervous or hormonal, have a think...

- If the response is really quick, it's probably nervous.
  Some information needs to be passed to effectors really quickly (e.g. pain signals, or information from your eyes telling you about a car heading your way), so it's no good using hormones to carry the message — they're too slow.

- If a response lasts for a long time, it's probably hormonal.
  For example, when you get a shock, a hormone called adrenaline is released into the body (causing the fight-or-flight response, where your body is hyped up ready for action). You can tell it's a hormonal response (even though it kicks in pretty quickly) because you feel a bit wobbly for a while afterwards.

Exam Tip
Try and learn to spell difficult words like 'pituitary'. In some questions you'll be marked on your spelling and, even when you're not, you still need to make sure the examiner knows what you're talking about.

Practice Questions — Fact Recall

Q1   How are hormones carried around the body?

Q2   True or false? Hormones affect all cells.

Q3   Name a hormone secreted from the pituitary gland.

Q4   Name a hormone secreted from the ovaries.

Q5   Which produces a faster response — nerves or hormones?

5. The Menstrual Cycle

Hormones secreted by the ovaries and the pituitary gland are responsible for controlling the changes that occur during a woman's menstrual cycle.

What is the menstrual cycle?

The menstrual cycle is the monthly sequence of events in which the female body releases an egg and prepares the **uterus** (womb) in case it receives a fertilised egg. This includes:

- The build-up of the protective lining in the uterus ready for the implantation of a fertilised egg.

- The release of an egg from the woman's ovaries.

- The breakdown of the uterus lining if a fertilised egg does not implant. This results in bleeding, which is known as menstruation (a period).

Learning Objectives:

- Know that hormones secreted by the ovaries and pituitary gland control the menstrual cycle.

- Know that follicle stimulating hormone (FSH), luteinising hormone (LH) and oestrogen are all involved in the menstrual cycle.

- Know that FSH promotes egg maturation and causes the ovaries to produce hormones such as oestrogen.

- Know that LH stimulates the release of an egg.

- Know that oestrogen inhibits FSH production.

Specification Reference
B1.2.2

The four stages of the menstrual cycle

The menstrual cycle has four stages. These are shown in Figure 1 and are explained below.

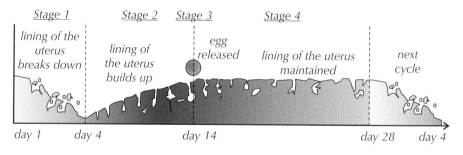

Figure 1: Diagram showing the four stages of the menstrual cycle.

- **Stage 1**
  Day 1 is when the bleeding starts.
  The uterus lining breaks down for about four days.

- **Stage 2**
  The lining of the uterus builds up again, from day 4 to day 14, into a thick spongy layer full of blood vessels, ready to receive a fertilised egg.

- **Stage 3**
  An egg is released from the ovary at day 14.

- **Stage 4**
  The wall is then maintained for about 14 days, until day 28.
  If no fertilised egg has landed on the uterus wall by day 28, the spongy lining starts to break down again and the whole cycle starts again.

Figure 2: A microscope image showing an egg (pink oval) being released from an ovary (brown).

Hormonal control of the menstrual cycle

You need to know about these three hormones that are involved in the menstrual cycle:

1. FSH (Follicle Stimulating Hormone)

- Produced by the pituitary gland.
- Causes an egg to mature in one of the ovaries and stimulates the ovaries to produce oestrogen (see Figure 3).

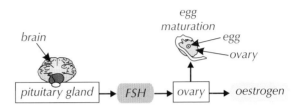

Figure 3: Diagram showing the role of FSH in the menstrual cycle.

2. Oestrogen

- Produced in the ovaries.
- Causes the pituitary gland to produce LH (see below) and inhibits the further release of FSH (see Figure 4).

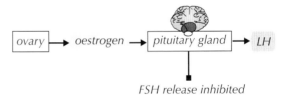

Figure 4: Diagram showing the role of oestrogen in the menstrual cycle.

3. LH (Luteinising Hormone)

- Produced by the pituitary gland.
- Stimulates the release of an egg at around the middle (day 14) of the menstrual cycle (see Figure 5).

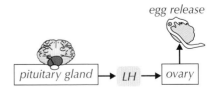

Figure 5: Diagram showing the role of LH in the menstrual cycle.

Levels of FSH, oestrogen and LH change throughout the menstrual cycle. So the level of one hormone can be used to predict the level of another hormone:

> **Example**
>
> FSH stimulates the ovaries to produce oestrogen, so if the FSH level rises, you'd expect the oestrogen level to rise too. The increasing oestrogen level will then inhibit FSH release, causing the FSH level to drop.

Practice Questions — Fact Recall

Q1   What is the hormone FSH responsible for in the menstrual cycle?

Q2   Which hormone inhibits the release of FSH?

Q3   What is the function of LH?

Q4   Which two glands secrete the hormones that control the menstrual cycle?

Practice Question — Application

Q1   The graph below shows the level of a hormone measured in the bloodstream of one woman during her 28 day menstrual cycle.

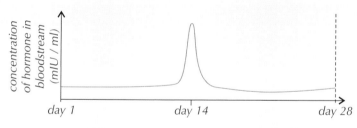

a) Which hormone do you think is shown on the graph? Give a reason for your answer.

b) Where is the hormone you gave in part a) produced?

c) The graph below shows the level of the same hormone measured in another woman during her 28 day menstrual cycle. This woman is struggling to have children. Suggest why this might be.

Tip: Think about what happens around the middle of the menstrual cycle.

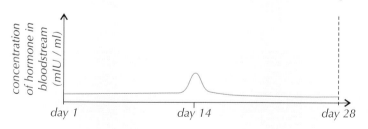

Tip: Both graphs are drawn to the same scale.

- Understand that hormones can be used to control fertility.
- Know that oestrogen and progesterone can be taken in oral contraceptives to inhibit FSH production, which prevents eggs from maturing, therefore reducing fertility.
- Know why oral contraceptives used to cause more significant side effects and how the number of side effects has now been reduced.
- Know that FSH and LH can be taken to increase fertility in women whose FSH levels are too low.
- Understand the steps involved in In Vitro Fertilisation (IVF).
- Be able to evaluate the use of IVF and hormones to control fertility.

Specification Reference
B1.2.2

6. Controlling Fertility

The hormones involved in the menstrual cycle can be used to increase or decrease a woman's fertility. This is useful for a whole load of reasons...

Reducing fertility

Contraceptives are used to prevent pregnancy. The hormones oestrogen and progesterone can be taken by women to reduce their **fertility** (their ability to get pregnant) and so are often used as contraceptives.

Oestrogen

Oestrogen can be used to prevent egg release. This may seem kind of strange (since naturally oestrogen helps stimulate the release of eggs — see page 50). But if oestrogen is taken every day to keep the level of it permanently high, it inhibits FSH production, and after a while egg maturation and therefore egg release stop.

Progesterone

Progesterone (another hormone involved in the menstrual cycle) also reduces fertility, e.g. by stimulating the production of thick cervical mucus which prevents any sperm getting through and reaching an egg. It can inhibit egg maturation and therefore the release of an egg too.

Oral contraceptives

The pill is an oral contraceptive (it can be taken by mouth to decrease fertility). The first version (known as the **combined oral contraceptive pill**) was made in the 1950s and contained high levels of oestrogen and progesterone.

However, there were concerns about a link between oestrogen in the pill and side effects like blood clots. The pill now contains lower doses of oestrogen so has fewer side effects.

There's also a **progesterone-only pill** — it has fewer side effects than the combined pill (but it's not as effective).

There are both positives and negatives associated with using the pill:

Benefits of the combined oral contraceptive pill

- The pill's over 99% effective at preventing pregnancy.
- It's also been shown to reduce the risk of getting some types of cancer.

Problems with the combined oral contraceptive pill

- It isn't 100% effective — there's still a very slight chance of getting pregnant.
- It can cause side effects like headaches, nausea, irregular menstrual bleeding, and fluid retention.
- It doesn't protect against STDs (sexually transmitted diseases).

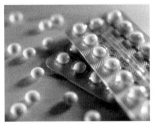

Figure 1: *The contraceptive pill is used to reduce fertility, decreasing the risk of pregnancy.*

Tip: Oral contraceptives are sometimes called birth-control pills.

Increasing fertility

Hormones can also be taken by women to increase their fertility.
For example, some women have an FSH level that is too low to cause their
eggs to mature. This means that no eggs are released and the women can't
get pregnant.

The hormones FSH and LH can be injected by these women to stimulate egg
maturation and release in their ovaries. These 'fertility drugs' can help a lot of
women to get pregnant when previously they couldn't. They are often used
during IVF too — see below.

> **Tip:** Flick back to page 50 for a reminder of what the hormones FSH and LH do.

Problems with fertility drugs

Using fertility drugs like FSH and LH has its problems:

- They don't always work — some women may have to use the treatment many times, which can be expensive.

- Too many eggs could be stimulated, resulting in unexpected multiple pregnancies (twins, triplets etc.).

> **Tip:** As well as being hard work, having multiple births puts a bigger stress on the mother and embryos' health during pregnancy.

In Vitro Fertilisation (IVF)

IVF is a process that can be used to help couples who are having difficulty having children.

IVF involves the following steps:

1. FSH and LH are given to the woman to stimulate the maturation of multiple eggs.

2. Eggs are then collected from the woman's ovaries.

3. The eggs are fertilised in a lab using the man's sperm.

4. The fertilised eggs then grow into embryos (small balls of cells).

5. Once the embryos have formed, one or two of them are transferred to the woman's uterus. Transferring more than one improves the chance of pregnancy.

This is summarised in Figure 2.

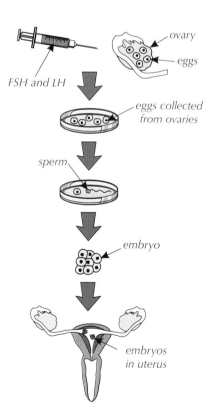

FSH and LH

ovary
eggs

eggs collected from ovaries

sperm

embryo

embryos in uterus

Figure 2: *Diagram showing the steps involved in IVF.*

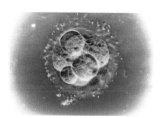

Figure 3: *An embryo ready for transfer into a uterus.*

The pros and cons of IVF

The main benefit of IVF is that it can give an infertile couple a child — a pretty obvious benefit. However there are negative sides to the treatment:

- Some women have a strong reaction to the hormones — e.g. abdominal pain, vomiting, dehydration.

- There have been some reports of an increased risk of cancer due to the hormonal treatment (though others have reported no such risk — the position isn't really clear at the moment).

- Multiple births can happen if more than one embryo grows into a baby — these are risky for the mother and babies (there's a higher risk of miscarriage, stillbirth...).

Practice Questions — Fact Recall

Q1 Explain the function of oestrogen in the combined contraceptive pill.

Q2 Apart from oestrogen, what hormone is found in the combined pill?

Q3 Why does the modern pill only contain small amounts of oestrogen?

Q4 FSH and LH can be given to women to stimulate egg maturation and release. Give a problem associated with using hormones in this way.

Q5 What is the next step after egg collection in IVF?

Q6 When are embryos transferred into the uterus during IVF?

Practice Question — Application

Q1 Jenny is 28 and is considering IVF as she and her partner are struggling to have children.

a) At the fertility clinic, the doctors discover that Jenny has an extremely low level of the hormone FSH. Explain how this may be preventing her from becoming pregnant.

b) The table shows some data about women aged 18-34 undergoing IVF in the UK in 2009 and 2010 using their own fresh eggs.

Year	Number of embryo transfers during IVF	Number of IVF pregnancies
2009	15813	6433
2010	16652	6695

Calculate the percentage of embryo transfers that resulted in pregnancy for 18-34 year olds undergoing IVF in 2010.

c) The average multiple pregnancy rate of women undergoing IVF in 2010 in the UK with their own fresh eggs was 22.2%. The multiple pregnancy rate of normal pregnancies was lower than this. Give a reason why this might be.

Tip: IVF can be done using a woman's own fresh eggs (eggs freshly collected from the woman), frozen eggs (eggs which have been extracted at an earlier date and frozen until needed), or using eggs from another woman.

Exam Tip
Read any data given to you carefully. In this question, make sure you're using the correct numbers from the table.

7. Plant Hormones

Like animals, plants have to respond to stimuli. Plant hormones control and coordinate the response of plants to light, moisture and gravity.

A plant's needs

Plants need to be able to detect and respond to stimuli (changes in the environment) in order to survive:

Examples

- Plants need light to make their own food. Plants can sense light, and grow towards it in order to maximise the amount of light they receive.

- Plants also need water to survive. They can sense moisture in the soil, so their roots grow towards it.

- Plants can sense and respond to gravity. This makes sure that their roots and shoots grow in the right direction.

Auxin

Auxin is a plant hormone that controls growth near the tips of shoots and roots. It controls the growth of a plant in response to different stimuli.

Auxin controls:

- **Phototropism** — plant growth in response to light.

- **Gravitropism** (also known as **geotropism**) — plant growth in response to gravity.

- Plant growth in response to moisture.

Auxin is produced in the tips of roots and shoots and moves backwards to stimulate the **cell elongation** process which occurs in the cells just behind the tips (see Figure 2). If the tip of a shoot is removed, no auxin is available and the shoot may stop growing.

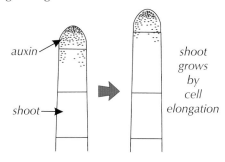

auxin

shoot

shoot grows by cell elongation

Figure 2: *Auxin release from the tips of shoots results in cell elongation and shoot growth.*

Learning Objectives:

- Understand that the hormone auxin controls phototropism and gravitropism (geotropism) in plants.

- Know that plants respond to light, gravity and moisture, because of the uneven distribution of auxin, which causes uneven growth rates in the shoots and roots.

- Know that plants' shoots grow towards light and away from gravity.

- Know that plants' roots grow towards moisture and gravity.

- Know that plant hormones are used as rooting compounds and weedkillers in agriculture and horticulture and be able to evaluate their use.

Specification Reference B1.2.3

Figure 1: *A plant displaying phototropism — its shoot is growing towards the light.*

Tip: Cell elongation just means that the cells of the plant get bigger (longer).

Shoot and root growth

Extra auxin promotes growth in the shoot but inhibits growth in the root. This, coupled with the unequal distribution of auxin in the shoot or root tip, produces the following results:

1. Shoots grow towards light

When a shoot tip is exposed to light, more auxin accumulates on the side that's in the shade than the side that's in the light. This makes the cells grow (elongate) faster on the shaded side, so the shoot bends towards the light (see Figure 3).

Tip: In <u>shoots</u>, more auxin on one side means that the cells on that side will <u>grow faster</u>. This will cause the plant to bend <u>away</u> from that side, e.g.

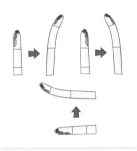

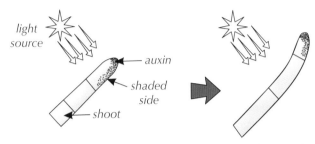

Figure 3: *Diagram to show how auxin causes shoot growth towards the light.*

2. Shoots grow away from gravity

When a shoot is growing sideways, gravity produces an unequal distribution of auxin in the tip, with more auxin on the lower side. This causes the lower side to grow faster, bending the shoot upwards, as shown in Figure 5.

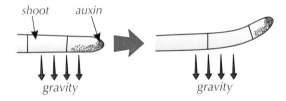

Figure 5: *Diagram to show how auxin causes shoot growth away from gravity.*

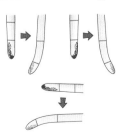

Figure 4: *A plant displaying gravitropism — its shoots are growing away from gravity.*

The distribution of auxin in response to gravity means that the shoot should always grow in the right direction (i.e. upwards), even in the absence of light.

3. Roots grow towards gravity

When a root is growing sideways, more auxin will accumulate on its lower side. In a root the extra auxin inhibits growth. This means the cells on top elongate faster, and the root bends downwards (see Figure 6).

Tip: In <u>roots</u>, more auxin on one side means that the cells on that side will <u>grow slower</u>. This will cause the plant to bend <u>towards</u> that side, e.g.

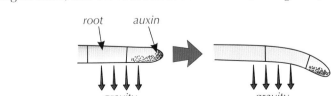

Figure 6: *Diagram to show how auxin causes root growth towards gravity.*

4. Roots grow towards moisture

An uneven amount of moisture either side of a root produces more auxin on the side with more moisture. This inhibits growth on that side, causing the root to bend in that direction, towards the moisture (see Figure 7).

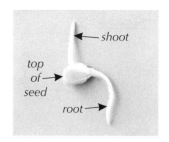

Figure 8: *This seed was grown sideways (not upright) and in the dark, but its shoot is growing upwards and its root downwards (i.e. in the right directions) because of gravitropism.*

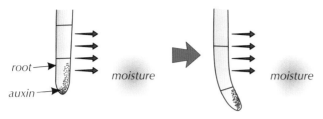

Figure 7: *Diagram to show how auxin causes root growth towards moisture.*

Uses of plant hormones

Plant hormones can be extracted and used by people in agriculture (farming) and horticulture (gardening). Artificial versions can also be made.

1. Selective weedkillers

Most weeds in crop fields are broad-leaved, unlike grasses and cereals which have very narrow leaves. Selective weedkillers are made of plant growth hormones — they only affect the broad-leaved plants. They disrupt their normal growth patterns, which soon kills them, but leave the crops untouched. You could be asked to interpret data on selective weedkillers in the exam:

Example

A farmer was studying the effect of selective weedkillers on barley yield. He grew the same type of barley in three fields of the same size and soil type. He used one type of selective weedkiller in Field A, another type in Field B, and left Field C untreated. He measured the crop yield of each field after one year. The results are shown in the graph.

Tip: Crop yield is a way of measuring the amount of crop produced by an area of land.

You could be asked to draw conclusions from the data...
From this graph, you can conclude that the crop yield for Field B was higher than the yields for Fields A and C. This could be because the weedkiller used to treat Field B was the most effective at removing weeds, which meant the crops had less competition, so the yield was greater.

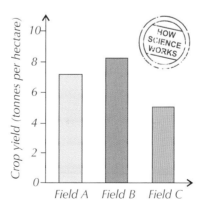

You could be asked why Field C was left untreated...
It was a control (see page 7) — the conditions were the same in Field C as the other fields (e.g. same sized field, same soil type, etc.) but no weedkiller was applied. This shows that the increased crop yield displayed in the other fields was likely to be due to the presence of weedkiller and nothing else.

Tip: Weeds compete with crops for resources, e.g. light and nutrients. If you remove the weeds, you remove the competition — so the crop will have more resources. This should mean that the crop grows more and produces a bigger yield. There's more on competition on p. 77.

2. Rooting powders

Plant cuttings won't always grow in soil. If you add rooting powder, which contains the plant hormone auxin, they'll produce roots rapidly and start growing as new plants. This helps growers to produce lots of clones of a really good plant very quickly.

Figure 9: *A gardener using rooting powder when planting cuttings.*

Practice Questions — Fact Recall

Q1   What is gravitropism?

Q2   What effect does auxin have on cell elongation in a plant root?

Q3   Explain how plant roots grow in response to moisture in the soil.

Practice Questions — Application

Q1   A scientist conducted an experiment to study phototropism in cress seedlings. 12 cress seeds were planted in Petri dish A and left directly under a light source. Another 12 cress seeds were planted in Petri dish B and provided with a light source placed to one side. The growth of the seeds after two weeks is shown in the diagram:

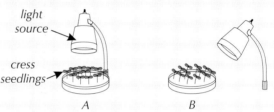

Tip: Don't forget to refer to the experiment in your answer to Q1 a). Don't just talk about what you know about auxin.

a) Describe how the distribution of auxin in the shoots of the cress seedlings will differ between Petri dish A and Petri dish B.

b) i)   Other than the position of the light source, the scientist tried to keep the conditions in both Petri dishes the same. Explain why she did this.

ii)   Give two conditions that the scientist needed to keep the same during the experiment.

Q2   Dan grows plants for a garden centre. He is trying to work out the best rooting powder to use for his cuttings. From the same type of plant, he grows 50 cuttings in rooting powder A, 50 in rooting powder B and 50 without rooting powder. He grows all the cuttings under the same conditions. His results are shown in the table.

		Powder A	Powder B	No powder
Average increase in root length (mm)	After 1 week	8	10	6
	After 2 weeks	17	19	14
	After 3 weeks	24	28	20

a) From these results, what can you conclude about which rooting powder is the best to use? Explain your answer.

b) Explain why Dan grew some cuttings without rooting powder.

Section Checklist — Make sure you know...

The Nervous System

☐ That the nervous system allows humans to respond to changes in the environment (stimuli) and to coordinate their behaviour.

☐ That receptor cells detect stimuli.

☐ That light receptor cells in the eyes contain a nucleus and cytoplasm, and are surrounded by a cell membrane, like most other animal cells.

☐ That receptor cells in the ears detect sound and aid balance, that chemical receptors in our nose and tongue allow us to smell and taste, and that receptors in our skin respond to touch, pressure, pain and changes in temperature.

☐ That information from receptors travels via neurones to the brain, where a response is coordinated.

☐ That effectors are muscles and glands, and that muscles respond to nervous impulses by contracting, and glands respond by secreting hormones.

Synapses and Reflexes

☐ That the connections between neurones are called synapses and that a nerve signal is transferred across a synapse by chemicals that diffuse across the gap.

☐ That reflexes are fast, automatic responses involving receptors, sensory neurones, relay neurones, motor neurones, synapses and effectors.

☐ That in a simple reflex, stimuli are detected by receptors and transmitted to the central nervous system as nervous impulses via sensory neurones. The impulses are then transferred via a relay neurone in the CNS to a motor neurone, which sends impulses to an effector. The effector then produces a response.

Homeostasis

☐ That internal conditions within the body, including body temperature, ion content, water content and blood glucose level need to be carefully controlled.

☐ That body temperature must be controlled to allow the enzymes involved in bodily processes to work at their best.

☐ That ions are removed from the body via the skin in sweat and via the kidneys in urine.

☐ That water leaves the body via the lungs in breath, the skin in sweat and the kidneys in the urine.

☐ That blood glucose must be regulated to ensure our cells get enough energy.

Hormones

☐ That hormones are chemical messengers which travel in the blood to activate target cells.

☐ That hormones are secreted by glands, e.g. follicle stimulating hormone (FSH) by the pituitary gland and oestrogen by the ovaries.

cont...

The Menstrual Cycle

❑ That the menstrual cycle (the monthly sequence of events in which the female body releases an egg and prepares the uterus in case it receives a fertilised egg) is controlled by hormones. These are secreted by the ovaries (e.g. oestrogen) and the pituitary gland (e.g. FSH and LH).

❑ That FSH causes eggs to mature and the ovaries to produce oestrogen, that luteinising hormone (LH) stimulates egg release and that oestrogen inhibits FSH production.

Controlling Fertility

❑ How the hormones oestrogen and progesterone can be used to decrease fertility.

❑ That oral contraceptives containing large doses of oestrogen used to cause many side effects, so oral contraceptives now contain lower doses of oestrogen or just progesterone.

❑ That progesterone-only pills cause fewer side effects than oral contraceptives containing oestrogen.

❑ How the hormones FSH and LH can be used as 'fertility drugs' to increase fertility.

❑ The pros and cons of using fertility drugs such as FSH and LH to control fertility, e.g. they may help women to get pregnant, but don't always work. They also increase the risk of multiple pregnancies.

❑ The basic process involved in In Vitro Fertilisation (IVF) — women are given FSH and LH to stimulate egg maturation and release. The eggs are collected and fertilised using sperm. The resulting embryos are grown until they are tiny balls of cells, at which point they are transferred into a uterus.

❑ The pros and cons associated with IVF, e.g. it can give a childless couple a child, but some women can react badly to the hormones and it's possible that the hormones may increase the risk of cancer. It also increases the risk of multiple births.

Plant Hormones

❑ That the plant hormone auxin is responsible for plant growth in response to light (phototropism), plant growth in response to gravity (gravitropism) and plant growth in response to moisture.

❑ How the uneven distribution of auxin leads to uneven rates of cell elongation, allowing plant shoots to grow towards light and away from gravity, and plant roots to grow towards moisture and gravity.

❑ That plant hormones are used as rooting compounds and weedkillers in agriculture and horticulture, and be able to evaluate their use.

Exam-style Questions

1   A scientist conducted an experiment on reaction time.

Subjects had an electrode placed on their upper arm to detect when their muscle contracted. The subjects were asked to place their finger on a metal disc, which gave out a small electric shock at random. This shock caused the muscle in the upper arm to contract.

The scientist measured reaction time as the time it took between the initiation of the shock and the contraction of the muscle in the upper arm.

The diagram shows the pathway taken in this reflex response.

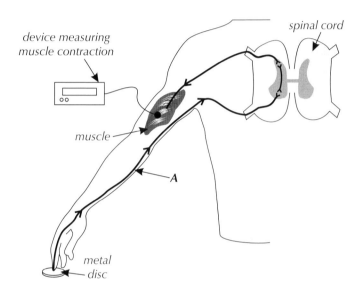

1 (a) (i)   What is the effector in this response?

(1 mark)

1 (a) (ii)   Name the neurone labelled **A** in the diagram.

(1 mark)

1 (b)   The average reaction time measured during the experiment was 0.024 s.

After he had recorded their reaction times, the scientist gave the subjects a drug which is known to increase the amount of chemical released at the synapses. He then repeated the experiment.

What do you think would happen to the average reaction time after administration of the drug? Explain your answer.

(2 marks)

1 (c)   Reflexes often help to protect us from injury.
Suggest and explain **two** features of reflexes that help them do this.

(4 marks)

2 The diagram shows a plant that has been kept in a cupboard for one week. While it was in the cupboard, it had three possible light sources (labelled **A**, **B** and **C** in the diagram).

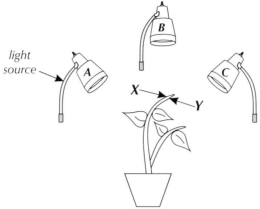

2 (a) (i) The plant only had one light source on during the week. Which light source do you think it was, **A**, **B** or **C**? Explain your answer.

(1 mark)

2 (a) (ii) Samples of the plant shoot are taken from point **X** and point **Y** and analysed for the presence of auxin. Which sample do you think will contain most auxin, sample **X** or sample **Y**? Explain your answer.

(3 marks)

2 (b) This plant was produced by taking a cutting from another plant and applying rooting powder to it before planting it in a pot. Explain why rooting powder was used.

(2 marks)

3 The combined pill (which contains both oestrogen and progesterone) and the progesterone-only pill are two types of oral contraceptive. Read the following information about them.

> The combined oral contraceptive pill is reported to have a failure rate of just 0.1%, if taken correctly and consistently. It should be taken around the same time every day, but is still effective if taken up to 12 hours late. The combined oral contraceptive pill increases the risk of blood clots and cannot be taken if the woman is breast feeding. It is taken by some women to control their periods if they experience heavy bleeding.
>
> The progesterone-only pill has to be taken at the same time everyday or within up to three hours, to be effective. If it is taken correctly the failure rate is reported to be 0.5%. The progesterone-only pill can lead to irregular bleeding, but it can be taken if breast feeding and can be taken by some women who have a history of blood clots.

In this question you will be assessed on the quality of your English, the organisation of your ideas and your use of appropriate specialist vocabulary.

Evaluate the use of the two types of oral contraceptive pill.

(6 marks)

1. Drugs and Drug Claims

Drugs can have positive effects on the body, e.g. they can help cure illness. But you have to be careful when looking at what drugs claim to do...

What are drugs?

Drugs are substances that alter what goes on in your body. Your body's essentially a seething mass of chemical reactions — drugs can interfere with these reactions, sometimes for the better, sometimes not.

Some of the chemical changes caused by drugs can lead to the body becoming **addicted to** (dependent on) the drug. If the drug isn't taken, an addict can suffer **withdrawal symptoms**.

> **Examples**
>
> **Heroin**, **cocaine**, nicotine and caffeine are all very addictive drugs and can all cause withdrawal symptoms. E.g. heroin withdrawal can cause symptoms of restlessness, muscle pain, vomiting and cold flushes. Caffeine withdrawal can cause headaches and drowsiness.

Types of drugs

There are many different types of drugs, including:

- **Medicinal drugs** — drugs that are medically useful, like antibiotics (see p. 29). For some of these drugs you don't need a prescription (e.g. paracetamol), but for others you do (e.g. morphine, a strong painkiller) because they can be dangerous if misused.

- **Recreational drugs** — drugs used for fun (see pages 69-70).

- **Performance-enhancing drugs** — drugs that can improve a person's performance in sport (see below).

Performance-enhancing drugs

Some athletes take performance-enhancing drugs to make them better at sport. There are different types of performance-enhancing drugs.

> **Examples**
>
> - **Anabolic steroids** — these increase muscle size, so the athlete is stronger.
> - **Stimulants** — these increase heart rate, so glucose and oxygen are transported to the athlete's muscles faster (giving them more energy).

Learning Objectives:

- Understand what drugs do and how they can lead to addiction and withdrawal symptoms.
- Know that heroin and cocaine are very addictive drugs.
- Know what performance-enhancing drugs are.
- Understand why anabolic steroids and stimulants are used as performance-enhancing drugs.
- Know that some performance-enhancing drugs are illegal and some can be prescribed legally, but that all are banned by sporting bodies.
- Be able to evaluate the use of performance-enhancing drugs, including the ethical issues around them.
- Know what statins do and be able to evaluate their effect.
- Be able to evaluate claims about prescribed and non-prescribed drugs.

Specification Reference
B1.3.1

Exam Tip
You need to learn these two examples of performance-enhancing drugs for the exam.

Exam Tip
If you're asked to name examples of performance-enhancing drugs in the exam, make sure you spell <u>stimulants</u> correctly. 'Stimuli' or a 'stimulus' are not drugs.

But these drugs can have negative health effects, e.g. steroids can cause high blood pressure and high doses of stimulants can cause an irregular heartbeat. Some performance-enhancing drugs are banned by law, some are prescription-only, but all are banned by sporting bodies.

Evaluating the use of performance-enhancing drugs

There are also ethical problems with taking performance-enhancing drugs:

<u>Against</u> drugs...	<u>For</u> drugs...
It's unfair if people gain an advantage by taking drugs, not just through training.	Athletes have the right to make their own decision about whether taking drugs is worth the risk or not.
Athletes may not be fully informed of the serious health risks of the drugs they take.	Drug-free sport isn't really fair anyway — different athletes have access to different training facilities, coaches, equipment, etc. You could argue that taking drugs makes things fairer.
It's unfair if athletes from wealthy countries can afford to buy the drugs and athletes from poorer countries can't.	It avoids a situation where athletes who take a banned substance without knowing are penalised (punished).

Evaluating drug claims

You might have to evaluate claims about prescribed or non-prescribed drugs in the exam. If so, you need to look at these claims critically.

Exam Tip
You need to know what statins are and what they do for your exam.

Tip: Heart and circulatory diseases include things like stroke and coronary heart disease.

Example

Statins are prescribed drugs used to lower the risk of heart and circulatory disease.

There's evidence that statins lower blood cholesterol and significantly lower the risk of heart disease in diabetic patients.

The original research was done by government scientists with no connection to the manufacturers. And the sample was big — 6000 patients.

It compared two groups of patients — those who had taken statins and those who hadn't (a control group, see p. 7). Other studies have since backed up these findings, so the results were reproducible (see p. 3).

HOW SCIENCE WORKS

But research findings aren't always so clear cut...

In 2012, it was claimed that taking a low dose of aspirin each day could help to prevent cancer.

But taking aspirin can have serious side-effects — for example, it can increase the risk of internal bleeding. And the data the claim was based on came from studies that weren't originally designed to look at the effect of aspirin on cancer risk.

So until more specific studies are done, there's not enough evidence to say whether the possible benefits of taking aspirin to prevent cancer outweigh the dangers.

Practice Questions — Fact Recall

Q1 Why may a person become addicted to a drug?

Q2 Give two examples of drugs that are very addictive.

Q3 a) Give one example of a performance-enhancing drug.

b) Describe one effect that the drug in part a) has on the body.

Q4 What are statins prescribed to do?

Practice Question — Application

Q1 Beth is an athlete. She is considering taking amphetamines. Amphetamines are a type of drug that increase heart rate and may help Beth to perform better.

a) i) What type of drug are amphetamines?

ii) Briefly explain how using amphetamines may help Beth to perform better.

Beth is due to take part in an international competition and has to have a drug test beforehand.

b) Suggest one reason why sporting bodies carry out drug testing.

Beth is not aware that the side effects of using amphetamines include increased blood pressure, reduced appetite, hallucinations and even heart attacks. These are serious health risks and are one reason why some people are against the use of these drugs in sport.

c) Give another reason why people may be against the use of amphetamines in sport.

d) Give one reason why people may support the use of performance-enhancing drugs in sport.

Exam Tip
Don't be put off if you're given a question in the exam about a drug you haven't heard of — just read the question carefully and apply what you know about drugs in general to answer the question.

Learning Objectives:
- Know that scientists are always developing new drugs.
- Understand why new medicinal drugs have to be tested before becoming available to the public (to check effectiveness, toxicity and dosage).
- Understand what happens when testing drugs in the laboratory and in clinical trials.
- Know what the terms 'optimum dose', 'placebo' and 'double-blind trials' mean.
- Know what the drug thalidomide was developed as.
- Understand what happened when thalidomide was used to relieve morning sickness in pregnant women without being tested for that use.
- Know how drug testing changed after the problems thalidomide caused.
- Know what thalidomide is used to treat today.

Specification Reference
B1.3.1

2. Testing Medicinal Drugs

Pharmacies stock lots of medicines that can prevent or cure diseases. But before they make it onto the pharmacy shelves the drugs have to be tested...

Laboratory testing

New drugs are constantly being developed. But before they can be given to the general public, they have to go through a thorough testing procedure — starting in the laboratory.

Cells and tissues

First of all, drugs are tested on human cells and tissues in the lab. However, you can't use human cells and tissues to test drugs that affect whole or multiple body systems, e.g. testing a drug for blood pressure must be done on a whole animal because it has an intact circulatory system.

Live animals

The next step is to test the drug on live animals. This is to see whether the drug works (produces the effect you're looking for), to find out about its **toxicity** (how harmful it is) and the best dosage (the dose at which it's most effective).

The law in Britain states that any new drug must be tested on two different live mammals. Some people think it's cruel to test on animals, but others believe this is the safest way to make sure a drug isn't dangerous before it's given to humans. Other people think that animals are so different from humans that testing on animals is pointless.

Clinical trials

If the drug passes the tests on animals then it's tested on human volunteers in a clinical trial.

First, the drug is tested on healthy volunteers. This is to make sure that it doesn't have any harmful side effects when the body is working normally. At the start of the trial, a very low dose of the drug is given and this is gradually increased.

If the results of the tests on healthy volunteers are good, the drugs can be tested on people suffering from the illness. The **optimum dose** is found — this is the dose of drug that is the most effective and has few side effects.

Placebos

To test how well the drug works, patients are put into two groups. One is given the new drug, the other is given a placebo (a substance that's like the drug being tested but doesn't do anything). This is so the doctor can see the actual difference the drug makes — it allows for the placebo effect (when the patient expects the treatment to work and so feels better, even though the treatment isn't doing anything).

Example

A pharmaceutical company has developed a drug, Drug X, to help people with high blood cholesterol to lower their cholesterol level. The drug was tested on 1500 patients with high cholesterol. The patients were divided into two groups and over six months each patient had one tablet per day. One group had a tablet containing Drug X and the other group had a tablet without Drug X — the placebo.

Tip: People in the control group of a clinical trial should be similar to people in the treatment group, e.g. of a similar age, gender, etc. This helps to make sure the study is a fair test — see How Science Works pages 6-7 for more on making a study a fair test.

Blind and double-blind trials

Clinical trials are blind — the patient in the study doesn't know whether they're getting the drug or the placebo. In fact, they're often double-blind — neither the patient nor the doctor knows until all the results have been gathered (see Figure 1). This is so the doctors monitoring the patients and analysing the results aren't subconsciously influenced by their knowledge.

	Blind trial	Double-blind trial
Does the **patient** know whether they're getting the drug or the placebo?	no	no
Does the **doctor** know whether the patient is getting the drug or the placebo?	yes	no

Figure 1: *Table summarising blind and double-blind trials.*

The importance of drug testing

It's really important that drugs are tested thoroughly before being used to make sure they're safe. An example of what can happen when drugs are not thoroughly tested is the case of **thalidomide**...

Example

Thalidomide is a drug that was developed in the 1950s. It was intended as a sleeping pill, and was tested for that use. But later it was also found to be effective in relieving morning sickness in pregnant women.

Unfortunately, thalidomide hadn't been tested as a drug for morning sickness, and so it wasn't known that it could pass through the placenta and affect the fetus, causing abnormal limb development. In some cases, babies were born with no arms or legs at all. About 10 000 babies were affected by thalidomide, and only about half of them survived.

The drug was banned, and more rigorous testing procedures were introduced. More recently thalidomide has been used in the treatment of leprosy and other diseases, e.g. some cancers.

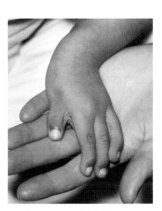

Figure 2: *This baby was born with a deformed hand due to thalidomide.*

Practice Questions — Fact Recall

Q1 Which comes first during drug testing — laboratory testing or clinical trials?

Q2 In the laboratory, what may drugs be tested on?

Q3 Give two reasons why drugs need to be tested in the laboratory.

Q4 a) In a clinical trial, what type of volunteer is the drug tested on first — healthy volunteers or people suffering from the illness?

b) Describe the dosage of drug that is first used in a clinical trial.

Q5 What is a placebo?

Q6 Briefly explain what is involved in a double-blind trial.

Exam Tip
If you're asked what a placebo is in the exam, remember that it's <u>not</u> a drug — this is because it doesn't actually do anything.

Practice Questions — Application

Q1 For each of the drugs below, suggest what would have been given as a placebo when that drug went through clinical trials.

a) a paracetamol capsule   b) a steroid inhaler

c) a cortisone injection

Q2 A new weight-loss pill has been developed called Drug X. The pill was tested in a double-blind clinical trial. It involved three groups of obese volunteers (50 per group), all of whom wanted to lose weight.
Each group member took a pill three times a day for a year, alongside diet and exercise. The first group took Drug X, the second group took a similar weight-loss pill already available (Drug Y) and the third group took a placebo. The average weight loss per person after one year is shown on the graph.

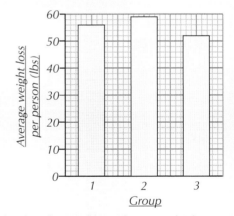

a) i) Would the doctors involved in this trial have known which patients were being given the placebo? Explain your answer.

ii) Suggest what could have been used as a placebo in this trial.

b) Why do you think Group 2 was included in the trial?

c) From these results, what can you conclude about Drug X? Use data from the graph to support your answer.

Exam Tip
When answering a question about a clinical trial in the exam, make sure you read all the information you're given. Here you need to have spotted that it's a double-blind trial — this will help you answer Q2 a) i).

3. Recreational Drugs

Some drugs are just used for fun. But with fun comes risk...

What are recreational drugs?

Recreational drugs are drugs used for fun. They can be legal or illegal.

Illegal recreational drugs

Illegal drugs are often divided into two main classes — soft and hard.
Hard drugs are usually thought of as being seriously addictive and generally
more harmful than soft drugs. But the terms "soft" and "hard" are a bit vague
— they're not scientific descriptions, and you can certainly have problems
with soft drug use.

> **Examples**
>
> - **Heroin** and **ecstasy** (hard drugs) and **cannabis** (a soft drug) can all
>   cause heart and circulatory system problems.
>
> - Recent studies suggest that for young people who are already more
>   at risk of developing mental health problems because of their genes,
>   using cannabis may increase this risk even further.

Reasons for using recreational drugs

So if all these recreational drugs are so dangerous, why do so many people
use them? There are various reasons why...

> **Example**
>
> When asked why they use cannabis, most users quote either simple
> enjoyment, relaxation or stress relief. Some say they do it to get stoned
> or for inspiration. Some multiple sclerosis sufferers say cannabis can
> relieve pain.
>
> But very often this turns out to be not the whole story. There may be other
> factors in the user's background or personal life which influence them in
> choosing to use drugs. It's a personal thing, and often pretty complicated.

Progression from soft drugs to hard drugs

Almost all users of hard drugs have tried cannabis first (though most users of
cannabis do not go on to use hard drugs). The link between cannabis and
hard drugs isn't clear, but three opinions are common...

1. Cannabis is a "stepping stone" — the effects of cannabis create a desire to
   try harder drugs.

2. Cannabis is a "gateway drug" — cannabis use brings people into contact
   with drug dealers.

3. It's all down to genetics — certain people are more likely to take drugs
   generally, so cannabis users will also try other drugs.

Learning Objectives:
- Know that heroin, ecstasy and cannabis are illegal recreational drugs and understand the health problems they cause.
- Be able to evaluate different types of drugs and know why some people use illegal recreational drugs.
- Understand why people might progress from using soft recreational drugs to using hard recreational drugs.
- Know that nicotine and alcohol are legal recreational drugs and understand that they can cause health problems.
- Be able to compare the overall impact on people's health of legal recreational drugs and illegal recreational drugs.

Specification Reference
B1.3.1

Legal recreational drugs

Legal recreational drugs can have a massive impact on people's health.

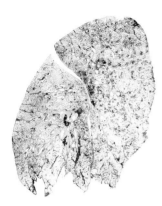

Figure 1: *A diseased lung from a smoker.*

Examples

Nicotine (the drug found in tobacco smoke) and **alcohol** are both legal recreational drugs. Smoking and drinking alcohol can have the following effects on a person's health:

Smoking	Alcohol
▪ Causes disease of the heart, blood vessels and lungs. ▪ Tobacco smoke also causes cancer. ▪ Nicotine is addictive so it's hard to stop smoking.	▪ Affects the nervous system and slows down the body's reactions. ▪ Too much alcohol leads to impaired judgement, poor coordination and unconsciousness. ▪ Excessive drinking can cause liver disease and brain damage. ▪ Alcohol is also addictive.

Tip: Nicotine and alcohol are not prescribed drugs, but some legal drugs are prescribed by doctors. These can also have a massive impact on health if people misuse them, e.g. people can become addicted to prescribed painkillers if they're overused.

Legal recreational drugs can also have a massive impact on society.

Examples

Smoking and alcohol have the following effects on our society:

▪ The National Health Service spends loads on treating people with lung diseases caused by smoking. Add to this the cost to businesses of people missing days from work, and the figures get pretty scary.

▪ The same goes for alcohol. The costs to the NHS are huge, but are pretty small compared to the costs related to crime (police time, damage to people/property) and the economy (lost working days etc.).

▪ And in addition to the financial costs, alcohol and smoking cause sorrow and anguish to people affected by them, either directly or indirectly.

Legal drugs, like nicotine and alcohol, have a bigger impact in the UK than illegal drugs, as so many people take them.

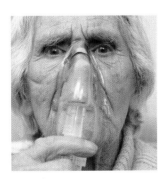

Figure 2: *A woman receiving oxygen therapy — a treatment for lung disease caused by smoking.*

Practice Questions — Fact Recall

Q1 Name two illegal and two legal recreational drugs.

Q2 Describe two opinions about the link between cannabis and hard drug use.

Q3 Do legal or illegal drugs have the biggest impact on people and society in the UK? Explain your answer.

Section Checklist — Make sure you know...

Drugs and Drug Claims

☐ That drugs cause chemical changes in the body, which can lead to addiction.

☐ That people addicted to drugs may suffer withdrawal symptoms without them.

☐ That heroin and cocaine are really addictive drugs.

☐ That performance-enhancing drugs are drugs that can improve a person's performance in sport.

☐ That anabolic steroids increase muscle growth and stimulants increase heart rate and how these can make a person better at sport.

☐ That some performance-enhancing drugs are illegal, some can be prescribed legally but that all are banned by sporting bodies.

☐ The issues surrounding the use of performance-enhancing drugs and how to evaluate them.

☐ That statins reduce the risk of heart and circulatory diseases and how to evaluate data on them.

☐ How to evaluate claims about prescribed and non-prescribed drugs.

Testing Medicinal Drugs

☐ That scientists are developing new drugs all the time, which have to be tested before use.

☐ That new medicinal drugs are first tested in the laboratory on human cells, tissues and animals.

☐ That drugs have to be tested to make sure they work, are safe and that the best dosage is known.

☐ That after lab testing, drugs are tested in clinical trials on healthy volunteers at low doses. They're then tested on ill volunteers to find the optimum dose of a drug (the dose the drug works best at).

☐ What a placebo is (a substance that's similar to the drug being tested but that doesn't do anything) and why they are used in clinical trials (to make sure the drug works).

☐ That in a double-blind trial neither the doctors nor the volunteers know which volunteers have been given the drug and who has been given the placebo.

☐ That the drug thalidomide was made for use as a sleeping pill. However, it was also used to relieve morning sickness in pregnant women without being tested for that use. As a result the drug caused abnormal limb development in many babies and even death. The drug was banned and now drug testing is much more thorough. Thalidomide is now used to treat leprosy and some cancers.

Recreational Drugs

☐ That heroin, ecstasy and cannabis are all illegal recreational drugs which can cause heart and circulatory system problems, and that cannabis may increase the risk of developing mental health problems in some people.

☐ That people use illegal recreational drugs for many reasons.

☐ The main opinions on why some people who use cannabis (a soft drug) may progress to using hard drugs.

☐ That nicotine and alcohol are legal recreational drugs and can cause many health problems.

☐ That legal drugs have a greater impact on people and society because far more people use them.

Exam-style Questions

1   Heroin is an illegal recreational drug.

1 (a)   Which of the following are also illegal drugs? Tick **two** boxes.

Cannabis   ☐

Nicotine   ☐

Statins   ☐

Ecstasy   ☐

(2 marks)

Alcohol is a legal recreational drug.

1 (b) (i)   Long-term, heavy drinkers of alcohol can feel nervous, depressed or irritable if they suddenly stop drinking. They may also be sick or sweat a lot.

What are these symptoms and why do they occur?

(2 marks)

(ii)   Excessive drinking of alcohol can lead to liver disease and brain damage.
Suggest **one** negative effect this may have on society.

(1 mark)

2   The drug thalidomide was developed in the 1950s.

2 (a)   What type of drug was thalidomide developed as?

(1 mark)

Thalidomide was given to pregnant women to stop morning sickness.

2 (b) (i)   Describe the effect this had on the women's babies and explain why this effect was not already known.

(2 marks)

2 (b) (ii)   Describe the consequences your answer to part **(b) (i)** had on the use of thalidomide and the future of drug testing.

(2 marks)

3   *In this question you will be assessed on the quality of your English, the organisation of your ideas and your use of appropriate specialist vocabulary.*

Scientists are developing new drugs all the time. Before the public can use these drugs they have to be thoroughly tested in the laboratory and in clinical trials.

Describe the process of testing a new medicinal drug, both in the laboratory and in clinical trials, and explain why the different testing procedures must be carried out.

(6 marks)

4 A study was done to find out if taking aspirin will reduce the risk of colorectal cancer in people who already have an increased risk of developing the disease (due to genetic factors).

Patients in the study were randomly put into two groups — a treatment group and a control group. The treatment group were given a 600 mg aspirin tablet per day. The control group were given a placebo.

4 (a) (i) Suggest what was used as a placebo in this study.

(1 mark)

4 (a) (ii) Explain why a placebo was included in this trial.

(1 mark)

The graph shows some of the results from the study:

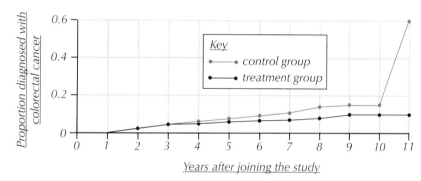

4 (b) How do the results from the control group compare to those from the treatment group? Use data from the graph to support your answer.

(3 marks)

Not everyone who took part in the trial continued to take the tablets they were given for the same length of time. The scientists behind the study decided to see what sort of effect this had on the likelihood of the participants developing cancer.

To do this, they split data from the treatment group and the control group into two further groups. The scientists then looked at the risk of developing cancer for each new group. The results are shown in the table:

	Treatment group		Control group	
	Aspirin taken daily for 2 years or more	Aspirin taken daily for less than 2 years	Placebo taken daily for 2 years or more	Placebo taken daily for less than 2 years
Risk of developing colorectal cancer (incidence rate per 100 person-years).	0.06	0.13	0.14	0.10

4 (c) A newspaper headline reported the study and wrote:
'An aspirin a day will halve your risk of cancer'.

Give **three** reasons why this headline is inaccurate.

(3 marks)

1. Adaptations and Competition

Organisms survive in many different environments because they are adapted to them and can compete for resources.

Animal adaptations

Adaptations are characteristics which increase an organism's chance of survival in the environment in which it lives. Animals that live in different environments have different adaptations.

Desert animals

The desert is a very hot and dry environment. Desert animals need to be able to save water and keep cool. Desert animals are adapted to their environment in the following ways:

- They have a large surface area compared to volume. This lets them lose more body heat, which helps to stop them overheating.

> **Example**
>
> The fennec fox has very large ears. This is an adaptation which increases its surface area and helps it to lose heat in its desert environment.
>
>
>
> **Figure 1:**
> *A fennec fox.*

- They are efficient with water — they lose less water by producing small amounts of concentrated urine and they also make very little sweat.

- They have thin layers of body fat and thin insulating coats — these adaptations help them to lose body heat.

- They have a sandy colour to give good camouflage — this helps them to avoid predators, or sneak up on prey.

> **Example**
>
> A camel is adapted to survive in desert conditions:
>
> *Camels are able to tolerate large changes in temperature, so they don't sweat much.*
>
>
>
> *Camels keep all their fat in their humps to help them lose heat from the rest of their body.*
>
> *Light-brown colour for camouflage.*

Learning Objectives:

- Know what an adaptation is.
- Understand how animals can be adapted to live in desert or arctic conditions, including the effect of surface area, insulation, body fat and camouflage.
- Understand how plants can be adapted to live in desert conditions, including the effect of surface area, water storage tissues and extensive roots.
- Know that some plants and animals have adaptations to help deter predators.
- Understand what is meant by the term 'extremophile'.
- Be able to identify adaptations in organisms and understand how they help the organism to survive.
- Understand that plants and animals need resources from their environment to survive and reproduce, and that they compete for these resources.

Specification Reference
B1.4.1

Arctic animals

The Arctic is a very cold environment. Arctic animals need to be able to reduce their heat loss. Arctic animals are adapted to their environment in the following ways:

- They have a small surface area compared to volume — they have a compact (rounded) shape to keep their surface area to a minimum, which reduces heat loss.

- They are well insulated — they have a thick layer of blubber (body fat) for insulation, which also acts as an energy store when food is scarce. They also have thick hairy coats to keep body heat in, and greasy fur which sheds water (this prevents cooling due to evaporation).

- They have white fur for good camouflage — this helps them to avoid predators, or sneak up on prey.

Tip: Generally, animals with a larger body mass will have a small surface area compared to volume and vice versa. This is why animals with larger body masses (e.g. polar bears) are found in cold environments.

Example

A polar bear is adapted to survive in arctic conditions. It has a rounded shape, which gives it a small surface area to volume ratio. It has a thick layer of blubber and a thick hairy coat for insulation. A polar bear also has white fur, for camouflage against the snowy conditions.

Figure 2: Polar bears are adapted for their arctic environment.

Plant adaptations

Plants also have adaptations to help them survive in their environment.

Desert plants

Desert plants have adapted to having little water in the following ways:

- They have a small surface area compared to volume. Plants lose water vapour from the surface of their leaves, so some desert plants have spines or smaller leaves to reduce water loss (by reducing the surface area). The total surface area of some desert plants is about 1000 times smaller than normal plants, which also reduces water loss.

- They have water storage tissues — this means they can save water for use during very dry periods.

- They maximise water absorption — some desert plants have shallow but extensive roots to absorb water quickly over a large area. Others have deep roots to access underground water.

Figure 3: The spines on a desert plant help to reduce water loss.

Example

A cactus is adapted to survive in desert conditions. It has:

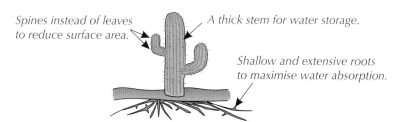

Spines instead of leaves to reduce surface area.

A thick stem for water storage.

Shallow and extensive roots to maximise water absorption.

Adaptations to deter predators

Some plants and animals have adaptations to help protect them against being eaten by other organisms.

Figure 4: *The aquatic coral snake has vibrant colours, warning predators that it is poisonous and shouldn't be eaten.*

> **Examples**
>
> - Some plants and animals have thorns (like roses) or sharp spines (like cacti and porcupines), which can hurt organisms that try to eat them.
>
> - Some produce poisons — like poison ivy and some tropical tree frogs. Tree frog poison can make a predator ill or even kill them. Predators soon learn to avoid eating similar organisms.
>
> - Some have amazing warning colours to signal to predators that they are dangerous — like wasps and aquatic coral snakes (see Figure 4).

Adaptations in microorganisms

Microorganisms have a huge variety of adaptations so that they can live in a wide range of environments. For example, some microorganisms (e.g. bacteria) are known as **extremophiles** — they're adapted to live in seriously extreme conditions like super hot volcanic vents, in very salty lakes or at high pressure on the sea bed.

Tip: A hydrothermal vent is an opening in the sea bed which sends out extremely hot water.

> **Example**
>
> *Thermococcus litoralis* is an extremophile. It's a bacterium that's found in deep sea hydrothermal vents. It's adapted to survive and reproduce at temperatures between 85 and 88 °C, which is much higher than most bacteria can tolerate.

Identifying and explaining adaptations

In the exam you might be given information about any organism and its environment and be asked to identify or explain its adaptations. Here's an example to show you how to do it...

Exam Tip
In the exam you could be asked to identify an animal's adaptations from explanations given. Therefore you need to think about what body features it needs. For example, if you're told that an adaptation helps an animal keep its balance when hopping then it will probably need to have a tail.

> **Example**
>
> **The Weddell seal lives in cold antarctic conditions and hunts fish in water covered by ice. Use this information and the diagram, to explain how the seal is adapted to live in the antarctic.**
>
>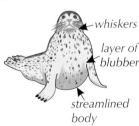
>
> You need to look at the adaptations labelled on the diagram and think about how they allow the seal to keep warm and hunt fish, for example:
>
> - Its whiskers help it to detect fish in the dark conditions under water.
>
> - Its layer of blubber helps insulate it in the cold water.
>
> - Its streamlined body helps reduce resistance from the water, so it can swim fast to catch fish.

Competition

Organisms need things from their environment and from other organisms in order to survive and reproduce. Plants need light, space, water and minerals (nutrients) from the soil to survive. Animals need space (territory), food, water and mates to be able to survive and reproduce. Organisms compete with other species (and members of their own species) for the same resources.

Tip: Organisms that are better adapted to their environment are better at competing for resources and will be more likely to survive than those that aren't as well adapted.

Examples

- Red and grey squirrels live in the same habitat and eat the same food. Competition with the grey squirrels for these resources means there's not enough food for the reds — so the population of red squirrels is decreasing.

- Weeds compete with crop plants for light and nutrients. Farmers use weedkillers to kill weeds so there is less competition and the crops get all the light and nutrients, which enables them to grow better.

Figure 5: The population size of red squirrels in Britain is decreasing due to increased competition from grey squirrels.

Practice Questions — Fact Recall

Q1 What is an adaptation?

Q2 How does having water storage tissues help a desert plant to survive?

Q3 Give two examples of adaptations that would help an organism to deter predators.

Q4 a) What is an extremophile?

b) Give two examples of the type of conditions in which you might find an extremophile.

Q5 What resources do plants compete for?

Q6 What resources do animals compete for?

Practice Question — Application

Q1 The table below gives descriptions of two different species of animal.

Species	Description
Equus assinus	Long ears, short fur and a grey or brown colour.
Alopex lagopus	Short ears and muzzle and a thick, white coat.

For each species, say whether you think they live in arctic or desert conditions. Explain your choices.

Tip: The muzzle is the mouth and nose area of an animal.

- Understand that changes in the environment are caused by living and non-living factors.
- Understand how changes in the environment can affect organisms.
- Be able to evaluate data showing the effect of environmental changes on organisms.

Specification Reference
B1.4.2

Tip: A change could be an increase or a decrease.

2. Environmental Change

Changes in the environment can have a big impact on living organisms...

Causes of environmental change

The environment in which plants and animals live changes all the time. These changes are caused by living and non-living factors.

Environmental changes caused by **living factors** include things such as:

- A change in the occurrence of infectious diseases.
- A change in the number of predators.
- A change in the number of prey or the availability of food sources.
- A change in the number or types of competitors.

Environmental changes caused by **non-living factors** include things such as:

- A change in average temperature.
- A change in average rainfall.
- A change in the level of air or water pollution.

How environmental change affects organisms

Environmental changes can affect animals and plants in these three ways:

Tip: A population is all the organisms of one species living in the same area.

1. Population size increases

An environmental change may cause the number of organisms of a particular species living in an area to increase.

> **Example**
>
> If the number of mice increases (an environmental change), then there's more food available for owls, so more owls survive and reproduce, and their numbers increase too.

2. Population size decreases

An environmental change may also cause the number of organisms of a particular species living in an area to decrease.

> **Example**
>
> The number of bees in the US is falling rapidly. Experts aren't sure why but it could be due to a number of different environmental changes such as:
>
> - Some pesticides (chemicals that kill pests) may be having a negative effect on bees.
> - There's less food available — there aren't as many nectar-rich plants around any more.
> - There's more disease — bees are being killed by new pathogens or parasites.

Figure 1: *The population size of bees is decreasing in the US due to environmental changes.*

3. Population distribution change

The distribution of an organism is where the organism is found.
Many different environmental changes can cause the distribution of a
population to change.

Example

The European Bee-Eater bird is a Mediterranean bird species. However,
this bird is now present in parts of Germany due to a rise in the average
temperature there.

Tip: Average
temperatures are
usually warmer in the
Mediterranean than in
Germany.

Practice Questions — Fact Recall

Q1 Give three examples of environmental changes caused by
living factors.

Q2 Give three examples of environmental changes caused by
non-living factors.

Practice Questions — Application

Q1 An environmental study was done on a lake over a number of years.
Over the course of the study the pH of the lake gradually decreased
due to the effect of acid rain. Mayfly cannot survive in water with a
low pH, whereas frogs which prey on mayfly can.

a) The population size of mayfly changed during the study.

   i) Suggest how the population size changed.

   ii) Was this change due to a living or non-living factor?

b) The population size of the frogs also changed during the study.
Suggest how and why the population size changed.

Q2 The graph shows the extent of arctic sea ice measured every
December between 1995 and 2012.

a) Calculate the percentage
change in the extent of sea
ice between 1995 and 2012.

b) Suggest what has caused
the change and say whether
this is a living or non-living
factor.

c) Polar bears depend on sea
ice for survival. Suggest how
the change in the extent of
sea ice has affected the polar
bear population.

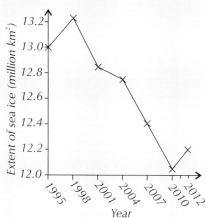

- Understand that
  lichens are living
  indicators and how
  they can be used to
  monitor air pollution.
- Understand that some
  invertebrate animals
  are living indicators
  and how they can be
  used to monitor water
  pollution.
- Understand
  that non-living
  indicators can be
  used to measure
  environmental
  changes such as
  temperature, rainfall
  and dissolved oxygen
  concentration.

Specification Reference
B1.4.2

Tip: An invertebrate animal is just an animal that does not have a backbone.

3. Measuring Environmental Change

Scientists can get some idea of how much our environment is changing using living and non-living indicators.

Living indicators

Some organisms are very sensitive to changes in their environment and so can be studied to see the effect of environmental change — these organisms are known as **living indicators**. They can be used to monitor pollution.

Air pollution

Air pollution can be monitored by looking at particular types of **lichen** that are very sensitive to the concentration of sulfur dioxide in the atmosphere (and so can give a good idea about the level of pollution from car exhausts, power stations, etc.). The number and type of lichen at a particular location will indicate how clean the air is (e.g. the air is clean if there are lots of lichen).

Water pollution

If raw sewage is released into a river, the bacterial population in the water increases and uses up the oxygen. Some **invertebrate animals**, like mayfly larvae, are good indicators for water pollution because they're very sensitive to the concentration of dissolved oxygen in the water. If you find mayfly larvae in a river, it indicates that the water is clean.

Other invertebrate species have adapted to live in polluted conditions — so if you see a lot of them you know there's a problem. For example, rat-tailed maggots and sludgeworms indicate a very high level of water pollution.

Non-living indicators

A non-living indicator is something that is not alive, but can be measured or monitored to give information about environmental change, e.g. temperature. Scientists use different methods and equipment to collect data about non-living indicators.

Examples

- Satellites are used to measure the temperature of the sea surface and the amount of snow and ice cover. These are modern, accurate instruments and give us a global coverage.

- Automatic weather stations are used to tell us the atmospheric temperature at various locations. These contain thermometers that are sensitive and accurate — they can measure to very small fractions of a degree.

- Rain gauges are used to measure rainfall, to find out how much the average rainfall changes year on year.

- Dissolved oxygen meters, which measure the concentration of dissolved oxygen in water, are used to discover how the level of water pollution is changing.

Figure 1: An automatic weather station can monitor temperature.

Practice Questions — Fact Recall

Q1 What is a living indicator?

Q2 What gas in the atmosphere are lichen sensitive to?

Q3 What type of organisms can be used to monitor water pollution?

Q4 Give three examples of non-living indicators of environmental change.

Practice Questions — Application

Q1 Lichen grow on tree trunks. One way of investigating the amount of lichen in an area is to measure how much of a sample of tree trunks are covered in lichen (percentage cover). In an experiment, scientists recorded the percentage cover of lichen on trees outside their laboratory (0 km) and at different locations up to a distance of 100 km away. A graph produced from their results is shown below.

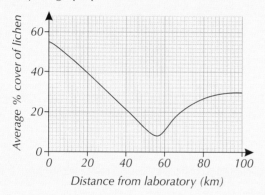

Figure 2: Lichen is commonly found growing on trees.

There is a power station somewhere within the area the scientists studied. By looking at the graph, how far from the laboratory would you expect the power station to be? Explain your answer.

Q2 The table below shows the levels of three types of invertebrate animals found in different areas of a river.

Organism	Area A	Area B	Area C
Stonefly larvae	High	Low	Low
Water louse	Low	High	Moderate
Sludgeworms	Low	High	High

Stonefly larvae can't tolerate a low concentration of dissolved oxygen in water.

a) Use the information available to explain which area of the river is the cleanest.

b) Which organism is most well adapted to live in polluted water? Explain your answer.

Exam Tip
Make sure you write <u>concentration</u> of dissolved oxygen in the exam — you could be throwing away marks if you write the 'amount' or 'level'.

Adaptations and Competition

☐ That an adaptation is a characteristic which helps an organism to survive in its environment.

☐ That desert animals have adaptations including a large surface area compared to volume, a thin layer of body fat, a thin insulating coat and camouflage.

☐ That arctic animals have adaptations including a small surface area compared to volume, a thick layer of body fat (blubber), a thick insulating coat and camouflage.

☐ That desert plants have adaptations including a small surface area compared to volume, water storage tissues and a wide or deep root system.

☐ That some plants and animals have adaptations to deter predators, such as thorns or spines, poisons and warning colours.

☐ That an extremophile is an organism that is adapted to survive in extreme conditions (e.g. at very high temperatures, in very high salt levels or at high pressure).

☐ How to identify adaptations of a given organism and explain how the adaptations help the organism to survive in its environment, e.g. help it to find food.

☐ That plants need light, space, water and nutrients to survive and reproduce.

☐ That animals need space, food, water and mates to survive and reproduce.

☐ That plants and animals compete with other species and members of their own species for the resources they need to survive and reproduce.

Environmental Change

☐ That environmental changes can be caused by living factors (e.g. a change in the number of competitors) and non-living factors (e.g. a change in average temperature or rainfall).

☐ That environmental changes can cause an increase or decrease in population size, or a change in the distribution of populations.

☐ How to evaluate data showing the effect of environmental changes on organisms.

Measuring Environmental Change

☐ That lichens are living indicators that can be used to monitor air pollution because they are sensitive to the concentration of sulfur dioxide in the atmosphere.

☐ That some invertebrate animals are living indicators that can be used to monitor water pollution because they are affected by the concentration of dissolved oxygen in water.

☐ That non-living indicators are not alive, but can be measured or monitored to give information about environmental change, e.g. sea surface temperature can be monitored by satellites, rainfall can be measured using rain gauges.

1. Pyramids of Biomass

Information about food chains can be shown on pyramid diagrams...

Food chains

A food chain shows what eats what. The first organism in a food chain is called a producer (i.e. a plant). The animal that eats the plant is called a primary consumer, and the animal that eats the primary consumer is called a secondary consumer.

| Example |

A food chain:

producer   *primary consumer*   *secondary consumer*

Each stage of a food chain is called a **trophic level**. There's less energy and less **biomass** (mass of living material) every time you move up a trophic level in a food chain. There are usually fewer organisms every time you move up a level too, although this isn't always true.

| Example |

In this food chain, the number of organisms increases as you move up the chain until the last stage — there 500 fleas feed on one fox.

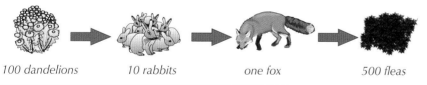

100 dandelions   *10 rabbits*   *one fox*   *500 fleas*

So a better way to look at the food chain is often to think about biomass instead of number of organisms. Biomass means the mass of living material.

Pyramids of biomass

Information about biomass can be used to construct a **pyramid of biomass** to represent the food chain. Each bar on a pyramid of biomass shows the mass of living material at that stage of the food chain — basically how much all the organisms at each level would "weigh" if you put them all together. The big bar along the bottom of the pyramid always represents the producer. The next bar will be the primary consumer, then the secondary consumer and so on up the food chain. Most of the biomass at each level is lost, so does not become biomass in the next level up. This is why biomass pyramids are practically always pyramid-shaped.

Learning Objectives:
- Know what 'biomass' is.
- Understand that biomass decreases at each trophic level moving up a food chain.
- Know how to draw a pyramid of biomass.
- Know how to interpret a pyramid of biomass.

Specification Reference B1.5.1

Tip: The reasons for there being less energy and biomass as you go up a food chain are shown on page 86.

Example

A pyramid of biomass of the 'fox' food chain:

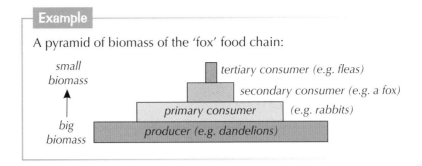

small
biomass

big
biomass

tertiary consumer (e.g. fleas)

secondary consumer (e.g. a fox)

primary consumer (e.g. rabbits)

producer (e.g. dandelions)

Constructing a pyramid of biomass

You need to be able to construct pyramids of biomass. Luckily it's pretty simple — they'll give you all the information you need to do it in the exam.

Example

A great tit feeds on 20 caterpillars, which in turn feed on a rose bush. Draw and label a pyramid of biomass to represent this food chain.

Here's what you need to remember when drawing a pyramid like this:

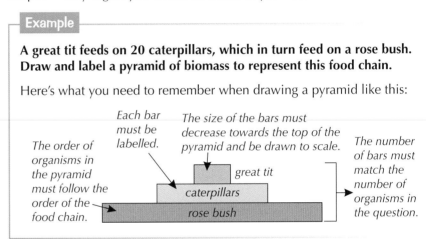

The order of organisms in the pyramid must follow the order of the food chain.

Each bar must be labelled.

The size of the bars must decrease towards the top of the pyramid and be drawn to scale.

The number of bars must match the number of organisms in the question.

great tit

caterpillars

rose bush

Interpreting a pyramid of biomass

You also need to be able to look at pyramids of biomass and explain what they show about the food chain.

Tip: Remember, pyramids of biomass represent food chains, so if the number of organisms in one trophic level changes (e.g. if their population size decreases), this will affect their biomass and the biomass of organisms elsewhere in the food chain.

Example

Look at the pyramid of biomass below:

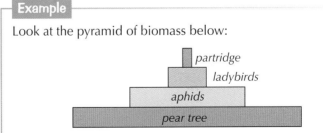

partridge

ladybirds

aphids

pear tree

Even if you know nothing about the natural world, you're probably aware that a tree is quite a bit bigger than an aphid. So what's going on here is that lots (probably thousands) of aphids are feeding on a few great big trees. Quite a lot of ladybirds are then eating the aphids, and a few partridges are eating the ladybirds.

Tip: Plants fix the Sun's energy during photosynthesis (the process by which plants make their own food).

Biomass and energy are still decreasing as you go up the levels — it's just that one tree can have a very big biomass, and can fix a lot of the Sun's energy using all those leaves.

You could also be expected to do a bit of maths, such as working out the ratio of the biomass at different levels.

Example

You might be given a pyramid of biomass like this one and be asked to work out the ratio of the biomass of ladybirds to the biomass of aphids.

So you need to count how many squares wide the ladybird and aphid bars are and then work out the ratio. Like this:

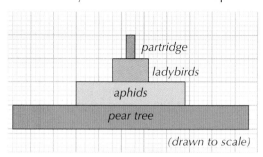

ladybird bar = 8 squares

aphid bar = 24 squares

(drawn to scale)

So the ratio of the ladybirds' biomass to the aphids' biomass is 8:24, which is the same as 1:3.

Practice Questions — Fact Recall

Q1   What is biomass?

Q2   Why is a pyramid of biomass nearly always pyramid shaped?

Practice Questions — Application

Q1   Caterpillars feed on cabbage plants.
Small birds eat the caterpillars and a bigger bird eats the small birds.
Draw and label a pyramid of biomass to represent this food chain.

Q2   Look at this pyramid of biomass.

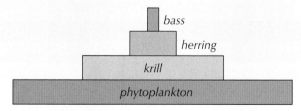

a) Which organism is the producer?

b) Which organism has the smallest biomass?

c) Why is the bar representing the herring smaller than the bar representing the krill?

- Understand that the source of energy for most food chains is the Sun.

- Understand how green plants and algae absorb light energy and convert it to chemical energy.

- Know that this chemical energy is stored in the cells of plants and algae.

- Understand the ways in which biomass and energy are lost at each stage of a food chain.

Specification Reference
B1.5.1

2. Energy Transfer in Food Chains

Energy is transferred along a food chain, but lots is lost along the way...

How does energy get into a food chain?

Energy from the Sun is the source of energy for nearly all life on Earth. Green plants and algae use a small percentage of the light energy from the Sun to convert carbon dioxide (from the air) and water (from the soil) into chemical energy (food) during **photosynthesis**. This energy's stored in the substances which make up the cells of plants and algae (biomass), and then works its way through the food chain as animals eat them and each other (see Figure 1).

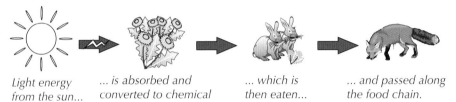

Light energy from the sun... ... is absorbed and converted to chemical energy in photosynthesis... ... which is then eaten... ... and passed along the food chain.

Figure 1: *Light energy from the Sun is the source of all energy in a food chain.*

Biomass and energy loss in food chains

Both biomass and energy are lost at each stage of the food chain. Biomass and energy are lost for a number of different reasons:

Respiration

Every organism in the food chain respires. Respiration supplies the energy for all life processes, including movement. Most of the energy released by respiration is eventually lost to the surroundings as heat. This is especially true for mammals and birds, whose bodies must be kept at a constant temperature which is normally higher than their surroundings.

Uneaten material

Some of the material which makes up plants and animals is inedible (e.g. bone), so it doesn't pass to the next stage of the food chain. Also some organisms die before they're eaten, so their remains are left to decay and their energy doesn't get passed along the food chain (instead the energy gets passed to the microorganisms that break down the remains).

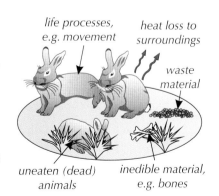

life processes, e.g. movement   heat loss to surroundings

waste material

uneaten (dead) animals   inedible material, e.g. bones

Figure 2: *Ways that biomass and energy are lost at each stage in a food chain.*

Waste products

Material and energy are also lost from the food chain in the organisms' waste materials, such as faeces (poo) and urine, which are generally not eaten — see Figure 2.

Length of food chains

The loss of energy at each stage of a food chain explains why you hardly ever get food chains with more than about five trophic levels. So much energy is lost at each stage that there's not enough left to support more organisms after four or five stages.

Q1 What sort of energy is at the start of nearly all food chains?

Q2 What sort of energy is stored in the cells of green plants and algae?

Q3 Explain how energy from the Sun gets passed along a food chain.

Q4 True or False? Energy is only lost between the first and second trophic levels of a food chain.

Practice Question — Application

Q1 In a food chain, duckweed is eaten by ducks, which are then eaten by a fox. Explain why not all of the energy the ducks get from the duckweed is passed on to the fox.

Section Checklist — Make sure you know...

Pyramids of Biomass

☐ That biomass is the mass of living material.

☐ That as you move up a food chain, there's less biomass at each level.

☐ That to draw a pyramid of biomass you need to draw a separate bar for each trophic level of a food chain, the size of the bars needs to decrease towards the top of the pyramid and be drawn to scale, the order of the bars must match the order in the food chain and all the bars must be labelled.

☐ How to interpret a pyramid of biomass, e.g. use one to explain what is happening in a food chain.

Energy Transfer in Food Chains

☐ That the source of energy at the start of most food chains is light energy from the Sun.

☐ That green plants and algae absorb some of the Sun's light energy and convert it into chemical energy when they photosynthesise.

☐ That green plants and algae store chemical energy from photosynthesis in their cells, and this is passed along a food chain when animals eat the plants and algae.

☐ That biomass and energy are lost at each stage of a food chain. This is because organisms respire and the energy released from respiration is used to fuel life processes or lost as heat. Also some of the organisms' material is not eaten (e.g. bones are inedible and some organisms die before being eaten) and some energy is lost in waste products (e.g. faeces and urine).

1. Decay

The process of decay is essential for keeping nature's cycle of nutrients going...

The cycle of elements

Living things are made of materials they take from the world around them. They need to take in materials for growth and other life processes. Plants take elements like carbon, oxygen, hydrogen and nitrogen from the soil or the air. They turn these elements into the complex compounds (carbohydrates, proteins and fats) that make up living organisms, and these compounds then pass through the food chain.

These elements are returned to the environment in waste products produced by the organisms, or when the organisms die. These materials decay because they're broken down (digested) by microorganisms — that's how the elements get put back into the soil.

Microorganisms work best in warm, moist conditions (and slower in cold or dry conditions). Many microorganisms also break down material faster when there's plenty of oxygen available for respiration. Respiration produces heat, which increases the temperature of their environment further.

All the important elements are thus recycled — they return to the soil, ready to be used by new plants and put back into the food chain again. In a **stable community** the materials taken out of the soil and used are balanced by those that are put back in. There's a constant cycle happening.

Compost

Kitchen waste (e.g. food peelings) and garden waste (e.g. dead leaves) can be made into compost. Compost is decayed remains of animal and plant matter that can be used as fertiliser. It recycles nutrients back into the soil — giving you a lovely garden.

Compost bins recreate the ideal conditions for decay — see Figure 1. Compost bins come in many shapes and sizes. There are also council recycling schemes that collect kitchen and garden waste and do the composting for you.

Extra decomposers added (compost maker)

Finely shredded waste is best

Warmth generated by microorganisms helps it all along

Mesh sides to let air in

Figure 1: *A compost bin provides the right conditions for microorganisms to work.*

Learning Objectives:

- Know that living organisms take in materials from their environment and use them for life processes.
- Understand how the materials that an organism takes in are returned to the environment.
- Know that microorganisms decay material.
- Know the conditions in which microorganisms work best to decay material.
- Know that the decay process releases materials back into the soil which plants can reuse.
- Know what is meant by the term, 'stable community'.
- Be able to evaluate schemes that recycle kitchen and garden waste.

Specification Reference B1.6.1

Tip: Some compost bins can be rotated so that the microorganisms get more oxygen. This means they'll respire more (which means they'll work faster).

Council-run composting schemes can be beneficial as they help to reduce the amount of space taken up by landfill sites. They can also make money for the council by producing compost, which can then be sold.

Tip: 'Landfill site' is just the posh term for a rubbish dump or tip.

Practice Questions — Fact Recall

Q1 Why do living organisms take in materials from their environment?

Q2 Elements are returned to the environment when an organism dies.

a) Describe how this happens.

b) Give one other way in which elements are returned to the environment.

Q3 Describe the conditions in which microorganisms are most active.

Q4 What is a stable community?

Q5 Compost is the decayed remains of animal and plant matter. Why is compost used on gardens?

Practice Question — Application

Gary recycles his garden waste by making it into compost. He does this in his garden using this compost bin:

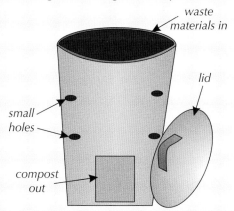

Figure 2: Compost bins can come in lots of different shapes and sizes.

Q1 Suggest why the compost bin has small holes in it.

Q2 Gary has found that compost is made more quickly if he puts his compost bin in a sunny area of the garden. Explain why this is.

Q3 Gary's neighbour told him that he should always keep the lid on his compost bin to stop water vapour escaping out of the bin. Explain how the presence of water vapour would help compost to be made.

Learning Objectives:
- Know what is meant by 'the carbon cycle'.
- Understand that carbon dioxide is removed from the atmosphere by photosynthesis and the carbon is used to make carbon compounds.
- Understand how carbon is passed along food chains.
- Understand the role of detritus feeders and microorganisms in decay.
- Understand how carbon is returned to the atmosphere as carbon dioxide by respiration.
- Understand how carbon is returned to the atmosphere as carbon dioxide by combustion.

Specification Reference
B1.6.2

2. The Carbon Cycle

Carbon is one of the elements in our environment that is constantly being recycled...

What is the carbon cycle?

Carbon is constantly being cycled — from the air, through food chains and eventually back out into the air again. The carbon cycle shows how carbon is recycled — see Figure 1.

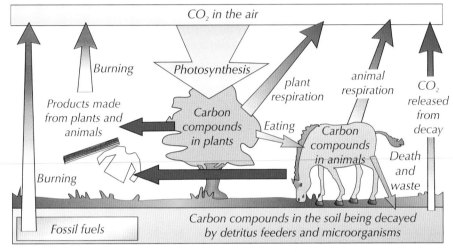

Figure 1: *The carbon cycle.*

Carbon is taken out of the air

The whole carbon cycle is "powered" by **photosynthesis**. CO_2 (carbon dioxide) is removed from the atmosphere by green plants and algae, and the carbon is used to make carbon compounds in the plants and algae, such as carbohydrates, fats and proteins.

Carbon moves through food chains

Some of the carbon becomes part of the fats and proteins in animals when the plants and algae are eaten. The carbon then moves through the food chain. The energy that green plants and algae get from photosynthesis is transferred up the food chain.

When plants, algae and animals die, other animals (called **detritus feeders**) and microorganisms feed on their remains. Animals also produce waste, and this too is broken down by detritus feeders and microorganisms. Compounds in the waste are taken up from the soil by plants as nutrients — they're put back into the food chain again.

Carbon is returned to the air

Some carbon is returned to the atmosphere as CO_2 when the plants, algae, animals (including detritus feeders) and microorganisms **respire**. Also CO_2 is released back into the air when some useful plant and animal products, e.g. wood and fossil fuels, are burnt (**combustion**).

Figure 2: *Woodlice are detritus feeders.*

Tip: Fossil fuels are made of decayed plant and animal matter.

Q1   What process removes carbon dioxide from the atmosphere?

Q2   What do plants use carbon for?

Q3   What happens to the carbon in green plants when the plants are eaten by animals?

Q4   How do detritus feeders put carbon back into the atmosphere?

Q5   How does the carbon contained within fossil fuels get back into the atmosphere?

Section Checklist — Make sure you know...

Decay

☐ That living things take the materials they need (e.g. carbon and nitrogen) from the environment and use them for growth and other life processes.

☐ That these materials are returned to the environment in the organism's waste products or when the organism dies.

☐ That when an organism dies, its remains are broken down by microorganisms and the elements it contains are returned to the soil where they can be used by new plants.

☐ That microorganisms are most active in warm, moist conditions with a good oxygen supply.

☐ That a stable community is one in which the materials taken out of the soil and used are balanced by those that are put back in — there's a constant cycle of materials.

☐ How to evaluate schemes for recycling kitchen and garden waste.

The Carbon Cycle

☐ That the carbon cycle shows how carbon is constantly recycled (from the air, through food chains, and back into the air again).

☐ That carbon is removed from the air as carbon dioxide when green plants and algae photosynthesise.

☐ That green plants and algae use the carbon in carbon dioxide to make carbohydrates, fats and proteins.

☐ That carbon is passed along the food chain when animals eat other organisms and in this way the energy that green plants and algae get from photosynthesis is transferred up the food chain.

☐ That animals use carbon to make fats and proteins in their body.

☐ That detritus feeders and microorganisms break down dead organisms and animal waste, which puts compounds back into the soil that can be taken up by plants as nutrients.

☐ That when green plants, algae, animals (including detritus feeders) and microorganisms respire, carbon dioxide is put back into the air.

☐ That the burning (combustion) of products made from plants and animals (e.g. wood) and fossil fuels puts carbon dioxide back into the air.

Exam-style Questions

1   The diagram below shows how a particular food chain is part of the carbon cycle.

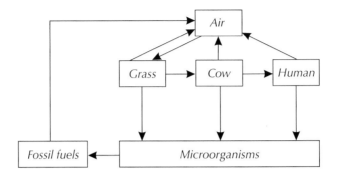

*In this question you will be assessed on the quality of your English,
the organisation of your ideas and your use of appropriate specialist vocabulary.*

Use the information in the diagram and your own knowledge to describe
the processes in which carbon is cycled between this food chain, other living
organisms and the air.

(6 marks)

2   Below is a pyramid of biomass.
It represents a food chain involving algae, fish and birds.

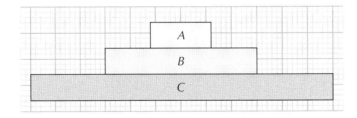

2 (a)   Explain why the Sun is needed at the start of all food chains.

(4 marks)

2 (b)   Which bar on the pyramid (A-C) represents the algae? Explain your answer.

(1 mark)

2 (c) (i)   The ratio of bar C to bar B is 2:1.
Calculate the ratio of bar B to bar A.

(2 marks)

2 (c) (ii)   Neither of the ratios in part (c) (i) are 1:1 because biomass is lost
as you go up a food chain. Explain how biomass is lost from a food chain.

(3 marks)

3 Scientists have been studying a species of wolf. The wolf lives in rocky mountains where the temperature at night can drop as low as –15°C. Its main source of prey is rodents that live in burrows beneath the ground. The wolf has adaptations to help it survive in the rocky mountains as shown on the diagram below.

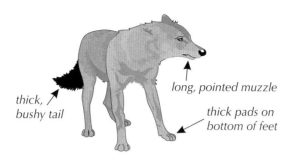

thick, bushy tail

long, pointed muzzle

thick pads on bottom of feet

3 (a) (i) What is an adaptation?

(1 mark)

3 (a) (ii) Use the information and the diagram above to suggest how the wolf is adapted to survive in the rocky mountains.

(3 marks)

3 (b) Scientists have been recording the total population size of the wolf over a number of years. Their findings and some other data are shown in the table and graph below.

Year	Total population size of wolf	Total population size of one type of prey (million)	Rabies outbreak in this year
2007	401	1.96	No
2008	327	2.01	Yes
2009	330	2.09	No
2010	341	2.06	No
2011	265	2.01	Yes
2012	269	1.99	No

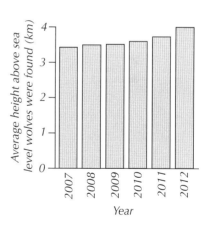

3 (b) (i) Describe the overall trend in the total population size of the wolf species studied.

(1 mark)

3 (b) (ii) Suggest the environmental change that's responsible for this trend. Use data from the table to support your answer.

(3 marks)

3 (b) (iii) Since 2007, the land higher than 3.5 km above sea level has gradually been taken over as farmland. Use data from the graph to suggest how this has affected the distribution of the wolf population.

(2 marks)

Learning Objectives:
- Understand why plants and animals have characteristics which are similar to their parents.
- Understand that differences between organisms can be due to their genes, their environment or both.

Specification Reference B1.7.1

1. Variation

These pages are all about the differences between you, me, and well... everyone else really. It's fascinating stuff...

What is variation?

Different species look... well... different — my dog definitely doesn't look like a daisy. But even organisms of the same species will usually look at least slightly different — e.g. in a room full of people you'll see different colour hair, individually shaped noses, a variety of heights, etc.

These differences are called the variation within a species — and there are two types of variation: **genetic variation** and **environmental variation**.

Genetic variation

All plants and animals have characteristics that are in some ways similar to their parents' (e.g. I've got my dad's nose, apparently). This is because an organism's characteristics are determined by the **genes** inherited from their parents. Genes are the codes inside your cells that control how you're made (there's more about genes on page 97). These genes are passed on in **sex cells** (**gametes**), which the offspring develop from (see page 98).

Most animals (and quite a lot of plants) get some genes from the mother and some from the father. This combining of genes from two parents causes genetic variation — no two of the species are genetically identical (other than identical twins).

Some characteristics are determined only by genes.

Figure 1: *Identical twins have exactly the same genes, which is why they look so alike.*

Examples
- Violet flower colour.   - Eye colour, blood group and inherited disorders (e.g. haemophilia or cystic fibrosis) in animals.

Environmental variation

The environment that organisms live and grow in also causes differences between members of the same species — this is called environmental variation.

Environmental variation covers a wide range of differences — from losing your toes in a piranha attack, to getting a suntan, to having yellow leaves and so on. Basically, any difference that has been caused by the conditions something lives in, is an environmental variation.

A plant grown on a nice sunny windowsill would grow luscious and green.  The same plant grown in darkness would grow tall and spindly and its leaves would turn yellow — these are environmental variations.

Tip: Plants are strongly influenced by environmental factors, e.g. sunlight, moisture level, temperature and soil mineral content.

Genetic and environmental variation

Most characteristics are determined by a mixture of genetic and environmental factors.

Examples

- Height — the maximum height that an animal or plant could grow to is determined by its genes. But whether it actually grows that tall depends on its environment, e.g. how much food it gets.

- Intelligence — one theory is that although your maximum possible IQ might be determined by your genes, whether or not you get to it depends on your environment, e.g. your upbringing and school life.

- Health — some people are more likely to get certain diseases (such as cancer or heart disease) because of their genes. But lifestyle also affects the risk, e.g. whether you smoke or how much junk food you eat.

Tip: Environmental factors aren't just the physical things around you. They can include things like the way you were brought up too.

Practice Questions — Application

Q1 Your sporting ability may be affected by your genes and your environment. Suggest one environmental factor that may affect your sporting ability.

Q2 Identical twins have exactly the same genes. Non-identical twins don't. Studies have shown that:

- identical twins tend to have more similar IQs than non-identical twins (Study 1).

- identical twins who are brought up together tend to have more similar IQs than identical twins who are brought up separately (Study 2).

What do the results of Studies 1 and 2 suggest about the influence of genes and the environment on IQ? Explain your answer.

Learning Objectives:

- Know that chromosomes are found in the cell nucleus.
- Know that chromosomes carry genes.
- Understand that genes control an organism's characteristics.

Specification Reference
B1.7.1

2. Genes, Chromosomes and DNA

Well, this is it. Probably the most important topic in the whole of biology — genes. It's certainly one of the most important topics in this section, so make sure you've got your head around it before you move on.

The cell nucleus

Most cells in your body have a structure called a **nucleus**. The nucleus contains your genetic material (the instructions you need to grow and develop). This material is stored in the form of chromosomes — see Figure 1.

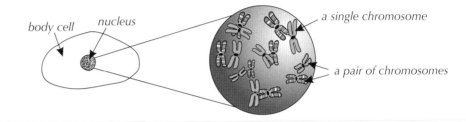

Figure 1: *Diagram to show that a cell nucleus contains chromosomes.*

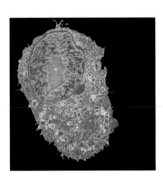

Figure 2: *A human cell (blue) and its nucleus (orange and green), seen under a microscope.*

In mammals, chromosomes come in pairs. The human cell nucleus contains 23 pairs of chromosomes. There are two No. 19 chromosomes, two No. 12s, two No. 3s, etc.

Chromosomes and DNA

Chromosomes are long lengths of a molecule called **DNA**.
The DNA is coiled up to form the arms of the chromosome (see Figure 4).

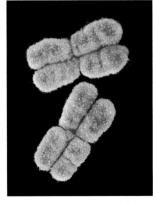

Figure 3: *A pair of human chromosomes seen under a microscope. (In fact, it's pair No. 3.)*

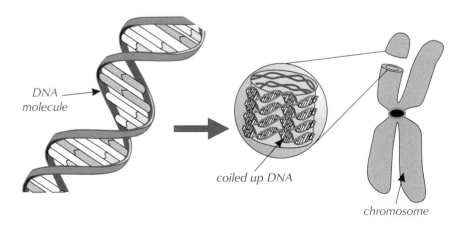

Figure 4: *Diagram to show how DNA coils up to form a chromosome.*

Chromosomes and genes

Chromosomes carry genes (see Figure 5). These are short sections of DNA. Genes control our characteristics. Different genes control the development of different characteristics, e.g. hair colour, eye colour.

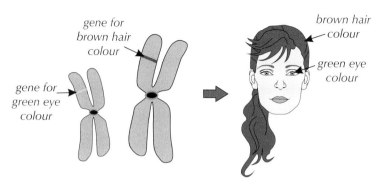

gene for brown hair colour

gene for green eye colour

brown hair colour

green eye colour

Figure 5: *Diagram showing relationship between chromosomes, genes and characteristics.*

Tip: A chromosome contains thousands of genes, not just one. This diagram is just to help show you what's going on.

There can be different versions of the same gene, which give different versions of a characteristic, like blue or brown eyes. The different versions of the same gene are called **alleles** instead of genes — it's more sensible than it sounds!

Tip: You might sometimes see chromosomes drawn like this:

That's because chromosomes only look like this:

just before a cell divides for reproduction and growth (see p. 99).

Practice Questions — Fact Recall

Q1 Where in the cell are chromosomes found?

Q2 a) What are genes?

   b) What do we need different genes for?

Practice Questions — Application

The photograph on the right was taken under a microscope. It shows a cell, its nucleus and chromosomes.

Q1 Which arrow is pointing to:

   a) the cell?

   b) the nucleus?

   c) a chromosome?

Q2 Suggest why it is not possible to see individual genes in this photograph.

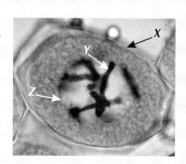

Exam Tip
Make sure you don't get genes and chromosomes mixed up in the exam if you have to label them — chromosomes are long lengths of DNA and they carry genes.

Learning Objectives:

- Understand that sexual reproduction involves the fusion of gametes and creates genetic variation in the offspring.
- Understand that asexual reproduction does not involve the fusion of gametes and creates genetically identical offspring (clones).

Specification Reference
B1.7.2

3. Reproduction

Organisms make more of themselves through reproduction.
There are two types: sexual and asexual. You need to know about both.

Sexual reproduction

Sexual reproduction is where genetic information from two organisms (a father and a mother) is combined to produce offspring which are genetically different to either parent.

Gametes

In sexual reproduction the mother and father produce gametes — e.g. egg and sperm cells in animals (see Figure 1). In humans, each gamete contains 23 chromosomes — half the number of chromosomes in a normal cell. (Instead of having two of each chromosome, a gamete has just one of each.)

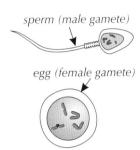
sperm (male gamete)
egg (female gamete)

Figure 1: *The sperm and egg cells.*

Fertilisation

The egg (from the mother) and the sperm cell (from the father) fuse together to form a cell with the full number of chromosomes (half from the father, half from the mother). The fusion of gametes is known as fertilisation (see Figure 3).

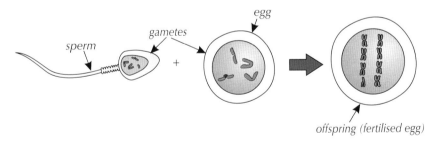
sperm
gametes
egg
offspring (fertilised egg)

Figure 3: *Diagram showing fertilisation.*

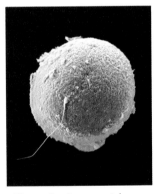

Figure 2: *A sperm (shown in blue) fertilising an egg (shown in yellow) as seen under a microscope.*

This is why the offspring inherits features from both parents — it's received a mixture of chromosomes from its mum and its dad (and it's the chromosomes that decide how you turn out). This mixture of genetic material produces variation in the offspring. Pretty cool, eh.

Here's the main thing to remember about sexual reproduction:

> Sexual reproduction involves the fusion of male and female gametes. Because there are two parents, the offspring contain a mixture of their parents' genes and are genetically different to their parents.

Exam Tip
You need to know the definition of sexual reproduction for the exam. The really important bit is that it involves the <u>fusion</u> of gametes.

Asexual reproduction

An ordinary cell can make a new cell by simply dividing in two. The new cell has exactly the same genetic information (i.e. genes) as the parent cell — this is known as asexual reproduction.

Here's how it works:

1. X-shaped chromosomes have two identical halves.

2. Each chromosome splits down the middle to form two identical sets of 'half chromosomes' (i.e. two sets of DNA strands). A membrane forms around each set.

3. The DNA then replicates (copies) itself to form two identical cells with complete sets of X-shaped chromosomes (ready to divide again).

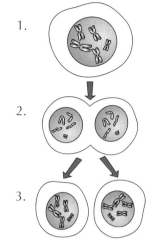

Figure 4: *Diagram showing the three main stages of asexual reproduction.*

This is how all plants and animals grow and produce replacement cells.

Some organisms also produce offspring using asexual reproduction, e.g. bacteria and certain plants.

Here's the main thing to remember about asexual reproduction:

> In asexual reproduction there's only one parent. There's no fusion of gametes, no mixing of chromosomes and no genetic variation between parent and offspring. The offspring are genetically identical to the parent — they're **clones**.

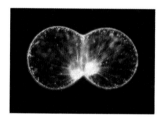

Figure 5: *A single-celled organism called a 'sea sparkle' undergoing asexual reproduction.*

Tip: There's more on clones on the next few pages.

Practice Question — Application

Q1 For each of the following examples, write down whether it's a case of sexual or asexual reproduction, and explain your answer.

a) A single-celled amoeba splits in two to form two genetically identical offspring.

b) Gametes from a male pea plant are crossed with gametes from a female pea plant to produce genetically varied offspring.

c) A lion and a tiger mate to produce an animal known as a 'liger'. The liger shares features with both its parents.

d) A single Brahminy blind snake lays a batch of unfertilised eggs. The offspring that hatch are clones of the mother snake.

Tip: To answer these questions, you need to think about the main differences between sexual and asexual reproduction — look back at the green summary boxes if you need clues.

Learning Objectives:

- Know that plants can be cloned by taking cuttings — and why this is beneficial.

- Know that plants can also be cloned through tissue culture.

- Understand the process by which animals can be cloned using embryo transplants.

- Understand the process by which animals can be cloned using adult cell cloning.

- Be able to interpret information about cloning methods.

- Be able to give informed opinions on the issues surrounding cloning.

Specification Reference
B1.7.2

4. Cloning

This topic is all about how humans can control reproduction. Read on...

What is cloning?

Cloning means making an exact (genetically identical) copy of an organism. It's basically just another term for asexual reproduction (see previous page). Plants which reproduce asexually are able to clone themselves naturally. Cloning can also be done artificially (by humans) — which is what the next few pages are all about.

Cloning plants

It's pretty easy to clone plants. Gardeners have been doing it for years. There are two ways of doing it:

1. Cuttings

Gardeners can take cuttings from good parent plants, and then plant them to produce genetically identical copies (clones) of the parent plant. These plants can be produced quickly and cheaply.

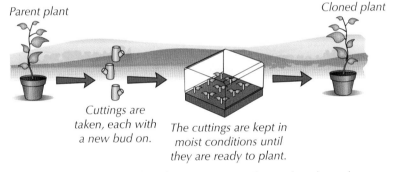

Parent plant

Cloned plant

Cuttings are taken, each with a new bud on.

The cuttings are kept in moist conditions until they are ready to plant.

Figure 1: *Diagram to show how cuttings can be used to clone plants.*

2. Tissue culture

This is a more modern method of cloning plants. A few plant cells are put in a growth medium with hormones, and they grow into new plants — clones of the parent plant. These plants can be made very quickly, in very little space, and be grown all year.

Figure 2: *A tobacco plant being grown by tissue culture (top). A room full of tissue cultures (bottom).*

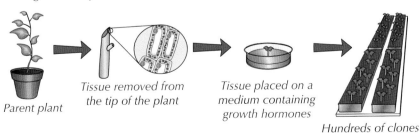

Parent plant

Tissue removed from the tip of the plant

Tissue placed on a medium containing growth hormones

Hundreds of clones can be made

Figure 3: *Diagram to show how tissue culture can be used to clone plants.*

Embryo transplants

You can produce animal clones using embryo transplants. An embryo is created, then split many times in the early stages to form clones. The cloned embryos are then implanted (inserted) into host mothers to continue developing.

Tip: Once an egg cell has been fertilised and starts dividing, it becomes an embryo. The embryo grows and develops into a baby.

Example

Farmers can use embryo transplants to produce cloned offspring from their best bull and cow:

1. Sperm cells are taken from a prize bull and egg cells are taken from a prize cow. The sperm are then used to artificially fertilise an egg cell.

2. The embryo that develops is then split many times (to form clones) before any cells become specialised.

3. These cloned embryos can then be implanted into lots of other cows...

4. ...where they grow into calves (which will all be genetically identical to each other).

Tip: A specialised cell is one that performs a specific function, e.g. a white blood cell defends against pathogens.

This is shown in Figure 4.

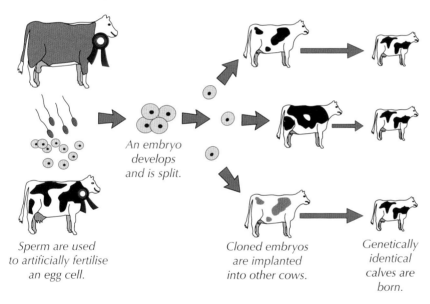

An embryo develops and is split.

Sperm are used to artificially fertilise an egg cell.

Cloned embryos are implanted into other cows.

Genetically identical calves are born.

Figure 4: *Diagram to show how genetically identical calves can be produced through embryo transplants.*

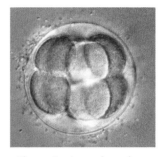

Figure 5: *An early embryo under the microscope — each ball is an individual cell. It's at this stage that the cells are separated in an embryo transplant.*

Tip: The calves here are clones of each other and of the original embryo — but they're not clones of the original bull and cow. Instead, they contain a mixture of genes from both parents.

Adult cell cloning

Adult cell cloning can also be used to make animal clones. Adult cell cloning involves taking an unfertilised egg cell and removing its genetic material (the nucleus). A complete set of chromosomes from an adult body cell (e.g. a skin cell) is inserted into the 'empty' egg cell. The egg cell is then stimulated by an electric shock — this makes it divide, just like a normal embryo.

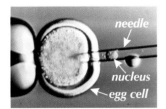

Figure 6: *A nucleus being injected into an egg cell during adult cell cloning.*

Tip: Remember, it's only the <u>nucleus</u> from the adult body cell that gets inserted into the empty egg cell.

When the embryo is a ball of cells, it's implanted into the uterus (womb) of an adult female (the surrogate mother). Here the embryo grows into a genetically identical copy (clone) of the original adult body cell (see Figure 7). This technique was used to create Dolly — the famous cloned sheep.

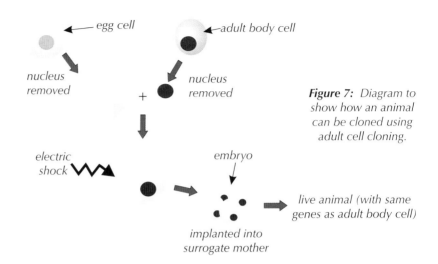

Figure 7: *Diagram to show how an animal can be cloned using adult cell cloning.*

Issues surrounding cloning

There are many social, economic and ethical issues surrounding cloning — you need to know what they are for your exam.

Benefits

- Cloning quickly gets you lots of "ideal" offspring with known characteristics. This can benefit farmers, e.g. if a farmer has a cow that produces lots of milk, he could clone it and create a whole herd of cows that all produce lots of milk relatively quickly.

- The study of animal clones could lead to greater understanding of the development of the embryo, and of ageing and age-related disorders.

- Cloning could be used to help preserve endangered species.

Concerns

- Cloning gives you a "reduced gene pool" — this means there are fewer different alleles in a population. If a population are all closely related and a new disease appears, they could all be wiped out — there may be no allele in the population giving resistance to the disease.

- It's possible that cloned animals might not be as healthy as normal ones, e.g. Dolly the sheep had arthritis, which tends to occur in older sheep (but the jury's still out on if this was due to cloning).

- Some people worry that humans might be cloned in the future. If it was allowed, any success may follow many unsuccessful attempts, e.g. children born severely disabled. Also, you'd need to consider the human rights of the clone — the clone wouldn't have a say in whether it wanted to be a clone or not, so is it fair to produce one?

Figure 8: *Dolly, the world's first cloned sheep, and the scientist who made her (he's the one on the right).*

Tip: Alleles are different forms of a gene (see page 97).

Tip: It's currently illegal to clone a human in the UK.

Practice Questions — Fact Recall

Q1 Plants can be cloned by taking cuttings.

    a) Give two benefits of taking cuttings to clone plants.

    b) Give one other way of cloning plants.

Q2 Name two methods of animal cloning.

Practice Questions — Application

Read the following passage and then answer the questions that follow.

Scientists in the US have been experimenting with cloning the African black-footed cat — an animal classed as 'threatened' on endangered species lists. Their aim is to take a skin cell nucleus from an adult black-footed cat and implant it into an empty egg cell provided by a domestic cat. Once dividing, the embryo will be implanted in the domestic cat in order to develop.

Figure 9: *The African black-footed cat.*

Q1 Once the black-footed cat nucleus has been implanted into the egg cell of the domestic cat, how will it be stimulated to divide?

Q2 Would an embryo created by the scientists' method share any genetic material with the domestic cat? Explain your answer.

Although no black-footed kittens have yet been born as a result of this method, the US team behind the project are confident that it will help to save endangered species.

Q3 Suggest how each of the following could help to save the black-footed cat:

    a) using common domestic cats as surrogate mothers rather than black-footed cats.

    b) being able to take skin cells from black-footed cats that have already died as well as ones that are still alive.

Many wildlife conservationists are against using cloning to save endangered species. Some argue that the money would be better spent on conserving the places in which endangered species live.

Q4 Suggest two more concerns people may have of using cloning to save an endangered species.

> **Tip:** Think about the number of domestic cats compared to how many black-footed cats there are likely to be.

Tip: Remember, DNA is what makes up chromosomes (see page 96).

5. Genetic Engineering

Humans are able to change an organism's genes through a process called genetic engineering. It's really quite clever...

What is genetic engineering?

The basic idea is to copy a useful gene from one organism's chromosome into the cells of another.

How genetic engineering works:

1. A useful gene is "cut" from one organism's chromosome using enzymes.

2. Enzymes are then used to cut another organism's chromosome and then to insert the useful gene.

Scientists use this method to do all sorts of things.

Example

The human insulin gene can be inserted into bacteria to produce human insulin:

1. The insulin gene is first cut out of human DNA using enzymes.

2. The same enzymes are then used to cut the bacterial DNA and different enzymes are used to insert the human insulin gene.

3. The bacteria are then allowed to multiply. The insulin they produce while they grow is purified and used by people with diabetes.

This is summarised in Figure 1.

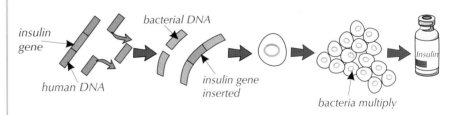

Figure 1: *Diagram showing how bacteria can be genetically engineered to produce insulin.*

Genetic engineering of plants and animals

Useful genes can be transferred into animals and plants at the very early stages of their development (i.e. shortly after fertilisation). This means they'll develop useful characteristics.

- **Genetically modified (GM) crops** are crops which have had their genes modified, e.g. to make them resistant to viruses, insects or herbicides (chemicals used to kill weeds).

- Sheep have been genetically engineered to produce substances, like drugs, in their milk that can be used to treat human diseases.

- Genetic disorders like cystic fibrosis are caused by faulty genes. Scientists are trying to treat these disorders by inserting working genes into sufferers. This is called gene therapy.

Tip: Herbicides kill weeds, but they can also end up killing crops. 'Selective herbicides' are usually used to stop this from happening, but they don't always kill all the weeds. If a crop is herbicide-resistant, more effective herbicides can be used to get rid of weeds — without risk to the crop.

The issues surrounding genetic engineering

Genetic engineering is an exciting new area in science which has the potential for solving many of our problems (e.g. treating diseases, more efficient food production etc.) but not everyone thinks it's a great idea.

There are worries about the long-term effects of genetic engineering — that changing a person's genes might accidentally create unplanned problems, which could then get passed on to future generations.

It's the same with GM crops...

The issues surrounding GM crops

(HOW SCIENCE WORKS)

Benefits

- On the plus side, GM crops can increase the yield of a crop, making more food. For example, insect-resistant crops shouldn't get eaten by insects so much — leaving more food for us.

- People living in developing nations often lack nutrients in their diets. GM crops could be engineered to contain the nutrient that's missing. For example, they're testing 'golden rice' that contains beta-carotene — a lack of this substance causes blindness.

Tip: 'Yield' just means the amount of product made. So the yield of a wheat field would be the amount of wheat produced. Insects eating the crop, disease, and competition with weeds all reduce crop yield.

Concerns

- Some people say that growing GM crops will affect the number of weeds and flowers (and so the population of insects) that live in and around the crops — reducing farmland biodiversity (the variety of living organisms on the farmland).

- Not everyone is convinced that GM crops are safe. People are worried they may develop allergies to the food — although there's probably no more risk for this than for eating usual foods.

- A big concern is that transplanted genes may get out into the natural environment. For example, the herbicide resistance gene may be picked up by weeds, creating a new 'superweed' variety.

Tip: GM crops are already being grown elsewhere in the world (not the UK) often without any problems.

Practice Questions — Fact Recall

Q1 In genetic engineering, useful genes are transferred into animals and plants in the early stages of their development. Explain why.

Q2 a) What does the 'GM' stand for in 'GM crop'?

b) Some GM crops are resistant to viruses.
What else can they be made resistant to? Give two examples.

Practice Questions — Application

B. thuringiensis is a species of bacteria. It produces a crystal protein, which is poisonous to insects when eaten. Some crop plants, including cotton and potatoes, have been genetically engineered to produce the *Bt* crystal protein.

Q1 Explain how enzymes would be used to make a cotton plant that can produce the *Bt* crystal protein.

Q2 Suggest a benefit of genetically engineering crop plants to produce the *Bt* crystal protein. Explain your answer.

Q3 Suggest a possible risk of growing crop plants that have been genetically engineered to produce the *Bt* crystal protein.

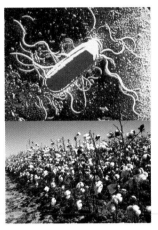

Figure 2: *A* B. thuringiensis *bacterium (top). GM cotton which produces the* Bt *crystal protein (bottom).*

Section Checklist — Make sure you know...

Variation

☐ That plants and animals have similar characteristics to their parents because an organism's characteristics are carried by genes, which are passed on from parents to their offspring in gametes.

☐ That differences between organisms can be determined by their genes, their environment or both.

Genes, Chromosomes and DNA

☐ That chromosomes are found in the cell nucleus and carry genes.

☐ That genes control characteristics in an organism and that different genes control different characteristics.

Reproduction

☐ That sexual reproduction involves the fusion of male and female gametes (e.g. sperm and egg cells) from two parents and creates offspring which contain a mixture of their parents' genes.

☐ That asexual reproduction involves no fusion of gametes, only one parent and no mixing of genes which creates offspring that are genetically identical to the parent (clones).

cont...

Cloning

☐ That plants can be cloned using cuttings and that this allows plants to be produced quickly and cheaply.

☐ That plants can also be cloned through tissue culture (a method of producing whole plants from plant cells grown on a growth medium).

☐ How cloned animals can be produced using embryo transplants — sperm is used to fertilise an egg, creating an embryo. The embryo is then split many times to produce clones before any cells become specialised. The cloned embryos are implanted into host mothers.

☐ How animals can be cloned using adult cell cloning — a nucleus from an adult body cell is inserted into an 'empty' egg cell. The egg cell is then stimulated to divide by electric shock and the embryo is implanted into the uterus of a surrogate mother.

☐ How to interpret information about cloning methods.

☐ The issues surrounding cloning and how to make judgements about them.

Genetic Engineering

☐ How genetic engineering works — enzymes are used to cut out useful genes from one organism's chromosome and then insert them into another's.

☐ That 'new' genes are often transferred into plants and animals at an early stage of their development, so that the plant or animal develops useful characteristics.

☐ How to interpret information about cloning methods.

☐ That GM (genetically modified) crops are examples of genetically engineered organisms and that some GM crops are resistant to insects or herbicides.

☐ The issues surrounding genetic engineering and how to make judgements about them.

☐ The issues surrounding GM crops, including: GM crops can increase yields; some people are concerned that they could negatively affect the weeds and insects that grow around GM crops; some people are concerned they could negatively affect human health.

Exam-style Questions

1 (a) Complete the paragraph below, using the correct words from the box.
You may only use each word once.

> chromosomes   gametes   variation   cloning   characteristics

Genes are found on .... Genes control an organism's

.... Genes are passed on from parents to offspring in the

.... The combining of genes from two parents creates genetic

.... in the offspring.

(4 marks)

1 (b) The girls shown below are identical twins. They have exactly the same genes.

1 (b) (i) Both twins have blue eyes. What determines the twins' eye colour?

(1 mark)

1 (b) (ii) The twin on the left is taller than the twin on the right.
Suggest **one** possible explanation for this difference in height.

(1 mark)

1 (c) The twins were born as a result of sexual reproduction.
Explain what sexual reproduction is.

(4 marks)

2   Cloned pigs may be created using embryo transplants.
         The diagram below shows the creation of a pig embryo for this purpose.

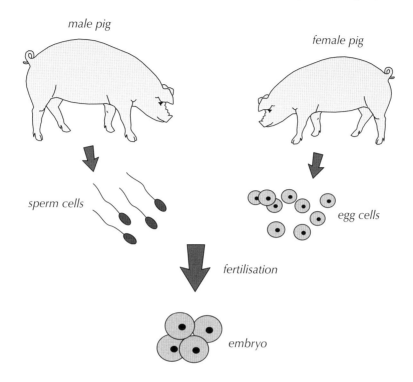

2 (a) (i)   Describe how genetically identical pigs will now be created using this embryo.

(3 marks)

2 (a) (ii)   Is this an example of sexual or asexual reproduction?
              Give **two** reasons for your answer.

(2 marks)

2 (b)   The pigs that are born as a result of this process will share characteristics with
          both the male pig and the female pig. Explain why.

(2 marks)

2 (c)   *In this question you will be assessed on the quality of your English,*
          the organisation of your ideas and your use of appropriate specialist vocabulary.

          Certain groups of people (e.g. farmers, scientists) may want to clone pigs.
          However, other people may have concerns about the cloning of pigs.

          Using your scientific knowledge, discuss the possible benefits and concerns of
          cloning pigs.

(6 marks)

1. Evolution and Natural Selection

This is it. The 'Big One' — how life on Earth began, and, um, kept on going...

Learning Objectives:

- Understand the theory of evolution — life on Earth began more than 3 billion years ago as simple organisms from which all more complex organisms evolved.
- Know that natural selection explains how evolution occurs.
- Know that Charles Darwin came up with the idea of natural selection.
- Understand the three main stages involved in natural selection.
- Know that mutations can result in new forms of a gene and how this can lead to changes in a species.

Specification Reference B1.8.1

The theory of evolution

The theory of evolution is this:

> More than 3 billion years ago, life on Earth began as simple organisms from which all the more complex organisms evolved.

It means that rather than just popping into existence, complex organisms like animals and plants 'developed' over billions of years from simpler single-celled organisms, such as bacteria.

Natural selection

Natural selection explains how evolution occurs. The scientist **Charles Darwin**, came up with the idea of natural selection in the 1800s. It works like this:

1. Individuals within a species show variation because of the differences in their genes.

   Example

   Some rabbits have big ears and some have small ones.

Figure 1: *Charles Darwin.*

Tip: Genetic differences are caused by sexual reproduction (see page 98) and mutations (see next page).

2. Individuals with characteristics that make them better adapted to the environment have a better chance of survival and so are more likely to breed successfully.

   Example

   Big-eared rabbits are more likely to hear a fox approaching them, and so are more likely to survive and have lots of offspring. Small-eared rabbits are more likely to get eaten.

3. So, the genes that are responsible for the useful characteristics are more likely to be passed on to the next generation.

Tip: Remember, it's the <u>genes</u> that get passed on to the next generation (not the characteristics themselves).

> **Example**
>
> All the baby rabbits are born with big ears.

Over time, the gene for a useful characteristic will become more common (accumulate) in a population. This will lead to changes in a species. The gradual changing of a species over time is evolution. Eventually, if the changes are great enough, a new species will evolve.

Mutations

Evolution can occur due to mutations.

> A mutation is a change in an organism's DNA (genes).

Most of the time mutations have no effect, but occasionally they can be beneficial by producing a useful characteristic. This characteristic may give the organism a better chance of surviving and reproducing — especially if the environment changes in some way. If so, the beneficial mutation is more likely to be passed on to future generations by natural selection. Over time, the beneficial mutation will accumulate in a population, sometimes changing a whole species.

Exam Tip
Don't get natural selection and evolution mixed up. Natural selection is when a useful characteristic (i.e. one that gives a better chance of survival) becomes more common in a population. Evolution is the gradual changing of a species over time (which happens as a result of natural selection).

> **Example**
>
> A mutation may make a bacterium resistant to an antibiotic (see page 29). If the antibiotic appears in the bacterium's environment (e.g. a person with a bacterial infection starts taking antibiotics), the mutation may give the bacterium a better chance of surviving, reproducing and passing the beneficial mutation on to future generations. Over time, the mutation will accumulate in the bacterial population.

Practice Questions — Fact Recall

Q1 According to the theory of evolution, how long ago did life on Earth begin?

Q2 According to the theory of evolution, how did complex organisms come to exist on Earth?

Q3 a) What is natural selection?

b) Who came up with the idea of natural selection?

Q4 a) What is a mutation?

b) Explain how a mutation can lead to changes in a species.

Exam Tip
Facts like how long ago life on Earth began and who came up with natural selection are dead easy to learn — and they could mean dead easy marks in the exam.

Practice Questions — Application

Q1 Warfarin is a chemical that was commonly used to kill rats. It is now used less often as many rats have become resistant to it.

Use the theory of evolution by natural selection to explain how most rats have become warfarin-resistant.

Q2 In 1810, a herd of reindeer were taken from the Arctic to an area with a warmer climate. The herd were then left to live and reproduce in the area and were revisited in 1960. Some information about the herd is shown in the graph.

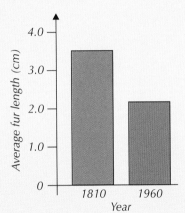

a) By roughly how much did the average fur length of the herd change between 1810 and 1960?

Tip: To help you answer Q2 b), think about how the change in fur length might affect the reindeer in their new environment.

b) Explain this change in terms of natural selection.

2. Ideas About Evolution

Darwin's ideas about natural selection are now pretty well established. But when they were first published, there wasn't as much evidence to support them.

Controversy

Darwin's theory of evolution by natural selection is widely accepted today. But Darwin's idea was very controversial at the time — for various reasons...

1. It went against common religious beliefs about how life on Earth developed — it was the first plausible explanation for our own existence without the need for a "Creator" (God).

2. Darwin couldn't give a good explanation for why these new, useful characteristics appeared or exactly how individual organisms passed on their beneficial characteristics to their offspring. But then he didn't know anything about genes or mutations — they weren't discovered 'til 50 years after his theory was published.

3. There wasn't enough evidence to convince many scientists, because not many other studies had been done into how organisms change over time.

For these reasons, Darwin's idea was only accepted gradually, as more and more evidence came to light.

Lamarck

Darwin wasn't the only person who tried to explain evolution. There were different scientific **hypotheses** around at the same time, such as Lamarck's:

Lamarck (1744-1829) argued that if a characteristic was used a lot by an organism then it would become more developed during its lifetime. E.g. if a rabbit used its legs to run a lot (to escape predators), then its legs would get longer.

Lamarck believed that these acquired characteristics would be passed on to the next generation, e.g. the rabbit's offspring would have longer legs.

Proving or disproving hypotheses

Often scientists come up with different hypotheses to explain similar observations. Scientists might develop different hypotheses because they have different beliefs (e.g. religious) or they have been influenced by different people (e.g. other scientists and their way of thinking)... or they just think differently.

The only way to find out whose hypothesis is right is to find evidence to support or disprove each one.

Learning Objectives:

- Know the reasons why Darwin's theory of evolution by natural selection wasn't accepted straight away.

- Understand that there have been other hypotheses about evolution, including Lamarck's — which was based on the idea that 'acquired characteristics' could be inherited.

- Know the differences between Darwin's theory and other hypotheses that try to explain evolution.

- Be able to suggest why scientists come up with different hypotheses based on the same observations.

- Understand that we now know Lamarck's hypothesis was wrong.

- Be able to interpret data about the development of evolutionary hypotheses.

Specification Reference B1.8.1

Figure 1: *Lamarck.*

Tip: There's more about hypotheses on page 1.

Example

Lamarck and Darwin both had different hypotheses to explain how evolution happens.

In the end Lamarck's hypothesis was rejected because experiments didn't support his hypothesis. You can see it for yourself, e.g. if you dye a hamster's fur bright pink (not recommended), its offspring will still be born with the normal fur colour because the new characteristic won't have been passed on.

The discovery of genetics supported Darwin's idea because it provided an explanation of how organisms born with beneficial characteristics can pass them on (i.e. via their genes).

There's now so much evidence for Darwin's idea that it's an accepted hypothesis (a theory).

Practice Questions — Application

Q1 Kyra is a geneticist — her work involves looking at how our genes affect us. Neil is a psychologist — his work involves looking at how our experiences influence our behaviour.

Kyra believes that alcohol addiction is down to the genes you inherit. Neil believes that alcohol addiction develops as a result of your upbringing and environment. Suggest a reason why Kyra and Neil have different opinions on the reasons for an alcohol addiction.

Q2 A farmer clips the flight feathers on the wings of his chickens. This makes the feathers shorter and stops the birds being able to fly. The offspring of these birds develop normal flight feathers and are able to fly. Explain how this scenario helps to disprove Lamarck's hypothesis about evolution.

Q3 Anteaters feed on insects such as ants. They have evolved extremely long tongues, which help them to reach inside ant nests and get at the ants.

a) Suggest how Lamarck may have explained the evolution of long tongues in anteaters.

b) How would scientists explain the evolution of long tongues in anteaters using the idea of natural selection?

Tip: To answer Q3b), you'll need to look back at the detail of Darwin's theory of evolution by natural selection on pages 110-111.

3. Classification

Classification means sorting things into groups. Like organisms, for example...

Classifying organisms

Looking at the similarities and differences between organisms allows us to classify them into groups.

Examples

- **Plants** make their own food (by a process called photosynthesis) and are fixed in the ground.

- **Animals** move about the place and can't make their own food.

- **Microorganisms** are different to plants and animals, e.g. bacteria are single-celled.

Studying the similarities and differences between organisms also help us to understand how all living things are related (**evolutionary relationships**) and how they interact with each other (**ecological relationships**).

Studying evolutionary relationships

Species with similar characteristics often have similar genes because they share a **recent common ancestor**. This makes them closely related. They often look very alike and tend to live in similar types of habitat.

Example

Whales and dolphins are closely related mammals that live in the sea.

Occasionally, genetically different species might look alike too.

Example

Dolphins and sharks look pretty similar because they've both adapted to living in the same habitat. But they're not closely related — they've evolved from different ancestors.

Evolutionary trees

Evolutionary trees show common (shared) ancestors and relationships between organisms. The more recent the common ancestor, the more closely related the two species. There are some examples of evolutionary trees on the next page.

Learning Objectives:

- Know that looking at the similarities and differences between organisms allows us to classify them into groups, e.g. plants, animals and microorganisms.

- Know that looking at the similarities and differences between organisms allows us to understand their evolutionary relationships.

- Understand how evolutionary trees show the relationships between organisms.

- Know that looking at the similarities and differences between organisms allows us to understand their ecological relationships.

Specification Reference B1.8.1

Tip: All organisms are related in some way, even if only distantly. That's because all life on Earth evolved from the same simple organisms.

Figure 1: *This shark (top) and dolphin (bottom) have similar streamlined bodies to help them move through the water, but aren't closely related.*

Example 1

This evolutionary tree shows that whales and dolphins have a recent common ancestor so are closely related. They're both more distantly related to sharks:

Tip: An evolutionary tree is a bit like a family tree — but instead of showing a mum, dad, grandparents, etc., it shows ancestors that existed many thousands or even millions of years ago.

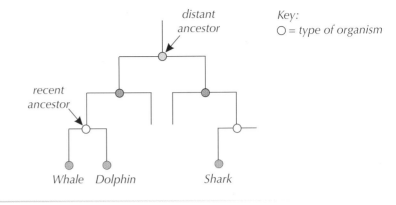

Example 2

This evolutionary tree shows the relationships between humans and some of the great apes. Each point at which the lines meet, indicates a common ancestor.

Tip: The distant ancestor is the 'oldest' organism on this evolutionary tree (i.e. it evolved first).

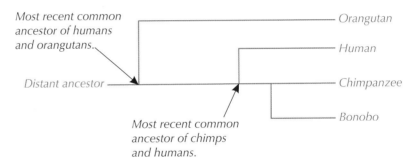

You can see that humans are more closely related to chimpanzees than to orangutans because they share a more recent common ancestor.

Studying ecological relationships

If we see organisms in the same environment with similar characteristics, it suggests they might be in competition.

Example

Dolphins and sharks often compete for the same food source (fish).

Differences between organisms in the same environment can show predator-prey relationships.

Example

Dolphins swim in small groups, but herring swim in giant shoals — this is because dolphins hunt herring, so the herring move around in large groups for protection.

Practice Questions — Fact Recall

Q1 How are we able to classify organisms into animals, plants and microorganisms?

Q2 Organisms in the same environment, often have similar characteristics, e.g. dolphins and sharks. What can this tell us about their ecological relationship?

Figure 2: A group of dolphins hunting a shoal of fish. The fish bunch together in a large ball for protection.

Practice Questions — Application

Q1 The picture below is of a sea cucumber.

The sea cucumber crawls along the sea bed feeding on the dead material it finds there (its only source of food). Is the sea cucumber an animal or a plant? Give two reasons for your answer.

Q2 The tree below shows the evolutionary relationships between some of the big cats.

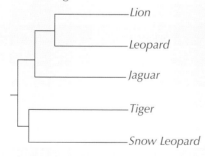

Lion

Leopard

Jaguar

Tiger

Snow Leopard

a) Which animal is most closely related to:

 i) the leopard? ii) the tiger?

b) Which animal evolved first, the jaguar or the lion?

c) Do the lion and the snow leopard share a common ancestor?

Evolution and Natural Selection

☐ The theory of evolution — life on Earth began more than 3 billion years ago as simple organisms from which all more complex organisms evolved.

☐ That Charles Darwin came up with the idea of natural selection to explain how evolution occurs.

☐ How natural selection works — individuals show variation, some individuals have characteristics that make them more likely to survive and breed, the genes for these characteristics are more likely to be passed onto the next generation.

☐ That a change in a gene is called a mutation.

☐ That a mutation may give rise to a beneficial characteristic, which helps the organism to survive and reproduce (especially if the environment changes).

☐ That a beneficial mutation can accumulate in a population and lead to a change in a species.

Ideas About Evolution

☐ The reasons why Darwin's theory of evolution by natural selection wasn't accepted straight away — it went against common religious beliefs; Darwin couldn't explain how characteristics were inherited (genes wouldn't be discovered for another 50 years); there wasn't enough evidence to support his theory.

☐ That there have been other hypotheses to explain how evolution occurs, including Lamarck's (which was based on the idea that 'acquired characteristics' could be inherited).

☐ The reasons why scientists might come up with different hypotheses based on the same observations, e.g. religious beliefs, personal backgrounds.

☐ How we came to reject Lamarck's hypothesis (experimental evidence didn't support it) and accept Darwin's (the discovery of genetics explained how characteristics could be inherited).

☐ How to interpret evidence about evolutionary hypotheses.

Classification

☐ How looking at the similarities and differences between organisms allows us to classify them as plants, animals and microorganisms.

☐ How looking at the similarities and differences between organisms allows us to understand their evolutionary relationships.

☐ How evolutionary trees show common ancestors and therefore the relationships between organisms.

☐ How looking at the similarities and differences between organisms allows us to understand their ecological relationships, e.g. competition, predator-prey relationships.

Exam-style Questions

1   The evolutionary tree shows how some groups of animals, including snakes, are related.

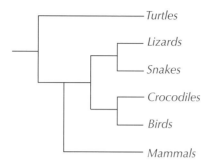

- Turtles
- Lizards
- Snakes
- Crocodiles
- Birds
- Mammals

1 (a)   Which of the following groups of animals are most closely related?
Tick the correct box below.

Turtles and lizards ☐   Snakes and crocodiles ☐

Crocodiles and birds ☐   Birds and mammals ☐

(1 mark)

1 (b)   According to the tree, which group of animals evolved first?

(1 mark)

The picture shows a type of snake called a Sinaloan milk snake.

The milk snake is relatively harmless, but it has evolved to have a very similar pattern and colouring to the deadly poisonous coral snake, which lives in the same environment. The coral snake's colouring warns predators that it is dangerous to eat.

1 (c)   Using the idea of natural selection, explain how the milk snake may have evolved to have a similar colouring to the coral snake.

(3 marks)

1 (d)   The theory of evolution by natural selection was proposed by Charles Darwin. Darwin's ideas about natural selection were only gradually accepted.
Give **three** reasons why this was the case.

(3 marks)

Learning Objectives:

- Know that everything is made up of atoms.
- Know the structure of an atom.
- Know the relative charges of protons, neutrons and electrons.
- Know that the number of electrons in an atom is the same as the number of protons, and that this means atoms are neutral.
- Know that an element is made up of only one type of atom.
- Recall that there are roughly 100 known elements.
- Understand that the atoms of an element contain the same number of protons and that atoms of different elements contain different numbers of protons.

Specification Reference
C1.1.1

1. Atoms and Elements

Atoms and elements are the basis of all of chemistry. So you really need to know what they are. Luckily, these pages are here to help out with that...

The structure of the atom

Atoms are the tiny particles that everything is made up of. There are quite a few different (and equally useful) models of the atom — but chemists tend to like the nuclear model best. The nuclear model shows atoms as having a small **nucleus** surrounded by **electrons** (see Figure 1). You can use the nuclear model to explain pretty much the whole of chemistry.

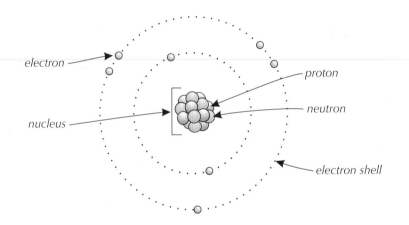

Figure 1: *The nuclear model of the atom.*

The nucleus

The nucleus is in the middle of the atom. It contains **protons** and **neutrons**. Protons are positively charged. Neutrons have no charge (they're neutral). So the nucleus has a positive charge overall because of the protons. But size-wise it's tiny compared to the rest of the atom.

The electrons

The electrons move around the nucleus. They're negatively charged. They're tiny, but they cover a lot of space. They occupy shells around the nucleus. Figure 2 shows the relative electrical charges of protons, neutrons and electrons.

Tip: A <u>shell</u> is just an area where electrons are found. At GCSE you'll usually see them drawn as circles around the nucleus. Shells are sometimes called <u>energy levels</u>.

Particle	Proton	Neutron	Electron
Charge	+1	0	−1

Figure 2: *The relative charges of protons, neutrons and electrons.*

Electrical charge

Atoms have no charge overall. They are neutral. The charge on the electrons (–1) is the same size as the charge on the protons (+1) — but opposite. This means the number of protons always equals the number of electrons in an atom.

Example

This atom has 7 protons. Each proton has a charge of +1, so the total charge of the nucleus is +7 (neutrons have no charge, remember).

The atom doesn't have a charge overall, so the total charge of the electrons must be –7, to cancel out the charge from the protons. As each electron has a charge of –1, this means there must be 7 electrons around the nucleus.

Tip: Don't worry about the way the electrons are arranged in the shells for now. You do need to know this stuff but it's all covered for you on pages 126-127.

If some electrons are added or removed, the atom becomes charged and is then an ion. (See page 129 for more on ions.)

Elements

Atoms can have different numbers of protons, neutrons and electrons. It's the number of protons in the nucleus that decides what type of atom it is.

Examples

An atom with one proton in its nucleus is hydrogen.

An atom with two protons is helium.

Tip: Protons, neutrons and electrons are all types of sub-atomic particle.

If a substance only contains one type of atom it's called an **element**.

Example

Lithium is an element. It's made up of lithium atoms only. Each lithium atom contains 3 protons.

Lithium is an element...   *...made of lithium atoms.*

Each lithium atom has the same number of protons.

Tip: Atoms of an element will also have the same number of electrons as each other, but it's the number of protons that's important — that's what determines what the element is.

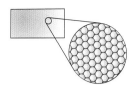

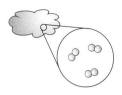

Figure 3: *Copper (top) and nitrogen (bottom) are both elements. Copper is made up of copper atoms only and nitrogen is made up of nitrogen atoms only.*

There are about 100 different elements — quite a lot of everyday substances are elements. For example, copper, iron, aluminium, oxygen and nitrogen are all elements. The important things to remember are...

- All the atoms of a particular element (e.g. nitrogen) have the same number of protons.
- Different elements have atoms with different numbers of protons.

Practice Questions — Fact Recall

Q1 Describe the structure of an atom. Use the terms 'proton', 'neutron', 'electron', 'nucleus' and 'shell' in your answer.

Q2 What is the relative charge of...

a) a proton?

b) a neutron?

c) an electron?

Q3 What feature of an atom determines what type of atom it is?

Q4 What is an element?

Q5 Approximately how many elements are there?

Practice Questions — Application

Q1 Neon is an element. How many types of atom does neon contain?

Q2 An atom of silver contains 47 protons. How many electrons does an atom of silver contain?

Q3 An atom of selenium contains 34 electrons. How many protons does an atom of selenium contain?

Q4 Look at the diagrams of Atom A and Atom B. Are they atoms of the same element or different elements? Explain your answer.

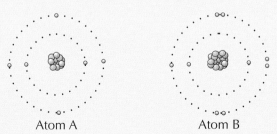

Atom A   Atom B

Q5 A particle contains 17 protons, 17 neutrons and 18 electrons.

a) What is the total charge of the nucleus?

b) What is the overall charge on the particle?

c) Is the particle an atom? Explain your answer.

2. The Periodic Table

Learning Objectives:
- Know that chemical symbols are used to represent atoms of different elements.
- Know what the periodic table is.
- Know where metals and non-metals are in the periodic table.
- Be able to work out the number of protons, electrons and neutrons in an atom from its atomic number and mass number.
- Know that elements in a group have the same number of electrons in their outer shell and so have similar properties.
- Know that Group 0 elements (the noble gases) have a full outer shell of electrons and that this makes them unreactive.

Specification Reference
C1.1.1, C1.1.2

The periodic table is a chemist's best friend. At first glance it might seem a bit intimidating but it's got loads of useful information in it. These pages will help you get a grip on exactly what that information is.

Chemical symbols

Atoms of each element can be represented by a one or two letter symbol — it's a type of shorthand that saves you the bother of having to write the full name of the element.

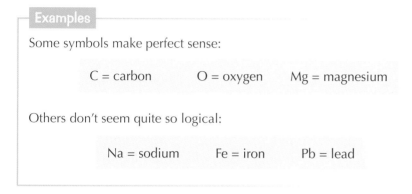

Examples

Some symbols make perfect sense:

C = carbon   O = oxygen   Mg = magnesium

Others don't seem quite so logical:

Na = sodium   Fe = iron   Pb = lead

What is the periodic table?

The **periodic table** is a table that contains all the known elements (about 100). The elements are represented by their symbols. The table is laid out so that elements with similar properties form columns. These vertical columns are called **groups**.

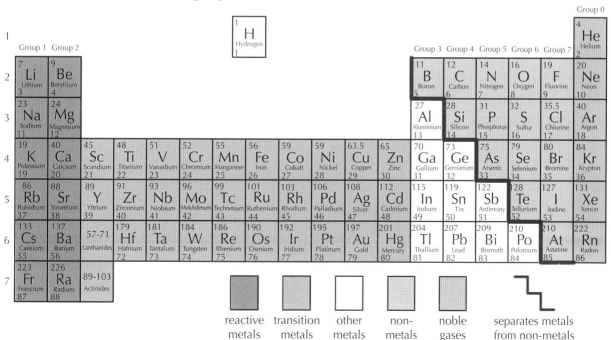

Figure 1: *The periodic table of the elements.*

Atomic numbers and mass numbers

Each symbol in the periodic table has two numbers by it. The smaller (bottom) number is the **atomic number**. This is the number of protons, which conveniently also tells you the number of electrons. The larger (top) number is the **mass number**. This is the total number of protons and neutrons.

Tip: The atomic number is sometimes called the proton number.

Tip: Sometimes the mass number isn't a whole number. For example, the mass number of chlorine is 35.5. This is because atoms of an element can have different numbers of neutrons, and an average number of neutrons is used in the mass number.

Exam Tip
You could be asked to calculate the number of protons, neutrons or electrons in an atom from its atomic number and mass number. So make sure you know how to do it.

Example

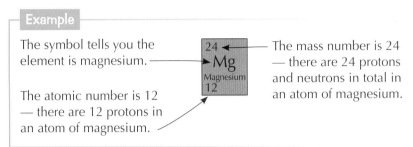

The symbol tells you the element is magnesium.

The atomic number is 12 — there are 12 protons in an atom of magnesium.

The mass number is 24 — there are 24 protons and neutrons in total in an atom of magnesium.

You can use the mass number and atomic number to work out the number of neutrons in an atom of an element. All you have to do is subtract the atomic number from the mass number.

Example

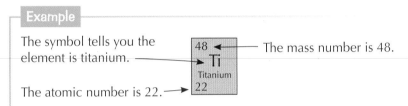

The symbol tells you the element is titanium.

The atomic number is 22.

The mass number is 48.

Number of protons in an atom of titanium = 22.

The total number of protons and neutrons in an atom of titanium is 48, so the number of neutrons = 48 – 22 = 26.

The number of electrons in an atom is equal to the number of protons, so the number of electrons in an atom of titanium is 22.

Groups in the periodic table

All of the elements in a group have the same number of electrons in their outer shell. This is why elements in the same group have similar properties. So, if you know the properties of one element, you can predict properties of other elements in that group.

Figure 2: Lithium, sodium and potassium are all in the same group so have similar properties. For example, they are all metals that are shiny when cut.

Example 1

The Group 1 elements are Li, Na, K, Rb, Cs and Fr.

They all have one electron in their outer shell.

They're all metals and they react the same way. For example:

- They all react with water to form an alkaline solution and hydrogen gas.
- They all react with oxygen to form an oxide.

The Group 0 elements (the **noble gases**) are He, Ne, Ar, Kr, Xe and Rn.

They all have eight electrons in their outer shell, apart from helium (which has two).

This means that they have a stable arrangement of electrons, which makes them unreactive.

Figure 3: Group 0 elements are all unreactive. This property means that helium can be safely used in balloons (top), and neon is safe to use in neon signs (bottom).

Practice Questions — Fact Recall

Q1   What information does an atomic number give you?

Q2   What information does a mass number give you?

Q3   Why do elements in the same group of the periodic table have similar chemical properties?

Q4   How many electrons do Group 1 elements have in their outer shell?

Q5   What is another name for the Group 0 elements?

Q6   Why are Group 0 elements unreactive?

Practice Questions — Application

Use the periodic table on page 382 to answer the following questions.

Q1   Name three metals and three non-metals.

Q2   Name all the elements in Group 2 of the periodic table.

Q3   What is the chemical symbol used to represent:

   a) sulfur?   b) chlorine?   c) potassium?

Q4   Give the atomic number of the following elements:

   a) calcium   b) copper   c) boron

Q5   Give the mass number of the following elements:

   a) bromine   b) potassium   c) helium

Q6   a) How many protons does an atom of sodium contain?

   b) How many electrons does an atom of sodium contain?

   c) How many neutrons does an atom of sodium contain?

Q7   a) How many protons does an atom of iron contain?

   b) How many electrons does an atom of iron contain?

   c) How many neutrons does an atom of iron contain?

Q8   Nitrogen (N) has five electrons in its outer shell.
How many electrons does Arsenic (As) have in its outer shell?

Learning Objectives:

- Know that electrons are found in shells, also known as energy levels.

- Know that electrons fill the shells closest to the nucleus first.

- Know how many electrons each shell can hold.

- Be able to draw and write out the electronic structures of the first 20 elements of the periodic table.

Specification Reference
C1.1.1

3. Electron Shells

So, you know that electrons are found in shells around the nucleus. The next thing you need to know is how they're arranged in these shells. Read on...

How are the electrons arranged in atoms?

Electrons always occupy **shells** (sometimes called **energy levels**). The electron shells with the lowest energy are always filled first — these are the ones closest to the nucleus. Only a certain number of electrons are allowed in each shell — see Figure 1.

Shell	Maximum number of electrons
1st	2
2nd	8
3rd	8

Figure 1: *Table showing how many electrons each electron shell can hold.*

Atoms are much happier when they have full electron shells — like the noble gases in Group 0. In most atoms the outer shell is not full and this makes the atom want to react to fill it.

Electronic structures

The **electronic structure** of an element is how the electrons are arranged in an atom of that element. You need to know the electronic structures for the first 20 elements (things get a bit more complicated after that). But they're not hard to work out. You just need to follow these steps:

1. Find the number of electrons in an atom of the element (using the periodic table).

2. Draw the first electron shell and add up to two electrons to it.

3. Draw the second electron shell and add up to eight electrons to it.

4. If you need to, draw the third electron shell and add up to eight electrons.

5. As soon as you've added enough electrons, stop.

Tip: Sometimes you'll see electrons drawn as dots (like on pages 120-121), other times you'll see them drawn as crosses. It doesn't matter which you use — they all represent electrons.

Tip: You'd usually draw the first four electrons in each shell spread out around the shell. Then you draw the next four electrons next to them to make pairs of electrons. But you don't need to worry about this for GCSE — just make sure you've got the right number of electrons in each shell.

> **Example**
>
> Draw the electronic structure of nitrogen.
>
> 1. The periodic table tells us nitrogen has seven protons... so it must have seven electrons.
>
> 2. Draw the first electron shell and add 2 electrons.
>
> 3. Draw the second shell and add the remaining five electrons.
>
> 4. Nitrogen only has seven electrons so you don't need to draw a third shell.

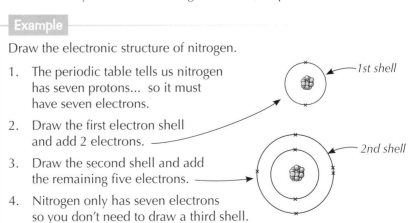

Drawing an atom is one way of showing its electronic structure, but you can also write out the electronic structure using numbers.

1. You can show the electronic structure of nitrogen using a diagram like this...

...or you can write it out like this.

2, 5

This shows that there are two electrons in the 1st shell...

...and 5 in the 2nd.

2. Argon has 18 electrons. Two can go in the first shell and eight can go in the second. That leaves eight to go into the third electron shell. So the electronic structure of argon is...   2, 8, 8.

Exam Tip
You need to be able to draw and write electronic structures for your exam, so make sure you know how to do it both ways.

Potassium and calcium

Beyond the third electron shell (after argon in the periodic table) things get a bit complicated. You could get asked for the electronic structures of potassium and calcium. All you need to know is that potassium has one electron in the fourth shell and calcium has two. So the electronic structure of potassium is 2, 8, 8, 1 and the electronic structure of calcium is 2, 8, 8, 2.

Tip: When you're working out the electronic structure of an element with lots of electrons (like argon), you may find it easier to write it out rather than drawing a diagram.

Practice Questions — Fact Recall

Q1 What is another name for an electron shell?

Q2 How many electrons can go in the first electron shell?

Q3 How many electrons can go in the second electron shell?

Q4 How many electrons can go in the third electron shell?

Q5 Which shell fills with electrons first?

Tip: An electronic structure is sometimes called an <u>electron configuration</u>.

Practice Questions — Application

Q1 This diagram shows the electronic structure of an element. Which element is it?

Q2 Which element has the electronic structure 2, 4?

Q3 Which element has the electronic structure 2, 8, 6?

Q4 Draw the electronic structure of oxygen.

Q5 Draw the electronic structure of boron.

Q6 Write out the electronic structure of phosphorus.

Q7 Write out the electronic structure of magnesium.

Tip: You'll need a periodic table to answer some of these questions — you'll find one on page 382.

Tip: You don't need to draw all the protons and neutrons out when you're drawing the electronic structure of an element. You can just draw a circle to represent the nucleus instead (as in Q1).

4. Compounds

Elements are substances that are made up of just one type of atom. If a substance is made up of more than one type of atom then it might be a compound — and that's what these pages are about.

What are compounds?

When different elements react, atoms form **chemical bonds** with other atoms to form **compounds**. It's usually difficult to separate the two original elements out again. Making bonds involves atoms giving away, taking or sharing electrons (there's more on bonding on page 130). If the different atoms aren't bonded together then it's not a compound — it's a mixture (see Figure 1).

An element.

A compound.

A mixture.

Figure 1: *Diagrams to represent the atoms in an element, a compound and a mixture.*

Properties of compounds

The properties of a compound are totally different from the properties of the original elements.

Figure 2: *Iron sulfide (bottom) is a compound of iron (top) and sulfur (middle).*

Tip: <u>Ions</u> are made when atoms lose or gain electrons — there's more about ions coming up on the next page.

> **Example**
>
> If iron (a lustrous magnetic metal) and sulfur (a nice yellow powder) react, the compound formed (iron sulfide) is a dull grey solid lump, and doesn't behave anything like either iron or sulfur.
>
>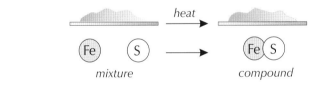
>
> mixture   compound

Compounds can be small **molecules** or great big structures called lattices (when I say big I'm talking in atomic terms).

> **Example**
>
>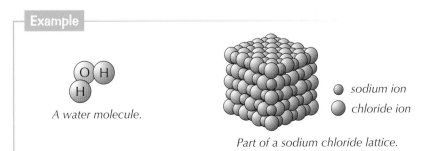
>
> *A water molecule.*
>
> ● sodium ion
> ● chloride ion
>
> *Part of a sodium chloride lattice.*

Ions

A compound which is formed from a metal and a non-metal consists of **ions**. Ions are charged particles. They are made when atoms lose or gain electrons. Metal atoms lose electrons to form positive ions and non-metal atoms gain electrons to form negative ions.

Tip: You can work out whether an element is a metal or a non-metal from its position in the periodic table (see page 123).

Example 1

Metal atoms form positive ions

A sodium atom has 11 protons and 11 electrons. Protons have a relative charge of +1 and electrons have a relative charge of -1, so the atom has no overall charge.

$$\underset{\text{total charge of protons}}{} 11 - 11 = 0 \quad \longleftarrow \text{ overall charge}$$

$$\text{total charge of electrons}$$

If a sodium atom loses an electron it will only have 10 electrons, but it will still have 11 protons. So the sodium will have an overall charge of +1, and is said to be a positively charged ion.

$$\underset{\text{total charge of protons}}{} 11 - 10 = +1 \quad \longleftarrow \text{ overall charge}$$

$$\text{total charge of electrons}$$

Example 2

Non-metal atoms form negative ions

A chlorine atom has 17 protons and 17 electrons, so has no overall charge.

$$\underset{\text{total charge of protons}}{} 17 - 17 = 0 \quad \longleftarrow \text{ overall charge}$$

$$\text{total charge of electrons}$$

If a chlorine atom gains an electron it will have 18 electrons, but it will still only have 17 protons. So it will have an overall charge of -1, and is said to be a negatively charged ion.

$$\underset{\text{total charge of protons}}{} 17 - 18 = -1 \quad \longleftarrow \text{ overall charge}$$

$$\text{total charge of electrons}$$

Tip: Ions can be represented using chemical symbols, but the charge on the ion needs to be shown as well. For example, a chloride ion is written as Cl^- and a sodium ion is written as Na^+.

Ionic bonding

Ions with opposite charges (positive and negative) are strongly attracted to each other. This is called **ionic bonding**.

Example

Sodium (a metal) reacts with chlorine (a non-metal) to form the compound sodium chloride.

A sodium atom has 1 electron in its outer shell. *A chlorine atom has 7 electrons in its outer shell.* *The sodium atom gives its outer electron to the chlorine atom. A sodium ion and a chloride ion are formed*

The sodium and chloride ions are oppositely charged and so are attracted to each other. This is ionic bonding, and results in the formation of the stable compound sodium chloride.

Tip: The + sign by the electronic structure of the sodium ion shows that it has a positive charge of 1 (+1). The − sign by the electronic structure of the chloride ion shows that it has a negative charge of 1 (−1).

Covalent bonding

Tip: A compound is two or more atoms of different elements held together by chemical bonds. A molecule is two or more atoms held together by covalent bonds. The atoms can be of the same element or different elements — it's the covalent bond that makes it a molecule.

A compound formed from non-metals consists of molecules. Each atom shares an electron with another atom — this is called a **covalent bond**. Each atom has to make enough covalent bonds to fill up its outer shell.

Example

Hydrogen and chlorine (both non-metals) react together and share an electron to form a molecule of hydrogen chloride. The molecule is made up of two different types of atom, so it's a compound.

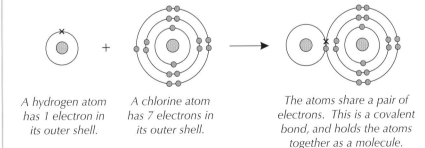

A hydrogen atom has 1 electron in its outer shell. *A chlorine atom has 7 electrons in its outer shell.* *The atoms share a pair of electrons. This is a covalent bond, and holds the atoms together as a molecule.*

Both the hydrogen atom and the chlorine atom now have full outer shells of electrons. This makes the molecule stable.

Tip: Diagrams showing covalent bonding like this are called <u>dot and cross diagrams</u>. (You won't be asked to draw diagrams like these in your GCSE Science exams.)

Formulae

A formula shows what atoms are in a compound.

Tip: Formulae' is just the plural of 'formula'. You may sometimes see it written as 'formulas'.

Examples

Carbon dioxide is a compound formed from a chemical reaction between carbon and oxygen. It contains one carbon atom and two oxygen atoms, so the formula is CO_2.

The formula of sulfuric acid is H_2SO_4. So, each molecule contains two hydrogen atoms, one sulfur atom and four oxygen atoms.

There might be brackets in a formula. For example, calcium hydroxide is $Ca(OH)_2$. The little number outside the bracket applies to everything inside the brackets. So in $Ca(OH)_2$ there is one calcium atom, two oxygen atoms and two hydrogen atoms.

Practice Questions — Fact Recall

Q1   What is an ion?

Q2   Do metal atoms form positive ions or negative ions?

Q3   Do non-metal atoms form positive ions or negative ions?

Q4   If a compound is formed from a metal and a non-metal, what type of bonding will be present in the compound?

Q5   What type of bonding holds the atoms in a molecule together?

Practice Questions — Application

Q1   The formula of carbon monoxide is CO.
      What atoms are in a molecule of carbon monoxide?

Q2   The formula of nitric acid is HNO_3.
      What atoms are in a molecule of nitric acid?

Q3   Look at diagrams A, B, C and D. Which one shows a compound?

A   B   C   D

Q4   Will bromine form positive or negative ions?

Q5   Will potassium lose or gain electrons to form ions?

Q6   Will lithium form positive or negative ions?

Q7   Will oxygen lose or gain electrons to form ions?

Q8   Magnesium oxide is made from the reaction between magnesium and oxygen. What type of bonding exists in magnesium oxide?

Q9   Sulfur dioxide is made from the reaction between sulfur and oxygen. What type of bonding exists in sulfur dioxide?

Tip: You can use the periodic table to help you work out if an atom is a metal or a non-metal. There's a periodic table on page 382.

Learning Objectives:

- Know that word equations and symbol equations can be used to represent reactions.
- Be able to write word equations.
- Understand why the mass of the products of a reaction is the same as the mass of the reactants.
- Be able to calculate the mass of a product or a reactant from the masses of other substances involved in the reaction.
- Understand symbol equations.
- **H** Be able to write balanced symbol equations.

Specification Reference
C1.1.3

5. Equations

Equations crop up again and again in chemistry. You need to know what they show and how to write them.

Word equations and symbol equations

Word equations and symbol equations show what happens in a chemical reaction. They show the **reactants** (the substances that react together) and the **products** (the substances that are made in a reaction).

Example

Magnesium and oxygen react to form magnesium oxide. This can be represented by a word equation or a symbol equation.

Word equation: magnesium   +   oxygen   →   magnesium oxide

Balanced symbol equation: $2Mg$ + O_2 → $2MgO$

Magnesium and oxygen are the reactants in this reaction. Magnesium oxide is the product.

Conservation of mass

During chemical reactions, things don't appear out of nowhere and things don't just disappear. You still have the same atoms at the end of a chemical reaction as you had at the start. They're just arranged in different ways.

Balanced symbol equations show the atoms at the start (the reactant atoms) and the atoms at the end (the product atoms) and how they're arranged.

Tip: You can think of the 2 before the Mg as meaning that there are two magnesium atoms. The 2 before the MgO means that there are two lots of MgO.

Example

Balanced symbol equation: $2Mg$ + O_2 → $2MgO$

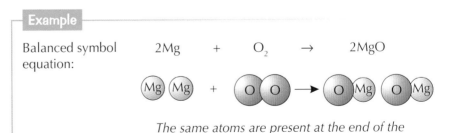

The same atoms are present at the end of the reaction as at the start — they're just rearranged.

Because atoms aren't gained or lost, the mass of the reactants equals the mass of the products. This is called conservation of mass. You can use this fact to work out the mass of individual reactants and products in a reaction.

1. 6 g of magnesium completely reacts with 4 g of oxygen.
    What mass of magnesium oxide is formed?

    The total mass of the reactants is 4 + 6 = 10 g, so the mass of the
    product (magnesium oxide) must be 10 g.

2. 30 g of magnesium oxide is formed from 18 g of magnesium.
    How much oxygen reacted?

    The total mass of the product is 30 g, so the total mass of the reactants
    must be 30 g. The mass of the magnesium is 18 g, so the mass of the
    oxygen must be 30 – 18 = 12 g.

> **Exam Tip**
> You could be asked to
> work out the mass of
> a product formed, or
> the mass of a reactant
> used. Just remember
> — the total mass of the
> products is exactly the
> same as the total mass of
> the reactants.

Balanced equations

There must always be the same number of atoms of each element on both
sides of an equation — they can't just disappear. If there aren't the same
number on each side then the equation isn't balanced.

Example

Sulfuric acid (H_2SO_4) reacts with sodium hydroxide (NaOH) to give sodium
sulfate (Na_2SO_4) and water (H_2O). To write the symbol equation start by
writing out the formulae in an equation:

$$H_2SO_4 \ + \ NaOH \ \rightarrow \ Na_2SO_4 \ + \ H_2O$$

The formulas are all correct but the numbers of some atoms don't match up
on both sides (e.g. there are three Hs on the left, but only two on the right).
So the equation isn't balanced.

Method for balancing equations Higher

You can balance equations by putting numbers in front of the formulas where
needed. All you do is this:

1. Find an element that doesn't balance and pencil in a number to try and
    sort it out.

2. See where it gets you. It may create another imbalance — if so, just
    pencil in another number and see where that gets you.

3. Carry on chasing unbalanced elements and it'll sort itself out pretty
    quickly.

> **Tip:** You <u>can't</u> change
> the small numbers inside
> formulas (like changing
> H_2O to H_3O). You can
> only put numbers in
> front of formulas (like
> changing H_2O to $3H_2O$).

> **Tip:** The more you
> practise balancing
> equations, the quicker
> you'll get...

In the equation below you're short of H atoms on the right-hand side — there are three H atoms on the left and only two on the right.

$$H_2SO_4 + NaOH \rightarrow Na_2SO_4 + H_2O$$

The only thing you can do about that is make it $2H_2O$ instead of just H_2O:

$$H_2SO_4 + NaOH \rightarrow Na_2SO_4 + 2H_2O$$

Exam Tip
If you're asked to write a symbol equation you always have to make sure it's balanced. If it's not balanced it's not a correct equation.

But now you have too many H atoms and O atoms on the right-hand side, so to balance that up you could try putting 2NaOH on the left-hand side.

$$H_2SO_4 + 2NaOH \rightarrow Na_2SO_4 + 2H_2O$$

And suddenly there it is! Everything balances. There are four H, one S, six O and two Na atoms on each side of the equation.

In the equation below we're short of Cl atoms on the left-hand side.

$$Al + Cl_2 \rightarrow AlCl_3$$

Try making it $3Cl_2$ instead of just Cl_2.

$$Al + 3Cl_2 \rightarrow AlCl_3$$

That causes too many Cl atoms on the left-hand side, so balance up the Cls by putting 2 before the $AlCl_3$.

$$Al + 3Cl_2 \rightarrow 2AlCl_3$$

Tip: If you made it '$2Cl_2$', you'd have four Cl on the left-hand side. There isn't a whole number that you could put in front of $AlCl_3$ to also give you four Cl on the right-hand side. So it's best to try $3Cl_2$.

Now you can balance the Al atoms by adding a 2 in front of the Al.

$$2Al + 3Cl_2 \rightarrow 2AlCl_3$$

Everything is now balanced. There are two Al atoms on each side and six Cl atoms on each side.

Symbol equations show how many atoms of one element there are compared to the number of atoms of other elements. So it's fine to double, or triple, or quadruple the number of atoms in a balanced equation, as long as you do the same to every term in the equation.

Balanced equation to show the reaction of aluminium and chlorine. $2Al + 3Cl_2 \rightarrow 2AlCl_3$

The numbers added to the equation to balance it have all been doubled. The equation is still balanced. $4Al + 6Cl_2 \rightarrow 4AlCl_3$

Practice Questions — Application

Q1   Copper sulfate and iron react to form iron sulfate and copper.

   a) What substances are the products in this reaction?

   b) What substances are the reactants in this reaction?

   c) Write a word equation for the reaction of copper sulfate and iron.

Q2   127 g of copper reacts with 32 g of oxygen to form copper oxide.

   a) Write a word equation for this reaction.

   b) What is the mass of copper oxide formed?

Q3 $N_2 + 3H_2 \rightarrow 2NH_3$ is the equation for the reaction between nitrogen (N_2) and hydrogen (H_2) to form ammonia (NH_3). 56 g of nitrogen are used in the reaction. 68 g of ammonia are formed. What is the mass of hydrogen that reacts?

Q4   Sodium hydroxide reacts with hydrochloric acid to give sodium chloride and water.

   a) Write a word equation for this reaction.

   b) 80 g of sodium hydroxide completely reacts with 73 g of hydrochloric acid. 36 g of water is formed. What is the mass of sodium chloride produced?

Q5   Balance the following equations:

   a) $Cl_2 + KBr \rightarrow Br_2 + KCl$

   b) $HCl + Mg \rightarrow MgCl_2 + H_2$

   c) $C_3H_8 + O_2 \rightarrow CO_2 + H_2O$

   d) $Fe_2O_3 + CO \rightarrow Fe + CO_2$

Q6   Sulfuric acid (H_2SO_4) reacts with lithium hydroxide (LiOH) to form lithium sulfate (Li_2SO_4) and water (H_2O). Write a balanced symbol equation for this reaction.

> **Exam Tip**
> Always check your equation is balanced properly. It's easy to make a mistake, so once you think you've balanced it correctly go back and count up again.

Section Checklist — Make sure you know...

Atoms and Elements

☐ That everything is made up of tiny particles called atoms.

☐ The structure of the atom, including the arrangement of protons, neutrons and electrons.

☐ The relative charges of protons (+1), neutrons (0) and electrons (–1).

☐ That atoms are neutral (have no overall charge) as they have equal numbers of protons and electrons.

☐ That an element is a substance made up of only one type of atom.

☐ That atoms of an element have the same number of protons.

☐ That atoms of different elements have different numbers of protons.

cont...

The Periodic Table

- [ ] That elements can be represented by symbols, e.g. C for carbon, Na for sodium, O for oxygen.
- [ ] That the periodic table contains all the known elements.
- [ ] Where the metals and non-metals are found in the periodic table.
- [ ] How to use the periodic table to find the atomic number and mass number of an element.
- [ ] What atomic number and mass number tell you about an element.
- [ ] How to work out the number of protons, neutrons and electrons in an element from its atomic number and mass number.
- [ ] That elements in a group of the periodic table have the same number of electrons in their outer shells and that this gives them similar chemical properties.
- [ ] That elements in Group 0 of the periodic table are called the noble gases.
- [ ] That the noble gases don't react with other elements because they have a full outer shell of electrons.

Electron Shells

- [ ] How to work out the electronic structure of the first 20 elements of the periodic table.

Compounds

- [ ] That a compound is formed when atoms of different elements react together and form chemical bonds.
- [ ] That when metals react with non-metals, the metal atoms give up electrons and form positively charged ions and the non-metal atoms gain electrons to become negatively charged ions.
- [ ] That oppositely charged ions are attracted to each other and that this attraction is known as ionic bonding.
- [ ] That when non-metals react together their atoms share pairs of electrons. These shared electrons hold the atoms together in a molecule. This is called covalent bonding.

Equations

- [ ] That word equations and symbol equations are used to show the reactants and products of a chemical reaction.
- [ ] How to write word equations for reactions.
- [ ] That the mass of the products of a reaction is equal to the mass of the reactants, because no atoms are gained or lost during a chemical reaction.
- [ ] How to work out the mass of a certain reactant or product when you're given the masses of the other substances involved in the reaction.
- [ ] That a symbol equation gives you information about the number of atoms of each element involved in a reaction.
- [ ] H How to balance symbol equations.

Exam-style Questions

1   Carbon monoxide (CO) and carbon dioxide (CO_2) both contain carbon atoms and oxygen atoms.

1 (a)   Draw a ring around the correct words to complete these sentences.

1 (a) (i)   Carbon and oxygen are both

non-metals.
metals.
noble gases.

(1 mark)

1 (a) (ii)   Carbon monoxide and carbon dioxide are both

elements.
compounds.
noble gases.

(1 mark)

1 (b)   This is the symbol equation for the reaction of carbon monoxide and oxygen:

$$2CO \; + \; O_2 \; \rightarrow \; 2CO_2$$

1 (b) (i)   Write a word equation for the reaction of carbon monoxide with oxygen.

(1 mark)

1 (b) (ii)   Using the symbol equation, describe the reaction of carbon monoxide and oxygen in terms of the number of molecules of each substance involved.

(3 marks)

1 (c)   Complete this diagram so that it shows the electronic structure of carbon.

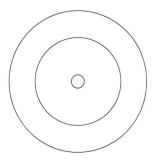

(2 marks)

2   Aluminium is a metal element that is used to make foil for cooking.

2 (a)   This table contains information about the atomic structure of aluminium.
Complete the table.

Atomic number	
Mass number	27
Number of protons	13
Number of electrons	
Number of neutrons	

(3 marks)

2 (b) (i)   Aluminium reacts with hydrochloric acid to form aluminium chloride and hydrogen.
Balance the symbol equation for this reaction.

$$......Al \ + \ ......HCl \ \rightarrow \ ......AlCl_3 \ + \ ......H_2$$

(2 marks)

2 (b) (ii) 135 g of aluminium reacted with 547.5 g of hydrochloric acid to make
667.5 g of aluminium chloride. What mass of hydrogen was produced?

(2 marks)

2 (b) (iii) Name the type of bonding that exists within hydrogen (H_2).

(1 mark)

2 (c)   Aluminium chloride can also be formed by reacting aluminium with chlorine.

2 (c) (i)   What group of the periodic table is chlorine in?

(1 mark)

2 (c) (ii) The reaction of aluminium and bromine is similar to the reaction of
aluminium and chlorine. Explain why.

(1 mark)

2 (c) (iii) Aluminium does not react with argon (Ar). Explain why not.

(2 marks)

1. Limestone and Other Carbonates

Learning Objectives:
- Know that limestone is quarried from the ground and can be used to build with.
- Know that limestone consists mainly of calcium carbonate ($CaCO_3$).
- Understand what thermal decomposition is.
- Know that metal carbonates such as calcium, magnesium, copper, zinc and sodium carbonates thermally decompose to form a metal oxide and carbon dioxide.
- Know that these carbonates react with acids to produce carbon dioxide, a salt and water.
- Know that limestone can be damaged by acid rain.
- Know that calcium oxide reacts with water to form calcium hydroxide.
- Know that calcium hydroxide can be used to neutralise acids.
- Understand how limewater can be used to test for carbon dioxide.

Specification Reference
C1.2.1

Limestone is a type of rock made from calcium carbonate.
Like other carbonates, it reacts in a number of different ways.

Limestone

Limestone is quarried out of the ground and made into blocks that can be used for building. Lots of old buildings like cathedrals are made from it. Limestone is mainly calcium carbonate — $CaCO_3$.

Thermal decomposition of metal carbonates

Thermal decomposition is when one substance chemically changes into at least two new substances when it's heated. Limestone thermally decomposes to make calcium oxide and carbon dioxide. Here's the equation for the reaction...

$$\text{calcium carbonate} \quad \rightarrow \quad \text{calcium oxide} \quad + \quad \text{carbon dioxide}$$
$$CaCO_3 \quad \rightarrow \quad CaO \quad + \quad CO_2$$

When magnesium, copper, zinc and sodium carbonates are heated, they decompose in the same way.

Example

Magnesium carbonate breaks down to form magnesium oxide and carbon dioxide when it's heated.

$$\text{magnesium carbonate} \quad \rightarrow \quad \text{magnesium oxide} \quad + \quad \text{carbon dioxide}$$
$$MgCO_3 \quad \rightarrow \quad MgO \quad + \quad CO_2$$

You might have difficulty doing some of these reactions in class — a Bunsen burner can't reach a high enough temperature to thermally decompose some carbonates of Group 1 metals.

Metal carbonates and acid

Calcium carbonate also reacts with acid to make a calcium salt, carbon dioxide and water. This reaction means that limestone is damaged by acid rain (see page 170).

Calcium carbonate reacts with acid as shown in this word equation:

$$\text{calcium carbonate} + \text{acid} \rightarrow \text{calcium salt} + \text{carbon dioxide} + \text{water}$$

The type of salt produced depends on the type of acid used.

Examples

If calcium carbonate reacts with sulfuric acid, a sulfate is produced.

$$\text{calcium carbonate} + \text{sulfuric acid} \rightarrow \text{calcium sulfate} + \text{carbon dioxide} + \text{water}$$

$$CaCO_3 + H_2SO_4 \rightarrow CaSO_4 + CO_2 + H_2O$$

If calcium carbonate reacts with hydrochloric acid, a chloride is produced.

$$\text{calcium carbonate} + \text{hydrochloric acid} \rightarrow \text{calcium chloride} + \text{carbon dioxide} + \text{water}$$

$$CaCO_3 + 2HCl \rightarrow CaCl_2 + CO_2 + H_2O$$

Exam Tip
You might be asked to write equations for the reactions of different carbonates with different acids, so make sure you can work them out. Remember, with sulfuric acid you always get a sulfate and with hydrochloric acid you always get a chloride.

Other carbonates that react with acids are magnesium, copper, zinc and sodium. In these reactions carbon dioxide and water are always produced, but the salt formed depends on which carbonate and which acid react.

Example

When zinc carbonate reacts with sulfuric acid, zinc sulfate is formed.

$$\text{zinc carbonate} + \text{sulfuric acid} \rightarrow \text{zinc sulfate} + \text{carbon dioxide} + \text{water}$$

$$ZnCO_3 + H_2SO_4 \rightarrow ZnSO_4 + CO_2 + H_2O$$

Reaction of calcium oxide with water

When limestone (mainly $CaCO_3$) is broken down, calcium oxide (CaO) can be formed. When you add water to calcium oxide you get calcium hydroxide. The word and symbol equations for this reaction are...

$$\text{calcium oxide} + \text{water} \rightarrow \text{calcium hydroxide}$$

$$CaO + H_2O \rightarrow Ca(OH)_2$$

Calcium hydroxide has two important uses:

1. Calcium hydroxide is an alkali which can be used to neutralise acidic soil in fields. Powdered limestone can be used for this too, but the advantage of calcium hydroxide is that it works much faster.

2. Calcium hydroxide can also be used in a test for carbon dioxide. If you make a solution of calcium hydroxide in water (called **limewater**) and bubble gas through it, the solution will turn cloudy if there's carbon dioxide in the gas (see Figure 1). The cloudiness is caused by the formation of calcium carbonate. The equation for this reaction is:

calcium hydroxide + carbon dioxide → calcium carbonate + water

$$Ca(OH)_2 \quad + \quad CO_2 \quad \rightarrow \quad CaCO_3 \quad + H_2O$$

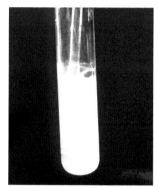

Figure 1: A test tube containing limewater. It has turned cloudy due to the presence of CO_2 in the gas being bubbled through it.

Practice Questions — Fact Recall

Q1 Which compound does limestone mainly consist of?

Q2 Write the word and symbol equations for the thermal decomposition of calcium carbonate.

Q3 What are the products of the reaction between a metal carbonate and an acid?

Q4 When calcium carbonate reacts with sulfuric acid, which salt is produced?

Q5 Which compound reacts with water to form calcium hydroxide?

Q6 Describe how calcium hydroxide can be used to test for carbon dioxide. Include the symbol equation for the reaction involved.

Practice Questions — Application

Q1 Write a word equation for the thermal decomposition of zinc carbonate.

Q2 a) What salt is produced when magnesium carbonate reacts with hydrochloric acid?

b) Balance the following equation:

$$MgCO_3 \quad + \quad HCl \quad \rightarrow \quad MgCl_2 \quad + \quad CO_2 \quad + \quad H_2O$$

- Know that limestone is an important building material and how it is used to make cement, mortar and concrete.

- Be able to weigh up the advantages and disadvantages of using limestone, cement and concrete as building materials.

- Understand that quarrying limestone and the production of cement and concrete have environmental, social and economic impacts. Some are positive and some are negative.

Specification Reference C1.2, C1.2.1

2. Using Limestone

Limestone is a really useful building material and necessary for the production of cement and concrete. The downside is that digging it up and processing it into cement and concrete causes a few problems...

Limestone as a building material

Limestone is a widely available building material and is cheaper than granite or marble. It's also a fairly easy rock to cut, which means it's pretty straightforward to make into different shapes, such as blocks. Limestone is also very hard-wearing.

Limestone can also be used to make other building materials. For example...

- Powdered limestone is heated in a kiln with powdered clay to make cement.

- Cement can be mixed with sand and water to make mortar. (Mortar is the stuff you stick bricks together with.)

- To make concrete you mix cement with sand and aggregate (water and gravel).

Limestone, concrete and cement have lots of qualities that make them great as building materials. They don't rot when they get wet like wood does. They can't be gnawed away by insects or rodents either. And to top it off, they're fire-resistant too.

Concrete can be poured into moulds to make blocks or panels that can be joined together. It's a very quick and cheap way of constructing buildings. Concrete also doesn't corrode like lots of metals do.

Figure 1: *Concrete being poured at a building site.*

Other uses and benefits of limestone

Limestone is a key material for providing things that people want — like houses, roads and even schools... but it's also useful in other ways.

- Limestone is used to make chemicals that are used in making dyes, paints and medicines.

- Limestone products are used to neutralise acidic soil. Acidity in lakes and rivers caused by acid rain is also neutralised by limestone products.

- Limestone is also used in power station chimneys to neutralise sulfur dioxide, which is a cause of acid rain.

- Limestone quarries and associated businesses provide jobs for people and bring more money into the local economy. This can lead to local improvements in transport, roads, recreation facilities and health.

Problems of using limestone

Quarrying limestone

Digging limestone out of the ground can cause environmental problems:

- Quarrying involves making huge ugly holes which permanently change the landscape.

- Quarrying processes, like blasting rocks apart with explosives, make lots of noise and dust in quiet, scenic areas.

- Quarrying destroys the habitats of animals and birds.

- The limestone needs to be transported away from the quarry — usually in lorries. This causes more noise and pollution.

- Waste materials produce unsightly tips.

Thankfully it's normally a requirement of the planning permission that once quarrying is complete, landscaping and restoration of the area are carried out.

Figure 2: A limestone quarry where limestone rock is extracted from the ground.

Limestone products

The production and use of limestone causes problems too.

- Cement factories make a lot of dust, which can cause breathing problems for some people.

- Energy is needed to produce cement. The energy is likely to come from burning fossil fuels, which causes pollution.

- Concrete is a hideously unattractive building material. It also has fairly low tensile strength and can crack — it can be reinforced with steel bars to make it much stronger though.

Figure 3: Air pollution from a cement factory.

Practice Questions — Fact Recall

Q1 Describe how you make...

a) Cement

b) Mortar

c) Concrete

Q2 Describe two benefits of using concrete as a building material.

Q3 Limestone can be used as a building material.
Give two other uses of limestone.

Q4 Limestone is extracted from the ground by quarrying.

a) Give three problems associated with quarrying limestone.

b) Describe two ways in which a quarry can benefit the local area.

Q5 Give one drawback of using concrete as a building material.

Q1 Richard is choosing materials for the floors of his conservatory and garage. Use the data in this table to answer the questions.

	Concrete	Wood	Marble
Cost (per m²)	£8.50	£25	£60
Appearance	Unattractive	Attractive	Attractive
Durability	Very hardwearing	Quite hardwearing	Very hardwearing

a) Suggest which material Richard should use in his garage and give reasons to support your choice.

b) Suggest which material Richard should use in his conservatory and give reasons to support your choice.

Section Checklist — Make sure you know...

Limestone and Other Carbonates

☐ That limestone is mostly calcium carbonate ($CaCO_3$) and is quarried from the ground.

☐ That thermal decomposition of calcium carbonate produces calcium oxide and carbon dioxide.

☐ That magnesium, copper, zinc and sodium carbonates thermally decompose to produce a metal oxide and carbon dioxide.

☐ That some Group 1 carbonates can't be decomposed in the school lab by a Bunsen burner.

☐ How to write word equations for the thermal decomposition of metal carbonates.

☐ That the reaction of calcium carbonate with acid produces a calcium salt, carbon dioxide and water.

☐ That limestone is damaged by acid rain.

☐ That magnesium, copper, zinc and sodium carbonates react with acids to produce a metal salt, carbon dioxide and water.

☐ How to write word equations for the reactions of metal carbonates with acids.

☐ That when calcium oxide reacts with water, calcium hydroxide is formed.

☐ That calcium hydroxide can be used to neutralise acidic soil.

☐ How calcium hydroxide in solution (limewater) can be used to test for carbon dioxide.

Using Limestone

☐ How cement, mortar and concrete are made from limestone.

☐ The advantages and disadvantages of using limestone, cement and concrete as building materials.

☐ The benefits of quarrying for limestone.

☐ The problems associated with limestone quarrying and manufacturing limestone building materials.

1. Metal Ores

To get hold of most metals you start by digging them out of the ground. Sometimes it's as simple as that, but it's usually a bit more complicated...

Extracting metals from ores

A few unreactive metals like gold are found in the Earth as the metal itself, rather than as a compound. The rest of the metals we get by extracting them from **metal ores**, which are mined from under the ground. A metal ore is a rock which contains enough metal to make it profitable to extract the metal from it. In many cases the ore is an oxide of the metal. For example, the main aluminium ore is called bauxite — it's aluminium oxide (Al_2O_3).

Most metals need to be extracted from their ores using a chemical reaction. The economics (profitability) of metal extraction can change over time.

> **Examples**
>
> If the market price of a metal drops a lot, it could cost more to extract than the price it's sold for. In this situation the metal wouldn't be worth extracting because there would be no profit to be made. If the market price increases a lot then it might be worth extracting more of it.
>
> As technology improves, it becomes possible to extract more metal from a sample of rock than was originally possible. So it might now be worth extracting metal that wasn't worth extracting in the past.

Learning Objectives:
- Know that a few unreactive metals are found in the earth as elements.
- Know that the majority of metals are found as compounds in a metal ore and that these ores are mined.
- Know that ores are rocks that contain enough of a metal to make it worthwhile to extract it.
- Understand that whether or not it is economical to extract a metal can change over time.
- Know that some ores are concentrated before the metal is extracted.

Specification Reference C1.3.1

Chemical methods of extraction

A metal can be extracted from its ore chemically — by **reduction** (see page 147) or by **electrolysis** (splitting with electricity, see page 147). Occasionally some metals are extracted from their ores using **displacement reactions** (see page 149). Some ores may have to be concentrated before the metal is extracted — this involves getting rid of the unwanted rocky material.

Figure 1: *A sample of bauxite, the main ore of aluminium.*

Practice Questions — Fact Recall

Q1 What is a metal ore?

Q2 Explain why a change in the market price of a metal could affect how much of that metal is extracted from its ores.

Q3 Name two chemical methods of extracting metals from their ores.

- Know that metals that are less reactive than carbon are extracted from their ores by reduction with carbon.
- Know that iron is extracted from its ore by reduction with carbon in the blast furnace.
- Understand what reduction is.
- Know that metals that are more reactive than carbon are extracted from their ores using electrolysis.
- Know that aluminium and titanium are examples of metals which can't be extracted by reduction with carbon.
- Understand why the extraction of aluminium and titanium from their oxides is expensive.

Specification Reference
C1.3.1

Exam Tip
You don't need to worry about remembering the reactivity series.
A copy of it will be given to you in the exam. Just remember what it shows and what that means for extracting metals.

Tip: Remember, the ore of a metal is usually the metal oxide.

2. Extracting Metals from Rocks

There are two main methods of extracting metals from metal ores. Which one to use is determined by how reactive the metal is...

The reactivity series

The **reactivity series** is a list of metals that are arranged in order of how reactive they are. The most reactive metals are at the top and the least reactive are at the bottom.

The position of each metal in the reactivity series is important. Whether a metal is higher or lower than carbon (the only non-metal in the series) determines the method that is used to extract it from its ore.

Even though carbon is a non-metal, it's included in the series so you can compare where metals are in relation to it.

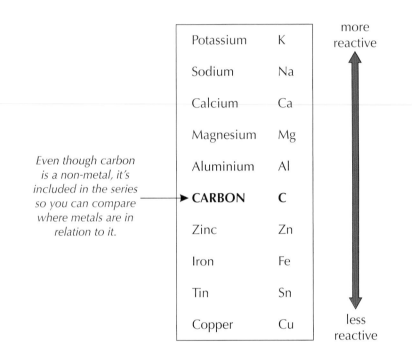

		more reactive
Potassium	K	
Sodium	Na	
Calcium	Ca	
Magnesium	Mg	
Aluminium	Al	
► CARBON	C	
Zinc	Zn	
Iron	Fe	
Tin	Sn	
Copper	Cu	less reactive

Figure 1: The reactivity series of metals.

The reactivity series and extracting metals

Metals that are below carbon in the reactivity series are less reactive than it. This means they can be extracted from their oxides by reduction using carbon (see next page).

Metals that are higher than carbon in the reactivity series are more reactive than carbon. They have to be extracted from their oxides using electrolysis (see next page), which is expensive.

Extraction by reduction with carbon

A metal below carbon in the reactivity series can be extracted from its ore by reacting it with carbon. The reaction that takes place is called a **reduction reaction**, which is where oxygen is removed from the metal ore.

Tip: During a reduction reaction, oxygen is removed from the ore and the ore is said to be reduced.

> **Example**
>
> Iron oxide (the ore of iron) is reduced in a blast furnace to make iron. Iron is less reactive than carbon so when iron oxide and carbon react the oxygen is removed from the iron ore, leaving iron metal.
>
> $$2Fe_2O_3 \quad + \quad 3C \quad \rightarrow \quad 4Fe \quad + \quad 3CO_2$$
> iron(III) oxide + carbon $\rightarrow$ iron + carbon dioxide

Extraction by electrolysis

Metals that are more reactive than carbon, such as aluminium, can't be extracted using carbon. So different processes, such as electrolysis have to be used. These processes are much more expensive than reduction with carbon because they have many stages and use a lot of energy.

Tip: Titanium isn't extracted by reduction with carbon or by electrolysis but all you need to know is that (like aluminium) it can't be extracted by reduction with carbon.

> **Example**
>
> Electrolysis can be used to extract aluminium from its oxide ore. A high temperature is needed to melt the aluminium oxide so that the aluminium can be extracted — this takes lots of energy, making it an expensive process.

Practice Questions — Fact Recall

Q1 Name the method used to extract a metal if it is...

  a) ...above carbon in the reactivity series.

  b) ...below carbon in the reactivity series.

Q2 Is an element at the top of the reactivity series more or less reactive than the elements below it?

Q3 When a metal ore is reduced by carbon, what is removed from it?

Q4 Why are other processes of extraction more expensive to carry out than reduction with carbon?

Q5 Give two examples of metals that are extracted using electrolysis.

Tip: Use the reactivity series on page 146 to help you with these Qs.

Practice Question — Application

Q1 What process is required to extract the following metals from their metal oxides? Use the reactivity series on page 146 to help you.

  a) Tin   b) Calcium

  c) Zinc   d) Potassium

- Know that smelting is a process whereby copper is extracted from copper-rich ores by heating in a furnace.

- Know how electrolysis can be used to purify copper.

- Know that there is a limited supply of copper-rich ores and that traditional methods of extraction are damaging to the environment.

- Know that new ways of extracting copper from low-grade ores include bioleaching and phytomining.

- Know that copper can be extracted from solution using a displacement reaction involving scrap iron.

Specification Reference
C1.3.1

3. Extracting Copper

Copper is a really important metal and you need to know about the different ways that it can be extracted.

Extracting copper from copper-rich ores

Copper extraction using carbon

Copper can be easily extracted by reduction with carbon (see page 147). The ore is heated in a furnace — this is called **smelting**. However, the copper produced this way is impure so electrolysis is used to purify it.

Copper purification by electrolysis

Electrolysis is the breaking down of a substance using electricity. It requires a liquid to conduct the electricity, called the **electrolyte**. Electrolytes are often metal salt solutions made from the ore (e.g. copper sulfate) or molten metal oxides. The electrolyte has free ions — these conduct the electricity and allow the whole thing to work.

In electrolysis there are two electrodes — one is positive and the other is negative. Electrons are lost or gained at the two electrodes — this allows ions to be formed at the positive electrode and atoms to bond at the negative electrode.

Here's how electrolysis is used to get copper:

1. The positive electrode is made of impure copper. Electrons are pulled off copper atoms at the positive electrode, causing them to go into solution as Cu^{2+} ions.

2. Cu^{2+} ions move towards the negative electrode, gain electrons and turn back into copper atoms.

3. The impurities are dropped at the positive electrode as a sludge, whilst pure copper atoms bond to the negative electrode.

Tip: You could extract copper straight from its ore by electrolysis if you wanted to, but it's more expensive than using reduction with carbon. A company will always pick the cheapest way unless there's a good reason not to.

Exam Tip
It's important to remember how the ions move in electrolysis — positive ions move towards the negative electrode, where they gain electrons and become copper atoms.

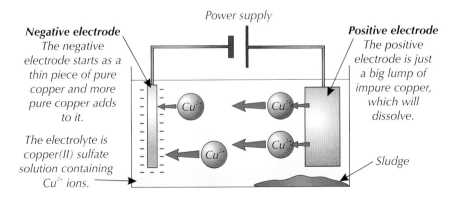

Power supply

Negative electrode
The negative electrode starts as a thin piece of pure copper and more pure copper adds to it.

The electrolyte is copper(II) sulfate solution containing Cu^{2+} ions.

Positive electrode
The positive electrode is just a big lump of impure copper, which will dissolve.

Sludge

Figure 1: *A diagram to show how electrolysis can be used to purify copper.*

Extracting copper from low-grade ores

The supply of copper-rich ores is limited and the demand for copper is growing — this could lead to shortages in the future. To help with this, scientists are looking into new ways of extracting copper from low-grade ores (ores that only contain small amounts of copper) or from the waste that is currently produced when copper is extracted. Using traditional methods to extract copper from these low-grade ores is very expensive. Examples of new methods to extract copper from low-grade ores are **bioleaching** and **phytomining**.

Tip: It's important to recycle as much copper as possible because supplies of copper-rich ores are limited (see pages 151-152).

Bioleaching

Bioleaching uses bacteria to separate copper from copper sulfide. The bacteria get energy from the bond between copper and sulfur, separating out the copper from the ore in the process. The leachate (the solution produced by the process) contains copper, which can be extracted, e.g. by filtering.

Phytomining

Phytomining involves growing plants in soil that contains copper. The plants can't use or get rid of the copper so it gradually builds up in the leaves. The plants can be harvested, dried and burned in a furnace. The copper can be collected from the ash left in the furnace.

Figure 2: *Bioleaching of copper sulfide ores at a copper mine.*

Bioleaching and phytomining — pros and cons

Traditional methods of copper mining are pretty damaging to the environment (see page 151). These new methods of extraction are cheap and have a much smaller environmental impact. For example, they require less energy which is good for the environment because energy use often contributes to climate change and other environmental problems. Phytomining is also more carbon neutral than traditional methods — even though carbon dioxide is released when the plants are burned, they only release the same amount of carbon dioxide as they absorbed when they were growing. The disadvantage of these new extraction methods is that they're slow. For example, in phytomining it takes a long time for plants to grow and take up copper.

Tip: Being able to weigh up the advantages and disadvantages of new techniques is an important skill for scientists to have.

Copper extraction by displacement

More reactive metals react more vigorously than less reactive metals. If you put a reactive metal into a solution of a dissolved metal compound, the reactive metal will replace the less reactive metal in the compound — this is a **displacement reaction**. This happens because the more reactive metal bonds more strongly to the non-metal bit of the compound and pushes out the less reactive metal.

Copper can be extracted from a solution using a displacement reaction.

One way this can be done is by using scrap iron. This is really useful because iron is cheap but copper is expensive. If some iron is put in a solution of copper sulfate, the more reactive iron will "kick out" the less reactive copper from the solution. You end up with iron sulfate solution and copper metal. The equation for this reaction is:

$$\text{copper sulfate} \quad + \quad \text{iron} \quad \rightarrow \quad \text{iron sulfate} \quad + \quad \text{copper}$$

If a piece of silver metal is put into a solution of copper sulfate, nothing happens. The more reactive metal (copper) is already in the solution.

Practice Questions — Fact Recall

Q1 What is the name given to the extraction of copper using a furnace?

Q2 Copper can be purified by electrolysis.

a) At which electrode do copper atoms go into solution as copper ions?

b) How are the copper ions formed?

c) Which electrode do the copper ions move towards?

Q3 a) Name two methods for extracting copper from low-grade ores.

b) Give one advantage of these methods over traditional methods.

Q4 Copper can be extracted from a solution of copper sulfate by adding scrap iron.

a) What type of reaction does this involve?

b) Give a benefit of using scrap iron in this reaction.

c) What are the two products of this reaction?

4. Impacts of Extracting Metals

Learning Objectives:
- Understand that the process of metal extraction has negative environmental impacts and these must be balanced against the social and economic benefits that extracting metal brings.
- Understand why it is important to recycle metals.

Specification Reference C1.3, C1.3.1

Metals are used in all sorts of different ways so it's important that we have good supplies of them. But getting hold of metals uses lots of energy and negatively affects the environment.

What are the impacts of metal extraction?

People have to balance the social, economic and environmental effects of mining metal ores. Most of the issues are exactly the same as those to do with quarrying limestone on page 143.

Positive impacts

Mining metal ores is good because it means that useful products can be made. It also provides local people with jobs and brings money into the area. This means services such as transport and health can be improved.

Negative impacts

Mining ores is bad for the environment. It causes noise and increased levels of traffic due to lorries visiting the mine. Mining destroys habitats, scars the landscape and leaves deep mine shafts that can be dangerous for a long time after the mine has been abandoned. The process of mining produces lots of solid waste (such as bits of rock that aren't ores) which can be an eyesore.

Mining and extracting metals also takes lots of energy, most of which comes from burning fossil fuels. Burning fossil fuels releases gases such as carbon dioxide and sulfur dioxide into the atmosphere which contribute to acid rain and climate change (see pages 170 and 171).

So, mining for metals has its benefits and drawbacks. It's likely that not many people would be against the jobs and other economic benefits that a mine brings, but these positives have got to be weighed up against the negative aspects of mining, such as increased pollution and habitat destruction.

Tip: It's important to be able to weigh up the social, environmental and economic consequences of processes such as metal mining and extraction.

Recycling metals

It's important to recycle metals. Here are some reasons why:

- Recycling metals only uses a small fraction of the energy needed to mine and extract new metal. For example, recycling copper takes 15% of the energy that's needed to mine and extract new copper. This is good for the environment because using energy usually has negative environmental impacts. Using less energy also helps to conserve fossil fuels — this is important as they are a non-renewable resource which is running out.

- Energy doesn't come cheap, so recycling saves money too.

Figure 1: *Compacted cans ready to be recycled at a recycling plant.*

- There's a finite amount of each metal in the Earth. Recycling conserves these resources.

- Recycling metal cuts down on the amount of rubbish that gets sent to landfill. Landfill takes up space and pollutes the surroundings. If all the aluminium cans in the UK were recycled, there'd be 14 million fewer dustbins to empty each year.

Practice Questions — Fact Recall

Q1   Give one social or economic benefit of mining for metals.

Q2   Give two environmental impacts of mining.

Q3   Explain how mining can contribute to acid rain, global dimming and climate change.

Q4   a) How does recycling metal save energy?

     b) State three other benefits of recycling metals.

Practice Question — Application

Q1   This table shows the amount of metal a council sent to landfill in two separate years. It costs the council £115 for every tonne of waste they send to landfill.

	Tonnes of waste metal to landfill	Cost (£)
Year 1	15 000	
Year 2	12 000	

   a) i) Work out the cost of sending the waste metal to landfill each year.

      ii) How much money did the council save from year 1 to year 2 by reducing the amount of metal they sent to landfill?

   b) Suggest one way the council could have reduced the amount of waste metal that was sent to landfill.

5. Properties and Uses of Metals

Once you've got hold of metals you can use them for all sorts of different things. What you use them for is determined by their individual properties, but all metals have some basic properties in common.

Basic properties of metals

Most elements are metals — so they cover most of the periodic table. In fact, only the elements on the far right are non-metals (see Figure 1).

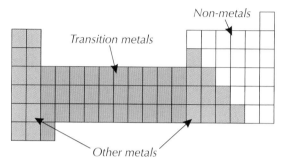

Figure 1: *A diagram of the periodic table showing the location of metals.*

All metals, including transition metals, have some fairly similar basic properties:

- They are strong (hard to break).

- They can be bent or hammered into different shapes.

- They're great at conducting heat.

- They conduct electricity.

Metals (and especially **transition metals**) have loads of everyday uses because of these properties...

- Their strength and 'bendability' makes them handy for making into things like bridges and car bodies.

- Their ability to conduct heat makes them ideal if you want to make something that heat needs to travel through, like a saucepan base.

- Their electrical conductivity makes them great for making things like electrical wires.

Copper, aluminium and titanium

The properties mentioned above are typical properties of metals. Not all metals are the same though — you need to learn the specific properties of copper, aluminium and titanium (see next page).

Learning Objectives:

- Know the location of the transition metals in the periodic table.

- Know that the transition metals have the same basic properties as other metals and know what these properties are.

- Understand that the properties of metals make them useful for many different uses.

- Know that the properties of copper make it ideal for use as electrical wiring and in plumbing.

- Know that aluminium and titanium are useful metals because of their low density and resistance to corrosion.

- Know that metals are useful structural materials but there are disadvantages to using them.

Specification Reference C1.3, C1.3.3

Figure 2: *Metals have to be bent into shape to make car bodies.*

Tip: Metal corrosion is where metals gradually break down as they react with their environment. Rusting is an example of corrosion — it's the corrosion of iron.

Tip: An alloy is a mixture of a metal with either another metal or a non-metal. There's more about them in the next topic (see page 156).

1. Copper

Copper is a good conductor of electricity. It's hard and strong but can be bent. It also doesn't react with water.

2. Aluminium

Aluminium is corrosion-resistant and has a low density — this low density means that it's lightweight. Pure aluminium isn't particularly strong, but it forms hard, strong alloys (see page 157).

3. Titanium

Titanium is another low density metal. Unlike aluminium it's very strong. It is also corrosion-resistant.

Uses of metals

Different metals are chosen for different uses because of their specific properties.

Examples

- If you were doing some plumbing, you'd pick a metal that could be bent to make pipes and tanks, and is below hydrogen in the reactivity series so it doesn't react with water. Copper is great for this.

- If you wanted to make electrical wires, you'd pick a metal that is a good conductor of electricity and can be drawn out into wires. Copper is an ideal choice for this.

- If you wanted to make an aeroplane, you'd probably use metal as it's strong and can be bent into shape. But you'd also need it to be lightweight, so an aluminium alloy would be a good choice.

- If you were making replacement hips, you'd use a metal that won't corrode when it comes in contact with water. It'd have to be light and not too bendy. Titanium has all of these properties so is used for this.

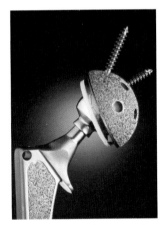

Figure 3: *A replacement hip joint made from titanium.*

Exam Tip
You might be asked to weigh up the advantages and disadvantages of using a metal for a particular purpose. You'll need to use your own knowledge and the information given in the question to answer it.

Metals are very useful structural materials, but some corrode when exposed to air and water, so they need to be protected — for example, by using paint. If metals corrode, they lose their strength and hardness.

Metals can also get 'tired' when stresses and strains are repeatedly put on them over time. This is known as **metal fatigue** and leads to metals breaking, which can be very dangerous. For example, in planes it's really important that metal components aren't fatigued so they are safe during flights. To help prevent fatigue, metal parts are specially designed and regularly checked.

HOW SCIENCE WORKS

Practice Questions — Fact Recall

Q1 Give the letter that corresponds to the transition metals on this periodic table.

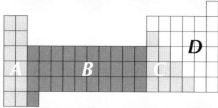

Q2 Metals are good at conducting electricity.

a) Suggest one metal product in which this property is important.

b) Give two other basic properties of metals.

Q3 Aluminium alloys are used to make lots of aeroplane parts. Why are they suitable for this use?

Q4 Give two reasons why copper is ideal for use in plumbing.

Q5 Which properties of titanium make it a suitable metal for replacement hips?

Q6 Give two disadvantages of using metals as structural materials.

Practice Question — Application

Q1 Rachel is buying a new bicycle. She can buy either a steel, aluminium or titanium frame. This table shows some properties of these metals.

	Steel	Aluminium	Titanium
Price	Low	Quite high	Very expensive
Strength	Very strong	Quite strong	Strong
Resistance to corrosion	Good	Excellent	Excellent
Relative density	High	Very low	Low

She would like a bike that's not too heavy or expensive. Use the table to suggest a type of frame for Rachel and give reasons for your choice.

- Know that iron straight out of the blast furnace is 96% iron and is used as cast iron.
- Know that cast iron is brittle due to the impurities it contains and this means its uses are limited.
- Know that most iron is made into steels (alloys containing iron and carbon).
- Know the properties of low-carbon, high-carbon and stainless steels.
- Know that most of the metals we use are alloys.
- Know that copper, gold, aluminium and iron are made into alloys to make them harder.
- Understand that alloys can be designed to have certain properties and for a specific purpose.

Specification Reference
C1.3.2

6. Alloys

Metals are often made into alloys. And that's what the next few pages are about — alloys. What they are, why they're made and some different types.

What is an alloy?

Alloys are mixtures of two or more metals, or a mixture of a metal and a non-metal. Iron is often used to make alloys. Before it's made into an alloy it needs to be extracted from its ore in a blast furnace and then purified.

Purification of iron

'Iron' straight from the blast furnace is only about 96% iron. The other 4% is impurities such as carbon. This impure iron is used as cast iron. It can be poured into shapes, so it's handy for making ornamental railings. It can also be used for structures that need to withstand being compressed, for example in columns. But cast iron has limited other uses because the impurities that it contains make it brittle.

To make the iron less brittle, the impurities are removed from most of the blast furnace iron to create pure iron. This pure iron has a regular arrangement of identical atoms. The layers of atoms can slide over each other (see Figure 1), which makes the iron soft and easily shaped. This iron is far too bendy for most uses, so most of it is converted into alloys.

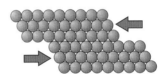

Figure 1: *The arrangement of atoms in pure iron.*

Figure 2: *A blast furnace in a steel foundry which is used to make iron.*

Conversion of iron to steel

Most of the pure iron is changed into alloys called steels. Steels are formed by adding small amounts of carbon and sometimes other metals to the iron. There are several different types of steel. They have different uses because of their different properties — see Figure 3.

Type of Steel	Properties	Uses
Low-carbon steel (0.1% carbon)	Easily shaped	Car bodies
High-carbon steel (1.5% carbon)	Very hard, inflexible	Blades for cutting tools, bridges
Stainless steel (chromium added, and sometimes nickel)	Corrosion-resistant	Cutlery, containers for corrosive substances

Figure 3: *Table showing the properties and uses of three different types of steel.*

Properties of alloys

Most metals in use today are actually alloys. Pure copper, gold, aluminium and iron (see previous page) are too soft for many uses so are made into alloys to make them more usable.

Alloys are harder than pure metals because they are made from atoms of different elements. Different elements have different sized atoms. So when an element such as carbon is added to pure iron, the smaller carbon atoms will upset the layers of pure iron atoms, making it more difficult for them to slide over each other.

Exam Tip
In the exam you might be given the properties of different alloys (including some you might not have come across before) and asked to work out which would be best for particular applications.

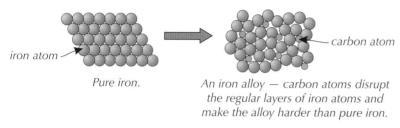

iron atom

carbon atom

Pure iron.

An iron alloy — carbon atoms disrupt the regular layers of iron atoms and make the alloy harder than pure iron.

Figure 4: *The arrangement of atoms in an iron alloy.*

In the past, the development of alloys was by trial and error. But nowadays we understand much more about the properties of metals, so alloys can be designed to have particular properties that make them suitable for a specific purpose.

Common alloys

Here are some examples of common alloys:

Bronze

Bronze is an alloy of copper and tin. It's harder than copper and it's good for making medals and statues from.

Cupronickel

Cupronickel is an alloy of copper and nickel. It's hard and corrosion-resistant. It's used to make "silver" coins.

Gold alloys

Gold alloys are used to make jewellery as pure gold is too soft. Metals such as zinc, copper, silver, palladium and nickel are used to harden the "gold".

Figure 5: *A bronze statue.*

Aluminium alloys

Aluminium alloys are used to make aircraft. Aluminium has a low density, but it's alloyed with small amounts of other metals to make it stronger.

Practice Questions — Fact Recall

Q1   What percentage of iron does iron from a blast furnace contain?

Q2   Why does cast iron have few uses?

Q3   Why is pure iron easily bent?

Q4   What element is added to iron to make steels?

Q5   Name a type of steel that is resistant to corrosion.

Q6   Why is pure aluminium made into an alloy?

Q7   Name the metals that form the following alloys.

a) Bronze

b) Cupronickel

Q8   Why isn't pure gold used to make jewellery?

Practice Questions — Application

Q1   Many car parts, such as axles, need to be hard and rigid.
Suggest a type of steel that could be used for this purpose.

Q2   Steel containers are used in kitchens and laboratories. They need to
be resistant to corrosion. Suggest a type of steel that could be used
for these containers.

Section Checklist — Make sure you know...

Metal Ores

☐ That some metals are found as the metal itself but most exist as compounds and need to be extracted from ores.

☐ That a rock with enough metal in to make it economic to extract the metal is called an ore.

☐ Why the economics of metal extraction can change over time.

☐ That most metals need to be extracted from their ores using a chemical reaction such as reduction, electrolysis or displacement.

Extracting Metals from Rocks

☐ That if a metal is below carbon in the reactivity series, it is extracted by reduction with carbon.

☐ That if a metal is above carbon in the reactivity series, it is extracted by electrolysis.

☐ That in a reduction reaction, oxygen is removed.

☐ That aluminium and titanium can't be extracted from their ores by reduction with carbon.

☐ That the extraction of aluminium and titanium from their ores is expensive because the processes used have lots of stages and need lots of energy.

cont...

Extracting Copper

☐ That copper can be extracted from its ore by smelting (heating it in a furnace).

☐ How electrolysis can be used to purify copper.

☐ That the supply of copper-rich ores is limited so it's important to recycle as much copper as possible.

☐ The two new methods that have been developed for extracting copper from low-grade ores — bioleaching (using bacteria) and phytomining (using plants that absorb copper from soil).

☐ The advantages and disadvantages of using bioleaching and phytomining instead of traditional extraction methods to extract copper from low-grade ores.

☐ How copper can be extracted from solution using a displacement reaction with scrap iron.

Impacts of Extracting Metals

☐ The social, economic and environmental impacts of mining for metal ores.

☐ That recycling metal, rather than extracting more metal, saves limited metal resources, requires less energy, saves fossil fuels and reduces the amount of waste going to landfill.

Properties and Uses of Metals

☐ Where the transition metals are in the periodic table.

☐ That metals have similar basic properties — they are strong, can be bent into shape, and conduct heat and electricity.

☐ What the specific properties of copper, aluminium and titanium are, and that these mean they are suitable for certain uses.

☐ That the downsides to using metals as structural materials are that they may corrode or break due to metal fatigue.

Alloys

☐ That an alloy is a mixture of two metals, or a mixture of a metal and a non-metal.

☐ That iron from a blast furnace needs to be purified as it contains impurities that make it brittle. It's then made into alloys because its softness means it has limited uses as a pure metal.

☐ That steel is an alloy of iron and carbon and that most iron is made into steel.

☐ The properties of low-carbon steel, high-carbon steel and stainless steel.

☐ That copper, gold and aluminium are made into alloys to make them harder and so more usable.

☐ That alloys can be designed for specific purposes.

Exam-style Questions

1   Car bodies can be made out of steel or aluminium alloys.

1 (a) (i)   Steel is an alloy. Define the term 'alloy'.

(2 marks)

1 (a) (ii)   Carbon is one element in steel. Name the other main element in steel.

(1 mark)

1 (a) (iii) Circle the correct word to complete the sentence.

Metals are often made into alloys to make them

softer.
harder.

(1 mark)

1 (b)   Low-carbon steel can be used to make car bodies.
Give **one** property that makes low-carbon steel suitable for this purpose.

(1 mark)

1 (c)   A disadvantage of using steel to make car bodies is that it can corrode. To help prevent this a layer of zinc is often applied to the steel — this process is called galvanisation.

1 (c) (i)   Galvanisation isn't necessary for aluminium car bodies.
Explain why this is the case.

(1 mark)

1 (c) (ii)   Give **one** other property of aluminium that makes it a better material for making car bodies from than steel.

(1 mark)

1 (c) (iii) Why would pure aluminium not be a suitable material for building car bodies?

(1 mark)

1 (c) (iv) Car bodies containing aluminium are more expensive than those made from steel as the extraction of aluminium from its ore is expensive. Explain why it is expensive to extract aluminium from its ore.

(2 marks)

2   Calcium hydroxide is an alkali that has many uses in industry and in agriculture.

2 (a) (i)   Name the **two** reactants involved in the formation of calcium hydroxide.

(1 mark)

2 (a) (ii)   Write the symbol equation for this reaction.

(2 marks)

2 (b) (i)   Calcium hydroxide can be dissolved in water to form a solution.
What is the common name for this solution?

(1 mark)

2 (b) (ii)   A solution of calcium hydroxide can be used to test for the presence of carbon dioxide.
If carbon dioxide was bubbled through the solution, what would you expect to see?

(1 mark)

2 (b) (iii)   Fill in the blanks in the equation for the reaction of calcium hydroxide
with carbon dioxide.

$$Ca(OH)_2 + CO_2 \rightarrow \underline{\hspace{1.5cm}} + \underline{\hspace{1.5cm}}$$

(2 marks)

2 (c)   The pH of soil can affect plant growth. Calcium hydroxide can be applied to fields
(a process called liming) to alter the pH of the soil. This graph shows soil pH in a field
during one year. During this time the farmer applied calcium hydroxide once.

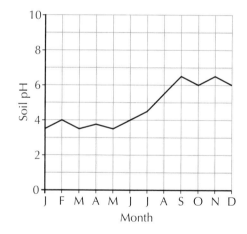

2 (c) (i)   What effect does calcium hydroxide have on soil pH?

(1 mark)

2 (c) (ii)   What type of reaction causes this effect?

(1 mark)

2 (c) (iii)   Using the graph, suggest the month when liming took place. Explain your answer.

(2 marks)

3 Malachite is a copper ore that contains 57% copper.
Copper can be extracted from malachite by the process shown below.

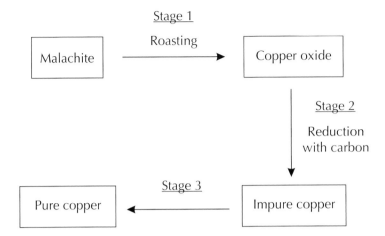

3 (a) Malachite is mostly copper carbonate.
Give the chemical formula of copper carbonate.

(1 mark)

3 (b) Stage 1 (roasting) takes place at a very high temperature. The copper carbonate breaks down to form copper oxide and one other product.

3 (b) (i) What type of reaction occurs during roasting?

(1 mark)

3 (b) (ii) Copper oxide is one product of roasting, what is the other?

(1 mark)

3 (c) Name the process used to obtain pure copper in Stage 3.

(1 mark)

3 (d) Chalcopyrite is another type of copper ore. It's a copper sulfide that is 10% copper.

3 (d) (i) Explain why copper isn't extracted from chalcopyrite using the method outlined in the diagram.

(2 marks)

3 (d) (ii) Suggest a method that could be used to extract copper from chalcopyrite and give **two** advantages of this method over the one outlined in the diagram.

(3 marks)

3 (e) Copper is used to make electrical wiring.

3 (e) (i) Give **two** reasons why copper is suitable for this use.

(2 marks)

3 (e) (ii) Give **one** other application of copper.

(1 mark)

4   Buildings and other structures can be made from a range of materials, including metals and products made from limestone.

4 (a)   Limestone can be made into a number of useful building materials.
Use the correct words from the box to complete the paragraph.

bauxite	sand	concrete	limestone	aggregate	clay

Limestone is heated with .... to make cement.

.... and water are added to cement to make mortar.

Sand and .... are added to cement to make ....

(4 marks)

4 (b)   Limestone based building materials can be used in combination with metals.
Iron is an example of a metal that is commonly used with limestone products.

4 (b) (i)   Iron is usually found as iron oxide. Describe how iron is extracted from iron oxide.

(3 marks)

4 (b) (ii)   Iron extracted from iron oxide with no further processing is usually brittle.
Explain why.

(1 mark)

4 (b) (iii)   Some metals do not need to be extracted from ores — they are found in the earth as the pure metal. Give one example of a metal found in its elemental form, and explain why it is not found as an ore.

(2 marks)

4 (c)   Mining for metal ores and quarrying for limestone have impacts on the environment.

4 (c) (i)   Tick **two** statements that are environmental impacts of extracting metal ores and limestone.

Statement	Environmental Impact Tick (✔)
Jobs are created in the local area.	
Traffic to and from the mine/quarry causes pollution.	
Habitats are destroyed.	
Dust from the site can cause health problems for local people.	

(2 marks)

4 (c) (ii)   Describe one way that mining and quarrying can contribute to global warming.

(2 marks)

Learning Objectives:
- Know that crude oil is a mixture of lots of different compounds.
- Know that the substances in a mixture are not chemically bonded to each other.
- Know that most of the compounds in crude oil are hydrocarbons.
- Know that the properties of substances are not changed when the substance is in a mixture.
- Know that mixtures can be separated using physical methods such as distillation.
- Understand how fractional distillation is used to separate crude oil into fractions.

Specification Reference
C1.4.1, C1.4.2

1. Fractional Distillation of Crude Oil

Crude oil is a fossil fuel that is formed deep underground from the remains of plants and animals. Loads of useful products can be made from crude oil using a technique called fractional distillation.

What is crude oil?

Crude oil is a **mixture** of many different compounds. A mixture consists of two (or more) elements or compounds that aren't chemically bonded to each other. Most of the compounds in crude oil are **hydrocarbon** molecules. Hydrocarbons are basically fuels such as petrol and diesel. They're made of only carbon and hydrogen.

Properties of mixtures

There are no chemical bonds between the different parts of a mixture, so the different hydrocarbon molecules in crude oil aren't chemically bonded to one another. This means that they all keep their original properties, such as their boiling points (the temperature at which they turn from a liquid into a gas). The properties of a mixture are just a mixture of the properties of the separate parts.

Separating mixtures

Because the substances in a mixture all keep their original properties, the parts of a mixture can be separated out by physical methods.

> **Example**
>
> Crude oil can be split up into its separate fractions by fractional distillation. Each fraction contains molecules with a similar number of carbon atoms to each other.

Fractional distillation

Crude oil can be split into separate groups of hydrocarbons using a technique called fractional distillation. The crude oil is pumped into piece of equipment known as a fractionating column, which works continuously (it doesn't get switched off). This fractionating column has a temperature gradient running through it — it's hottest at the bottom and coldest at the top.

Figure 1: *A fractionating column.*

The crude oil is first heated so that it vaporises (turns into a gas) and is then piped in at the bottom of the column. The gas rises up the column and gradually cools. Different compounds in the mixture have different boiling points, so they condense (turn back into a liquid) at different temperatures. This means they condense at different levels in the fractionating column.

Hydrocarbons that have a similar number of carbon atoms in have similar boiling points, so they condense at similar levels in the column.

| Example |

- Hydrocarbons with lots of carbon atoms in have high boiling points, so they condense near the bottom of the column.

- Hydrocarbons with a small number of carbon atoms in have low boiling points, so they condense near the top of the column.

Tip: There's more about how the number of carbon atoms affects the properties of a hydrocarbon coming up on page 168.

The groups of hydrocarbons that condense together are called **fractions**. The various fractions are constantly tapped off from the column at the different levels where they condense.

The process of fractional distillation is illustrated in Figure 2.

Tip: The temperature at which a compound condenses is the same as its boiling point. E.g. If a compound had a boiling point of 120 °C, it would condense at 120 °C.

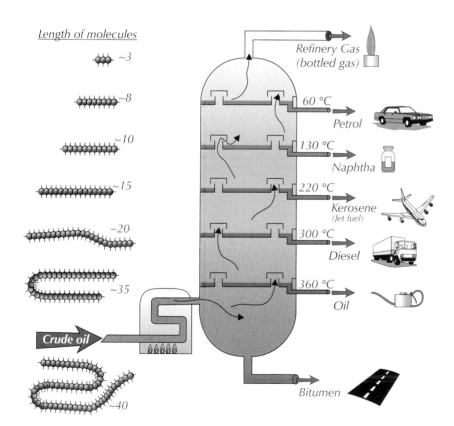

Length of molecules

~3
~8
~10
~15
~20
~35
Crude oil
~40

Refinery Gas (bottled gas)

60 °C Petrol

130 °C Naphtha

220 °C Kerosene (Jet fuel)

300 °C Diesel

360 °C Oil

Bitumen

Figure 2: *The process of fractional distillation.*

Exam Tip
Don't worry — you don't need to know the names, lengths or condensing temperatures of specific fractions. Just make sure you understand the general principles of fractional distillation for the exam.

Practice Questions — Fact Recall

Q1 What is a mixture?

Q2 What is a hydrocarbon?

Q3 Name the process that is used to separate crude oil into fractions.

Q4 Where do compounds with a small number of carbon atoms leave the fractionating column — near the bottom or near the top?

Practice Questions — Application

Q1 This table shows the number of carbon atoms in some of the hydrocarbons found in crude oil.

Hydrocarbon	Number of carbon atoms
Butane	4
Decane	10
Icosane	20
Tetracontane	40

Tip: Don't forget — the fractionating column is hottest at the bottom and coolest at the top.

a) Which of the hydrocarbons in the table will condense at the lowest temperature?

b) Which of the hydrocarbons in the table will condense nearest the bottom of a fractionating column?

Q2 This table contains data on some of the fractions of crude oil that are separated out during fractional distillation.

Fraction	Approximate boiling temperature range (°C)
Petrol	30 – 80
Naphtha	80 – 190
Kerosene	190 – 250
Diesel	250 – 350

a) Which of the fractions in the table will be removed closest to the top of the fractionating column?

b) Octane has a boiling point of 125 °C.

i) At what temperature will octane condense?

ii) In which of the fractions in the table will octane be found?

2. Properties and Uses of Crude Oil

The different fractions that you get when you separate crude oil have very different properties. This means they can be used for different things.

Alkanes

Most of the fractions of crude oil consist of hydrocarbons called alkanes. Alkanes are made up of chains of carbon atoms surrounded by hydrogen atoms. Different alkanes have chains of different lengths.

> **Example**
>
> The first four alkanes are methane (natural gas), ethane, propane and butane.
>
> Methane has just one carbon atom and four hydrogen atoms, so its chemical formula is CH_4. The displayed structure of methane is shown in Figure 1. The green lines in this structure represent covalent bonds. 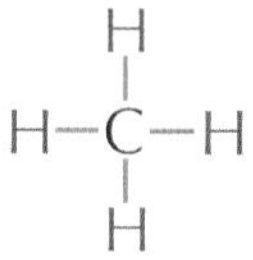
>
>
>
> *Figure 1: Methane.*
>
> Ethane (C_2H_6) has a chain of two carbon atoms, propane (C_3H_8) has three carbon atoms and butane (C_4H_{10}) has four carbon atoms. Their displayed structures are shown in Figure 2. 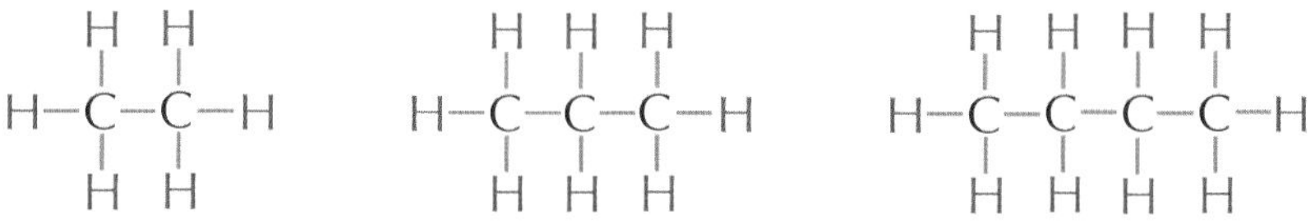
>
> Ethane
>
> Propane
>
> Butane
>
> *Figure 2: The structures of ethane, propane and butane.*

Carbon atoms form four bonds and hydrogen atoms only form one bond. In alkanes, there are no carbon-carbon double bonds so all the atoms have formed bonds with as many other atoms as they can — this means they're saturated.

General formula of alkanes

Alkanes all have the general formula C_nH_{2n+2}. In this formula, n is the number of carbon atoms. If an alkane has n carbon atoms, it will always have 2n + 2 hydrogen atoms.

> **Example**
>
> If an alkane has 5 carbons, it's got to have (2 × 5) + 2 = 12 hydrogens. So the chemical formula of an alkane with 5 carbon atoms is C_5H_{12}.

Learning Objectives:
- Know that most of the hydrocarbons in crude oil are alkanes.
- Be able to recognise alkanes from their chemical and displayed formulae.
- Know that alkanes are saturated hydrocarbons.
- Know that alkanes have the general formula C_nH_{2n+2}.
- Know how the boiling point, viscosity and flammability of alkanes change depending on the size of the molecules.
- Understand how the properties of an alkane influence how it is used as a fuel.

Specification Reference C1.4.1, C1.4.2

Exam Tip
You need to be able to recognise methane, ethane, propane and butane in the exam, so make sure you learn these structures and formulas.

Tip: Saturated means a compound only has single carbon-carbon bonds.

Tip: You can work out the chemical formula of any alkane using the general formula, as long as you know how many carbon atoms it has.

Properties of alkanes

The properties of alkanes change depending on how long the carbon chain is. There are three trends in the properties of alkanes that you need to know.

- The shorter the molecules, the more runny the hydrocarbon is — that is, the less **viscous** it is.

- The shorter the molecules, the more **volatile** they are. "More volatile" means they turn into a gas at a lower temperature. So, the shorter the molecules, the lower the temperature at which that fraction vaporises or condenses — and the lower its boiling point.

- The shorter the molecules, the more **flammable** the hydrocarbon is.

So, alkanes with very long carbon chains are viscous, have very high boiling points and are not very flammable.

Tip: How <u>flammable</u> something is just means how easy it is to ignite.

Uses of hydrocarbons

The uses of hydrocarbons depend on their properties.

Examples

The volatility helps decide what the fraction is used for.

- The refinery gas fraction has the lowest boiling point — in fact it's a gas at room temperature. This makes it ideal for using as bottled gas. It's stored under pressure as liquid in 'bottles'. When the tap on the bottle is opened, the fuel vaporises and flows to the burner where it's ignited.

- The petrol fraction has a higher boiling point. Petrol is a liquid which is ideal for storing in the fuel tank of a car. It can flow to the engine where it's easily vaporised to mix with the air before it is ignited.

The viscosity also helps decide how the hydrocarbons are used.

- The really gloopy, viscous hydrocarbons are used for lubricating engine parts or for covering roads.

Figure 3: *Bottled gas.*

Practice Questions — Fact Recall

Q1 Draw the displayed structure of methane.

Q2 Name the alkane that has the chemical formula C_3H_8.

Q3 Why are alkanes described as being "saturated"?

Q4 Describe the trend in flammability of the alkanes.

Practice Questions — Application

Q1 Octane has eight carbon atoms in it. What is its chemical formula?

Q2 Hexadecane is an alkane with long carbon chains. Explain why hexadecane is a suitable alkane to use in lubricating oil.

3. Environmental Problems

Crude oil, coal and natural gas are all fossil fuels. Fossil fuels make great fuels, but burning them to release energy can be bad for the environment.

Burning fuels (combustion)

We burn **fossil fuels** (coal, oil and natural gas) to get energy for lots of different processes. Power stations burn huge amounts of fossil fuels to make electricity. Cars are also a major culprit in burning fossil fuels.

Fossil fuels contain carbon and hydrogen. During **combustion** (when the fuel is burnt), the carbon and hydrogen react with oxygen from the air so that carbon dioxide and water vapour are released into the atmosphere. The carbon and hydrogen are said to be oxidised. Energy (heat) is also released.

Complete and partial combustion

When there's plenty of oxygen, all the fuel burns — this is called complete combustion. When a fuel is completely combusted only carbon dioxide and water are produced. This is the equation for the complete combustion of a hydrocarbon:

hydrocarbon + oxygen → carbon dioxide + water vapour

If there's not enough oxygen, some of the fuel doesn't burn completely — this is called partial combustion. Under these conditions, solid particles (called particulates) of soot (carbon) and unburnt fuel may be released, as well as carbon dioxide and water. Carbon monoxide (a poisonous gas) is also released

Writing equations for combustion

In the exam, you could be asked to write a balanced symbol equation for the complete combustion of a particular fuel. All you have to do is put the chemical formula of your fuel and O_2 for oxygen on one side, CO_2 for carbon dioxide and H_2O for water on the other side and then make sure the equation balances.

Example — **Higher**

Write an equation for the complete combustion of propane.

Propane has the chemical formula C_3H_8 (you saw this on page 167.)

If you put C_3H_8 and O_2 on one side of the equation and CO_2 and H_2O on the other side of the equation you get:

$$C_3H_8 + O_2 \rightarrow CO_2 + H_2O$$

Balancing the equation gives you:

$$C_3H_8 + 5O_2 \rightarrow 3CO_2 + 4H_2O$$

This is the equation for the complete combustion of propane.

Learning Objectives:
- Know that most fuels contain carbon and/or hydrogen.
- Know that when fuels are burnt, the carbon and hydrogen in the fuels are oxidised and energy is released.
- Know that the substances released when fuels are burnt can include carbon dioxide, water, carbon monoxide, sulfur dioxide, oxides of nitrogen and solid carbon particulates.
- Know that sulfur dioxide and nitrogen oxides can cause acid rain.
- Know that it's possible to remove the sulfur from fuels before they are burned.
- Know that sulfur dioxide can be removed from waste gases after a fuel has been burned.
- Know that carbon dioxide contributes to global warming and solid carbon particulates contribute to global dimming.
- Understand the social, economic and environmental impacts of using fuels.

Specification Reference C1.4.3

Tip: **H** See page 133 for more on balancing chemical equations.

You could also be asked to write an equation for the partial combustion of a fuel. If so, you'll be told in the question what the products of the reaction are and you'll just need to balance the equation.

Other products of combustion

If the fuel contains sulfur impurities, the sulfur will be released as sulfur dioxide when the fuel is burnt. Oxides of nitrogen will also form if the fuel burns at a high temperature. This is because at very high temperatures, nitrogen and oxygen in the air react with one another.

Acid rain

Sulfur dioxide is one of the gases that causes acid rain. When the sulfur dioxide mixes with the water in the clouds it forms dilute sulfuric acid. This then falls as acid rain (see Figure 1).

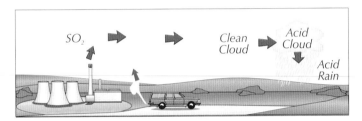

Figure 1: *The formation of acid rain.*

Oxides of nitrogen cause acid rain by forming dilute nitric acid in clouds.

Consequences of acid rain

Acid rain causes lakes to become acidic and many plants and animals die as a result. Acid rain also kills trees (see Figure 2), damages limestone buildings and ruins stone statues (see Figure 3). Links between acid rain and human health problems have also been suggested.

Reducing acid rain

The benefits of electricity and travel have to be balanced against the environmental impacts. Governments have recognised the importance of this and international agreements have been put in place to reduce emissions of air pollutants such as sulfur dioxide.

One way to reduce sulfur dioxide emissions is to remove the sulfur from fuels before they're burnt. The problem is, this costs money. Also, removing sulfur from fuels takes more energy. This usually comes from burning more fuel, which releases more of the greenhouse gas carbon dioxide. Nevertheless, petrol and diesel are starting to be replaced by low-sulfur versions.

Another way to reduce sulfur dioxide emissions is to remove the sulfur dioxide from waste gases before they are released. Power stations now have Acid Gas Scrubbers to take the harmful gases out before they release their fumes into the atmosphere. The other way of reducing acid rain is simply to reduce our usage of fossil fuels.

Figure 2: *Trees that have been killed by acid rain.*

Figure 3: *A statue that has been damaged by acid rain.*

Global warming and climate change

The level of carbon dioxide in the atmosphere is increasing — because of the large amounts of fossil fuels humans burn. There's a scientific consensus that this extra carbon dioxide has caused the average temperature of the Earth to increase — global warming (see Figure 4).

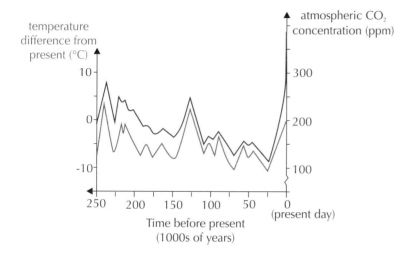

Figure 4: *Graph showing how the atmospheric concentration of CO_2 and the temperature have changed over the last 250 000 years.*

Global warming is a type of climate change and causes other types of climate change, e.g. changing rainfall patterns. It could also cause severe flooding due to the polar ice caps melting.

Global dimming

In the last few years, some scientists have been measuring how much sunlight is reaching the surface of the Earth and comparing it to records from the last 50 years. They have been amazed to find that in some areas nearly 25% less sunlight has been reaching the surface compared to 50 years ago. They have called this global dimming.

They think that it is caused by particles of soot and ash that are produced when fossil fuels are burnt. These particles reflect sunlight back into space, or they can help to produce more clouds that reflect the sunlight back into space. However, there are many scientists who don't believe the change is real and blame it on inaccurate recording equipment.

Figure 5: *Thick black smoke being released into the air. The particulate carbon in this smoke could contribute to global dimming.*

Practice Questions — Fact Recall

Q1 a) What two products are formed when a hydrocarbon fuel is completely combusted?

b) What other products may be released if a hydrocarbon fuel undergoes partial combustion?

Q2 What gas other than carbon dioxide and water vapour will be formed if a fuel containing sulfur impurities is burnt in air?

Q3 Under what conditions will nitrogen oxides form when a hydrocarbon fuel is burned?

Q4 a) Name two gases that can cause acid rain.

b) Give two ways in which acid rain can damage the environment.

c) Suggest one way of reducing acid rain.

Q5 a) What is global warming?

b) Suggest one consequence of global warming.

Practice Questions — Application

Exam Tip
You could get a question like this in the exam where you're asked to consider the environmental impacts of a fuel you've never heard of before. Just read the question carefully — all the information you need is there.

Q1 Hexadecane ($C_{16}H_{34}$) can be used as a fuel. When it undergoes complete combustion carbon dioxide and water vapour are released.

a) Will using hexadecane as a fuel contribute to climate change? Explain your answer.

b) Could burning hexadecane result in acid rain? Explain your answer.

Q2 A study by scientists at a local weather station has shown that over the last 50 years, the amount of sunlight reaching the weather station has decreased. Suggest a possible explanation for this finding.

Q3 Write a balanced symbol equation for the complete combustion of pentane (C_5H_{12}).

Q4 Some hexane (C_6H_{14}) burns incompletely producing carbon monoxide and water as the only products. Write a balanced symbol equation for this combustion.

4. Alternative Fuels

There are lots of problems with using fossil fuels, so scientists are developing some alternative fuel sources. The trouble is, there are advantages and disadvantages to using all of these alternative fuels too.

Learning Objectives:
- Know that ethanol and biodiesel are biofuels, and that biofuels are produced from plants.
- Know that hydrogen gas can also be used as an alternative fuel.
- Understand the advantages and disadvantages of using alternative fuels.

Specification Reference C1.4.3

Developing alternative fuels

Some alternative fuels have already been developed, and there are others in the pipeline (so to speak). Many of them are renewable fuels so, unlike fossil fuels, they won't run out. However, none of them are perfect — they all have pros and cons.

Biofuels

Biofuels are fuels that are made from plant material. There are two types of biofuel you need to know about — ethanol and biodiesel.

Ethanol

Ethanol's made by fermentation of plants and is used to power cars in some places. It's often mixed with petrol to make a better fuel. Here are some of the advantages of using ethanol as a fuel.

- The CO_2 released when ethanol is burnt was taken in by the plant as it grew, so it's 'carbon neutral'. The only other product when ethanol burns is water and the process of making ethanol doesn't require much energy, so ethanol is better for the environment than fossil fuels.

- Ethanol is a renewable resource because it's made from plants.

- Growing the crops to make ethanol is labour intensive so provides employment for local people.

Disadvantages of using ethanol include:

- Engines need to be converted before they'll work with ethanol fuels.

- Ethanol fuel isn't widely available.

- There are worries that as demand for it increases, farmers will switch from growing food crops to growing crops to make ethanol — this will increase food prices.

Tip: Fuels are described as carbon neutral if there is no net release of carbon dioxide when the fuel is burnt — any carbon dioxide released into the atmosphere when the fuel burns was taken out of the atmosphere when the fuel was made.

Biodiesel

Biodiesel can be produced from vegetable oils such as rapeseed oil and soybean oil. It can be mixed with ordinary diesel fuel and used to run a diesel engine. Here are some of the advantages of using biodiesel.

- Like ethanol, biodiesel is 'carbon neutral', renewable and provides jobs for local people.

- Engines don't need to be converted before they can run on biodiesel.

- Biodiesel produces much less sulfur dioxide and 'particulates' than ordinary diesel or petrol.

Figure 1: *A biodiesel fuel pump.*

Disadvantages of using biodiesel include:

- We can't make enough to completely replace diesel.
- Biodiesel is expensive to make.
- It could increase food prices like using more ethanol could.

Hydrogen gas

Tip: Electrolysis of water means using electricity to split water up into hydrogen and oxygen.

Hydrogen gas can also be used to power vehicles. You get the hydrogen from the electrolysis of water — but it takes electrical energy to split it up. This energy can come from a renewable source, e.g. solar. Some of the advantages of using hydrogen gas include:

- Hydrogen combines with oxygen in the air to form just water — so it's very clean.
- The hydrogen gas comes from water and there's lots of water about.

Here are some of the disadvantages of using hydrogen gas:

- You need a special, expensive engine to use hydrogen as a fuel.
- Hydrogen isn't widely available as a fuel.
- You still need to use energy from another source to make it.
- Hydrogen's hard to store because it is extremely flammable.

Figure 2: *Hydrogen powered vehicles.*

Practice Questions — Fact Recall

Q1 What is a biofuel? Give two examples of biofuels.

Q2 Give one advantage and one disadvantage of using ethanol as a fuel.

Q3 What is biodiesel made from?

Practice Questions — Application

Q1 A distribution company wants to reduce its impact on the environment. Its fleet of distribution vans currently runs on diesel fuel. Suggest a way that this company could become more environmentally friendly without having to replace all of the vans it already has.

Q2 A company makes hydrogen gas from the electrolysis of water. The electricity needed for this process comes from a fossil fuel power station. The company claims that their hydrogen is a completely clean fuel because the only product formed when hydrogen burns is water.

a) Explain why this claim is incorrect.

b) What could the company do to make its hydrogen a completely clean fuel?

Section Checklist — Make sure you know...

Fractional Distillation of Crude Oil

☐ That crude oil is a mixture of many different compounds, most of which are hydrocarbons (compounds made from only hydrogen and carbon).

☐ That the substances in a mixture are not chemically bonded to each other.

☐ That the substances in a mixture keep all of their original properties (e.g. boiling point) and so can be separated from each other using physical methods (e.g. distillation).

☐ How crude oil can be separated into fractions using fractional distillation.

Properties and Uses of Crude Oil

☐ That most of the compounds in crude oil are a type of hydrocarbon known as alkanes and how to recognise alkanes from either their chemical formula or their displayed structure.

☐ The chemical formulae and displayed structures of methane, ethane, propane and butane.

☐ That alkanes have the general formula C_nH_{2n+2} and are described as saturated hydrocarbons because all of the atoms in an alkane have formed bonds with as many other atoms as they possibly can.

☐ That the shorter the molecules the less viscous a hydrocarbon is, the more volatile a hydrocarbon is and the more flammable a hydrocarbon is.

☐ Why alkanes with different properties are used in different ways.

Environmental Problems

☐ That most fuels (including the fossil fuels coal, oil and natural gas) contain carbon and hydrogen.

☐ That when fuels are burnt, the carbon is oxidised to carbon dioxide, the hydrogen is oxidised to water and energy is released.

☐ That carbon monoxide, carbon particulates and unburnt fuel can be released if there is not enough oxygen available when a fuel burns (this is called partial combustion).

☐ **H** How to write balanced symbol equations for the complete and partial combustion of fuels.

☐ That sulfur dioxide can be released when a fuel burns if the fuel contains sulfur impurities and oxides of nitrogen can be released if the fuel burns at a high temperature.

☐ That sulfur dioxide and nitrogen oxides can cause acid rain if they mix with the water in clouds.

☐ That acid rain can be reduced by removing sulfur from fuels before they are burnt, or by removing sulfur dioxide from waste gases before they are released.

☐ That carbon dioxide contributes to global warming (a type of climate change) and that carbon particulates in the atmosphere may have caused global dimming.

Alternative Fuels

☐ That ethanol and biodiesel are examples of biofuels (fuels that are produced from plant material).

☐ That hydrogen gas (produced by electrolysis of water) can be used as a fuel source.

☐ The advantages and disadvantages of using each of these alternative fuels.

Exam-style Questions

1   Many modern cars use petrol as their fuel source.
Petrol is produced from crude oil via a process known as fractional distillation.

1 (a) (i) Describe the process of fractional distillation.

(4 marks)

1 (a) (ii) Petrol is removed from near the top of the fractionating column.
What does this tell you about the hydrocarbons that make up petrol?

(1 mark)

1 (b)   *In this question you will be assessed on the quality of your English,
the organisation of your ideas and your use of appropriate specialist vocabulary.*

Outline the environmental impacts of using petrol as a fuel.

(6 marks)

2   Many scientists are developing alternatives to fossil fuels, such as biofuels.

2 (a)   Give **two** reasons why an alternative to fossil fuels is needed.

(2 marks)

2 (b)   Ethanol is an example of a biofuel. Ethanol is described as being 'carbon neutral'.

2 (b) (i) Explain why ethanol is a 'carbon neutral' fuel.

(1 mark)

2 (b) (ii) Suggest **two** reasons why most people have not switched to using
ethanol powered cars.

(2 marks)

2 (c)   Biodiesel is another example of a biofuel.

2 (c) (i) Biodiesel produces much less sulfur dioxide when it is burned
than normal diesel does. Explain why this is an advantage.

(2 marks)

2 (c) (ii) Discuss **one** positive and **one** negative social impact of producing
and using biodiesel.

(4 marks)

3   Alkanes are a type of saturated hydrocarbon.

3 (a)   What is the general formula of the alkanes?

(1 mark)

3 (b)   This table contains information about some common alkanes.

Alkane	Formula	Length of carbon chain
Propane	C_3H_8	3
Heptane	C_7H_{16}	7
Decane	$C_{10}H_{22}$	10

3 (b) (i)   Which of the alkanes in the table is likely to be the least flammable?
Explain your answer.

(1 mark)

3 (b) (ii)   Which of the alkanes in the table would be most suitable to use in bottled gas?
Explain your answer.

(2 marks)

3 (c)   Heptane is often found in fuels such as petrol.

3 (c) (i)   Write a balanced symbol equation for the complete combustion of heptane.

(3 marks)

3 (c) (ii)   Under what conditions would carbon monoxide form when heptane is burned?

(1 mark)

3 (c) (iii) Describe how oxides of nitrogen could be formed when heptane is burned.

(2 marks)

4   A town council wants to be more environmentally friendly and is planning to swap
its diesel powered buses for a fleet of buses that are powered by hydrogen gas.

4 (a)   Why is using hydrogen more environmentally friendly than using diesel?

(1 mark)

4 (b)   At a meeting, a number of the town's residents voiced concerns about the plan.
One of the main concerns raised was the cost of replacing all the town's buses.

4 (b) (i)   Suggest **two** other concerns (besides cost) that the town's residents might have.

(2 marks)

4 (b) (ii)   Suggest a cheaper option the town council could use for making its buses more
environmentally friendly. Explain your answer.

(3 marks)

Learning Objectives:

- Know that cracking is a process used to convert large hydrocarbon molecules into smaller, more useful hydrocarbons.
- Know that cracking produces some products that can be used as fuels.
- Know that cracking is a thermal decomposition reaction.
- Know that cracking involves heating the hydrocarbon and passing it over a catalyst or mixing it with steam at very high temperatures.
- Know that cracking produces alkanes and alkenes.

Specification Reference
C1.5.1

1. Cracking Crude Oil

Some fractions of crude oil are more useful than others — for example, short-chain hydrocarbons are often more useful than long-chain hydrocarbons. Cracking is used to break long-chain hydrocarbons down into shorter ones.

What is cracking?

Long-chain hydrocarbons form thick gloopy liquids like tar which aren't all that useful, so a lot of the longer molecules produced from fractional distillation are turned into smaller ones by a process called **cracking**.

Some of the products of cracking are useful as fuels, like petrol for cars and paraffin for jet fuel. Cracking also produces substances like ethene, which are needed for making plastics (see page 184). The process of cracking is illustrated in Figure 1.

Figure 1: *Cracking. In this example, diesel (a long-chain hydrocarbon) is being broken down into the shorter-chain hydrocarbons petrol, paraffin and ethene.*

Figure 2: *A catalytic cracker at an oil refinery.*

Tip: Broken pottery can be used as a catalyst for cracking because the pottery contains aluminium oxide.

How cracking works

Cracking is a **thermal decomposition** reaction — breaking molecules down by heating them. The first step is to heat the long-chain hydrocarbon to vaporise it (turn it into a gas). The vapour can then be passed over a powdered catalyst at a temperature of about 400 °C – 700 °C. Aluminium oxide is one of the catalysts used. The long-chain molecules split apart or "crack" on the surface of the specks of catalyst — see Figure 3.

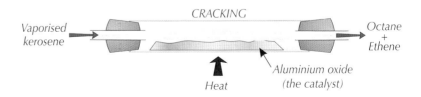

Figure 3: *The cracking of kerosene into octane and ethene using an aluminium oxide catalyst.*

Alternatively, the vapour can be mixed with steam and heated to a very high temperature. This will also lead to thermal decomposition of long-chain hydrocarbon molecules to form smaller ones.

Products of cracking

Most of the products of cracking are **alkanes** and unsaturated hydrocarbons called **alkenes**.

Tip: See page 167 for more about alkanes and page 182 for more about alkenes.

Example

Kerosene is a long-chain hydrocarbon molecule (it has 10 carbon atoms). There's lots of kerosene in crude oil, but kerosene itself isn't that useful. Cracking is used to break kerosene down into octane and ethene (see Figure 5). Octane is a shorter-chain alkane which is useful for making petrol. Ethene is an alkene which is useful for making plastics.

Figure 4: Kerosene — one of the less useful products from crude oil.

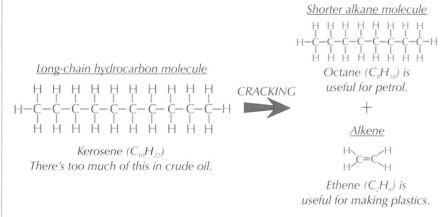

Shorter alkane molecule

Octane (C_8H_{18}) is useful for petrol.

Long-chain hydrocarbon molecule

CRACKING

+

Kerosene ($C_{10}H_{22}$)
There's too much of this in crude oil.

Alkene

Ethene (C_2H_4) is useful for making plastics.

Figure 5: The cracking of kerosene into an alkane (octane) and an alkene (ethene).

Tip: Kerosene is also known as decane.

Practice Questions — Fact Recall

Q1 a) What is cracking and why is it useful?

   b) Give two things that the products of cracking can be used for.

Q2 What type of reaction is cracking?

Q3 a) Describe how an aluminium oxide catalyst can be used to crack a long-chain hydrocarbon.

   b) How can cracking be performed without using a catalyst?

Q4 Name two types of hydrocarbon that are produced in cracking.

2. Using Crude Oil

We use fractions of crude oil for loads of different things, but we need to watch out — there are problems with using it.

Why do we use crude oil?

There are lots of advantages to using crude oil. Crude oil fractions release lots of energy when they burn and they burn cleanly, so they make good fuels. Most modern transport is fuelled by crude oil fractions, e.g. cars, boats, trains and planes. Parts of crude oil are also burned in central heating systems in homes and in power stations to generate electricity.

There's a massive industry with scientists working to find oil reserves, take it out of the ground, and turn it into useful products. As well as fuels, crude oil also provides the raw materials for making various chemicals, including plastics.

Often, alternatives to using crude oil fractions as fuel are possible. For example, electricity can be generated by nuclear power or wind power, there are ethanol-powered cars, and solar energy can be used to heat water. But things tend to be set up for using oil fractions so crude oil fractions are often the easiest and cheapest thing to use.

Figure 1: An offshore oil rig.

> **Example**
>
> Cars are designed for petrol or diesel and it's readily available. There are filling stations all over the country, with storage facilities and pumps specifically designed for these crude oil fractions.

Crude oil fractions are often more reliable than other energy sources too. For example, solar and wind power won't work without the right weather conditions, whereas crude oil can be used any time. Nuclear energy is reliable, but there are lots of concerns about its safety and the storage of radioactive waste.

Disadvantages of using crude oil

There are two major disadvantages to using crude oil.

1. It's bad for the environment

Oil spills can happen as the oil is being transported by tanker — this spells disaster for the local environment. Birds get covered in the stuff and are poisoned as they try to clean themselves. Other creatures, like sea otters and whales, are poisoned too.

You also have to burn oil to release the energy from it. But burning oil is thought to be a major cause of global warming, acid rain and global dimming.

Figure 2: Volunteers cleaning up an oil spill.

Tip: See pages 170 and 171 for more on acid rain, global warming and global dimming.

2. Crude oil is non-renewable

Most scientists think that oil will run out — it's a non-renewable fuel. No one knows exactly when it'll run out but there have been heaps of different predictions — for example, about 40 years ago, scientists predicted that it'd all be gone by the year 2000. New oil reserves are discovered from time to time and technology is constantly improving, so it's now possible to extract oil that was once too difficult or expensive to extract.

In the worst-case scenario, oil may be pretty much gone in about 25 years — and that's not far off. Some people think we should immediately stop using oil for things like transport, for which there are alternatives, and keep it for things that it's absolutely essential for, like some chemicals and medicines.

It will take time to develop alternative fuels that will satisfy all our energy needs (see pages 173-174 for more info). It'll also take time to adapt things so that the fuels can be used on a wide scale. For example, we might need different kinds of car engines, or special storage tanks built.

One alternative is to generate energy from renewable sources — these are sources that won't run out. Examples of renewable energy sources are wind power, solar power, tidal power and biofuels. So however long oil does last for, it's a good idea to start conserving it and finding alternatives now.

Tip: Deciding whether or not to continue using non-renewable resources like crude oil is an important decision that society has to make.

Practice Questions — Fact Recall

Q1 Why do crude oil fractions make good fuels?

Q2 a) Suggest an alternative energy source that can be used instead of crude oil.

b) Give two reasons why crude oil fractions are still used for fuels even though alternatives are available.

Q3 Give two reasons why using crude oil can be bad for the environment.

Q4 40 years ago, scientists predicted that all the crude oil would be gone by the year 2000. Explain why this prediction did not come true.

Q5 Some people think that we should stop using oil as a fuel for transport immediately. Explain why people might think this.

Learning Objectives:

- Know that alkenes are a type of unsaturated hydrocarbon with the general formula C_nH_{2n}.
- Be able to recognise alkenes from their chemical and displayed formulae.
- Know how to test for alkenes using bromine water.
- Know how ethene can be used to produce ethanol.
- Know how ethanol can be produced from sugars by fermentation.
- Understand the advantages and disadvantages of making ethanol from both ethene and sugar.

Specification Reference
C1.5, C1.5.1, C1.5.3

3. Alkenes and Ethanol

Alkenes are really useful. You can make alkenes by cracking long-chain hydrocarbon molecules that come from crude oil. Once you have an alkene, you can use it to make loads of cool stuff, including ethanol.

What are alkenes?

Alkenes are hydrocarbons which have a double covalent bond between two of the carbon atoms in their chain — see Figure 1.

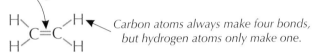

This is a double bond — so each carbon atom is still making four bonds.

Carbon atoms always make four bonds, but hydrogen atoms only make one.

Figure 1: *An alkene — all alkenes have a double bond in them.*

Alkenes are known as **unsaturated** because you can add more atoms to them — the double bond can open up, allowing the two carbon atoms to bond with other atoms. The first two alkenes are ethene (with two carbon atoms) and propene (three carbon atoms) — see Figure 2.

Ethene (C_2H_4)   *Propene (C_3H_6)*

Figure 2: *The structures of ethene and propene.*

All alkenes have the general formula C_nH_{2n} — they have twice as many hydrogens as carbons. You can use this general formula to recognise alkenes in your exam. If a molecule only has hydrogen and carbon atoms in it, and there are twice as many hydrogens as carbons, then it must be an alkene. You can also recognise alkenes from a displayed formula by looking out for the carbon-carbon double bond.

Testing for alkenes

You can test for an alkene by adding the substance to bromine water. An alkene will decolourise the bromine water, turning it from orange to colourless — see Figures 3 and 4. This is because the double bond has opened up and formed bonds with the bromine.

Figure 3: *The orange to colourless colour change when an alkene is added to bromine water.*

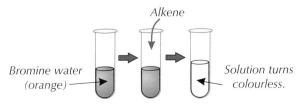

Alkene

Bromine water (orange)   *Solution turns colourless.*

Figure 4: *Using bromine water to test for alkenes.*

Making ethanol from ethene

Ethene (C_2H_4) can be reacted with steam (H_2O) in the presence of a catalyst to make ethanol. This is called a hydration reaction. At the moment this is a cheap process, because ethene's fairly cheap and not much of it is wasted. The trouble is that ethene's produced from crude oil, which is a non-renewable resource that could start running out fairly soon. This means using ethene to make ethanol will become very expensive.

Making ethanol from sugars

The alcohol in beer and wine, etc. isn't made from ethene — it's made by **fermentation**. The raw material for fermentation is sugar. This is converted into ethanol using yeast. The word equation for this is:

$$\text{sugar} \rightarrow \text{carbon dioxide} + \text{ethanol}$$

This process needs a lower temperature and simpler equipment than when making ethanol using ethene. It also requires less energy and therefore results in less CO_2 production, so fermentation is better for the environment. Another advantage is that the raw material is a renewable resource. Sugar is grown as a major crop in several parts of the world, including many poorer countries.

The ethanol produced this way can also be used as quite a cheap fuel in countries which don't have oil reserves for making petrol. There are disadvantages though. The ethanol you get from this process needs to be purified and it isn't very concentrated, so if you want to increase its strength you have to distil it (as in whisky distilleries). There are also concerns that growing more sugar to make ethanol could lead to more deforestation.

Tip: Weighing up the relative advantages and disadvantages of two techniques (like these two techniques for making ethanol) is an important skill that all scientists need.

HOW SCIENCE WORKS

Practice Questions — Fact Recall

Q1   Draw the chemical structure of propene.

Q2   Explain why alkenes are described as unsaturated.

Q3   a) Give two techniques that can be used to produce ethanol.

b) Discuss the advantages and disadvantages of each of these techniques.

Practice Questions — Application

Q1   A chemist has mixed up his bottles of propane and propene. When he adds bromine water to bottle A the resulting solution is colourless. When he adds bromine water to bottle B the resulting solution is orange. Which bottle contains propene and which contains propane?

Q2   Which of these is an alkene?

A: C_5H_{12} B: $C_3H_6Cl_2$ C: C_4H_8 D: C_2H_4O

- Know that alkenes can undergo polymerisation reactions to form polymers.

- Know how to show the formation of polymers from monomers.

- Know some of the main uses of polymers.

- Know that many polymers are difficult to dispose of because they aren't biodegradable.

- Know that biodegradable polymers are being developed and understand why this is important.

Specification Reference
C1.5, C1.5.2

4. Using Alkenes to Make Polymers

Ethanol isn't the only thing you can make from alkenes. Lots of alkenes are used to make polymers. Plastics are polymers... and we all know how useful plastics are.

Polymerisation

Probably the most useful thing you can do with alkenes is **polymerisation**. This means joining together lots of small alkene molecules (**monomers**) to form very large molecules — these long-chain molecules are called **polymers**.

> **Example**
>
> Many ethene molecules can be joined up to produce poly(ethene) or "polythene". 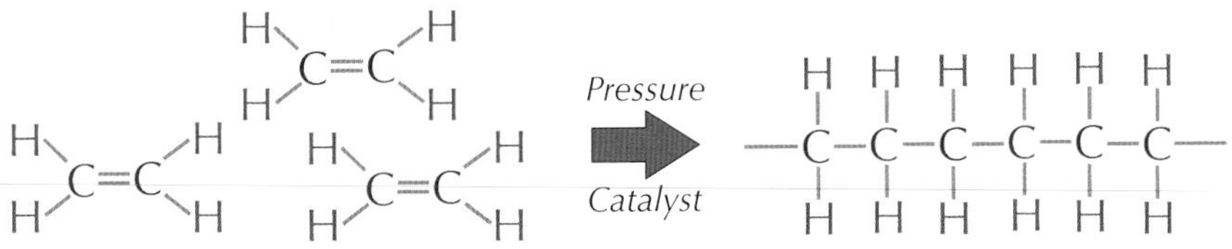
>
>
> *Many ethene monomers*   *A section of poly(ethene)*
>
> This reaction can be shown like this... 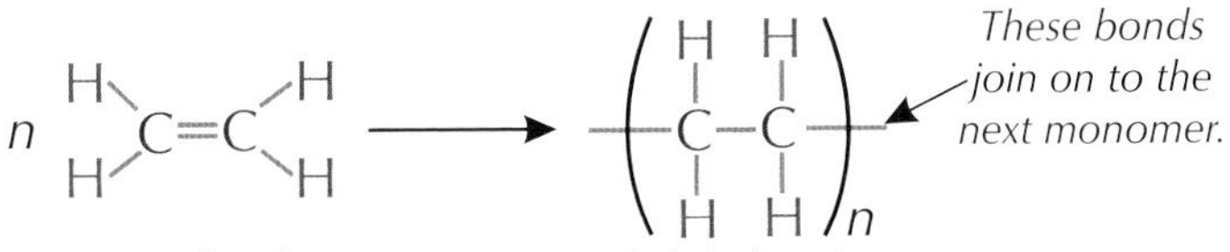
>
>
> *Many single ethenes*   *Poly(ethene)*
>
> These bonds join on to the next monomer.
>
> ... where n is a very large number of monomers.

Tip: The polymers that are made from alkenes are called <u>addition polymers</u>, because they're formed by <u>adding</u> lots of alkenes together.

For the exam you need to know the structures of poly(ethene) and one other polymer, called poly(propene). Poly(propene) is made when lots of propene monomers join together (see Figure 1).

Tip: The names of polymers can be written with or without brackets. E.g. poly(ethene) or polyethene.

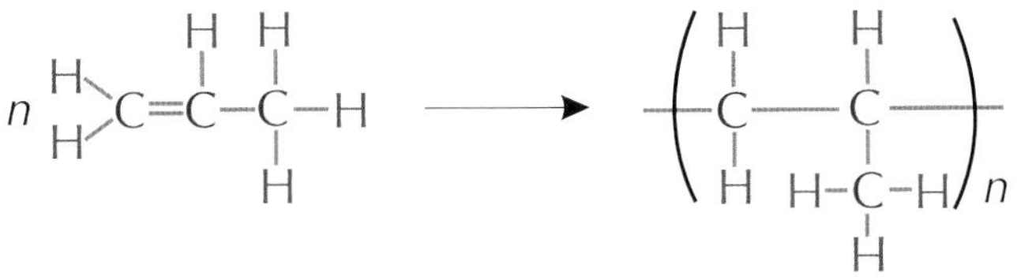

Many single propenes   *Poly(propene)*

Figure 1: *The polymerisation of propene monomers to form poly(propene).*

Finding monomers and naming polymers

In the exam, you might be given a polymer and asked to draw the monomer that makes it. All you have to do is take the bit of the polymer that repeats, remove the bonds from either side and add a double bond into it.

The monomer that makes this polymer is...

Polymer → Remove outside bonds → Add double bond → Monomer

Tip: To find the polymer that is made from a monomer you do the opposite — take out the double bond and add bonds to either side.

You could also be asked to name a polymer that you haven't come across before. Naming polymers is easy. All you have to do is put 'poly' in front of the name of the monomer.

The polymer that is formed from but-2-ene is called poly(but-2-ene).

The polymer that is formed from bromoethene is called poly(bromoethene).

Exam Tip
You don't have to learn any of these names. You'll be given the name of the monomer if you need to name a polymer in the exam — you just need to remember to add 'poly' to it.

Properties and uses of polymers

The physical properties of a polymer depend on what it's made from. Polyamides are usually stronger than poly(ethene), for example.

A polymer's physical properties are also affected by the temperature and pressure of polymerisation. Poly(ethene) made at 2000 atmospheres pressure and 200 °C is flexible, and has low density. But poly(ethene) made at 60 °C and a few atmospheres pressure with a catalyst is rigid and dense.

The fact that different polymers have different properties means they are useful for different things.

- Light, stretchable polymers such as low density poly(ethene) are used to make plastic bags.

- Elastic polymer fibres are used to make super-stretchy LYCRA® fibre for tights.

New uses for polymers are developed all the time. Some waterproof coatings for fabrics are made of polymers, and so are many new packaging materials. Dental polymers are used in resin tooth fillings. Polymer hydrogel wound dressings keep wounds moist.

Memory foam is an example of a **smart material**. It's a polymer that gets softer as it gets warmer. Mattresses can be made of memory foam — they mould to your body shape when you lie on them.

Problems with using polymers

HOW SCIENCE WORKS

Most polymers aren't "**biodegradable**" — they're not broken down by microorganisms, so they don't rot. This means it's difficult to get rid of them — if you bury them in a landfill site, they'll still be there years later. The best thing is to reuse them as many times as possible and then recycle them if you can. However, new biodegradable packaging materials are being developed. Plastic bags and other biodegradable plastics made from polymers and cornstarch are being produced.

Things made from polymers are usually cheaper than things made from metal. However, as crude oil resources get used up, the price of crude oil will rise. Crude oil products like polymers will get dearer. It may be that one day there won't be enough oil for fuel and plastics and all the other uses. Choosing how to use the oil that's left means weighing up advantages and disadvantages on all sides.

Figure 2: *Plastic waste in a landfill site.*

Practice Questions — Fact Recall

Q1 Describe what happens during a polymerisation reaction.

Q2 Give two factors that affect the physical properties of a polymer.

Q3 What property of memory foam makes it a good material to make mattresses out of?

Q4 a) What does the term biodegradable mean?

b) Are most polymers biodegradable or non-biodegradable?

Q5 Explain why the cost of making things from polymers is likely to rise in the future.

Practice Questions — Application

Q1 What is the name of the polymer that is formed from chloroethene?

Q2 Draw the monomers that each of these polymers are made from:

a) $\left(\begin{array}{cc} F & H \\ | & | \\ -C-C- \\ | & | \\ H & H \end{array}\right)_n$

b) $\left(\begin{array}{cc} F & F \\ | & | \\ -C-C- \\ | & | \\ F & F \end{array}\right)_n$

Q3 Draw the polymer that would be formed from each of these monomers:

a) $\underset{H}{\overset{H}{\diagdown}}C=C\underset{Br}{\overset{H}{\diagup}}$

b) $\underset{H}{\overset{H}{\diagdown}}C=C\underset{OH}{\overset{H}{\diagup}}$

Section Checklist — Make sure you know...

Cracking Crude Oil

☐ That long-chain hydrocarbons can be broken down into shorter, more useful hydrocarbons using a process known as cracking.

☐ That some of the products that are made when long-chain molecules are cracked are useful as fuels, while others are useful as raw materials for making other substances, such as plastics.

☐ That cracking is a type of thermal decomposition reaction (a reaction where molecules are broken down by heating them).

☐ That the first step in the cracking process is to vaporise the long-chain hydrocarbon (turn it into a gas). The vapour is then passed over an aluminium catalyst at high temperatures (around 400 - 700 °C) or mixed with steam and heated to a very high temperature.

☐ That cracking can be used to produce alkanes and alkenes.

Using Crude Oil

☐ That using crude oil is bad for the environment because oil spills can occur when the oil is transported and burning crude oil contributes to global warming, global dimming and acid rain.

☐ That crude oil is a non-renewable resource and will eventually run out.

☐ Some of the advantages and disadvantages of using products from crude oil.

Alkenes and Ethanol

☐ That alkenes are unsaturated hydrocarbons that contain a carbon-carbon double bond and have the general formula C_nH_{2n}.

☐ That alkenes are described as unsaturated because the double bond can open up, allowing the two carbon atoms to bond with other atoms.

☐ How to recognise alkenes like ethene and propene from their chemical and displayed formulae.

☐ How bromine water can be used to test for the presence of alkenes in a solution.

☐ That ethanol can be made by hydrating ethene with steam in the presence of a catalyst.

☐ That ethanol can also be produced by fermenting sugars.

☐ The relative advantages and disadvantages of using ethene and fermentation to produce ethanol.

Using Alkenes to Make Polymers

☐ That many small alkene molecules (monomers) can be joined together to form long polymers.

☐ How to represent polymerisation reactions using diagrams and how to find the monomer that is used to make a particular polymer (and vice versa).

☐ How the properties of a polymer influence what the polymer is used for.

☐ That most polymers are non-biodegradable and this makes them difficult to dispose of.

☐ That new biodegradable polymers are being developed that contain cornstarch.

Exam-style Questions

1   Polyvinyl chloride (PVC) is a very commonly used type of plastic.
     This diagram shows the structure of PVC.

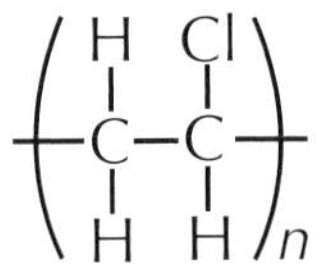

$$\left(\begin{array}{cc} H & Cl \\ | & | \\ -C & -C- \\ | & | \\ H & H \end{array}\right)_n$$

1 (a)   Draw the monomer that can be used to make PVC.

(2 marks)

1 (b)   The monomer used to make PVC can be made from ethene (C_2H_4).
     Ethene is produced from fractions of crude oil by a process called cracking.

1 (b) (i)   What type of hydrocarbon is ethene?

(1 mark)

1 (b) (ii)   Describe how a fraction of crude oil could be cracked.

(4 marks)

1 (b) (iii)   Ethene can be used to make many things other than polymers.
     Name the product that is made when ethene is reacted with steam
     in the presence of a catalyst.

(1 mark)

2   Propene is an alkene. Like other alkenes, propene can undergo polymerisation.

2 (a) (i)   What is the general formula of an alkene?

(1 mark)

2 (a) (ii)   Are alkenes saturated or unsaturated? Explain your answer.

(2 marks)

2 (a) (iii)   Describe a chemical test that can be used to show that alkenes
     are present in a solution

(2 marks)

2 (b) (i)   Give the name of the polymer that will be formed form propene.

(1 mark)

2 (b) (ii)   Describe what happens when propene undergoes polymerisation.

(2 marks)

2 (c)   Lots of people recycle polymers. Explain why it is important to
     reduce the amount of polymer waste going into landfill sites.

(2 marks)

1. Plant Oils

You can get oils from lots of different plants. They're pretty useful too — they go into all sorts of food products and you can even turn them into fuels.

Extracting oils from plants

Some fruits, nuts and seeds contain a lot of oil.

> **Examples**
>
> - Avocados and olives are oily fruits.
>
> - Sesame oil, rapeseed oil and sunflower oil are all made from seeds.
>
> - Peanuts, almonds and walnuts are used to make nut oils.

Oil can be extracted from plant material by crushing and pressing it, or using distillation.

Crushing and pressing

One way to get the oil out is to crush the plant material. The crushed plant material is then pressed between metal plates to squash the oil out — see Figure 1. This is the traditional method of producing olive oil.

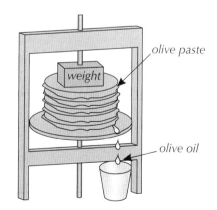

Figure 1: Extracting olive oil.

The oil needs to be separated from any water and crushed plant material that has been collected with it. This is often done using a centrifuge — the oily paste is spun round at very high speeds and this causes the oil and the water to separate out.

Learning Objectives:

- Know that you can extract oil from some plant material.

- Understand how oils can be extracted from oily fruits, seeds and nuts by crushing and pressing them.

- Understand how plant oils can be extracted using distillation.

- Know that vegetable oils are good foods because they contain energy and important nutrients.

- Be able to explain why vegetable oils are used to cook food.

- Know that vegetable oils can be turned into fuels.

Specification Reference C1.6.1

Figure 2: A working olive oil press.

Distillation

Another way to extract oils from plant material is **distillation**. This is when you heat the plant material until the oils that are in it **evaporate**. Then you collect the vapour and cool it down so that it **condenses** back into pure liquid oil.

The plant material is usually heated using steam. Water is boiled to make the steam, which is then passed down a pipe and over the plant material. This method is usually used to extract oils from delicate plant material, like lavender flowers. The apparatus that you need for steam distillation is shown in Figure 3.

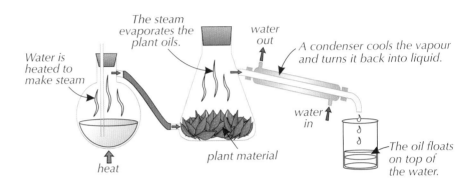

The steam evaporates the plant oils.

Water is heated to make steam

water out

A condenser cools the vapour and turns it back into liquid.

water in

heat

plant material

The oil floats on top of the water.

Figure 3: *Extracting plant oil using steam distillation.*

Often the oil and water is collected in a funnel with a tap on the bottom, called a separating funnel. This means that you can just open the tap and run the water off, leaving the layer of pure oil behind.

Uses of plant oils

Plant oils are used for lots of things. They are used to flavour or cook food, and they can even be turned into fuels.

Using plant oils in food

Vegetable oils make good foods because they provide us with a lot of energy — they have a high energy content. There are lots of useful nutrients in vegetable oils too.

> **Examples**
>
> - Oils from seeds contain vitamin E.
> - Vegetable oils contain essential fatty acids, which the body needs for many metabolic processes.

Figure 4: *Cooking a stir fry. Because of the high temperature of the vegetable oil, the food cooks very quickly.*

Using plant oils to cook

There are a number of advantages of using oils to cook food. Vegetable oils have higher boiling points than water, so they can be used to cook foods at higher temperatures. This means that the food cooks faster.

Cooking with vegetable oil also gives food a different flavour. This is because of the oil's own flavour, but it's also down to the fact that many flavours come from chemicals that are soluble in oil. This means the oil 'carries' the flavour, making it seem more intense.

Using oil to cook food increases the energy we get from eating it. This makes it fattening — eating lots of food cooked in oil makes us put on weight.

Using plant oils as fuels

Vegetable oils such as rapeseed oil and soybean oil can be processed and turned into fuels. Because vegetable oils can provide a lot of energy they're really suitable for use as fuels.

Example

A particularly useful fuel made from vegetable oils is called **biodiesel**. Biodiesel has similar properties to ordinary diesel fuel — it burns in the same way, so you can use it to fuel a diesel engine.

Tip: There's more about biodiesel on page 173.

Practice Questions — Fact Recall

Q1   Plant oils can be extracted from fruits like olives by pressing them.

a) Outline the basic method that is used to extract oil from olives.

b) Give one way that the oil could be separated from any water and plant material that has been collected with it.

Q2   Some plant oils can't be extracted just by crushing the plant. Name one other way of extracting oils from plants.

Q3   Vegetable oils in food provide us with a lot of energy. Give one other reason why vegetable oils make good foods.

Q4   Cooking food in vegetable oil is quicker than cooking it in boiling water.

a) Explain why food cooks quicker in vegetable oil than in water.

b) Give one other advantage of cooking food in vegetable oil.

c) Give one disadvantage of cooking food in vegetable oil.

Q5   Vegetable oils can be turned into fuels.

a) Why are vegetable oils suitable for use as fuels?

b) Name one example of a fuel that is made from vegetable oils.

Tip: There's more about the advantages and disadvantages of using oils and fats in food coming up in the next topic.

Learning Objectives:

- Know that unsaturated oils contain carbon-carbon double bonds.
- Be able to describe a simple test for unsaturation in oils using bromine water.
- **H** Understand how unsaturated oils react with hydrogen in the presence of a nickel catalyst at 60 °C.
- **H** Know that the reaction with hydrogen is used to harden vegetable oils.
- **H** Be able to explain why hardened vegetable oils are useful.
- Know some of the health effects of using different oils and fats in foods.

Specification Reference C1.6, C1.6.3

Exam Tip
If an exam question asks you to give the result of the bromine water test, make sure you only use the words decolourised or colourless. <u>Don't</u> say 'clear' or 'transparent' — you won't get the mark.

2. Unsaturated Oils

Vegetable oils, like olive oil, are liquids at room temperature, whereas animal fats, like lard, tend to be solid instead. This is down to whether they're saturated or unsaturated, and it affects what they can be used for.

What is an unsaturated oil?

Oils and fats contain long-chain molecules with lots of carbon atoms. They can be either **saturated** or **unsaturated**. Unsaturated oils contain double bonds between some of the carbon atoms in their carbon chains. Saturated fats don't contain any carbon-carbon double bonds.

There are two types of unsaturated fat. **Monounsaturated fats** contain one C=C double bond somewhere in their carbon chains. **Polyunsaturated fats** contain more than one C=C double bond.

Testing for unsaturation

You can test for unsaturation using bromine water. Bromine water is orange, but it will decolourise when you add an unsaturated oil to it (see Figure 1).

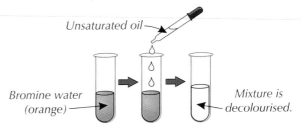

Unsaturated oil

Bromine water (orange)

Mixture is decolourised.

Figure 1: *An unsaturated oil decolourises bromine water.*

Hydrogenation of unsaturated oils   Higher

Unsaturated vegetable oils are liquid at room temperature. They can be hardened by reacting them with hydrogen in the presence of a nickel catalyst at about 60 °C. This is called **hydrogenation**. The hydrogen adds to the double-bonded carbons, opening out the double bonds.

> **Example** **Higher**
>
> Hydrogenating the unsaturated hydrocarbon ethene makes the saturated hydrocarbon ethane.
>
>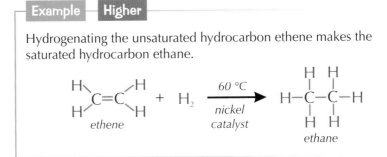
>
> *ethene*   *60 °C nickel catalyst*   *ethane*

Hydrogenated oils have higher melting points than unsaturated oils, so they're more solid at room temperature. This means that they can be used as spreads — many margarines are made from hydrogenated vegetable oils.

Hydrogenated oils are used in the food industry for baking cakes and pastries. The oils are a lot cheaper than butter and they keep longer — this makes the products cheaper and gives them a long shelf life.

The more you hydrogenate an oil, the more saturated fat it will contain and the harder it will become. Fats are often only partially hydrogenated so that they don't become too solid.

| Example | Higher |

Margarine is usually made from partially hydrogenated vegetable oil — turning all the double bonds in vegetable oil to single bonds would make margarine too hard and difficult to spread. Hydrogenating most of them gives margarine a nice, buttery, spreadable consistency.

Vegetable oils and health

Vegetable oils tend to be unsaturated, while animal fats tend to be saturated. In general, saturated fats are less healthy than unsaturated fats, as saturated fats increase the amount of cholesterol in the blood, which can block up the arteries and increase the risk of heart disease. Unsaturated fats like olive oil reduce the amount of blood cholesterol.

Cooking food in oil, whether saturated, unsaturated or partially hydrogenated, makes it more fattening. That's why it's healthier to use cooking methods that don't involve oil.

Figure 2: A food information label. The markings show that this pie contains high levels of fat and saturated fat.

Practice Questions — Fact Recall

Q1 What is the difference between a saturated oil and an unsaturated oil?

Q2 Describe a test that you could do to find out if an oil is unsaturated.

Q3 Unsaturated vegetable oils can by hydrogenated to harden them.

a) Give the catalyst and the temperature used for this reaction.

b) Give one use of hydrogenated vegetable oils.

Q4 Explain why unsaturated fats are healthier than saturated fats.

Practice Question — Application

Q1 The melting points of two samples of sunflower oil are shown in the table. One has been hydrogenated and the other has not.

Sample	Melting point (°C)
X	38
Y	−17

a) Which sample is the hydrogenated oil? Explain your answer.

b) Which sample will contain a higher proportion of unsaturated fat?

c) What would you expect to see if bromine water was added to sample Y? Explain your answer.

Tip: H Remember, hydrogenating oils gets rid of double bonds.

- Know that oils will not dissolve in water.
- Understand what an emulsion is.
- Know how to make an emulsion.
- Understand that an emulsion will have different properties from the liquids used to make it.
- Know some examples of emulsions.
- Know that an emulsifier will stop an emulsion from separating out.
- **H** Understand how emulsifier molecules can stop an emulsion separating out.
- Know the advantages and disadvantages of using emulsifiers in foods.

Specification Reference
C1.6, C1.6.2

3. Emulsions

When you mix a watery liquid and an oily fat together and shake you end up with an emulsion. Emulsions have loads of uses, especially in foods.

Making emulsions

Oils don't dissolve in water. However, you can mix an oil with water to make an **emulsion**. Emulsions are made up of lots of droplets of one liquid suspended in another liquid. You can make an emulsion by putting two liquids that don't mix (like oil and water) into a sealed container and giving it a really good shake.

There are two main types of emulsion — an oil-in-water emulsion (oil droplets suspended in water) or a water-in-oil emulsion (water droplets suspended in oil) — see Figure 1.

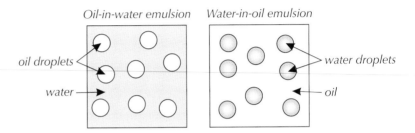

Oil-in-water emulsion   *Water-in-oil emulsion*

oil droplets

water

water droplets

oil

Figure 1: *An oil-in-water emulsion and a water-in-oil emulsion.*

Figure 2: *Some vinegar and oil in a bottle (left) and the emulsion that is formed when the bottle is shaken (right).*

Uses of emulsions

Emulsions are thicker than either oil or water. Generally, the more oil you've got in an oil-in-water emulsion, the thicker it is. The physical properties of emulsions make them suited to lots of uses in food.

> **Examples**
>
> - Some salad dressings and sauces are emulsions. A salad dressing made by shaking olive oil and vinegar together forms an emulsion that coats salad better than plain oil or plain vinegar. An emulsified salad dressing has a smooth and glossy appearance too.
>
> - Mayonnaise is an emulsion of sunflower oil (or olive oil) and vinegar — it's thicker than either.
>
> - Milk is an oil-in-water emulsion with not much oil and a lot of water. There's about 3% oil in full-fat milk. Single cream has a bit more oil (about 18%). Double cream has lots of oil (nearly 50%) — that's why it's so much thicker than single cream.
>
> - Whipped cream and ice cream are oil-in-water emulsions with an extra ingredient — air. Air is whipped into cream to give it a fluffy, frothy consistency for use as a topping. Whipping air into ice cream gives it a softer texture, which makes it easier to scoop out of the tub.

Emulsions also have non-food uses. Most moisturising lotions are oil-in-water emulsions. The smooth texture of an emulsion makes it easy to rub into the skin. Some paints are emulsions too — their creamy texture makes them easy to apply to the wall and gives them a smooth, even appearance when they dry.

Emulsifiers

Oil and water mixtures naturally separate out. **Emulsifiers** can be added to emulsions to make them more stable and stop them from separating.

> **Examples**
>
> ▪ Lots of salad dressings contain emulsifiers, like egg yolk or lecithin. They help to keep the emulsion stable, so the dressing can sit on the shelf of a shop (or your cupboard) for a long time without separating out.
>
> ▪ Ice creams often contain emulsifiers too — they help keep the texture of the product nice and smooth.

Tip: Lecithin is a substance that acts as an emulsifier. It's found naturally in egg yolks, which is why egg yolks make good emulsifiers.

Tip: Texture is just how something feels.

How emulsifiers work   Higher

Emulsifiers are molecules with one part that's attracted to water and another part that's attracted to oil or fat (see Figure 3). The bit that's attracted to water is called **hydrophilic**, and the bit that's attracted to oil is called **hydrophobic**.

Hydrophilic head
(likes water, hates oil).

Hydrophobic tail
(likes oil, hates water).

Figure 3: An emulsifier molecule.

The hydrophilic end of each emulsifier molecule latches onto water molecules. The hydrophobic end of each emulsifier molecule attaches to oil molecules.

When you shake oil and water together with a bit of emulsifier, the oil forms droplets, surrounded by a coating of emulsifier with the hydrophilic bit facing outwards. Other oil droplets are repelled by the hydrophilic bit of the emulsifier, while water molecules latch on. So the emulsion won't separate out (see Figure 4).

Exam Tip H
Hydro- means 'water'.
-phobic means 'hating' (like a phobia) and -philic means 'loving'. So hydrophobic = 'water hating' and hydrophilic = 'water loving'.
It's important to use technical terms correctly in exams.

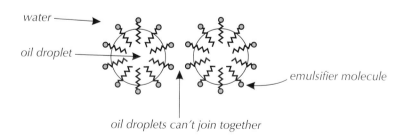

water

oil droplet

emulsifier molecule

oil droplets can't join together

Figure 4: How emulsifier molecules prevent an emulsion separating out.

Figure 5: Emulsifiers in action. The salad dressing without an emulsifier (left) has separated out. The salad dressing with an emulsifier (right) has not separated.

Advantages and disadvantages of emulsifiers

You need to know the advantages and disadvantages of using emulsifiers.

Advantages

- Emulsifiers stop emulsions from separating out and this gives them a longer shelf-life.

- Emulsifiers allow food companies to produce food that's lower in fat but that still has a good texture.

Disadvantages

- Some people are allergic to certain emulsifiers. For example, egg yolk is often used as an emulsifier — so people who are allergic to eggs need to check the ingredients very carefully.

Tip: Low fat margarines contain less fat and more water than normal margarines. Emulsifiers help them to keep a nice spreadable texture. Otherwise you'd end up with a gunky mess of separated water, oils and hard fats.

Practice Questions — Fact Recall

Q1 Do oils dissolve in water?

Q2 a) Draw a simple diagram showing an oil-in-water emulsion.

b) Give one way that the physical properties of an oil-in-water emulsion will be different to the properties of either oil or water.

Q3 a) Name two food products that are emulsions.

b) Name one non-food product that is an emulsion.

Q4 a) What job does an emulsifier do?

b) Give one advantage and one disadvantage of using emulsifiers in food products.

Q5 a) Draw and label an emulsifier molecule.

b) Explain how emulsifier molecules stop an emulsion separating.

Practice Questions — Application

Exam Tip
Make sure you can remember how to make an emulsion — it's a simple little detail, but it might just come up.

Q1 Kevin has 30 ml of olive oil and 10 ml of vinegar.
He wants to make them into an emulsion to use as a salad dressing.

a) Describe how Kevin could prepare the emulsion.

Anna is also making a salad dressing. She has the same amount of oil and vinegar as Kevin, but she decides not to mix them.

b) Which method will make a better salad dressing?
Explain your answer.

Q2 Polysorbate 80 is a commonly used emulsifier. What does this tell you about the structure of a molecule of Polysorbate 80?

Section Checklist — Make sure you know...

Plant Oils

☐ That some plants contain oils, which you can extract.

☐ How to get oils out of nuts, seeds and fruits by crushing and pressing them.

☐ How to get oils out of other plant material using distillation.

☐ That vegetable oils in food provide you with energy and useful nutrients.

☐ Why you might choose to cook food in vegetable oil rather than boiling water.

☐ That you can make fuels (like biodiesel) from vegetable oils because they contain lots of energy.

Unsaturated Oils

☐ That unsaturated oils have double bonds in their carbon chains.

☐ That an unsaturated oil will decolourise bromine water.

☐ H That an unsaturated oil will react with hydrogen in the presence of a nickel catalyst at 60 °C, opening out its double bonds. This is called hydrogenation.

☐ H That hydrogenation makes oils harder.

☐ H Some of the uses of hydrogenated vegetable oils.

☐ Why unsaturated oils are better for you than saturated fats.

☐ That all oils are fattening because they contain lots of energy.

Emulsions

☐ That oil does not dissolve in water.

☐ That an emulsion is a mixture where lots of tiny droplets of one liquid are suspended in another liquid.

☐ That you can make an emulsion by shaking water and oil in a sealed container.

☐ That an emulsion will be thicker than either the oil or water it was made from.

☐ That salad dressings, mayonnaise, ice creams, moisturisers and paints are examples of emulsions.

☐ That emulsifiers make emulsions more stable and stop them from separating out.

☐ H That an emulsifier molecule has a hydrophilic end and a hydrophobic end.

☐ H How emulsifier molecules stops emulsions from separating out.

☐ Some of the advantages and disadvantages of using emulsifiers in food products.

Exam-style Questions

1 A student tested whether some common kitchen substances could act as emulsifiers.

1 (a) Explain why you might add an emulsifier to an emulsion.

(1 mark)

The student measured out oil and water into six test tubes. He added his test substances and shook each tube well. Then he timed how long it took for each emulsion to separate out. His results are shown below.

Tube	A	B	C	D	E	F
Substance added to oil and water	Nothing	Washing-up liquid	Salt	Sugar	Mustard	Vinegar
Time taken to separate (mins)	5	40	4.5	5	42	4.5

1 (b) (i) Name the substance(s) in the table that can act as emulsifiers.

(1 mark)

1 (b) (ii) Explain your answer to part **(i)**.

(2 marks)

2 Cottonseed oil is used in the food industry to make biscuits and as a cooking oil.

2 (a) Suggest how oil could be extracted from cottonseeds.

(1 mark)

2 (b) Cottonseed oil contains 25% saturated fat. Olive oil contains 15% saturated fat. Explain why cottonseed oil might be considered less healthy than olive oil.

(2 marks)

2 (c) Give **one** reason you might choose to cook a food in cottonseed oil rather than water.

(1 mark)

2 (d) Before cottonseed oil can be used in baking it needs to be hardened. Describe how this could be done.

(3 marks)

1. Plate Tectonics

When a scientist puts forward a theory it can be ages before that theory is generally accepted by the scientific community. A perfect example of this is Alfred Wegener and his theory of continental drift. Read on to find out more.

Wegener's theory of continental drift

The Earth's surface isn't smooth — it's covered in mountains and valleys. In the olden days, scientists thought that these structures were formed due to the surface of the Earth shrinking as the Earth cooled down after it was formed. But scientists now think that the Earth's surface is split up into big chunks called **tectonic plates** and that mountains are formed when these tectonic plates collide.

The idea that the Earth's surface is not stable and is made up of parts that move was first put forward by Alfred Wegener. He proposed a theory known as the theory of **continental drift**.

Wegener said that about 300 million years ago, there had been just one 'supercontinent'. This landmass, called Pangaea (see Figure 1), broke into smaller chunks which moved apart. He claimed that these chunks (our modern-day continents) were still slowly 'drifting' apart.

Evidence for continental drift

Alfred Wegener came across some work listing the fossils of very similar plants and animals which had been found on opposite sides of the Atlantic Ocean (see Figure 2).

Figure 1: *Pangaea — what the Earth looked like 300 million years ago according to Wegener's theory.*

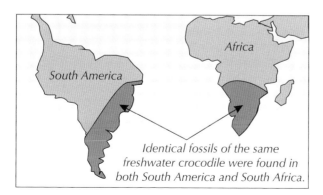

Identical fossils of the same freshwater crocodile were found in both South America and South Africa.

Figure 2: *Map showing the locations of identical fossils found in Africa and South America.*

Tip: This discovery suggested to Wegener that South America and Africa were once close together.

He investigated further, and found other cases of very similar fossils on opposite sides of oceans.

Wegener had also noticed that the coastlines of Africa and South America seemed to 'match' like the pieces of a jigsaw. He wondered if these two continents had previously been one continent which then split. He started to look for more evidence, and found it.

Figure 3: A Mesosaurus fossil. Fossils like this were used as evidence for continental drift.

Example

There were matching layers in the rocks in different continents and fossils had been found in the 'wrong' places. Fossils of tropical plants had been discovered on Arctic islands, where the present climate would clearly have killed them off.

In 1915, Wegener felt he had enough evidence and he published his theory of "continental drift".

The reaction to Wegener's theory

The reaction from other scientists to Wegener's theory was mostly very hostile. A few scientists supported Wegener, but most of them didn't see any reason to believe such a strange theory. There were two main reasons why other scientists thought that Wegener's theory was wrong.

1. Wegener couldn't explain how the continents moved

The main problem was that Wegener's explanation of how the 'drifting' happened wasn't very convincing. At the time, other scientists thought that the continents were fixed and couldn't move and Wegener didn't have any evidence that the continents were moving.

Tip: Wegener's story is a classic example of how science works — someone puts forwards a theory, other scientists test the theory and when there's enough evidence to support it, the theory is accepted.

HOW SCIENCE WORKS

Wegener thought that the continents were 'ploughing through' the sea bed, and that their movement was caused by tidal forces and the earth's rotation. Other geologists said this was impossible. One scientist calculated that the forces needed to move the continents like this would also have stopped the Earth rotating. (Which it hadn't.) Wegener had used inaccurate data in his calculations, so he'd made some rather wild predictions about how fast the continents ought to be moving apart.

2. Land bridges could explain a lot of Wegener's evidence

Lots of Wegener's evidence for continental drift was based on things like similar fossils being found on the opposite sides of oceans and matching layers of rock on different continents.

Other people had noticed this too and in 1920, scientists came up with an alternative theory to explain Wegener's evidence. They thought that there had once been land bridges linking the continents — so animals had been able to cross (see Figure 4). The bridges had 'sunk' or been covered over since then.

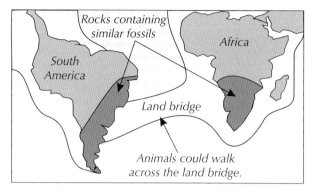

Figure 4: *Map showing how a land bridge could have once existed between South America and Africa.*

Tip: Scientists accepted the land bridge theory because at the time it was the only explanation that made sense. We now know that the continents aren't fixed and it seems unlikely that land bridges would have existed... how times change.

If Wegener's evidence could be explained by a different, more believable theory, why should they believe Wegener's theory of continental drift? It probably didn't help that Wegener wasn't a 'proper' geologist — he'd studied astronomy.

Acceptance of Wegener's theory

In the 1950s, scientists were able to investigate the ocean floor and found new evidence to support Wegener's theory. He wasn't right about everything, but his main idea was correct. By the 1960s, geologists were convinced. We now think the Earth's crust is made of several chunks called tectonic plates which move about, and that colliding chunks push the land up to create mountains.

Practice Questions — Fact Recall

Q1 a) How did scientists think that mountains were formed before Wegener's theory of continental drift?

b) How do scientists think that mountains are formed now?

Q2 Outline Wegener's theory of continental drift.

Q3 Wegener said that finding similar fossils on opposite sides of oceans was evidence that the continents were once close together. Suggest an alternative explanation.

- Be able to describe the structure of the Earth with reference to the crust, mantle and core.
- Know that the Earth is surrounded by the atmosphere.
- Know that the heat generated by radioactive decay in the mantle causes convection currents.
- Know that the Earth's crust, atmosphere and oceans are the source of all our resources, including minerals.
- Understand that the Earth's crust is split up into tectonic plates.
- Know that movement of the tectonic plates is driven by convection currents.
- Understand that the tectonic plates mostly move very slowly, just a few cm per year, but that movements can be sudden.
- Know that earthquakes and volcanic eruptions occur at plate boundaries and understand why they are unpredictable.

Specification Reference
C1.7, C1.7.1

2. The Earth's Structure

Wegener's theory of continental drift really made people think about what the structure of the Earth might be like. Now we know loads about the structure of the Earth... here's a summary.

The layers of the Earth

The Earth is almost spherical and it has a layered structure. The bit we live on, the **crust**, is very thin (it varies between 5 km and 50 km) and is surrounded by the **atmosphere**.

At the centre of the Earth is the **core**, which we think is made of iron and nickel. The core is the thickest layer of the Earth.

Surrounding that is the **mantle**. The mantle is about 2900 km thick and has all the properties of a solid, except that it can flow very slowly in convection currents. These convection currents are caused by the large amounts of heat produced by radioactive decay in the core below. The structure of the Earth is shown in Figure 1.

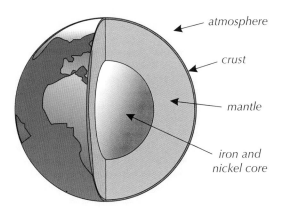

atmosphere

crust

mantle

iron and nickel core

Figure 1: *Structure of the Earth.*

The Earth's resources

The Earth's crust, oceans and atmosphere are the ultimate source of minerals and resources — we can get everything we need from them.

> **Examples**
>
> - Metals like gold and silver can be mined from the Earth's crust.
> - We can get salt from the Earth's oceans.
> - Gases like oxygen and nitrogen can be extracted from the atmosphere.

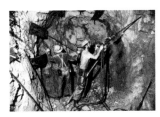

Figure 2: *Silver being mined from the Earth's crust.*

Tectonic plates

The crust and the upper part of the mantle are cracked into a number of large pieces called **tectonic plates**. These plates are a bit like big rafts that 'float' on the mantle.

The plates don't stay in one place though. That's because the convection currents in the mantle cause the plates to drift. The map in Figure 3 shows the edges of the plates as they are now, and the directions they're moving in (blue arrows).

Tip: The term 'mantle dynamics' can be used to describe the convection currents within the mantle.

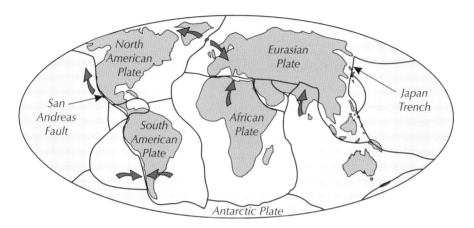

Figure 3: The tectonic plates that make up the surface of the Earth.

Exam Tip
Don't panic! You don't need to know the names and locations of the plates for your exam. As long as you get the general concept you'll be fine.

Most of the plates are moving at speeds of a few centimetres per year relative to each other. Occasionally, the plates move very suddenly, causing an earthquake. Volcanoes and earthquakes often occur at the boundaries between two tectonic plates.

Tip: Alfred Wegener was the first person to suggest that the continents may drift. See page 199 for more on Wegener's theory of continental drift.

Predicting earthquakes

HOW SCIENCE WORKS

Tectonic plates can stay more or less put for a while and then suddenly lurch forwards. Earthquakes are impossible to predict accurately because we can't see what's happening deep underground, but scientists are trying to find out if there are any clues that an earthquake might happen soon — things like strain in underground rocks.

Scientists can use these clues to predict that an earthquake will happen, but these predictions are sometimes ignored by local people and governments. Here are the reasons why.

- Even with all their clues scientists can only say that an earthquake's likely to happen, not that it definitely will happen. Scientists make many earthquake predictions every year and not all of them are right.

- If the earthquake does happen, it's impossible to predict exactly when. The earthquake could happen months after the initial prediction.

Figure 4: Damage to buildings following an earthquake.

- There's no way to accurately predict the strength of the earthquake. Many earthquakes cause little or no damage.

- Scientists can't accurately predict exactly where the earthquake will happen — it could be miles away from where it was initially predicted to happen.

- There's no way to stop an earthquake, so the only way that people can respond to a predicted earthquake is to evacuate. This is expensive and very inconvenient, so people don't want to evacuate unless they are sure that the earthquake will happen imminently, will happen where they live and will be strong enough to cause some serious damage and put their lives at risk.

Figure 5: A volcano erupting.

Predicting volcanic eruptions

There are some clues that say a volcanic eruption might happen soon. Before an eruption, molten rock rises up into chambers near the surface, causing the ground surface to bulge slightly. This causes mini-earthquakes near the volcano. But sometimes molten rock cools down instead of erupting, so mini-earthquakes can be a false alarm.

Practice Questions — Fact Recall

Q1 What is the outer layer of the Earth (the bit we live on) called?

Q2 Describe the properties of the mantle in terms of whether it is a solid or a liquid.

Q3 What do we think the Earth's core is made from?

Q4 What drives the movement of tectonic plates?

Q5 How quickly are most tectonic plates moving?

Q6 Where do earthquakes and volcanoes usually occur?

Q7 Give three things that scientists cannot accurately predict about an earthquake.

Practice Questions — Application

Q1 Catania is a city in Italy that is located near to an active volcano. In the last few days there have been some mini-earthquakes in the city and some of the residents are starting to evacuate.

a) Why are some of the residents evacuating?

b) Suggest why not all of the residents are evacuating.

Q2 Palmdale is a city in the USA. It lies on the San Andreas Fault, the location of which is shown in Figure 3 on page 203. Lots of earthquakes happen in Palmdale. Explain why.

3. The Evolution of the Atmosphere

The Earth's atmosphere is really important — without it, life would never have evolved. This is the story of how the atmosphere came into being.

The atmosphere today

The Earth's **atmosphere** has been roughly as it is now for the last 200 million years or so. The main gases in the atmosphere are nitrogen and oxygen. Nitrogen is by far the most abundant gas — about four-fifths (80%) of the atmosphere is nitrogen. About one-fifth (20%) of the atmosphere is oxygen. There are small amounts of other gases in the atmosphere too. These include carbon dioxide, water vapour and noble gases (see page 125).

Formation of the early atmosphere and oceans

The Earth's surface was originally molten for many millions of years. It was so hot that any atmosphere just 'boiled away' into space. Eventually things cooled down a bit and a thin crust formed, but volcanoes kept erupting.

There was intense volcanic activity for the first billion years after the Earth was formed, and the volcanoes gave out lots of gas. Scientists think this was how the oceans and atmosphere were formed. There are lots of different theories, but the most popular theory suggests that the early atmosphere was probably mostly carbon dioxide (CO_2), with virtually no oxygen (O_2). There was probably water vapour too, and small amounts of methane (CH_4) and ammonia (NH_3). This is quite like the atmospheres of Mars and Venus today.

As the Earth cooled, the water vapour in the atmosphere condensed, forming the oceans.

Changes to the atmosphere

Although the early atmosphere was mostly carbon dioxide, it didn't stay that way for long. Most of the carbon dioxide was gradually removed from the atmosphere. This happened in a number of ways.

Absorption by the oceans

The oceans are a natural store of carbon dioxide. When the oceans formed, a lot of the carbon dioxide from the atmosphere dissolved into them.

Absorption by plants and algae

Green plants and algae evolved over most of the Earth. They absorbed some of the carbon dioxide in the atmosphere and used it for a process called **photosynthesis**. Photosynthesis produces oxygen as a by-product, so when the green plants and algae evolved, carbon dioxide was gradually removed from the atmosphere and oxygen was added.

Learning Objectives:

- Know that the composition of the atmosphere hasn't changed much in the last 200 million years.
- Know the relative abundances of nitrogen, oxygen and other gases in the atmosphere.
- Know that the early atmosphere and the oceans were formed due to volcanic activity.
- Know that one theory suggests that the early atmosphere was mainly made up of carbon dioxide.
- Know how carbon dioxide was removed from the atmosphere and that much of the carbon is now locked up in sedimentary rocks and fossil fuels.
- Know that the oxygen in the atmosphere was produced by plants and algae.
- Know that burning fossil fuels releases carbon dioxide back into the atmosphere and the environmental impacts this can have.
- H Understand how the gases in air can be separated using fractional distillation.

Specification Reference C1.7.2

Locking away the carbon

When the plants and algae that had absorbed the carbon dioxide died, they were buried under layers of sediment, along with the skeletons and shells of marine organisms that had slowly evolved. Some of the carbon inside these marine organisms was locked away as insoluble carbonates in sedimentary rocks.

Figure 1: *Limestone containing the fossilised remains of early marine organisms.*

> **Example**
>
> Limestone is a sedimentary rock that is formed from the shells and skeletons of marine organisms. A lot of the carbon from the carbon dioxide in the early atmosphere is now locked away in limestones.

Some of the carbon was locked away in fossil fuels such as coal and oil. These fossil fuels contain carbon and hydrocarbons that are the remains of plants and animals.

Problems of increasing carbon dioxide emissions

There is virtually no carbon dioxide left in the atmosphere now, but when we burn fossil fuels today, this 'locked-up' carbon is released and the concentration of carbon dioxide in the atmosphere rises. As the world has become more industrialised, more fossil fuels have been burnt in power stations and in car engines. This carbon dioxide is thought to be altering our planet in a couple of ways.

Global Warming

An increase in carbon dioxide is causing **global warming** — an increase in the average temperature of the Earth. Global warming is a type of **climate change** and it could lead to dramatic changes in our weather.

Tip: See page 171 for more on global warming and climate change.

Acidic oceans

The oceans are a natural store of carbon dioxide — they absorb it from the atmosphere. However the extra carbon dioxide we're releasing is making them too acidic. This could lead to the death of many marine organisms including corals and shellfish. It also means that in the future the oceans won't be able to absorb any more carbon dioxide and this could accelerate global warming.

Fractional distillation of air   Higher

Tip: Carbon dioxide that is extracted from the air in this way is used in some fire extinguishers.

You can fractionally distil air to get a variety of products (e.g. nitrogen and oxygen) that can be used as raw materials in industry. The air is first filtered to remove dust. It's then cooled to around −200 °C and becomes a liquid. During cooling water vapour condenses and is removed. Carbon dioxide freezes, so that can be removed too.

The remaining gases are separated by **fractional distillation**. The fractional distillation of air is possible because the gases in air have different boiling points. This means that they will condense at different temperatures.

The liquefied air (with the water vapour and CO_2 removed) enters the fractionating column and is heated slowly so that it vaporises again. The gas then travels up the column and gradually cools. The different gases are extracted at the different levels in the column where they condense. Oxygen and argon come out together so another column is used to separate them.

The process of separating air is shown in Figure 2.

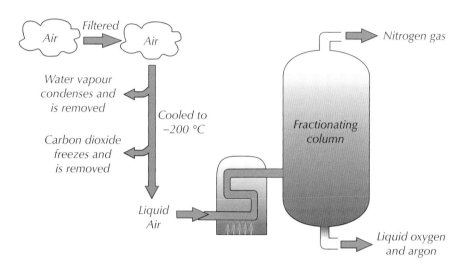

> **Tip:** The fractional distillation of air is very similar to the fractional distillation of crude oil (see pages 164-165).

Figure 2: *Separating air using fractional distillation.*

Practice Questions — Fact Recall

Q1   What are the two most abundant gases found in the Earth's atmosphere today?

Q2   Describe the likely composition of the Earth's early atmosphere.

Q3   How did the Earth's oceans form?

Q4   Why did the evolution of green plants and algae lead to a decrease in the concentration of carbon dioxide in the atmosphere?

Q5   What happened to most of the carbon from the carbon dioxide in the early atmosphere?

Q6   a) Name the gas released when fossil fuels are burnt that is thought to be contributing to global warming.

   b) How is the increase in the concentration of this gas in the atmosphere affecting the Earth's oceans?

Q7   Name the process that can be used to separate air into its component gases.

Figure 3: *A fossil fuel power station.*

Practice Question — Application

Tip: This graph is an estimate of how the composition of the atmosphere has changed over time. No one knows for sure how the atmosphere has changed so scientists have to use the evidence they have to make the best guess they can. *(HOW SCIENCE WORKS)*

Q1 This graph shows how the composition of gases in the atmosphere has changed over the last 4.5 billion years.

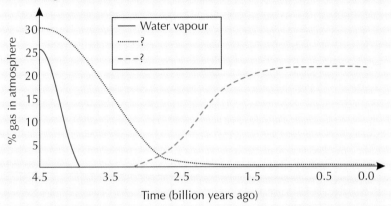

a) Describe and explain the change in the concentration of water vapour in the atmosphere between 4.5 and 4 billion years ago.

b) The other two lines on the graph are not labelled. Suggest which gases these lines represent, giving reasons for your answers.

Q2 This graph shows how the acidity of the oceans has changed over the last 150 years.

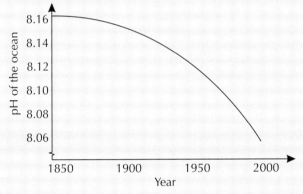

Tip: pH is a measure of how acidic something is — the lower the pH, the more acidic it is.

a) Describe how the pH of the oceans has changed over the last 150 years.

b) Suggest a possible explanation for this change.

c) What consequences could these changes have in the long term?

4. Life on Earth

Living organisms have been around for billions of years. No one really knows how life on Earth started, but there have been lots of theories.

Evolution of life

There are lots of different theories to explain how life might have evolved.

> **Example** — **Higher**
>
> The **primordial soup theory** states that billions of years ago, the Earth's atmosphere was rich in nitrogen, hydrogen, ammonia and methane (a hydrocarbon). Lightning struck, causing a chemical reaction between the gases, resulting in the formation of amino acids. The amino acids collected in a 'primordial soup' — a body of water out of which life gradually crawled. The amino acids gradually combined to produce organic matter which eventually evolved into simple living organisms.
>
> In the 1950s, Miller and Urey carried out an experiment to prove this theory. They sealed a mixture of the relevant gases in their apparatus, heated them and applied an electrical charge for a week. They found that amino acids were made, but not as many as there are on Earth. This suggests the theory could be along the right lines, but isn't quite right.

The mystery of life Higher

All the theories to explain how life began are just that — theories. We may never know for certain how or why life began. The problem is, life started about 3 billion years ago, so it's unlikely that any evidence of the earliest life forms will still be around today. We can guess, but we can't really know for sure what the conditions were like when life started and we don't yet have the capability to test a lot of the theories.

Learning Objectives:
- Know that there are many theories to explain how life on Earth might have started.
- H Know that one of these theories is the primordial soup theory.
- H Understand why we don't know for certain how life began.

Specification Reference
C1.7, C1.7.2

Practice Questions — Fact Recall

Q1 How did life begin according to the 'primordial soup' theory?

Q2 Explain why we can't be certain how life began.

Section Checklist — Make sure you know...

Plate Tectonics

☐ How scientists used to think mountains were formed and how they think mountains are formed now.

☐ That Alfred Wegener's theory of continental drift suggested that our modern day continents were originally one land mass (called Pangaea) which broke into chunks that gradually drifted apart.

☐ Why it took a long time for Wegener's theory of continental drift to be accepted.

cont...

The Earth's Structure

☐ That the Earth has a layered structure consisting of a core, a mantle and a crust and that the Earth is surrounded by an atmosphere.

☐ That the mantle is mostly solid but can flow very slowly and that radioactive decay in the core generates heat which drives convection currents in the mantle.

☐ That we can get all the minerals and other resources that we need from the Earth's crust, the atmosphere and the Earth's oceans.

☐ That the Earth's crust is divided into chunks called tectonic plates and that the movement of these tectonic plates is driven by the convection currents in the mantle.

☐ That movement of most tectonic plates is very slow (a few cm per year) but that earthquakes and volcanic eruptions can occur at the boundaries between tectonic plates if the plates move suddenly.

☐ Why earthquakes and volcanoes are difficult to predict and why scientists' predictions of earthquakes and volcanic eruptions are often ignored.

The Evolution of the Atmosphere

☐ That the composition of the atmosphere has been roughly the same for the last 200 million years — 80% nitrogen, 20% oxygen, with small amounts of carbon dioxide, water vapour and noble gases.

☐ That the early atmosphere was formed from gases that were released by volcanoes and that the oceans were formed when the Earth cooled, allowing the water vapour in the air to condense.

☐ That according to one theory, the early atmosphere was mostly carbon dioxide with small amounts of water vapour, methane (a hydrocarbon) and ammonia, but very little oxygen.

☐ That a lot of the CO_2 in the early atmosphere either dissolved into the oceans or was absorbed by green plants and algae when they evolved — there is now very little CO_2 left in the atmosphere.

☐ That green plants and algae used the CO_2 in photosynthesis — a process that produces oxygen.

☐ That when ancient plants, algae and marine organisms died, the carbon from the CO_2 they had absorbed was locked away in fossil fuels and as carbonates in sedimentary rocks.

☐ That burning fossil fuels today releases carbon dioxide back into the atmosphere.

☐ That the concentration of carbon dioxide in the atmosphere is increasing and that this is causing global warming and the oceans (which absorb CO_2) to become more acidic.

☐ 🄷 That fractional distillation can be used to separate air into it's component gases, according to their boiling point — these gases can then be used as raw materials in industry.

☐ 🄷 That prior to fractional distillation, air is filtered to remove dust and cooled to −200 °C so the water vapour and carbon dioxide can be removed from it.

Life on Earth

☐ That there are many theories as to how life on Earth might have begun.

☐ 🄷 That one theory is the primordial soup theory. This states that lightning struck causing a chemical reaction between nitrogen, hydrogen, hydrocarbons (like methane) and ammonia in the air, which led to the formation of amino acids.

☐ 🄷 Why it is impossible to know exactly how life started billions of years of ago.

Exam-style Questions

1 This diagram shows the structure of the Earth.

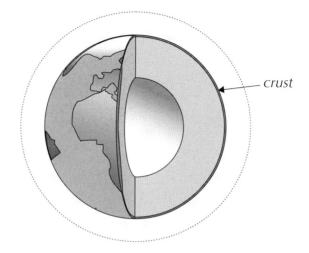

crust

1 (a) Complete the diagram by labelling the atmosphere, the core and the mantle.

(3 marks)

1 (b) The Earth's crust is divided into tectonic plates that move relative to one another.

1 (b) (i) The idea that the continents move was first proposed by Alfred Wegener in 1915. Give **two** pieces of evidence that supported Wegener's theory of continental drift.

(2 marks)

1 (b) (ii) Suggest why Wegener's theory was not initially accepted by other scientists.

(1 mark)

1 (c) Scientists now know that the movement of tectonic plates is driven by convection currents in the mantle.

1 (c) (i) What process produces the heat that drives the convection currents in the mantle?

(1 mark)

1 (c) (ii) Complete the sentence below describing the movement of tectonic plates.

Most tectonic plates move very ...., at a rate of a

few .... per year.

(2 marks)

1 (d) The movement of tectonic plates can be sudden. In 2011, sudden movements of tectonic plates caused an earthquake that resulted in a tsunami hitting Japan.

Put an X on this map to mark a possible location of the earthquake.

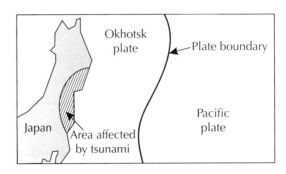

(2 marks)

2 The composition of the Earth's atmosphere has changed a lot over the last 4.5 billion years.

2 (a) Name the gas that is most abundant in our atmosphere today.

(1 mark)

2 (b) Scientists think that the most abundant gas in the atmosphere 4.5 billion years ago was carbon dioxide. Now, there is almost no carbon dioxide in our atmosphere.

2 (b) (i) Where did the gases that formed the early atmosphere come from?

(1 mark)

2 (b) (ii) Give **two** reasons why the concentration of carbon dioxide in the atmosphere decreased to the level that it is at today.

(2 marks)

2 (c) The burning of fossil fuels is now causing the concentration of carbon dioxide in the atmosphere to rise again. Give **two** environmental impacts that increased levels of carbon dioxide in the atmosphere may cause.

(2 marks)

2 (d) Some scientists believe that life may have evolved from the gases in the early atmosphere. Describe **one** theory to explain how life may have begun.

(3 marks)

1. Infrared Radiation

When you feel the heat from a fire, what you're actually feeling is the infrared radiation given off by it. The temperature, colour and shininess of a surface all affect how much infrared radiation something emits...

What is heat radiation?

Heat radiation is the transfer of heat energy by **infrared (IR) radiation**. Infrared radiation can be emitted by solids, liquids and gases.

All objects are continually emitting and absorbing infrared radiation. Infrared radiation is emitted from the surface of an object.

Rate of infrared transfer

Several factors affect the rate at which radiation is emitted or absorbed by an object.

Temperature

An object that's hotter than its surroundings emits more radiation than it absorbs (as it cools down). And an object that's cooler than its surroundings absorbs more radiation than it emits (as it warms up).

The hotter an object is, the more radiation it radiates in a given time.

Example

You can feel this infrared radiation if you stand near something hot like a fire or if you put your hand just above the bonnet of a recently parked car.

The engine and bonnet of a recently parked car is hotter and so emits more infrared radiation.

Figure 1: *The amount of infrared radiation emitted from the bonnet of a recently parked car (left) and the same car an hour after parking (right).*

Learning Objectives:

- Know that all materials emit and absorb infrared radiation.
- Understand that the hotter an object is, the higher its rate of emission of infrared radiation.
- Know that matt and dark-coloured surfaces are good at absorbing and emitting infrared radiation.
- Know that shiny and light-coloured surfaces are poor at absorbing and emitting infrared radiation.
- Know that shiny and light-coloured surfaces are good at reflecting infrared radiation.

Specification Reference P1.1.1

Tip: Remember, the car bonnet is also absorbing infrared radiation. All objects absorb and emit infrared radiation all the time. The car bonnet is just emitting more infrared radiation than it absorbs because it's warmer than its surroundings.

Figure 2: *Many houses have
roofs lined with metallic foil
to reflect infrared radiation
and stop it escaping from the
house.*

Surface colour and texture

The amount of infrared radiation emitted or absorbed by a surface depends on its colour and texture, as well as its temperature.

Dark, matt surfaces absorb infrared radiation falling on them much better than light, shiny surfaces, such as gloss white or silver. They also emit much more infrared radiation (at any given temperature).

Light, shiny surfaces reflect a lot of the infrared radiation falling on them. This makes them great for reducing the amount of energy transferred by radiation.

Example

Vacuum flasks (see p.226) have silver inner surfaces to keep heat in or out, depending on whether it's storing hot or cold liquid.

Practice Questions — Fact Recall

Q1 What is heat radiation?

Q2 Will an object that's hotter than its surroundings emit or absorb more infrared radiation overall?

Q3 How will increasing an object's temperature affect the rate at which it emits infrared radiation?

Q4 Describe a surface that would be good at absorbing infrared radiation.

Q5 Describe a surface that would be poor at emitting infrared radiation.

Q6 What type of surface is good at reflecting infrared radiation?

Practice Question — Application

Q1 The diagram below shows two ball bearings attached to two metal plates with wax. Each metal plate is put at the same distance from a Bunsen burner. The plates are identical, except that one plate has a matt black back surface, while the other has a shiny silvered surface.

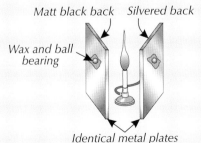

Matt black back   Silvered back

Wax and ball
bearing

Identical metal plates

Eventually the heat from the Bunsen burner will heat up the metal plates, melt the wax and cause the ball bearings to drop. Which ball bearing will drop first? Explain your answer.

2. Kinetic Theory

Kinetic theory isn't as hard as it sounds — it's just about describing the jiggling about of particles in solids, liquids and gases...

States of matter

The three states of matter are solid (e.g. ice), liquid (e.g. water) and gas (e.g. water vapour). The particles of a particular substance in each state are the same — only the arrangement and energy of the particles are different. The energy an object (or particle) has because of its movement is called its kinetic energy (see p.240).

Solids

In solids, strong forces of attraction hold the particles close together in a fixed, regular arrangement. The particles don't have much energy so they can only vibrate about their fixed positions.

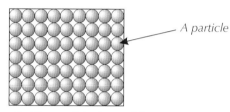

— *A particle*

Figure 1: *The particles in a solid.*

Liquids

There are weaker forces of attraction between the particles in liquids. The particles are close together, but can move past each other, and form irregular arrangements. They have more energy than the particles in a solid — they move in random directions at low speeds.

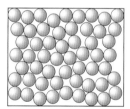

Figure 2: *The particles in a liquid.*

Gases

There are almost no forces of attraction between the particles in a gas. The particles have more energy than those in liquids and solids — they are free to move, and travel in random directions and at high speeds.

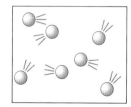

Figure 4: *The particle arrangement in a gas.*

Learning Objectives:

- Know the three states of matter — solid, liquid and gas.
- Know that the particles in each state of matter have different amounts of energy.
- Be able to use kinetic theory to explain the properties of solids, liquids and gases.
- Understand and recognise simple models showing the differences between the particles in different states of matter.

Specification Reference P1.1.2

Exam Tip
You might be asked to use a picture or model in the exam to describe a state of matter — so make sure you know this page inside out.

Figure 3: *The three states of water — ice, water and water vapour.*

Figure 5: *The heat energy from this person's hand is enough to melt the gallium metal they are holding.*

When you heat a substance, you give its particles more kinetic energy (E_k) — they vibrate or move faster. This is what eventually causes solids to melt and liquids to boil.

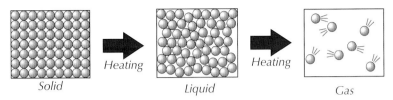

Figure 6: *A diagram to show how heating can change the state of a substance, and the particle arrangement in each state.*

Example

As a solid is heated, its particles gain energy and vibrate more. If the solid is heated enough, eventually the particles have enough energy to be able to move past each other. At this point the solid melts and becomes a liquid.

Tip: Remember, a substance has the same type of particles whether it's a solid, liquid or gas — only the arrangement and energy of the particles change.

Properties of solids, liquids and gases

You can use kinetic theory to explain the properties of different states of matter.

- Gases and liquids can flow because their particles can move past each other. The particles in a solid can't move anywhere — they can only vibrate in their fixed positions, so solids can't flow.

- Gases are compressible. The particles in a gas are very spread out, which means you can squash a gas into a smaller volume — you're just reducing the distance between particles. The particles in liquids and solids can't really get much closer together, which is why only gases are compressible.

Practice Questions — Fact Recall

Q1 What are the three states of matter?

Q2 Describe the arrangement and energy of the particles in a solid.

Q3 Describe how the arrangement of particles in a liquid is different to that in a solid.

Q4 In which state of matter do particles have the most energy?

Q5 A solid is heated and melts. In terms of particles, explain why:

a) the solid becomes a liquid.

b) a liquid can flow, but a solid can't.

The diagram below shows a box filled with small light polystyrene balls. A small fan is fitted at the bottom of the box. This apparatus can be used to model the particles in different states of matter.

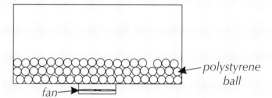

Q1   What state of matter is modelled by the balls at the bottom of the box when the fan is turned off? Explain your answer.

Q2   The fan is turned on, causing the small balls to fly around the inside of the box at high speeds.

   a) What state of matter do the balls now model?

   b) Name one property of the balls that has been increased by turning on the fan that is also increased when the particles of a substance are heated.

- Know that conduction and convection are both processes where energy is transferred by particles colliding with each another.
- Understand that whether a substance is a good insulator or conductor depends on the arrangement and movement of its particles.
- Understand the process of conduction and that it is the main method of heat transfer in solids.
- Understand that metals are good conductors because they contain free electrons.
- Describe how energy is transferred by convection in a liquid or gas.

Specification Reference
P1.1.3

Tip: The closer you have to be to people in a crowd, the more likely you are to bump into someone. It's the same idea with particles — the closer together they are, the more likely it is they'll bang into each other when they're vibrating.

3. Conduction and Convection

Energy is mostly transferred through solids by conduction, and through liquids and gases by convection. Both types of heat transfer happen because the particles in a substance move about...

Conduction

When you heat a solid, you give its particles extra kinetic energy and cause them to vibrate more. The particles collide with their neighbouring particles and pass some of their extra energy on to them. This is called **conduction**.

This process continues throughout the solid and gradually some of the extra kinetic energy (or heat) is passed all the way through the solid. This causes a rise in temperature at the other side of the solid, and hence an increase in the amount of heat radiating from the solid's surface.

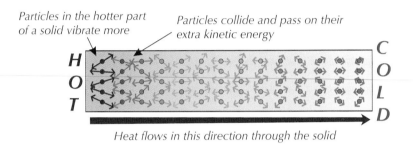

Particles in the hotter part of a solid vibrate more

Particles collide and pass on their extra kinetic energy

Heat flows in this direction through the solid

***Figure 1**: Conduction of energy through a solid.*

Rate of conduction

Usually conduction is faster in denser solids, because the particles are closer together and so will collide more often and pass energy between them. Materials that have relatively large spaces between their particles conduct heat energy much more slowly — these materials are insulators.

Conduction in metals

Metals are very good conductors. They "conduct" so well because they contain free electrons that are able to move inside the metal. At the hot end the electrons move faster and collide with other free electrons, transferring energy (see Figure 2). These other electrons then pass on their extra energy to other electrons and particles in the solid... and so it goes on.

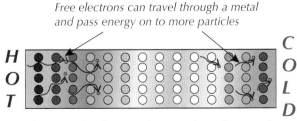

Free electrons can travel through a metal and pass energy on to more particles

***Figure 2**: Conduction of energy through a metal.*

Because the electrons can move freely, this is obviously a much faster way of transferring the energy through the metal than slowly passing it between jostling neighbouring atoms. This is why heat energy travels so quickly through metals.

Example

Saucepans are usually made from metal so energy from the cooker is transferred quickly to the pan and its contents.
Pan handles are usually made of an insulator so you don't end up burning your hand when touching the pan.

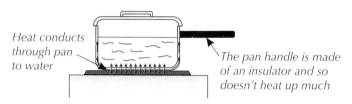

Heat conducts through pan to water

The pan handle is made of an insulator and so doesn't heat up much

Figure 3: Conduction of energy through a saucepan.

Convection

Convection occurs when the more energetic particles in a liquid or gas move from a hotter region to a cooler region — and take their heat energy with them.

Gases and liquids are usually free to slosh about — and that allows them to transfer heat by convection. Convection simply can't happen in solids because the particles can't move about as much, they can only vibrate.

Immersion heaters in kettles and hot water tanks and (unsurprisingly) convector heaters work using convection currents (see next page).

Immersion heaters

Figure 4 on the next page shows how an immersion heater heats water using convection. Here's how it works:

- Heat energy is transferred from the heater coils at the bottom of the tank to the water by conduction (see p 218). The particles near the coils get more energy, so they start moving around faster.

- This means there's more distance between them, i.e. the water expands and becomes less dense. This reduction in density means that the hotter water tends to rise above the denser, cooler water.

- As the hot water rises, the colder water sinks towards the heater coils. This cold water is then heated by the coils and rises — and so it goes on.

- You end up with convection currents going up, round and down, circulating the heat energy through the water.

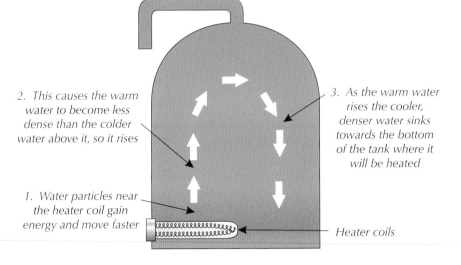

2. This causes the warm water to become less dense than the colder water above it, so it rises

3. As the warm water rises the cooler, denser water sinks towards the bottom of the tank where it will be heated

1. Water particles near the heater coil gain energy and move faster

Heater coils

Figure 4: *Heating by convection in an immersion heater. The white arrows show the flow of water inside the heater.*

Figure 5: *You can see convection currents by sticking some potassium permanganate crystals in the bottom of a beaker of cold water. Heat the beaker gently over a Bunsen flame — the potassium permanganate will start to dissolve and make a gorgeous bright purple solution that gets moved around the beaker by the convection currents as the water heats. It's real pretty.*

Convection currents are all about changes in density. Because the hot water rises (because of the lower density) you only get convection currents in the water above the heater. The water below it stays cold because there's almost no conduction.

Radiators

Heating a room with a radiator relies on convection currents too. Hot, less dense air by the radiator rises and denser, cooler air flows to replace it.

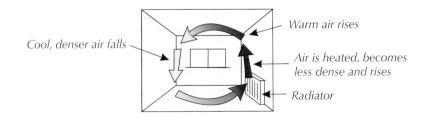

Warm air rises

Cool, denser air falls

Air is heated, becomes less dense and rises

Radiator

Figure 6: *A radiator heating a room by convection.*

Tip: The key thing to remember is that convection happens because a heated liquid or gas becomes less dense. This means it moves away from the hotter region to a cooler one, taking its energy with it.

Practice Questions — Fact Recall

Q1 What is conduction?

Q2 Which is more likely to be a good conductor — a material with smaller or larger spaces between its particles? Explain your answer.

Q3 Explain why metals are faster conductors than most other types of solid.

Q4 What is convection?

Q5 In which state of matter does convection not happen?

Q6 Describe how an immersion heater uses convection to heat water.

Practice Question — Application

Q1 A warm room has a window in its roof. The temperature of the window is lower than the rest of the room and cools the air near it. This sets up a convection current in the room and over time causes the temperature of the air in the room to drop.

In terms of particles, describe how and why the convection current is set up and how this cools the room.

- Know that energy transfers by evaporation and condensation involve particles.
- Be able to describe evaporation and condensation using kinetic theory.
- Be able to explain the cooling effect of evaporation.
- Know what factors will change the rate of evaporation or condensation of a substance.

Specification Reference
P1.1.3

Figure 1: *The water vapour leaving a kettle is invisible. It becomes visible when it condenses, which is why there's a gap between the steam and kettle spout seen here.*

Tip: Remember, the boiling point is the temperature at which a liquid becomes a gas.

4. Condensation and Evaporation

Just like conduction and convection, condensation and evaporation can both be explained through the joy of particle movements...

Condensation

When a gas cools, the particles in the gas slow down and lose kinetic energy. The attractive forces between the particles pull them closer together.

If the temperature gets cold enough and the gas particles get close enough together that condensation can take place, the gas becomes a liquid.

Examples

Water vapour in the air condenses when it comes into contact with cold surfaces, e.g. drinks glasses.

The steam you see rising from a boiling kettle is actually invisible water vapour condensing to form tiny water droplets as it spreads into cooler air (see Figure 1).

Evaporation

Evaporation is when particles escape from a liquid and form a gas. Particles can evaporate from a liquid at temperatures that are much lower than the liquid's boiling point.

Particles near the surface of a liquid can escape and become gas particles if:

- The particles are travelling in the right direction to escape the liquid.

- The particles are travelling fast enough (they have enough kinetic energy) to overcome the attractive forces of the other particles in the liquid.

Figure 2 shows the position and velocity of some particles in a beaker of liquid.

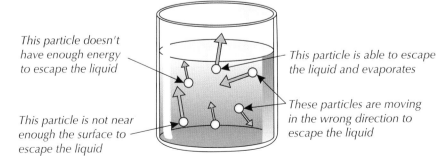

This particle doesn't have enough energy to escape the liquid

This particle is able to escape the liquid and evaporates

This particle is not near enough the surface to escape the liquid

These particles are moving in the wrong direction to escape the liquid

Figure 2: *A diagram to show why certain particles in a liquid can or cannot evaporate from a liquid. The arrows show the velocity of each particle.*

The cooling effect of evaporation

The fastest particles (with the most kinetic energy) are most likely to evaporate from the liquid — so when they do, the average speed and kinetic energy of the remaining particles decreases.

This decrease in average particle energy means the temperature of the remaining liquid falls — the liquid cools. This cooling effect can be really useful.

> **Example**
>
> Sweating when you exercise or get hot helps your body keep cool.
> As the water from the sweat on your skin evaporates, it cools you down.

Tip: This is tricky stuff, but you need to make sure you can explain why evaporation from a liquid causes it to cool. Remember, it's usually the particles with the highest energies that escape, so the energy of a typical particle in the liquid left behind is likely to be lower.

Rates of evaporation and condensation

The rates of evaporation and condensation of liquids and gases can vary.

Evaporation

The rate of evaporation will be faster if the...

- Temperature is higher.
  The average particle energy will be higher, so more particles will have enough energy to escape.

- Density of the liquid is lower.
  The forces between the particles will usually be weaker, so more particles will have enough energy to overcome these forces and escape the liquid.

- Surface area of the liquid is larger.
  More particles will be near enough to the surface to escape the liquid. The nearer to the surface a particle is, the less energy it needs to be able to escape. So having more particles near the surface means more of them will have the energy to escape.

Tip: The average energy of the particles in both liquids in Figure 3 is the same, but the nearer a particle is to the surface of a liquid, the less energy it needs to escape. More particles will be near the surface of the liquid with the greater surface area, so more particles will have enough energy to evaporate.

Only one of these particles can escape

Many more particles have enough energy to escape the water with the higher surface area because they're nearer the surface.

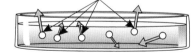

Figure 3: *Two beakers containing the same volume of water at the same temperature, but with different surface areas.*

- Airflow over the liquid is greater.
  The lower the concentration of an evaporating substance in the air it's evaporating into, the higher the rate of evaporation. A greater airflow means air above the liquid is replaced more quickly, so the concentration in the air will be lower.

Figure 4: *Condensation of water vapour on a window. The colder the window, the higher the rate of condensation of water onto it.*

Condensation

The rate of condensation will be faster if the...

- Temperature of the gas is lower.
  The average particle energy in the gas is lower — so more particles will slow down enough to clump together and form liquid droplets.

- Temperature of any surface the gas touches is lower (see Figure 4).

- Concentration is higher.
  Concentration is just a measure of the number of particles of the gas per unit volume. The higher the concentration of a gas, the stronger the forces between the particles will be. Fewer particles will have enough energy to overcome these forces and so more particles will clump together and form a liquid.

Practice Questions — Fact Recall

Q1 In terms of particles, explain what happens when a gas condenses.

Q2 What is responsible for water vapour becoming visible steam — evaporation or condensation?

Q3 What is evaporation?

Q4 What does a particle need to be able to escape a liquid at a temperature below the liquid's boiling point?

Q5 Explain why evaporation from a liquid causes the liquid left behind to cool down.

Q6 Give four ways you could increase the rate of evaporation of a liquid.

Q7 Give three ways you could increase the rate of condensation of a gas.

Practice Question — Application

Q1 In terms of particles, explain why blowing air across a hot drink will cause it to cool quicker than if it is just left to cool unaided.

5. Rate of Energy Transfer

Different objects can lose or gain heat much faster than others — even in the same conditions. Here are some of the many fascinating differences that can cause different energy transfer rates — enjoy.

What affects rate of energy transfer?

The temperature of the object and its surroundings

The bigger the temperature difference between a body and its surroundings, the faster energy is transferred by heating. Kinda makes sense.

> **Example**
>
> Food cools quicker if you put it in the fridge rather than leaving it out in a warm room, as the temperature difference between the food and its surroundings is greater.

Surface area

Heat energy is radiated from the surface of an object. The bigger the surface area, the more infrared waves that can be emitted from (or absorbed by) the surface — so the quicker the transfer of heat.

> **Examples**
>
> Radiators have large surface areas to maximise the amount of heat they transfer. This is why car and motorbike engines often have 'fins' — they increase the surface area so heat is radiated away quicker so the engine cools quicker.
>
> Heat sinks are devices designed to transfer heat away from objects they're in contact with, e.g. computer components (see Figure 2). They have fins and a large surface area so they can emit heat as quickly as possible.

***Figure 1**: Cooling fins on a motorbike engine.*

Surface area to volume ratio

The higher the proportion of an object that's in contact with its surroundings, the more radiation it will emit per second, i.e. the rate of energy transfer will be higher. This proportion is given by the **surface area to volume ratio** of the object.

> The higher the surface area to volume ratio, the higher the rate of energy transfer between an object and its surroundings.

Learning Objectives:

- Know how the rate of energy transfer from an object depends on many factors, including: surface area, volume, the material it is made from, the substance(s) the object is in contact with.

- Know that the rate of energy transfer between an object and its surroundings is higher the bigger the temperature difference is between them.

- Be able to explain the design of objects designed to maximise or reduce the rate of heat energy transfer.

- Be able to explain how animals have adapted to their environments, in terms of heat transfer.

Specification Reference P1.1.3

The smaller the surface area to volume ratio of an object is, the smaller the proportion of the object's energy that will be given out per second.

Type of material

Objects made from good conductors (see p.218) transfer heat away more quickly than insulating materials, e.g. plastic.

It also matters whether the materials in contact with it are insulators or conductors. If a hot object is in contact with a conductor, the heat will be conducted away much faster than if it is in contact with a good insulator.

Figure 2: *A heat sink on a computer's motherboard. The heat sink is made of a conductor and has many flat fins to maximise its surface area to volume ratio. It transfers heat at a very high rate and keeps the computer components cool.*

Controlling heat transfer — products

You need to know about heat energy transfers and how products can be designed to reduce them. The vacuum flask is the classic example of a product designed to minimise heat transfer.

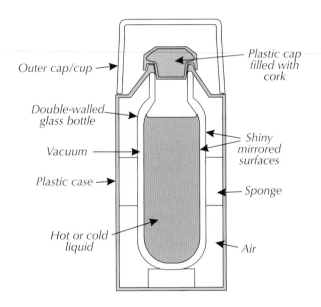

Outer cap/cup

Plastic cap filled with cork

Double-walled glass bottle

Vacuum

Shiny mirrored surfaces

Plastic case

Sponge

Hot or cold liquid

Air

Figure 3: *The structure of a vacuum flask.*

Exam Tip
If they ask you about energy transfer in the exam, you must always say which form of heat transfer is involved at any point — conduction, convection or radiation. You've got to show them that you know your stuff — it's the only way to get top marks.

- The glass bottle is double-walled with a vacuum between the two walls. This stops all conduction and convection through the sides.

- The walls either side of the vacuum are silvered to keep heat loss by radiation to a minimum.

- The bottle is supported using insulating foam. This minimises heat conduction to or from the outer glass bottle.

- The stopper is made of plastic and filled with cork or foam to reduce any heat conduction through it.

Controlling heat transfer — humans and animals

Humans and animals have different ways of controlling their rate of heat transfer to keep themselves at the right temperature.

- In the cold, the hairs on your skin 'stand up' to trap a thicker layer of insulating air around the body. This limits the amount of heat loss by convection. Some animals do the same using fur.

- When you're too warm, your body diverts more blood to flow near the surface of your skin so that more heat can be lost by radiation — that's why some people go pink when they get hot.

- Generally, animals in warm climates have larger ears than those in cold climates to help control heat transfer.

Example

Arctic foxes have evolved small ears, with a small surface area to minimise heat loss by radiation and conserve body heat.

Fennec foxes live in the desert — they have huge ears with a large surface area to allow them to lose heat by radiation easily and keep cool.

***Figure 4**: An arctic fox (left) and a fennec fox (right).*

- Animals in colder climates are also often larger than those in warmer climates. This gives them a smaller surface area to volume ratio, and so minimises the proportion of their energy they transfer to the surroundings each second (see p 225).

Practice Question — Fact Recall

Q1 How would increasing each of the following properties of an object and its surroundings affect the rate of energy transfer between them? (Assume all other factors affecting energy transfer remain the same.)

a) Decreasing the surface area to volume ratio of the object, for a given volume.

b) Increasing the temperature difference between the object and its surroundings.

c) Making the object from a material that's a better conductor.

d) Putting the object in contact with a better insulating material.

e) Increasing the temperature of both the object and its surroundings by the same amount.

Tip: Keeping all the other factors the same means only the variable you're changing affects the rate of energy transfer.

HOW SCIENCE WORKS

Practice Questions — Application

Q1 Antelope squirrels live in the desert and can survive in temperatures over 40 °C. They are much smaller in size than the grey squirrels found in the UK.

In terms of energy transfer, describe and explain one way antelope squirrels have adapted to their environment.

Q2 The picture shows an iron household radiator.

Suggest two ways the radiator has been designed to maximise the amount of energy it transfers to its surroundings.

6. Saving Energy in the Home

It's important to try and save energy where you can — it can help the environment as well as saving you some cash. One way of cutting down your bills is to install insulation in your home...

Types of building insulation

Different methods of insulation help reduce the amount of energy lost from your home in different ways. Here are some examples...

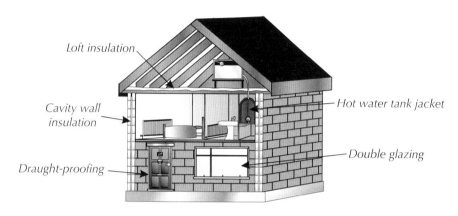

Figure 1: Different methods of insulating a home.

Cavity wall insulation

Houses usually have cavity walls made up of two layers of bricks separated by an air gap. Foam squirted into the gap between the bricks stops convection currents being set up in the gap and reduces the amount of radiation across the gap.

The insulating foam (and the air pockets trapped in it — air is an insulator) also helps reduce heat loss by conduction.

Loft insulation

Fibreglass is an insulating material made of thin strands of glass that trap pockets of air. A thick layer of fibreglass wool laid out across the whole loft floor reduces conduction, as the material (and the trapped air) are insulators. It also reduces heat loss by radiation, as heat no longer radiates directly from the loft floor surface into the roof space (see Figure 2).

Draught-proofing

Putting strips of foam and plastic around doors and windows stops draughts of cold air blowing in, i.e. they reduce heat loss due to convection.

Double glazing

Double-glazed windows are made up of two layers of glass or plastic, with a gap between them filled with air. This air gap helps reduce heat loss by conduction through the window, as air is a gas and does not conduct well.

Learning Objectives:
- Understand how types of building insulation reduce energy transfer.
- Understand the term 'payback time' and be able to calculate it for a type of insulation.
- Be able to evaluate how effective and cost-effective different types of insulation and materials are.
- Know that U-values are a measure of how insulating a material is.
- Know that the lower the U-value a material has, the better insulator it is.
- Know that solar hot water panels heat water using radiation from the Sun, and that this water can be used to heat a building or supply it with hot water.

Specification Reference P1.1.4

Figure 2: Loft insulation.

Tip: Make sure you know how each type of insulation helps reduce the energy lost from a home.

Hot water tank jacket

Putting fibreglass wool around a hot water tank reduces the heat lost from the tank by conduction and radiation in the same way as loft insulation.

Thick curtains

Big bits of cloth over the window to reduce heat loss by convection. The curtains trap air between them and the windows and separate it from the rest of the room. This means a convection current is only set up in this small region, rather than in the whole room.

Figure 3: *A hot water tank jacket.*

Exam Tip
Make sure you learn this equation — it won't be on the equations sheet you get given in the exam.

Effectiveness and cost-effectiveness

The most effective methods of insulation are ones that give you the biggest annual saving — they save the most energy and so save you the most money each year on your heating bills.

Eventually, the money you've saved on heating bills will equal the initial cost of putting in the insulation (the amount it cost to buy). The time it takes is called the **payback time**.

$$\text{payback time} = \frac{\text{inital cost}}{\text{annual saving}}$$

Example

Buying and installing cavity wall insulation costs £490 and will give an annual saving of £70 on energy bills. Calculate the payback time.

$$\text{payback time} = \frac{490}{70} = 7 \text{ years}$$

The most **cost-effective** methods of insulation tend to be the cheapest. They are cost-effective because they have a short payback time — this means the money you save covers the amount you paid really quickly.

Example

This table shows the payback times for two different types of insulation.

Type of insulation	Double glazing	Loft insulation
Initial cost (£)	3000	200
Annual saving (£)	60	50
Payback time (years)	50	4

Installing double glazing would save you more money each year than putting in loft insulation — it's a more effective method of insulation.

The payback time for loft insulation is much shorter than for double glazing, which makes it a much more cost-effective method of insulation.

U-values

U-values measure how effective a material is at insulating. Heat transfers faster through materials with higher U-values than through materials with low U-values. So the better the insulator (see p.218) the lower the U-value.

Tip: A material with a U-value of zero would be a perfect insulator — no energy would be able to transfer through it.

Example

The U-value of a typical duvet is about 0.75 W/m^2K, whereas the U-value of loft insulation material is around 0.15 W/m^2K.

Tip: For home insulation, you want to use materials with low U-values as they'll be good insulators.

Solar hot water panels

Another way of saving money on your energy bills is to use free energy sources to heat your home, such as energy from the Sun.

Solar hot water panels contain water pipes under a black surface (or black painted pipes under glass). Radiation from the Sun is absorbed by the black surface to heat the water in the pipes. This water can be used for washing or pumped to radiators to heat the building.

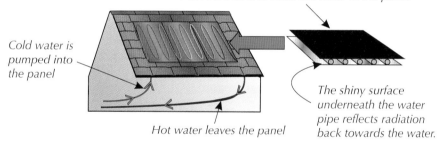

The matt, black outer surface absorbs radiation from the Sun and heats the water in the panel.

Cold water is pumped into the panel

The shiny surface underneath the water pipe reflects radiation back towards the water.

Hot water leaves the panel

Tip: Remember black, matt surfaces are good absorbers of infrared radiation, and silver, shiny surfaces are good reflectors (see p.214).

Figure 4: *A solar hot water panel has different surfaces to maximise the amount of heat energy transferred to the water inside it.*

Practice Questions — Fact Recall

Q1 Explain how installing each of the following types of insulation helps reduce energy loss from a home.

    a) Cavity wall insulation

    b) Loft insulation

    c) Double glazing

Q2 What is the equation for payback time?

Q3 What is the difference between the effectiveness and cost-effectiveness of building insulation?

Q4 What is U-value a measure of?

Q5 Give two possible uses for the water from a solar hot water panel.

Q1 The table shows the initial cost of installing three types of insulation and the annual saving each would give.

Type of insulation	Double glazing	Hot water tank jacket	Cavity wall insulation
Initial cost (£)	4500	15	432
Annual saving (£)	60	30	72

a) Use the data in the table to answer the following questions.

   i) Which type of insulation would be the most effective to install? Give a reason for your answer.

   ii) Would it be more cost-effective to install a hot water tank jacket or cavity wall insulation? Show your working.

b) A homeowner chooses to install a hot water tank jacket. They need to choose between materials to make the jacket. Material 1 has a U-value of 0.2 W/m^{2}K and material 2 has a U-value of 0.13 W/m^{2}K. Which material should they choose? Explain your answer.

7. Specific Heat Capacity

Some materials are easier to heat up than others. Specific heat capacity is a measure of how much energy it takes to change the temperature of a material.

Learning Objectives:

- Know that specific heat capacity is the amount of energy needed to change the temperature of 1 kg of a substance by 1 °C.

- Be able to use the equation $E = m \times c \times \theta$.

Specification Reference P1.1.4

What is specific heat capacity?

It takes more heat energy to increase the temperature of some materials than others. For example, you need 4200 J to warm 1 kg of water by 1 °C, but only 139 J to warm 1 kg of mercury by 1 °C.

Materials which need to gain lots of energy to warm up also release loads of energy when they cool down again. They can 'store' a lot of heat.

The measure of how much energy a substance can store is called its **specific heat capacity**.

> Specific heat capacity is the amount of energy needed to raise the temperature of 1 kg of a substance by 1 °C.

The formula for specific heat capacity

You'll have to do calculations involving specific heat capacity. This is the equation to use:

E = energy transferred (J) ⟶ $E = m \times c \times \theta$ ⟵ θ = temperature change (°C)

m = mass (kg) c = specific heat capacity (J/kg°C)

Tip: [H] If you're doing the higher paper, you'll need to be able to rearrange this equation. Using a formula triangle like this one can really help.

See page 381 for more on how to use formula triangles.

Example

Water has a specific heat capacity of 4200 J/kg°C.
How much energy is needed to heat 2 kg of water from 10 °C to 100 °C?

First work out the temperature difference, θ, between the starting and finishing temperatures.

$\theta = 100\ °C - 10\ °C = 90\ °C$

Then plug the numbers for m, c and θ into the formula to find E.

$E = m \times c \times \theta = 2 \times 4200 \times 90 = 756\ 000$ J

An empty 200 g aluminium kettle cools down from 115 °C to 10 °C, losing 19 068 J of heat energy. What is the specific heat capacity of aluminium?

Convert the mass of the kettle from grams to kilograms: 200 g = 0.2 kg.
The temperature difference, θ = 115 °C − 10 °C = 105 °C

Then rearrange the formula and plug in the values:

$$E = m \times c \times \theta, \text{ so } c = \frac{E}{m \times \theta} = \frac{19\,068}{0.2 \times 105} = 908 \text{ J/kg}°\text{C}$$

Using specific heat capacity

When picking a material to do a job, it can be worth thinking about its specific heat capacity. For example, if you wanted an object to be able to store a lot of energy or not heat up very quickly in hot conditions, a material with a high specific heat capacity would be best to use.

Figure 1: A household radiator. Central heating systems use pipes and radiators to pipe hot water around a building to heat it.

Heaters

The materials used in heaters usually have high specific heat capacities so that they can store large amounts of heat energy.

- Water has a really high specific heat capacity. It's also a liquid, so it can easily be pumped around in pipes — ideal for central heating systems in buildings.

- Electric storage heaters are designed to store heat energy at night (when electricity is cheaper), and then release it during the day. They store the heat using concrete or bricks, which (surprise surprise) have a high specific heat capacity (around 880 J/kg°C).

- Some heaters are filled with oil, which has a specific heat capacity of around 2000 J/kg°C. Because this is lower than water's specific heat capacity, oil heating systems are often not as good as water-based systems. Oil does have a higher boiling point though, which usually means oil-filled heaters can safely reach higher temperatures than water-based ones.

Practice Questions — Fact Recall

Q1 What is specific heat capacity?

Q2 Do materials used in heaters usually have a low or high specific heat capacity? Explain why these materials are used.

Q3 Give three examples of materials used in heaters because of their specific heat capacity.

Practice Questions — Application

Q1 A kettle heats 0.3 kg of water from a temperature of 20 °C to 100 °C. Water has a specific heat capacity of 4200 J/kg°C. How much energy does it take to heat the water?

Q2 This table shows the specific heat capacities of 3 different materials.

Material	Specific heat capacity in J/kg°C
water	4200
glass	837
steel	490

Use the information in the table to answer the following questions.

a) A fire lighter needs to cool down very quickly. Which material would be best to use to make a lighter? Explain your answer.

b) Which material would be the most effective to use in a heater? Explain your answer.

c) Placing a hot object on a heat mat stops heat being transferred and damaging the surface below it. Which material from the table would be the best to make a heat mat from? Explain your answer.

Q3 A chef heats 400 g of oil to a temperature of 113 °C. The oil is left to cool until it reaches a temperature of 25 °C. The oil transfers 70.4 kJ of energy to its surroundings. Calculate the specific heat capacity of the oil.

Section Checklist — Make sure you know...

Infrared Radiation

- [ ] That all objects absorb and emit infrared radiation all the time.
- [ ] The higher the temperature of an object, the more infrared radiation it will emit in a particular time.
- [ ] That dark and matt surfaces are good emitters and absorbers of infrared radiation.
- [ ] That light, shiny surfaces are poor emitters and absorbers of infrared radiation, but reflect it well.

Kinetic Theory

- [ ] That the three states of matter are solid, liquid and gas.
- [ ] How to describe the differences between the arrangement of particles in each state of matter.
- [ ] That gas particles of a substance have more energy than liquid particles, and both have more energy than the particles in a solid.
- [ ] How to recognise and use simple models to describe the differences between particles in different states of matter.

Conduction and Convection

- [ ] That conduction is the main method of heat transfer in solids.
- [ ] That the smaller the spaces between the particles in a solid, the better a conductor it is likely to be.
- [ ] That conduction is caused by vibrating particles colliding and passing on their extra kinetic energy to neighbouring particles.
- [ ] How free electrons are involved in conduction through a metal.
- [ ] That convection is the main method of heat transfer in liquids and gases.
- [ ] That convection happens when heating causes particles to gain extra kinetic energy and move apart, causing the heated liquid or gas to become less dense.

Condensation and Evaporation

- [ ] What condensation is.
- [ ] What evaporation is.
- [ ] How evaporation has a cooling effect on a liquid.
- [ ] How to vary the rate of evaporation of a liquid.
- [ ] How to vary the rate of condensation of a gas.

Rate of Energy Transfer

- [ ] How different factors affect the rate of energy transfer between an object and its surroundings.
- [ ] How to explain how the design of a device helps it reduce or maximise heat transfer.

cont...

☐ How to explain, in terms of heat transfer, how animals have adapted to their environments.

Saving Energy in the Home

☐ How different types of insulation help to reduce energy loss from a building.

☐ How to calculate the payback time for types of insulation.

☐ How to evaluate how effective and cost-effective installing different types of insulation is.

☐ That U-values are a measure of how good an insulator a material is. The better the insulator, the lower its U-value will be.

☐ How solar hot water panels heat water using radiation from the Sun.

Specific Heat Capacity

☐ That the specific heat capacity of a material is the amount of energy needed to change the temperature of 1 kg of that material by 1 °C.

☐ How to evaluate the use of different materials based on their specific heat capacities.

☐ How to use the equation $E = m \times c \times \theta$ to calculate the energy transferred to or from a material.

☐ 🅗 How to use the equation $E = m \times c \times \theta$ to calculate m, c or θ.

Exam-style Questions

1   A homeowner decides to insulate their loft using fibreglass loft insulation topped with a layer of silver foil.

1 (a) (i)   Complete the sentence by drawing a circle around the correct word.

The layer of silver foil helps reduce energy transferred from the house by
| conduction. |
| convection. |
| radiation. |

(1 mark)

1 (a) (ii)   Explain how the foil helps reduce energy transfer by this method.

(1 mark)

1 (b)   Describe how laying fibreglass insulation on the floor of the loft will help reduce the rate of energy transfer from the house to its surroundings.

(2 marks)

1 (c)   Explain why it's important for the homeowner to use a material with a low U-value to insulate his loft.

(1 mark)

1 (d)   The loft insulation costs £54 to install and will save the homeowner £30 a year on his energy bills. Calculate the payback time for the loft insulation.

(2 marks)

2   The diagram shows a metal heat sink used to keep a computer component cool.

2 (a)   Explain how the design of the heat sink helps it to control the temperature of the computer component.

(4 marks)

2 (b)   Many heat sinks are fitted with a fan to cool the air around them. In terms of energy transfer, explain why this is a useful feature for a heat sink to have.

(2 marks)

3   When people get hot, they sweat to control their rate of energy transfer. The liquid water that makes up sweat evaporates from the skin and helps to cool the person down. Standing in front of a fan can help a person to cool down more quickly.

3 (a)   Which of these pictures, A, B or C, shows the arrangement of particles in a liquid?

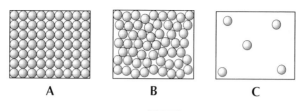

               A   **B**   **C**

Write your answer in the box.

(1 mark)

3 (b)   Describe the difference in energies between the particles in a gas and a liquid.

(1 mark)

3 (c)   *In this question you will be assessed on the quality of your English, the organisation of your ideas and your use of appropriate specialist vocabulary.*

    Explain, in terms of particles, how sweating helps to cool a person down and why using a fan can speed up this process.

(6 marks)

4   A kettle uses a heating coil at its base to heat water.

4 (a)   The coil transfers energy to the water next to it by conduction. Energy is transferred throughout the water by convection. Describe how the process of convection causes the water to heat up.

(4 marks)

4 (b)   The kettle holds 1.2 kg of water when it is filled. Water has a specific heat capacity of 4200 J/kg°C. Calculate the energy required to heat the water in a full kettle from 10 °C to 100 °C.

    Use the correct equation from the equations listed on page 381.

    Clearly show how you work out your answer. Give your answer in joules.

(3 marks)

4 (c)   A small amount of water vapour escapes from the spout of the kettle. The water vapour becomes visible a short distance away from the kettle.

4 (c) (i)   Name the process shown by water vapour becoming visible.

(1 mark)

4 (c) (ii)   Explain, in terms of particles, why the water vapour becomes visible a short distance from the kettle.

(3 marks)

Learning Objectives:

- Know that energy can't be created or destroyed — it is transferred usefully, stored or dissipated.
- Be able to describe the energy transfers that take place in different appliances, and the main ways they waste energy.

Specification Reference
P1.2, P1.2.1

1. Energy Transfer

Energy comes in loads of different forms, but it doesn't have to stay put — it can be converted into other types.

Types of energy

There are nine different types of energy. You need to know what they all are and where they're found. Handily, they're all in this table...

Type of energy	Example of where it is found or comes from
Electrical	Whenever a current flows
Light	From the Sun, light bulbs, etc
Sound	From loudspeakers or anything noisy
Kinetic (or movement)	Anything that's moving has it
Nuclear	Released only from nuclear reactions
Thermal (or heat)	Flows from hot objects to colder one
Gravitational potential	Possessed by anything which can fall
Elastic potential	Stretched springs, elastic, rubber bands, etc.
Chemical	Possessed by foods, fuels, batteries etc.

Gravitational potential, elastic potential and chemical are forms of **stored energy**. The energy is not obviously doing anything — it's kind of waiting to happen, i.e. waiting to be turned into one of the other forms.

The conservation of energy principle

There are plenty of different types of energy, but they all obey the principle below:

Energy can be transferred usefully from one form to another, stored or dissipated — but it can never be created or destroyed.

Tip: Dissipated is a fancy way of saying the energy is spread out and lost.

Examples

In a solar hot water panel, light energy from the Sun is transferred to heat energy (see page 231).

When an object falls, gravitational potential energy is transferred to kinetic energy. Some will be lost as heat and sound energy.

Energy transfer in devices

All the types of energy can be transferred to other types by different devices. Often a device transfers one type of energy into two or more different types.

Energy transfers in a device can be shown as arrows in a diagram, between the types of input and output energy.

Exam Tip
In the exam, they can ask you about any device or energy transfer system they feel like. If you understand a few different examples, it'll be easier to think through whatever they ask you about in the exam.

Examples

A television:

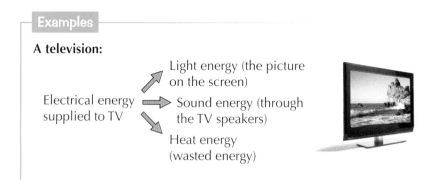

A battery-powered alarm:

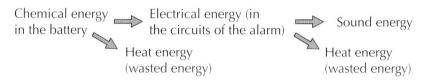

Tip: Anything that's battery powered will first transfer the chemical energy of the battery into electrical energy, then into other forms of energy.

Practice Questions — Fact Recall

Q1   What are the nine different types of energy?

Q2   What is the principle of conservation of energy?

Practice Questions — Application

Q1   Give an example of a device that causes the following energy transfers to occur.

a) Electrical energy to sound energy.

b) Elastic potential energy to kinetic energy.

c) Kinetic energy to sound energy.

Q2   Suggest what the main energy transfers are when each of the following devices are used.

a) A bow and arrow.   b) A computer.

c) A battery-powered torch.

Tip: Don't forget about the energy that's dissipated.

- Know that when
  energy is transferred,
  only some of it is
  transferred usefully
  and the rest is wasted.
- Be able to calculate
  the efficiency of a
  device as a decimal or
  a percentage.
- Understand that
  wasted energy
  eventually spreads out
  into the surroundings,
  causing them to
  become warmer.
- Be able to compare
  methods for reducing
  energy consumption
  in terms of efficiency
  and cost-effectiveness.
- Understand how
  'wasted' energy can
  be made useful, for
  example in heat
  exchangers.

Specification Reference
P1.2, P1.2.1

2. Efficiency of Machines

*Sometimes it's really handy to know how much energy a device wastes
compared to how much it usefully transfers — that's efficiency for you.*

Energy input and energy output

Useful devices are only useful because they can transform energy from one
form to another. In doing so, some of the energy that's supplied to the device
is always lost or wasted, often as heat.

The energy that's supplied to a device is called the **energy input**. The energy
that's transferred usefully is called its **useful energy output**. You can draw an
energy flow diagram like Figure 1 to show the useful (and wasteful) energy
transfers in a device — it's pretty much the same for all devices.

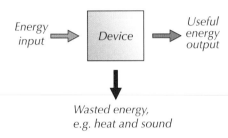

Figure 1: *An energy flow diagram for a device, showing the
input energy, useful output energy and waste energy.*

What counts as 'useful energy' depends on what the device is and what it's
meant to do.

Figure 2: *A radio is a useful
device because it transfers
most of the energy supplied
to it into sound energy (and
a small amount of light
energy). Some of the energy
is lost as heat.*

Example

A washing machine transfers electrical
energy to heat, kinetic and sound energy.
The sound energy isn't useful because it
doesn't help to clean the clothes, but the
kinetic and heat energy do.

Calculating efficiency

A machine is a device which turns one type of energy into another. The
less energy that is 'wasted', the more **efficient** the device is said to be. The
efficiency of any device is defined as:

$$\text{efficiency} = \frac{\text{useful energy out}}{\text{total energy in}}$$

You might not know the energy inputs and outputs of a machine, but you can still calculate the machine's efficiency as long as you know the power input and output. Power is the amount of energy transferred per second (see p.251).

$$\text{efficiency} = \frac{\text{useful power out}}{\text{total power in}}$$

You can give efficiency as a decimal or you can multiply your answer by 100 to get a percentage, i.e. 0.75 or 75%.

Exam Tip
An exam question will either tell you how much useful energy the machine delivers or it will tell you how much it wastes.

Tip: The units you use for power (or energy) aren't important here, as long as you use the same ones for in and out.

Example 1

A motor is supplied with 257 W of power and gives out 120 W of useful power. What is the efficiency of the motor? Give your answer as a decimal.

$$\text{efficiency} = \frac{\text{useful power out}}{\text{total power in}}$$
$$= \frac{120}{257}$$
$$= 0.467 \text{ (to 3 s.f.)}$$

So, the motor has an efficiency of 0.467 (to 3 s.f.)

Tip: The actual answer you'd get on your calculator would be something like 0.46692607. When you get a long number answer you need to round it. Both pieces of data given in example 1 are given to 3 s.f., so it's sensible to round your answer to 3 s.f.. There's more on significant figures on page 331.

Example 2

An electric fan is supplied with 2000 kJ of energy. 600 kJ of that is wasted as heat and sound. What is the percentage efficiency of the fan?

Total energy in = 2000 kJ
Useful energy out = total energy in – wasted energy
= 2000 – 600 = 1400 kJ

Start by working out the efficiency as a decimal:

$$\text{efficiency} = \frac{\text{useful energy out}}{\text{total energy in}}$$
$$= \frac{1400}{2000}$$
$$= 0.7$$

Then, multiply this by 100 to get the efficiency of the fan as a percentage:

$$\text{percentage efficiency} = 0.7 \times 100 = 70\%$$

Figure 3: An electric fan will always have an efficiency of less than 1 (or 100%) because some of the energy it transfers is wasted, e.g. as heat and sound.

Rearranging the efficiency formula Higher

Tip: If you need help with formula triangles, take a look at page 381.

The other way they might ask it is to tell you the efficiency and the input energy and ask for the energy output — so you need to be able to swap the formula round. As usual, a formula triangle will come in handy for rearranging the formulas.

Example **Higher**

A lamp with an efficiency of 0.74 is supplied with 350 J of energy. What will its useful energy output be?

Rearrange the equation $\text{efficiency} = \dfrac{\text{useful energy out}}{\text{total energy in}}$ to give:

useful energy out = efficiency × total energy in = 0.74 × 350 = 259 J

Efficiency and cost-effectiveness

It may sound like the best thing to do is to always pick the most efficient machine. But sometimes efficiency isn't everything — there are other factors to consider too. When you're choosing an appliance you need to consider cost-effectiveness (see p.230) as well as efficiency.

New, efficient appliances are cheaper to run than older, less efficient appliances. But new appliances can be expensive to buy. You've got to work out if it's cost-effective to buy a new appliance. To work out how cost-effective a new appliance will be you need to work out its payback time and compare this to the timescale over which you plan to use the device.

A payback time of one year might sound good, but not if you plan to replace the device after 6 months. On the other hand, a payback time of one year on a device that breaks after 18 months is less cost-effective than a payback time of two years on a device that will last 10 years, assuming you plan to use it until it breaks.

Figure 4: *(From left to right) An LED light bulb, a low-energy light bulb and an ordinary light bulb.*

Example

One way to reduce your energy consumption in the home is to replace ordinary light bulbs with more efficient low-energy bulbs or LED light bulbs.

A low-energy bulb is about 4 times as efficient as an ordinary light bulb, and LED light bulbs are even more efficient than that. These energy-efficient light bulbs also last much longer than ordinary light bulbs. The downsides are that they're both more expensive to buy, and LED bulbs don't always give out as much light as the other two types of bulb.

Even though low-energy and LED light bulbs are more expensive to buy initially, they are more efficient, use less energy and last longer. This means switching to using them from an ordinary light bulb can save you money over time — they are usually more cost-effective.

As you saw on page 230, the quicker the payback time, the more cost-effective something usually is. For example, a low-energy bulb that costs £3 and will save you £12 a year has a payback time of:

$$\text{payback time} = \frac{\text{initial cost}}{\text{annual saving}} = \frac{3}{12} = 0.25 \text{ years (or three months)}$$

Low-energy bulbs typically last around 10 years. Ordinary light bulbs usually only last a year. So over 10 years, not only would you save money on your energy bills, but you also wouldn't have to splash out and pay for nine more bulbs.

Tip: Remember, the payback time is the time it takes for the money saved by using the energy-saving light bulb to equal its initial cost.

Wasted energy

For any given example you can talk about the types of energy being input and output, but remember this:

> No device is 100% efficient and the wasted energy is usually spread out as heat.

Electric heaters are the exception to this. They're usually 100% efficient because all the electricity is converted to "useful" heat.

Useful energy is concentrated energy. The entire energy output of a device, both useful and wasted, eventually ends up as heat. This heat is transferred to cooler surroundings, which then become warmer. As the heat is transferred to cooler surroundings, the energy becomes less concentrated — it dissipates.

The total amount of energy stays the same. The energy is still there, but as it becomes increasingly spread out, it can't be easily used or collected back in again.

Tip: A Sankey diagram can be used to show the proportion of energy that's transferred to useful and wasted energy in a machine (see pages 247-248).

Tip: Remember — 'dissipates' just means that the energy is spread out and 'lost'.

Using 'waste' energy

Heat exchangers reduce the amount of heat energy that is 'lost'. They do this by pumping a cool fluid through the escaping heat. The temperature of this fluid rises as it gains heat energy. The heat energy in the fluid can then be converted into a form of energy that's useful again — either in the original device, or for other useful functions.

Tip: Not all the wasted energy can be converted back to useful energy. Some will still be dissipated as heat, and some will be lost as sound energy.

Example

Some of the heat from a car's engine can be transferred to the air that's used to warm the passenger compartment.

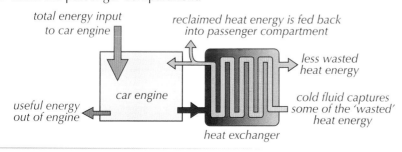

Q1   What does it mean to say a machine is efficient?

Q2   Why is it not possible for a device to be 100% efficient?

Q3   a) What eventually happens to all the energy wasted by a device?

b) What effect does this wasted energy have on the surroundings?

c) Why is this energy not useful?

d) Suggest one way some of this energy can be made useful.

Practice Questions — Application

Q1   Work out the efficiency of the following devices as a decimal.

a) One where total power in = 90 W and useful power out = 54 W.

b) A machine supplied with 800 J of energy that wastes 277 J.

Q2   Work out the efficiency of the following devices as a percentage.

a) One where total power in = 36 W and useful power out = 12.6 W.

b) A lamp that transfers 7.5 kJ of electrical energy into 4.5 kJ of light energy, 2.9 kJ of heat energy and 100 J of sound energy.

Q3   A TV is supplied with 650 kJ of electrical energy. It transfers 275 kJ to light energy, 190 kJ to sound energy and the rest to heat energy.

a) What is the total useful energy out?

b) How much energy is wasted by the TV?

c) What is the efficiency of the TV as a decimal?

Q4   Ben is comparing two types of energy-saving light bulbs. Data for the two bulbs is shown in the table. The annual saving shown is the amount of money Ben would save each year by switching from using an ordinary bulb to each of these bulbs.

	Average lifetime	Cost	Useful power output	Power input	Annual saving on energy bills
Low-energy light bulb	8 years	£3.50	7 W	10 W	£5.60
LED bulb	12 years	£16.00	7 W	8 W	£10.00

a) Calculate the payback time for each bulb.

b) Which bulb would it be most cost-efficient to buy if you plan to use it until it needs replacing?

c) State which bulb is more efficient.

d) Give one reason Ben may choose to buy the low-energy bulb instead of the LED bulb.

Q5   A machine with an efficiency of 68% outputs 816 J of useful energy. What is the total energy input?

Tip: When working out efficiency, always divide the smaller number by the bigger number. A percentage efficiency must always be less than 100% and a decimal efficiency must always be less than 1.

Exam Tip
You'll be given the formula for efficiency in the exam, but if you're doing the Higher Tier you need to know how to rearrange it.

3. Sankey Diagrams

It's time to get your pencils and graph paper out — it's time to talk about Sankey diagrams. They're good for making efficiency data look prettier.

What are Sankey diagrams?

The idea of Sankey diagrams is to make it easy to see at a glance how much of the total energy in is being usefully employed compared with how much is being wasted.

The thicker the arrow, the more energy it represents — so you see a big thick arrow going in, then several smaller arrows going off it to show the different energy transformations taking place.

Example

This Sankey diagram for a TV shows that most of the energy supplied to it is wasted as heat energy. Some is transferred to useful sound energy and a small amount is converted to useful light energy.

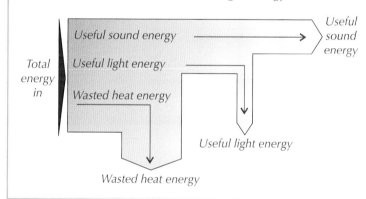

Sankey diagrams can be drawn as sketches. They show what energy transfers take place and roughly how much energy is given out in different forms.

Exam Tip
If you're asked to draw a Sankey diagram in the exam, it's really important to label the input and outputs, otherwise you'll miss out on easy marks.

Example

This is a sketch of a Sankey diagram for a simple motor. It shows that the energy supplied is transferred to kinetic, sound and heat energy.

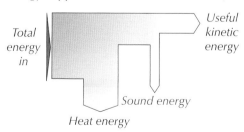

You don't know the actual amounts, but you can see that most of the energy is being wasted — and that it's mostly wasted as heat.

Exam Tip
With sketches, they're likely to ask you to compare two different devices and say which is more efficient. You generally want to be looking for the one with the thickest useful energy arrow(s).

Sankey diagrams can also be detailed, where the width of each arrow is proportional to the number of joules it represents (see next example). You can use detailed diagrams to work out the efficiency (see p.242) of a device.

Example

This is a detailed Sankey diagram for the same motor. You can use it to calculate the useful energy output and efficiency of the motor.

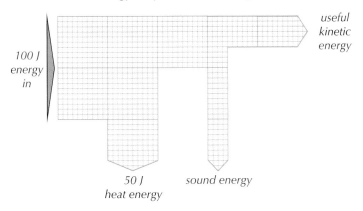

Start by working out how much energy each output arrow on the diagram represents.

- The energy input arrow represents 100 J of energy and is 20 squares wide.

Tip: You could also find how much each square is worth using the width of the heat energy arrow. It's 10 squares wide and represents 50 J, so each square is worth 50 ÷ 10 = 5 J.

- To work out how much energy each square in the arrow represents, you divide the total energy by the number of squares. So, each square represents 100 ÷ 20 = 5 J. This is the same for the whole diagram.

- Now, work out how much the kinetic energy arrow represents — it's 6 squares wide. Useful kinetic energy out = 6 × 5 = 30 J.

Once you've got all the numbers, plug them into the efficiency formula:

$$\text{efficiency} = \frac{\text{useful energy out}}{\text{total energy in}} = \frac{30}{100} = 0.3$$

The motor has an efficiency of 0.3 (or 0.3 × 100 = 30%).

Practice Questions — Application

Q1 Look at these Sankey diagrams for two different washing machines.

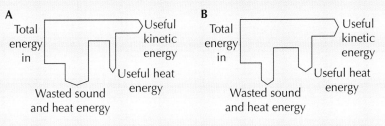

Which of the machines, A or B, is more efficient? Explain your answer.

Q2   Look at this Sankey diagram for an electric fan.

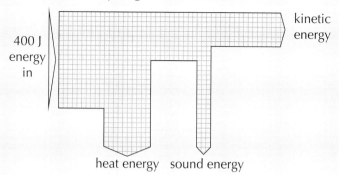

a) How much energy does each square represent?

b) How much energy is wasted?

c) What is the efficiency of the fan?

Exam Tip
If the question doesn't ask for the efficiency as a decimal or a percentage, you can give your answer as either and get the marks.

Section Checklist — Make sure you know...

Energy Transfer

☐ That the different types of energy are electrical, light, sound, kinetic, nuclear, thermal, gravitational potential, elastic potential and chemical.

☐ That energy is always conserved — energy can be transferred usefully from one form to another, stored or dissipated, but can never be created or destroyed.

☐ The types of energy transfers that occur in different appliances.

Efficiency of Machines

☐ That when energy is transferred, some energy is always wasted.

☐ How to use the formulas $\text{efficiency} = \dfrac{\text{useful energy out}}{\text{total energy in}}$ and $\text{efficiency} = \dfrac{\text{useful power out}}{\text{total power in}}$ to calculate efficiency as either a decimal or a percentage.

☐ How to use efficiency and cost-effectiveness to compare different ways of reducing energy consumption, e.g. comparing LED and low-energy light bulbs.

☐ That eventually wasted energy spreads out into the surroundings, which makes them warmer.

☐ That there are ways to make 'wasted' energy useful, e.g. heat exchangers.

Sankey Diagrams

☐ How to draw a Sankey diagram and be able to explain what it shows you.

☐ How to calculate efficiency from a Sankey diagram.

Exam-style Questions

1   This Sankey diagram shows the energy transferred by Television A every second.

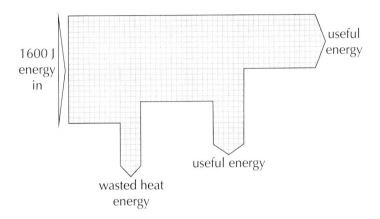

1 (a)   Suggest what the **two** types of useful energy output by Television A are.

(2 marks)

1 (b) (i)   How much energy is transferred into heat energy by the television?
Clearly show how you work out your answer.

(2 marks)

1 (b) (ii)   Calculate the efficiency of Television A as a decimal.
Use the correct equation from the equations listed on page 381.
Clearly show how you work out your answer.

(3 marks)

1 (c)   A consumer wants to buy Television A or B. The table below shows data on Television A, and another television, B.

	Input energy (each second) in J	Efficiency	Initial cost to buy	Lifetime	Annual saving on energy bills
Television A	1600		£200	5 years	£50
Television B	1700	30%	£300	8 years	£40

1 (c) (i)   Television B outputs 400 J of light energy and 110 J of sound energy each second.
Sketch a Sankey diagram for Television B.

(3 marks)

1 (c) (ii)   The consumer decides to buy Television A. Use the information in the table to suggest **three** reasons why he may have made this choice

(4 marks)

1. The Cost of Electricity

Electricity can be expensive stuff — and the more you use, the more it costs. Powerful appliances are very good at transferring electrical energy quickly.

Electrical energy

Electrical appliances are designed to transfer electrical energy into other forms (see page 241).

> **Examples**
>
> A radio is designed to convert electrical energy into sound energy. It also wastes some of the electrical energy as heat energy.
>
> A washing machine is designed to convert electrical energy into heat and kinetic energy, but it will also waste some by producing sound energy.

The **power** of an appliance is the amount of energy it transfers in a given time. Power is usually measured in watts (W) or kilowatts (kW). 1 kW = 1000 W.

The amount of energy that is transferred by an appliance depends on its power and the amount of time that the appliance is switched on. Energy is usually measured in joules (J) — 1 J is the amount of energy transferred by a 1 W appliance in 1 s. A 5 kW appliance transfers 5000 J in 1 s.

You can calculate the energy transferred by an appliance using this equation:

$$E = P \times t$$

E = energy transferred (J) t = time (s) P = power (W)

> **Example**
>
> **A 500 W washing machine is used for 5400 s. How much energy does it transfer?**
>
> You just need to put the numbers into the formula:
>
> $E = P \times t = 500 \times 5400 = 2\ 700\ 000$ J

Kilowatt-hours

When you're dealing with large amounts of electrical energy (e.g. the energy used by a home in one week), it's easier to think of the power and time in kilowatts and hours — rather than in watts and seconds.

Learning Objectives:

- Be able to give examples of energy transfers that common electrical appliances are designed to make happen.
- Know how to calculate the amount of electrical energy transferred by an appliance using $E = P \times t$.
- Be able to read an electricity meter and use it to calculate electricity cost.

Specification Reference P1.3.1

Tip: 1 kJ = 1000 J, so you could also write this as 2700 kJ.

Tip: Make sure you know which units you should be using for which situations. If you mix up the units (and start multiplying kW by s, for example) you'll get the wrong answer.

The standard units of electrical energy are kilowatt-hours (kWh) — not joules.

> A kilowatt-hour is the amount of electrical energy used by a 1 kW appliance left on for 1 hour.

You can use exactly the same equation as before to calculate large amounts of energy — only the units are different.

$$E = energy\ transferred\ (kWh) \longrightarrow E = P \times t \longleftarrow t = time\ (h)$$

$$P = power\ (kW)$$

Tip: You don't need to be able to convert between kilowatt-hours and joules.

Example — Higher

A 1.3 kW heater transfers 75 kWh of electrical energy. How long is it switched on for?

Rearrange $E = P \times t$ to get $t = E \div P$, then plug in the values for E and P:

$t = E \div P$, $= 75 \div 1.3 = 58$ hours (to 2 s.f.)

Tip: There's more on significant figures on page 331.

Calculating the cost of electricity

Mains electricity is usually measured in kilowatt-hours. Electricity companies normally charge a set price per kilowatt-hour. You can work out how much the electricity costs using this formula:

Exam Tip
You won't be given this formula in the exam so make sure you learn it.

> cost of electricity = number of kWh used × price per kWh

Example

An electricity supplier charges 14p per kWh. What's the cost of leaving a 60 W light bulb on for: a) 30 minutes? b) one year?

a) First, find the energy transferred by the bulb in 30 minutes in kWh.
    60 W = 0.06 kW, 30 minutes = 0.5 h
    So, $E = P \times t = 0.06 \times 0.5 = 0.03$ kWh

    Then work out the cost of the electricity used:
    cost = number of kWh × price per kWh = 0.03 × 14 = 0.42p

b) one year = 365 days = (365 × 24) hours = 8760 hours
    So the energy transferred is $E = P \times t = 0.06 \times 8760 = 525.6$ kWh

    cost = number of kWh × price per kWh
    $= 525.6 \times 14 = 7358.4p = £73.58$ (to the nearest penny)

Each kWh of electricity costs 14p.
How long can a 5 kW heater be used for 14p?

Start by working out how many units of electricity you can use for 14p.
This one's quite straightforward — the cost of 1 kWh is 14p,
so for 14p you can use 1 kWh.

Then calculate how long it'll take the heater to transfer 1 kWh of electricity.
Rearrange the formula $E = P \times t$ to get $t = E \div P$.

Then just plug the numbers in: t = 1 ÷ 5 = 0.2 hours = 12 minutes.

So, the heater can be used for 12 minutes for 14p.

Tip: **H** If you need help with rearranging formulas take a look at page 381.

Tip: There are 60 minutes in an hour, so to convert from hours to minutes just multiply by 60.

Reading an electricity meter

The amount of electricity you use in the home is measured by an electricity meter. The meter basically just counts how many kWh of electricity you use — and that's how many kWh the electricity supplier will charge for.

They might ask you to read values off an electricity meter in the exam — but don't worry, it's pretty straightforward. You may be given something like this:

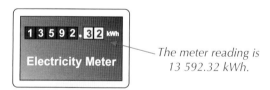

The meter reading is 13 592.32 kWh.

Figure 1: A domestic electricity meter showing a reading of 11 483.09 kWh.

You could be given two meter readings and be asked to work out the total energy that's been used over a particular time period. Just subtract the meter reading at the start of the time (the smaller one) from the reading at the end to work this out.

An electricity meter showed a reading of 10 382.66 kWh.

One month later, the reading was 10 496.73 kWh.

So, in one month, 10 496.73 – 10 382.66 = 114.07 kWh of electricity were used.

An electricity supplier charges 13p per kWh of electricity. Look at the following electricity meter readings and work out the cost of the electricity used between 1st March and 31st March.

1st March | 1 6 8 9 4 . 3 6 kWh | *31st March* | 1 7 4 8 4 . 3 6 kWh |

Electricity meter reading on 1st March: 16 894.36 kWh.
Electricity meter reading on 31st March: 17 484.36 kWh.

Amount of electricity used = 17 484.36 – 16 894.36 = 590 kWh

Cost = number of kWh used × price per kWh = 590 × 13 = 7670p = £76.70

Practice Questions — Fact Recall

Q1 What does the amount of energy transferred by an electrical appliance depend on?

Q2 Write down the formula that relates energy, power and time. This formula can be used with two different sets of units — what are they?

Q3 What's the formula for working out the cost of electricity used?

Q4 What units are usually used to measure the amount of electricity used in a home?

Practice Questions — Application

Q1 Work out how much electrical energy (in J) is transferred by the following appliances:

a) A 60 W light bulb turned on for 60 s.

b) A 0.1 W clock radio turned on for 24 hours.

Q2 Work out how many units of electrical energy (in kWh) are transferred by the following appliances:

a) A 2 kW vacuum cleaner turned on for 0.5 hours.

b) A 2800 W hair dryer used for 15 minutes.

Q3 An electricity supplier charges 15p per kWh. Calculate the cost of the following:

a) 17 kWh of electricity.   b) A 3 kW appliance left on for 1 hour.

c) A 2.4 kW toaster used for 6 minutes.

Q4 A 1.1 kW microwave transfers 480 kJ of energy in the time it takes to cook a potato. How long does it take to cook the potato?

2. Choosing Electrical Appliances

Electrical appliances are great — as long as you have an electricity supply. Even if you do though, picking the best appliance isn't always straightforward.

Comparing different appliances

There are often a few different appliances that do the same job. In the exam, they might ask you to weigh up the pros and cons of different appliances and decide which one is most suitable for a particular situation.

You might need to work out whether one appliance uses less energy or is more cost-effective than another.

You might also need to think about the practical advantages and disadvantages of using different appliances. E.g. 'Can an appliance be used in areas with limited electricity supplies?'

You might get asked to compare two appliances that you haven't seen before. Just take your time and think about the advantages and disadvantages — you should be able to make a sensible judgement.

Example

These are the kinds of things you'll need to think about if you were asked to compare battery radios and clockwork radios:

- Battery radios and clockwork radios are both handy in areas where there is no mains electricity supply.

- Clockwork radios work by storing elastic potential energy in a spring when someone winds them up. The elastic potential energy is slowly released and used to power the radio.

- Batteries can be expensive, but powering a clockwork radio is free.

- Battery power is also only useful if you can get hold of some new batteries when the old ones run out. You don't get that problem with clockwork radios — but it can get annoying to have to keep winding them up every few hours to recharge them.

- Clockwork radios are also better for the environment — a lot of energy and harmful chemicals go into making batteries, and they're often tricky to dispose of safely.

Figure 1: *A clockwork radio. Because it's powered by winding it up, it's better for the environment than a battery-powered radio — but much harder work.*

You might be asked to use data to compare two appliances. Make sure you look carefully at the data you're given. You might need to use it to do some calculations, for example to work out which appliance costs more to run.

Learning Objectives:

- For a given situation, evaluate the advantages and disadvantages of using different electrical appliances.

- Understand how access to electricity can affect people's standard of living.

Specification Reference P1.3

Tip: See page 244 for an explanation of cost-effectiveness.

A company is deciding whether to install a 720 W low-power heater, or a high-power 9 kW heater. The heater they choose will be on for 30 hours each week. Their electricity provider charges 7p per kWh of electricity. How much money per week would they save by choosing the low-power heater?

Calculate the electricity used in a week by the low-power heater:
720 W = 0.72 kW
$E = P \times t = 0.72 \times 30 = 21.6$ kWh

The electricity used in a week by the high-power heater is:
$E = P \times t = 9 \times 30 = 270$ kWh

Total saving per week:
   saving = number of kWh × price per kWh
          = $(270 - 21.6) \times 7$ = £17.39 (to the nearest penny)

Access to electricity

Most people in developed countries have access to mains electricity. However, many people living in the world's poorest countries don't — this has a big effect on the amount of facilities, services and goods available to them.

Here are a few examples of how differing access to electricity affects people's lives:

Convenience and safety

In the UK, our houses are full of devices that transform electrical energy into other useful types of energy. For example, not only is electric lighting useful and convenient, but it can also help improve safety at night (see Figure 2).

Figure 2: *Electric street lighting. Good lighting makes a street safer for people walking and driving around.*

Refrigeration

Refrigerators keep food fresh for longer by slowing down the growth of bacteria. Refrigerators are also used to keep vaccines cold. Without refrigeration it's difficult to distribute important vaccines — this can have devastating effects on a country's population.

Health

Electricity also plays an important role in improving public health in other ways. Hospitals in developed countries rely heavily on electricity, e.g. for X-ray machines (see Figure 3). Without access to these modern machines, the diagnosis and treatment of patients would be poorer and could reduce life expectancy.

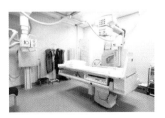

Figure 3: *An X-ray machine in a hospital. Hospitals in developed countries rely on electricity for all kinds of things, including refrigeration and machinery to treat and diagnose medical problems.*

Communication

Communications are also affected by a lack of electricity. No electricity means no internet or phones — making it hard for people to keep in touch, or for people to send and receive news and information.

Q1 Describe three ways having no access to electricity can affect people's lives.

Practice Questions — Application

Q1 Look at the information in the table about two different freezers.

Model	A	B
Price	£400	£250
Power	300 W	550 W

A consumer wants to buy one of these freezers. The freezer chosen would be on for 168 hours per week. The consumer is charged 10p per kWh.

a) How much electricity would be used by Freezer A per week?

b) How much would it cost to run Freezer A for a week?

c) How much would it cost to run Freezer B for a week?

d) What is the total saving per week if Freezer A is chosen over Freezer B?

e) Give one advantage and one disadvantage of choosing Freezer A over Freezer B.

Q2 A mobile phone company develops a solar-powered battery pack for charging a phone. Give an advantage and a disadvantage of using this battery pack over a charger that uses UK mains electricity.

Section Checklist — Make sure you know...

The Cost of Electricity

☐ Some examples of electrical appliances and the energy transfers they're designed to make happen.

☐ How to use $E = P \times t$ to calculate electrical energy transferred in both joules and kilowatt-hours.

☐ How to calculate the cost of electricity used.

☐ How to read an electricity meter.

Choosing Electrical Appliances

☐ How to compare the advantages and disadvantages of electrical appliances, depending on their use.

☐ The ways differing access to mains electricity can affect people's lives.

Exam-style Questions

1 The diagram shows the reading on a home electricity meter.

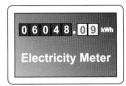

The electricity supplier charges 9p per kilowatt-hour of electricity.

1 (a) One month later, another meter reading was taken. The homeowner
was billed £167.59 for the electricity she had used between the meter readings.
What was the second meter reading?
Clearly show how you work out your answer.

(3 marks)

1 (b) The homeowner is considering replacing her current washing machine with a newer
machine. The table shows data for three different washing machines, R, S and T.

Washing machine	R	S	T
Price (£)	400	215	649
Power (kW)	2.6	2.5	2.8
Time for one wash cycle (h)	1.8	2.5	1
Efficiency (%)	65	48	72

1 (b) (i) How much energy would be transferred from the mains electricity supply during one
wash cycle by machine S?
Use the correct equation from the equations listed on page 381.
Clearly show how you work out your answer. Give your answer in joules.

(2 marks)

1 (b) (ii) How much would it cost to run machine S for one cycle?
Clearly show how you work out your answer.

(3 marks)

1 (b) (iii) The homeowner uses her washing machine for four cycles per week. She works out
that machine R instead of her current one would save 20p per wash cycle.
What is the payback time for machine R? Give your answer in number of wash cycles.

(2 marks)

1 (b) (iv) Give **one** advantage and **one** disadvantage of choosing machine T over
machines R and S.

(2 marks)

1. Energy Sources and Power Stations

Learning Objectives:

- Know the difference between non-renewable and renewable energy resources.

- Know that non-renewable energy resources include fossil fuels (coal, oil and gas) and nuclear fuels (uranium and plutonium).

- Know that many power stations generate electricity by heating water or air to drive a turbine coupled to a generator.

- Know that fossil fuels are burned to heat water or air to generate electricity.

- Know that electricity is generated in nuclear power stations from the fission of uranium or plutonium.

Specification Reference P1.4.1

There are lots of different energy resources that we use to generate electricity, and you need to know about 12 of them. But before we get stuck into that, first you need to know your non-renewables from your renewables...

Non-renewable energy resources

Non-renewable energy resources are the three **fossil fuels** and nuclear:

- Coal
- Natural gas
- Oil
- Nuclear fuels (uranium and plutonium)

Non-renewable fuels will all run out one day. They all do damage to the environment through emissions or because of issues with their mining, storage and disposal (see pages 269-270 for more), but they do provide most of our energy.

Renewable energy resources

Renewable energy resources are:

- Wind
- Tides
- Solar
- Biofuels
- Waves
- Hydroelectric
- Geothermal

Renewable energy resources will never run out. Most of them do damage to the environment, but in less nasty ways than most non-renewables. The trouble is they don't provide much energy and some of them are unreliable because they depend on the weather.

Burning fuels

Most of the electricity we use is generated from the four non-renewable sources of energy (coal, oil, gas and nuclear) in big power stations, which are all pretty much the same apart from the boiler. Figure 1 shows how electricity is generated in a typical fossil fuel power station.

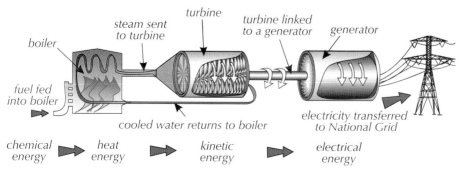

boiler — steam sent to turbine — turbine — turbine linked to a generator — generator

fuel fed into boiler

cooled water returns to boiler

electricity transferred to National Grid

chemical energy → heat energy → kinetic energy → electrical energy

Figure 1: *Electricity generation in a fossil fuel power station and the energy transfers involved.*

- The fossil fuel is burned to convert its stored chemical energy into heat (thermal) energy.

- The heat energy is used to heat water (or air in some power stations) to produce steam.

- The steam turns a turbine, converting heat energy into kinetic energy.

- The turbine is connected to a generator, which transfers kinetic energy into electrical energy.

Nuclear energy

A nuclear power station is mostly the same as the one used for burning fossil fuels (see previous page), but with nuclear fission of uranium or plutonium producing the heat to make steam to drive turbines. The difference is in the boiler, as shown in Figure 2. Nuclear power stations take the longest time of all the power stations to start up.

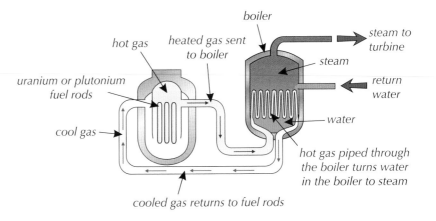

Figure 2: A nuclear reactor and boiler of a typical nuclear power station. Energy from nuclear fission heats gas in the reactor, which is sent to a boiler to heat water and produce steam.

Figure 3: A nuclear power station at night. You can see the steam condensing as it leaves the cooling tower.

Practice Questions — Fact Recall

Q1 What are the three fossil fuels?

Q2 a) Name four renewable energy sources.

   b) Give one reason why renewable energy resources aren't always used instead of non-renewable energy resources.

Q3 a) Name two fuels used in nuclear power stations.

   b) What process releases energy from nuclear fuels?

Q4 In many fossil fuel power stations, water is heated to form steam.

   a) How is the water heated?

   b) Describe how electricity is generated using steam.

2. Wind and Solar Power

Here's the first of many topics on the pros and cons of using different renewable energy resources to generate electricity. First up, wind and solar radiation...

Generating electricity using wind

Generating electricity from wind involves putting up lots of windmills (wind turbines) where they're exposed to the weather, like on moors or around coasts.

Each wind turbine has its own generator inside it. The electricity is generated directly from the wind turning the blades, which turn the generator.

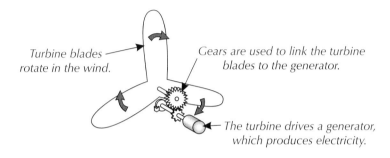

Turbine blades rotate in the wind.

Gears are used to link the turbine blades to the generator.

The turbine drives a generator, which produces electricity.

Figure 1: The structure of a wind turbine. The blades of the wind turbine rotate in the wind and directly drive a generator, which generates electricity.

Advantages and disadvantages

Wind turbines produce no **atmospheric pollution** (except for a little bit when they're manufactured), but according to some they do spoil the view (see Figure 2). You need about 1500 wind turbines to replace one coal-fired power station and 1500 of them cover a lot of ground — which will have a big effect on the scenery. This negative impact on the landscape is called **visual pollution**.

Wind turbines also produce **noise pollution** — they can be very noisy, which can be annoying for people living nearby. There's no permanent damage to the landscape though — if you remove the turbines, you remove the noise and the view returns to normal.

There's also the problem of no power when the wind stops, and it's impossible to increase supply when there's extra demand. The initial costs are quite high, but there are no fuel costs and minimal running costs.

Solar cells

Solar cells generate electric currents directly from the Sun's radiation (see Figure 3). They're expensive to produce but they cause no environmental damage, except maybe a bit when they're actually produced.

Learning Objectives:
- Know that electricity can be generated by using wind to drive turbines directly.
- Know that solar cells produce electricity directly from the Sun's radiation.
- Know that electricity generated by solar cells is useful in remote areas or when only small amounts of electricity are needed.
- Understand the advantages and disadvantages of using wind and the Sun's radiation to generate electricity compared to other energy sources.

Specification Reference
P1.4.1

Figure 2: A wind farm in the countryside.

Exam Tip
There are lots of types of pollution (see page 274), so make sure you say using wind to generate electricity causes no 'atmospheric pollution', not just 'pollution', otherwise you won't get the marks.

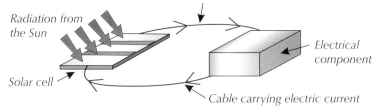

The solar cell generates electric current directly from the Sun's radiation and so can be plugged straight into electrical components like batteries.

Radiation from the Sun

Solar cell

Electrical component

Cable carrying electric current

Figure 3: *A solar cell generating electric current from the Sun's radiation, connected directly to electrical components.*

Solar cells are often the best source of energy for devices that don't use a lot of energy, or in remote places where it would be difficult to get power from other sources.

Figure 4: *A solar panel generates electricity during the day, then uses it to power a lamp that lights up the road sign at night.*

Examples

- Calculators, road signs and watches don't use much energy, so solar cells are ideal for powering them — see Figure 4.

- Space is probably the ultimate remote location — you can't just nip up to a space satellite and top it up with fuel. Instead, satellites use large solar panels to generate the electricity they need.

Solar cells cause no atmospheric pollution, although they do need quite a lot of energy to manufacture in the first place. In sunny countries solar power is a very reliable source of energy — but only in the daytime.

Solar power can still be cost-effective even in cloudy countries like Britain. Initial costs are high but after that the energy is free and running costs almost nil. Solar cells are usually used to generate electricity on a relatively small scale, e.g. powering individual homes (see Figure 5).

It's often not practical or too expensive to connect them to the **National Grid** — the network that distributes electricity around the country (see page 276). The cost of connecting them to the National Grid can be enormous compared with the value of the electricity generated.

Figure 5: *Solar cells and a wind turbine being used to power a house in Hamburg, Germany.*

Practice Questions — Fact Recall

Q1   How is electricity generated by a wind turbine?

Q2   What's the biggest advantage of generating electricity using wind turbines rather than fossil fuels?

Q3   Give two disadvantages of generating electricity using wind.

Q4   What's the energy source used by a solar cell?

Q5   Why are solar cells often used to power devices in remote locations?

Q6   Why are solar cells very rarely connected to the National Grid?

3. Hydroelectricity and Tides

Whether it's in a hydroelectric scheme or a tidal barrage, the principle is always the same — water falls through turbines that are connected to electrical generators, which surprisingly enough generate electricity.

Learning Objectives:

- Know that water can be used in a hydroelectric power station to drive turbines directly.
- Know that hydroelectricity can be useful in remote areas with little access to other sources of energy.
- Understand how pumped storage is used to store energy that can be used to provide electricity at times of peak demand.
- Know how tidal barrages are used to generate electricity.

Specification Reference P1.4.1

Hydroelectric power stations

Generating electricity using hydroelectric power usually requires the flooding of a valley by building a big dam. Rainwater is caught and allowed out through turbines — see Figure 1.

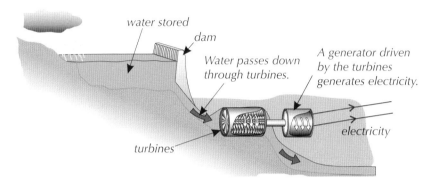

water stored

dam

Water passes down through turbines.

A generator driven by the turbines generates electricity.

electricity

turbines

Figure 1: *A hydroelectric power station. Water is held back behind a dam. When it's released it passes through turbines, which turn a generator and generates electricity.*

There is no atmospheric pollution, but there is a big impact on the environment due to the flooding of the valley (rotting vegetation releases methane and CO_2) and possible loss of habitat for some species (sometimes the loss of whole villages).

The reservoirs can also look very unsightly when they dry up. Putting hydroelectric power stations in remote valleys tends to reduce their impact on humans.

A big advantage is it can provide an immediate response to an increased demand for electricity. There's no problem with reliability except in times of drought — but remember this is Great Britain we're talking about. Initial costs are high, but there's no fuel and minimal running costs. It can be a useful way to generate electricity on a small scale in remote areas. However, in these cases it's often not practical or economical to connect it to the National Grid.

Figure 2: *The Hoover Dam on the Colorado River in the USA — possibly the most well-known hydroelectric power station in the world.*

Pumped storage

Most large power stations have huge boilers which have to be kept running all night even though demand is very low. This means there's a surplus of electricity at night. It's surprisingly difficult to find a way of storing this spare energy for later use — **pumped storage** is one of the best solutions.

In pumped storage, 'spare' night-time electricity is used to pump water up to a higher reservoir. This can then be released quickly during periods of **peak demand** such as at teatime each evening, to supplement the steady delivery from the big power stations (see Figure 3).

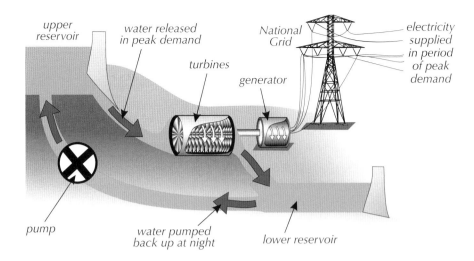

Figure 3: A pumped-storage system. Water flows from an upper reservoir to a lower reservoir and generates electricity. A pump is used to carry water back up to the upper reservoir.

Figure 4: The inside of the Dinorwig pumped-storage hydroelectric power station in Wales. It's built deep inside a mountain to preserve the natural beauty of the Snowdonia National Park.

Remember, pumped storage uses the same idea as hydroelectric schemes, but it isn't a way of generating power — it's simply a way of storing energy which has already been generated.

At times of low demand (e.g. at night) electricity is relatively cheap, so it doesn't cost much to pump water into the upper reservoir. At other times, such as the end of a popular TV programme (that's a lot of kettles boiling all at once), electricity is much more expensive and there's a surge in demand.

By generating electricity only at times of peak demand, pumped-storage systems can make a profit even though there's a slight overall loss in energy (it's impossible to make them 100% efficient).

Tidal barrages

Tidal barrages are big dams built across river estuaries, with turbines in them. The turbines, as ever, are connected to electrical generators which turn and generate electricity. As the tide comes in it fills up the estuary to a height of several metres — it also drives the turbines. This water can then be allowed out through the turbines at a controlled speed when there's a height difference of water between the two sides of the barrage. The source of the energy is the gravity of the Sun and the Moon, as this is what causes tides.

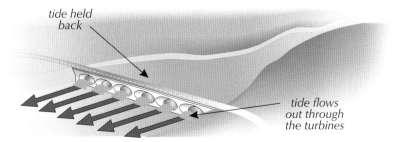

Figure 5: The structure of a tidal barrage. Tide water is held back behind the barrage, then allowed to flow through turbines connected to generators, generating electricity.

This form of electricity generation causes no atmospheric pollution — the main problems are preventing free access by boats, spoiling the view and altering the habitat of the wildlife, e.g. wading birds, sea creatures and beasties who live in the sand.

Tides are pretty reliable in the sense that they happen twice a day without fail, and always near to the predicted height. The only drawback is that the height of the tide is variable so lower (neap) tides will provide significantly less energy than the bigger 'spring' tides. They also don't work when the water level is the same either side of the barrage — this happens four times a day because of the tides.

Tidal barrages are excellent for storing energy ready for periods of peak demand. Initial costs are moderately high, but there are no fuel costs and minimal running costs. Even though it can only be used in some of the most suitable estuaries, tidal power has the potential for generating a significant amount of energy.

Figure 6: *A tidal barrage on the Rance River in France.*

Practice Questions — Fact Recall

Q1 Describe how electricity is generated in a hydroelectric power station.

Q2 Give two environmental problems that can be caused by hydroelectric power stations.

Q3 Explain why hydroelectric schemes are often used to generate electricity in remote areas.

Q4 a) Explain how surplus energy is stored in pumped storage.

b) Pumped storage is used to store energy despite the fact that it uses more energy than it provides. Why is this?

Q5 Briefly explain how a tidal barrage can be used to generate electricity.

Learning Objectives:

- Know how electricity can be generated using waves.

- Know how hot steam that rises to the surface in some volcanic areas can be used to generate electricity, and know that this is known as geothermal energy.

- Know that biofuels can be used to produce electricity in the same way as fossil fuels.

Specification Reference
P1.4.1

4. Other Renewable Resources

If you thought that was it for renewable energy resources, think again. Last but not least — generating electricity using waves, geothermal energy and biofuels.

Waves

To generate electricity using waves, you need lots of small wave-powered turbines located around the coast. As waves come in to the shore they provide an up and down motion which can be used to drive a generator (see Figure 1).

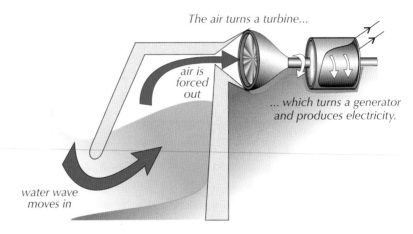

The air turns a turbine...

air is forced out

... which turns a generator and produces electricity.

water wave moves in

Figure 1: *A diagram showing how waves can be used to generate electricity. Waves force air through the turbine, which turns a generator and generates electricity.*

There is no atmospheric pollution produced — the main problems are spoiling the view and being a hazard to boats. They are fairly unreliable, since waves tend to die out when the wind drops. Initial costs are high, but there are no fuel costs and minimal running costs. Waves are never likely to provide energy on a large scale, but they can be very useful on small islands.

Figure 2: *The Islay LIMPET wave power station on the coast of Islay, a Scottish Hebridean island.*

> ### Example
>
> - The Scottish island of Islay lies on the western coast of Scotland and is exposed to the full force of the northern Atlantic Ocean. Because of this and the fact that the island is fairly remote, it's an ideal location for a wave-powered station.
>
> - In 2000 the Islay LIMPET (Land Installed Marine Power Energy Transmitter) was built. This was the first commercial wave power device to be connected to the UK National Grid. It provides enough energy to power a few hundred homes.
>
> - As a wave hits the structure, air is forced up through a turbine. When the wave drops, air is sucked back through the turbine. This process repeats every time a wave hits, and electricity is generated.

Geothermal energy

Geothermal energy is heat energy from hot underground rocks — it can be used to generate electricity. This is only possible in volcanic areas where hot rocks lie near to the surface. The source of much of the heat is the slow decay of various radioactive elements, including uranium, deep inside the Earth.

Steam and hot water rise to the surface and are used to drive a turbine, which is connected to a generator. This is actually brilliant free energy with no real environmental problems.

Figure 3: *The Nesjavellir geothermal power station in Iceland.*

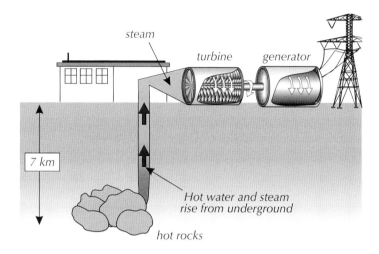

Figure 4: *The structure of a geothermal power station. Hot water and steam from underground drive a turbine, which is connected to a generator.*

In some places, geothermal heat is used to heat water or buildings directly, without being converted to electrical energy. The main drawback with geothermal energy is there aren't very many suitable locations for power stations. Also, the cost of building a power station is often high compared to the amount of energy we can get out of it.

Biofuels

Biofuels are renewable energy resources — they're made from plants and waste. They're used to generate electricity in exactly the same way as fossil fuels (page 259) — they're burned to heat up water. They can also be used in some cars — just like fossil fuels. Biofuels are a relatively quick and 'natural' source of energy and are theoretically **carbon neutral** (see page 270).

Tip: 'Carbon neutral' means they absorb just as much carbon dioxide as they release — i.e. there's no overall atmospheric pollution. Biofuels release CO_2 when they're burned, but they absorb it when they're grown.

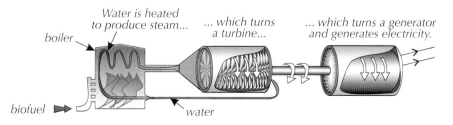

Figure 5: *A diagram of how biofuels are used to generate electricity. Biofuels are burned to heat water, which produces steam. The steam drives a turbine, which drives a generator and generates electricity.*

Biofuels can be solids, liquids or gases. We can get biofuels from organisms that are still alive or from dead organic matter.

Figure 6: *An algae biofuel culture system being used to make ethanol and biodiesel.*

- Solid biofuels are usually just naturally occuring products, e.g. straw, nutshells and wood chips.

- Crops can be grown to produce liquid biofuels, e.g. ethanol from fermented sugar cane and biodiesel from modified plant oils.

- Gas biofuels are usually generated from some kind of natural fermentation process, e.g. methane biogas from sludge digesters.

Practice Questions — Fact Recall

Q1   Briefly explain how electricity can be generated from waves.

Q2   Give one environmental advantage of generating electricity from waves rather than fossil fuels.

Q3   The total amount of electricity that can be generated by waves is fairly low. Give one other disadvantage of generating electricity using waves.

Q4   How electricity is generated using geothermal energy?

Q5   Why are geothermal power stations only found in certain parts of the world?

Q6   How is electricity generated in a biofuel power station?

5. Energy Sources and the Environment

Generating electricity from any energy source, renewable or not, can have an impact on the environment. You need to know what the impacts of each energy source are and how we might be able to reduce them in the future.

Non-renewable resources and the environment

In the UK, we currently generate most of our electricity using non-renewable energy sources. These can really harm the environment in a number of ways.

Releasing harmful gases

All three fossil fuels (coal, oil and gas) release CO_2 into the atmosphere when they're burned. For the same amount of energy produced, coal releases the most CO_2, followed by oil then gas. All this CO_2 adds to the **greenhouse effect** and contributes to global warming. The greenhouse effect is where gases in the Earth's atmosphere trap thermal (heat) radiation from the Sun. This causes the overall temperature of the atmosphere to rise (i.e. global warming).

Burning coal and oil releases sulfur dioxide, which causes acid rain. Acid rain can be harmful to trees and soils and can have far-reaching effects in ecosystems. Acid rain can be reduced by taking the sulfur out before the fuel is burned, or cleaning up the emissions.

Damage to habitats and landscapes

Coal mining makes a mess of the landscape, especially "open-cast mining" where huge pits are dug on the surface of the Earth. Oil spillages cause serious environmental problems, affecting animals that live in and around the sea. We try to avoid them, but they'll always happen.

> **Example**
>
> In 2010, an explosion at the oil drilling station Deepwater Horizon in the Gulf of Mexico resulted in the largest accidental oil spill in history. This resulted in thousands of miles of coastline being covered in crude oil, making the area uninhabitable for many local species of animals and plants.

Figure 1: A pelican covered in oil from the oil spill.

Nuclear power

Nuclear power is 'clean', in that it doesn't cause the release of any harmful gases or other chemicals into the atmosphere. (Transporting nuclear material and waste to and from sites does cause a small amount atmospheric pollution though, e.g. from transport lorries burning fossil fuels.)

Learning Objectives:

- Know that burning fossil fuels releases harmful substances into the atmosphere.

- Know that extraction of fuels and generation of electricity from the fuels can result in destruction of the landscape and wildlife habitats.

- Know that generating electricity from nuclear fuels produces harmful waste products that are expensive and difficult to dispose of.

- Understand the disadvantages of burning biofuels.

- Understand what is meant by carbon capture and storage, and why it is important to limit the amount of carbon dioxide in the atmosphere.

- Know some examples of locations where the carbon dioxide from carbon capture and storage can be stored.

Specification Reference P1.4.1

The biggest problem with generating electricity using nuclear fuel is that the nuclear waste produced is very dangerous and difficult to dispose of. This is because it stays highly radioactive for a long time and so needs to be sealed in lead containers far away from people's homes.

Nuclear fuel (e.g. uranium and plutonium) is relatively cheap but the overall cost of nuclear power is high due to the cost of the power station and final **decommissioning** — shutting down the power station so it's completely safe and poses no risk to people or the environment. Nuclear power always carries the risk of an equipment failure leading to major catastrophe, like the Chernobyl disaster in 1986 (see the following example).

Tip: You don't need to know all the detail in the example, just remember the problems that can crop up with using nuclear power.

Example

In 1986, overheating in the nuclear reactor of a nuclear power station in Chernobyl, Ukraine, caused the control rods to jam in place. This resulted in the fission chain reaction escalating out of control and causing an explosion, as well as melting of the equipment inside the reactor.

Harmful radioactive particles were released across the surrounding area for hundreds of miles. This had an immediate and long-lasting effect on the environment. Many people had to evacuate their homes, areas of farmland had to be abandoned due to contamination and the radiation released was directly linked to deaths and cancer cases.

Biofuels and the environment

Biofuels (see page 267) are a relatively quick and 'natural' source of energy and are supposedly carbon neutral. There is still debate into the impact of biofuels on the environment, once the full energy that goes into the production is considered.

- The plants that grow to produce the waste (or to feed the animals that produced the dung) absorb carbon dioxide from the atmosphere as they are growing.

- When the waste is burned, this CO_2 is re-released into the atmosphere. So it has a neutral effect on atmospheric CO_2 levels (although this only really works if you keep growing plants at the same rate you're burning things).

Using biofuels to generate electricity doesn't just produce carbon dioxide. Biofuel production also creates methane emissions — a lot of this comes from the animals.

Figure 2: An oil palm plantation in Indonesia. These crops can be used to make biodiesel.

In some regions, large areas of forest have been cleared to make room to grow biofuels (see Figure 2), resulting in lots of species losing their natural habitats. The decay and burning of this vegetation also increases CO_2 and methane emissions.

Biofuels have potential, but their use is limited by the amount of available farmland that can be dedicated to their production.

Carbon capture and storage

Carbon capture and storage (CCS) is used to reduce the amount of CO_2 building up in the atmosphere and reduce the strength of the greenhouse effect.

CCS works by collecting the CO_2 from power stations before it is released into the atmosphere. The captured CO_2 can then be pumped into empty gas fields and oil fields like those under the North Sea, where it can be safely stored without it adding to the greenhouse effect (see Figure 3).

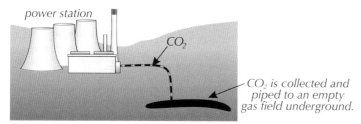

power station

CO_2

CO_2 is collected and piped to an empty gas field underground.

Figure 3: *Carbon dioxide being pumped from a power station to an empty gas field for storage.*

CCS is a new technology that's developing quickly. New ways of storing CO_2 are being explored, including storing CO_2 dissolved in seawater at the bottom of the ocean and capturing CO_2 with algae, which can then be used to produce oil that can be used as a biofuel.

Practice Questions — Fact Recall

Q1 Name two harmful gases that are released into the atmosphere by burning coal.

Q2 a) Which non-renewable resource doesn't directly release harmful gases into the atmosphere when used to generate electricity?

    b) Give two problems with using this fuel to generate electricity.

Q3 a) What is meant by a 'carbon neutral' process?

    b) Explain how using biofuels to generate electricity can be a carbon neutral process. Why might it not be?

Q4 a) Why is it important to limit the amount of CO_2 released into the atmosphere?

    b) Describe carbon capture and storage.

    c) Give two examples of where the carbon dioxide caught in this process can be stored.

6. Choosing Energy Sources

Before deciding which power station to set up you need to evaluate the pros and cons of each type. These can involve cost, time, and environmental issues.

Learning Objectives:

- Know that different power stations have different start-up times, and gas has the shortest start-up time of all the fossil fuels.

- Understand that different sources of energy cause different environmental issues, including noise and visual pollution and the destruction of habitats.

- Be able to evaluate the advantages and disadvantages of using different energy sources to generate electricity.

- Know the ways in which power companies can try to match supply with demand.

Specification Reference
P1.4.1

Setting up a power station

Because coal and oil are running out fast, many old coal- and oil-fired power stations are being taken out of use. Often they're being replaced by gas-fired power stations because these have the shortest **start-up time** of all the fossil fuel power stations — they don't take very long to build and get going from scratch. There's also still quite a lot of gas left, and gas doesn't pollute as badly as coal and oil.

But gas is not the only option. When looking at the options for a new power station, there are several factors to consider:

- How much it costs to set up and run.

- How long it takes to build.

- How much power it can generate.

Then there are also the trickier factors like damage to the environment and impact on local communities. And because these are often very contentious issues, getting permission to build certain types of power station can be a long-running process, and hence increase the overall start-up time.

The time and cost of decommissioning (shutting down) a power station can also be a crucial factor.

Other considerations

There are countless other factors that need to be considered when looking at our options for generating electricity. Here are some of the most important ones...

Start-up costs

Renewable resources often need bigger power stations than non-renewables for the same output. And, as you'd expect, the bigger the power station, the more expensive it is to build.

Nuclear reactors and hydroelectric dams also need huge amounts of engineering to make them safe, which bumps up the costs.

Start-up and decommissioning time

These are both affected by the size of the power station, the complexity of the engineering and also the planning issues (e.g. discussions over whether a nuclear power station should be built on a stretch of beautiful coastline can last years). Gas is one of the quickest to start up. Nuclear power stations take by far the longest (and cost the most) to decommission.

Reliability issues

All the non-renewables are reliable energy providers (until they run out). Many of the renewable sources depend on the weather, which means they're pretty unreliable here in the UK. The exceptions are tidal power and geothermal (which don't depend on weather).

Tip: Although tides and geothermal energy don't depend on the weather, they do depend on location — they can only be used in very specific places

Running and fuel costs

Renewables usually have the lowest running costs, because there's no actual fuel involved — with the exception of biofuels.

Location issues

This is fairly common sense — a power station has to be near to the stuff it runs on.

- Solar — pretty much anywhere, though the sunnier the better.

- Gas — pretty much anywhere there's piped gas (most of the UK).

- Hydroelectric — hilly, rainy places with floodable valleys, e.g. the Lake District, Scottish Highlands.

- Wind — exposed, windy places like moors and coasts or out at sea.

- Oil — near the coast (oil transported by sea).

- Waves — on the coast.

- Coal — near coal mines, e.g. Yorkshire, Wales.

- Nuclear — away from people (in case of disaster), near water (for cooling).

- Tidal — big river estuaries where a dam can be built.

- Geothermal — fairly limited, only in volcanic areas where hot rocks are near the Earth's surface.

Figure 1: Wind turbines don't need a fuel supply, so they can be built out at sea where winds are strong.

Example

- On a mountain in a volcanic area might be an ideal location for a wind farm or a geothermal power station.

- However, it's unlikely that you'd be able to build a tidal power station there, or one that requires a constant supply of fuel such as coal or nuclear (as it would be difficult and costly to get the fuel there).

Environmental issues

As you've already seen in this section, any energy resource will affect the environment in one way or another. If there's a fuel involved, there'll be waste pollution and you'll be using up resources. If it relies on the weather, it's often got to be in an exposed place where it sticks out like a sore thumb.

On the next page you'll find a nice roundup of all the environmental impacts you can expect to be caused by each type of energy resource.

- Atmospheric pollution — this is caused by burning coal, oil, gas and biofuels (pages 259 and 267). It can also be argued that it's caused by nuclear, because the fuel needs to be transported to and from sites and the vehicles used to do this burn fossil fuels.

- Using up resources — this is an issue with the non-renewables, i.e. coal, oil, gas and nuclear. Mining the resources can also ruin the landscape and release harmful gases such as CO_2 and methane into the atmosphere.

- Visual pollution — different people have different views on what's unsightly and what isn't, but you could argue a case for any of the methods of generating electricity causing visual pollution.

- Noise pollution — anything that involves driving a turbine can cause noise pollution, so this applies to everything but solar cells. It's particularly an issue with wind farms, as they're sometimes built near to where people live.

- Disruption of habitats — caused by hydroelectric dams, tidal barrages and the growing of biofuels.

- Disruption of leisure activities — boats, etc. can be disrupted by tidal barrages or offshore wind farms.

- Other problems — nuclear reactors produce dangerous waste and carry a risk of explosions and contamination from radioactive material. Hydroelectric can result in floods due to dams bursting or overtopping (when the water spills over the top of the dam).

Supply and demand

The National Grid (see page 276) needs to supply and direct all the energy that the country needs — our energy demands keep on increasing too. In order to meet these demands in the future, the energy supplied to the National Grid will need to increase, or the energy demands of consumers will need to decrease.

In the future, supply can be increased by opening more power stations or increasing their power output (or by doing both). Demand can be reduced by consumers using more energy-efficient appliances, and being more careful not to waste energy in the home (e.g. turning off the lights or running washing machines at cooler temperatures).

Practice Questions — Fact Recall

Q1 a) Which type of fossil fuel power station has the shortest start-up time?

b) Which type of power station takes the longest to decommission?

Q2 Give two resources that can only be used to generate electricity in particular locations. Explain each of your answers.

Q3 How can supply be made to match the demand for electricity if a country's demand for electricity is increasing?

Q1 A country's energy demands see a sudden increase and a solution needs to be found fast. The government decides the solution is to set up a large non-renewable power station as quickly as possible. Suggest what type of power station should be built and explain your answer.

Q2 This table compares some of the different factors that need to be taken into account when using the different methods of generating electricity listed.

	Start-up time	Reliability of supply	Amount of power provided	Emissions	Disruption to wildlife habitats
Coal	Moderate	Excellent	High	High	Moderate
Nuclear	Long	Excellent	High	None	Moderate
Wind	Short	Poor	Low	None	Low
Hydroelectric	Long	Good	Moderate	None	High
Solar	Short	Poor	Low	None	Low

a) A power station needs to be built to supply a remote town located between two tidal river estuaries. The funders of the power station want to minimise the amount of atmospheric pollution caused by the power station.

i) Use information in the table to suggest which of the energy resources listed would be the most suitable to build. Explain your answer.

ii) Give one advantage and one disadvantage of building a tidal barrage to generate electricity for the town rather than the method you chose in a) i).

b) A small, temporary research station deep in heart of the Chihuahuan Desert, USA, needs an electricity supply as soon as possible. Which type of energy source listed in the table would be most suitable to use? Give reasons for your answer.

7. Electricity and the National Grid

- Know that the National Grid transmits electricity from power stations to consumers.

- Know the basic structure of the National Grid.

- Know that for a given amount of power transmitted, increasing the voltage decreases the current through the wires and so decreases the energy lost through heating.

- Understand that the energy lost through heating can be reduced with the use of step-up and step-down transformers.

- Be able to compare the advantages and disadvantages of using overhead and underground cables to transmit electricity in the National Grid.

Specification Reference
P1.4.2

There's no use in generating a load of electricity if you can't get it to people's homes — that's where the National Grid steps in to do all the hard work.

Distribution of electricity

The National Grid takes electrical energy from power stations to where it's needed in homes and industry. It's the network of pylons and cables that covers the whole of Britain — whoever you pay for your electricity, it's the National Grid that gets it to you. It enables power to be generated anywhere on the grid, and then be supplied anywhere else on the grid.

To transmit the huge amount of power needed, you need either a high voltage or a high current. The problem with a high current is that you lose loads of energy through heat in the cables — the energy loss is proportional to the square of the current, so if the current doubles the energy loss is multiplied by four. It's much cheaper to boost the voltage up really high (to 400 000 V) and keep the current very low.

Transformers

A **transformer** is a device used in the National Grid to change the voltage of a current supply. To get the voltage to 400 000 V to transmit power requires transformers as well as big pylons with huge insulators — but it's still cheaper than transmitting it through smaller wires at a low voltage.

The transformers have to step the voltage up at one end, for efficient transmission, and then bring it back down to safer, usable levels at the other end. The voltage is increased ('stepped up') using a step-up transformer. It's then reduced again ('stepped down') at the consumer end using a step-down transformer (see Figure 1).

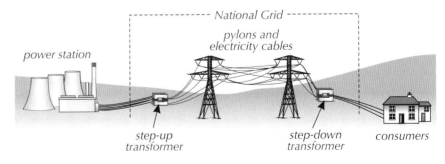

Figure 1: A diagram of the National Grid distributing electricity from a power station to consumers.

Figure 2: An electricity substation where step-down transformers are used to reduce electricity voltage before it's supplied to consumers.

Transmitting electricity

Electrical energy can be moved around by cables buried in the ground like those in Figure 3, as well as in overhead power lines supported by pylons like those in Figure 4. Both of these options have their pros and cons...

Figure 3: Exposed underground electricity cables. The cables have a thick layer of insulation to prevent them from causing electric shocks.

Thermal insulation

Even when you transmit electricity using a low current, there will still be a small amount of resistance in a transmission cable that will cause it to heat up.

Overhead cables are surrounded by air, which cools them down and stops them from overheating. Underground cables need cooling systems to do this — which is one of the factors that makes them more difficult and expensive to install than overhead cables.

Electrical insulation

Air also acts as an electrical insulator around overhead cables, which means the cables themselves don't need any electrical insulation. Underground cables need a thick layer of electrical insulation to stop electrical energy being lost (and stop anyone near them getting an electric shock), which also makes them much thicker than overhead cables.

Figure 4: Overhead electricity cables carried by pylons.

Installation and maintenance

Overhead cables aren't exactly easy to set up, but they're easier and less expensive than underground cables to install. Once they're set up, it's also a lot quicker and easier to access overhead cables to carry out maintenance and repairs than underground cables (see Figure 5).

Figure 5: Repairs being made to overhead cables.

One advantage of having underground cables is that they're protected from the weather and are unlikely to be affected by it. Overhead cables are exposed and can be damaged by severe weather conditions such as high winds.

Underground cables generally need less maintenance than overhead cables once they've been installed. However, when you do have to repair them you have the hassle of having to dig down to them — it takes longer and is more expensive to repair them than overhead cables.

Risks and hazards

Because they're more exposed and they're not insulated, there is a greater risk of getting a fatal electric shock from overhead cables than underground cables. Underground cables are insulated and buried deep underground, so usually they're not a danger to anyone.

Overhead cables can also be a hazard to low-flying aircraft, e.g. helicopters.

Disturbance to land and visual impact

Digging up land to install underground cables disrupts the land and may damage animal habitats, which doesn't happen when overhead cables are installed.

Overhead cables and electricity pylons aren't particularly easy on the eye, so people might not be happy when they're built near homes. However, one of the big pluses of using underground cables is that once they're installed, you can't see them — there's no visual pollution (see page 274).

Land restrictions

Installing underground cables means you can't use the land around the cables for certain things, e.g. placing the foundations for new buildings, so the land has restricted use. With overhead cables you can use the land around the pylons for anything you like, as long as it doesn't get in the way of the pylons or the cables overhead.

Tip: There's a lot to take in on these pages. Just keep going over them until you know all the advantages and disadvantages of using each type of cabling.

Practice Questions — Fact Recall

Q1 a) What does a transformer do?

b) Why are transformers used in the National Grid?

Q2 What does each label A-E represents in this diagram?

Q3 For each of the following, say whether the statement applies to overhead electricity lines or underground cables.

a) Cheaper to set up.

b) Easier to set up.

c) Easier to maintain.

d) More reliable.

e) Easier to access.

f) Requires less insulation.

g) Poses less danger.

h) Causes less visual pollution.

i) Causes less disturbance to land.

Section Checklist — Make sure you know...

Energy Sources and Power Stations

☐ That non-renewable energy resources will eventually run out and renewable ones won't.

☐ That the fossil fuels (coal, oil and gas) and nuclear fuel are non-renewable resources.

☐ That electricity is generated in some power stations by heating air or water to produce steam. The steam turns a turbine connected to a generator, which produces electricity.

☐ That fossil fuels are burned to heat water or air to generate electricity.

☐ That energy generated from the fission of uranium or plutonium is used to heat water in nuclear power stations.

Wind and Solar Power

☐ That wind can be used to drive rotor blades connected to a turbine directly. This drives a generator inside the wind turbine, which generates electricity.

☐ The advantages and disadvantages of using wind to generate electricity.

☐ That electricity can be produced directly from the Sun's radiation using solar cells.

☐ The advantages and disadvantages of using solar energy to generate electricity.

☐ That solar cells are a useful electricity source in remote locations or in situations where a small amount of electricity is needed. It's usually uneconomical or impractical to connect these solar cells to the National Grid.

Hydroelectricity and Tides

☐ That in a hydroelectric power station, water drives turbines directly to generate electricity.

☐ That hydroelectric power can be useful in remote areas.

☐ That pumped storage can be used to store energy to meet peak electricity demands. Water is pumped into a higher reservoir at off-peak times, then released through turbines to generate electricity when demand is high.

☐ That tidal barrages are dams built across estuaries, where turbines are driven by tide water as it fills and leaves the estuary.

Other Renewable Resources

☐ That wave power can be generated using the motion of waves.

☐ That in volcanic areas hot water and steam that rise to the surface can be used to drive turbines and generators to generate electricity.

☐ That biofuels can be burned to heat water to generate electricity.

cont...

Energy Sources and the Environment

❏ That burning fossil fuels releases harmful gases into the atmosphere, such as CO_2 and sulfur dioxide.

❏ That obtaining fuels can have a major impact on the environment, through mining or as a result of accidents such as oil spillages.

❏ That using nuclear fuels to generate electricity produces harmful waste materials that are difficult and expensive to dispose of.

❏ That generating electricity using biofuels can be a carbon neutral process, but isn't necessarily.

❏ That growing biofuels can release methane and carbon dioxide into the atmosphere, and might also require areas of forest to be cleared.

❏ That carbon capture and storage (CCS) is a process in which carbon dioxide emissions are captured and stored. CCS is becoming more common as the technology is advancing quickly.

❏ That some of the best stores for carbon dioxide are in old oil and gas fields, e.g. under the North Sea.

Choosing Energy Sources

❏ That different types of power station have different start-up and decommissioning times that affect their overall cost and suitability.

❏ That of the fossil fuels (coal, oil and gas), gas power stations have the shortest start-up time. Nuclear power stations, on the other hand, have by far the longest of all decommissioning times.

❏ How to evaluate the use of different energy sources to generate electricity and suggest what method of generating electricity would be most suitable to use in a given situation.

❏ That the UK is faced with the constant problem of matching electricity supply with demand, and that the two ways of matching an increasing demand are increasing supply or finding ways of reducing the demand.

Electricity and the National Grid

❏ That the National Grid distributes electricity from power stations to consumers around the country.

❏ That pylons, cables and transformers are all used in the National Grid.

❏ That to transmit a given amount of power, increasing the voltage of the electricity supply decreases the current. This decreases the energy lost by heating in the cables transmitting electric current. This is why electricity is transmitted at a high voltage across the National Grid.

❏ That step-up transformers are used in the National Grid to increase the voltage of the supply before it's transmitted.

❏ That step-down transformers are used to reduce the voltage back to safer levels before the electricity is supplied to consumers.

❏ That electricity is transmitted by the National Grid using overhead power lines and underground cables, and be able to compare the pros and cons of using each method.

Exam-style Questions

1   Complete the following sentences using words from the box.

large	turbines	remote	cells	crowded	small

Solar .... use radiation from the Sun to generate electricity.

They can be useful energy sources in .... locations,
e.g. in space, where getting access to other energy sources is difficult.

They usually generate a .... amount of electricity, so it is often too
expensive or difficult to connect them to the National Grid.

(3 marks)

2   The table below shows the percentage of the total electricity produced from each of six
energy sources in two different countries of roughly the same size.

	Coal	Oil	Gas	Nuclear	Hydroelectric	Wind
Country 1	49.9%	2.4%	20.3%	19.6%	6.0%	1.8%
Country 2	3.9%	4.0%	4.5%	3.1%	84.2%	0.3%

2 (a)   What percentage of electricity in Country 1 is generated from non-renewable
energy sources?

(2 marks)

2 (b)   Both countries generate the same amount of electricity each year. Suggest which
country will emit more atmospheric pollution by generating electricity.
Explain your answer.

(2 marks)

2 (c)   Country 1 is considering reducing the amount of coal it burns and generating some of
its electricity from biofuels instead.

2 (c) (i)   Give **one** environmental advantage of switching to generating electricity using biofuels
from coal.

(1 mark)

2 (c) (ii) Give **one** disadvantage of switching to generating electricity using biofuels from coal.

(1 mark)

3   Coal is the most commonly used resource for generating electricity in the UK.

3 (a)   Coal is a fossil fuel. Which of the energy sources listed is **not** a fossil fuel?
Draw a circle around the correct answer.

wind   **gas**   **oil**

(1 mark)

3 (b)   Describe how electricity is generated in a coal-fired power station.

(3 marks)

3 (c)   Suggest **one** reason why coal is the most common source used for electricity generation in the UK.

(1 mark)

3 (d)   Some modern coal-fired power stations are built with carbon capture and storage (CCS) technology to reduce the damage that generating electricity using coal does to the environment.

3 (d) (i)   Name the substance caught and stored by carbon capture and storage systems.

(1 mark)

3 (d) (ii)   Name **one** environmental problem this substance causes.

(1 mark)

---

4   A small village is connected to the National Grid using overhead power cables.
The cables have to be repaired regularly as they are often damaged by high winds.

4 (a)   Give **two** advantages of replacing the overhead power cables with underground cables.

(2 marks)

4 (b)   Some of the villagers are concerned about the high voltages used to transmit electricity in the cables and want the voltage of the supply to be reduced.

4 (b) (i)   Name a device that could be used to reduce the voltage in the cables.

(1 mark)

4 (b) (ii)   The electricity supplier tells them that transmitting electricity at low voltages wastes more energy than transmitting it at high voltages. Explain why this happens.

(2 marks)

---

5   A government wants to build a number of new power stations that produce a large, reliable supply of electricity, but don't produce atmospheric pollution. Ideally, they would also want the power stations to be relatively quick and cheap to build.

5 (a)   Name **two** polluting gases that can be produced when generating electricity.

(2 marks)

5 (b)   Give **one** reason why using waves would not be a suitable method of generating electricity for the government to choose, assuming the country has a coastline.

(1 mark)

5 (c)   *In this question you will be assessed on the quality of your English, the organisation of your ideas and your use of appropriate specialist vocabulary.*

The government is advised to build hydroelectric power stations. Evaluate how well this method of generating electricity matches the government's needs.

(6 marks)

1. Wave Basics

Learning Objectives:

- Know that a wave transfers energy without transferring matter.
- Understand the terms amplitude, wavelength and frequency as measurements of waves.
- Know that all waves obey the wave equation: $v = f \times \lambda$.
- Know how to calculate wave speed using the wave equation.

Specification Reference
P1.5.1

Waves move through substances carrying energy from one place to another — and once they've gone, it's as if they were never there.

What is a wave?

A **wave** is a vibration that transfers energy without transferring any matter, by making the particles of the substance (or fields) that it is travelling through vibrate.

Waves can be represented on axes showing the **displacement** of one particle from its rest position as the wave moves along over time — see Figure 1. Crests and troughs are just points of maximum and minimum displacement from the particle's rest position.

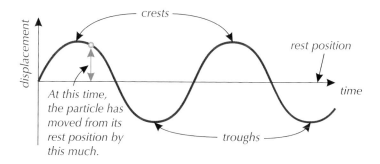

Figure 1: A diagram showing how the displacement of a particle in a wave change as the wave travels.

They can also be represented on axes of displacement against distance (see Figure 2). The shape is the same, but this graph shows a 'snap shot' of the displacements of several particles along the wave.

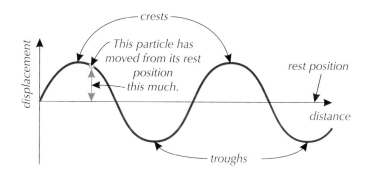

Figure 2: A diagram showing the displacements of particles along the wave.

Wave measurements

There are a few measurements that you can use to describe waves...

Amplitude

Tip: Amplitude is <u>not</u> the distance from a trough to a crest — it's an easy mistake to make so watch out...

The **amplitude** is the displacement from the rest position to a crest or a trough.

Wavelength

The **wavelength** is the length of a full cycle of the wave, e.g. the distance from crest to crest.

Tip: Amplitude can also be measured on a displacement-time graph (but wavelength can't).

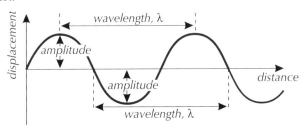

Figure 3: *A diagram showing the amplitude and wavelength of a wave.*

They could give you the distance between several crests and get you to find the wavelength — you just need to divide the distance by the number of wave cycles that cover that distance.

Frequency

Frequency is the number of complete waves passing a certain point per second or the number of waves produced by a source each second. Frequency is measured in hertz (Hz). 1 Hz is 1 wave per second.

Figure 4: *An oscilloscope screen showing a waveform. The amplitude, wavelength and frequency can be measured from it..*

The wave equation

The equation below applies to all waves. You need to learn it — and practise using it.

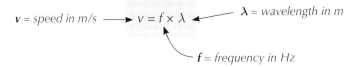

v = speed in m/s $\longrightarrow v = f \times \lambda \longleftarrow \lambda$ = wavelength in m

f = frequency in Hz

Tip: The symbol for wavelength is the Greek letter λ, which is called 'lambda'.

Example

A paddle vibrating up and down in a pool is used to produce waves on the water. The wavelength of each wave is 1.2 m and exactly 2 complete waves are produced per second. Calculate the speed of the wave.

The number of waves produced per second is the frequency.

So f = 2 Hz and λ = 1.2 m.

Substitute these into the wave equation:

$v = f \times \lambda = 2 \times 1.2 = 2.4$ m/s

A wave has a frequency of 4.0×10^7 Hz and a speed of 3.0×10^8 m/s. Find its wavelength.

You're trying to find λ using f and v, so you've got to rearrange the equation.

So $\lambda = v \div f = (3.0 \times 10^8) \div (4.0 \times 10^7) = 7.5$ m

$$\frac{v}{f \times \lambda}$$

Practice Questions — Fact Recall

Q1 What do waves transfer?

Q2 What is

a) the amplitude of a wave?   b) the wavelength of a wave?

Q3 What term gives the number of waves produced by a wave source per second?

Q4 Write down the wave equation. Say what each symbol stands for and the units that it is measured in.

Practice Questions — Application

Q1 The diagram below shows a man shaking a slinky up and down to produce a wave. The waves stop at the wall and do not bounce back along the rope. What is the wavelength of the wave?

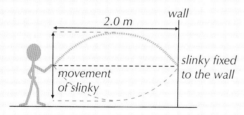

Q2 Calculate the speed of a wave with a wavelength of 0.45 m and a frequency of 15 Hz.

Q3 An oscilloscope is used to display the wave below.

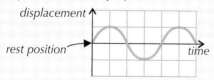

Copy the grid and draw the oscilloscope trace if:

a) the amplitude of the wave is increased.

b) the frequency of the wave is increased.

Q4 A light wave has a wavelength of 7.5×10^{-7} m and travels at 3.0×10^8 m/s. What is its frequency?

Learning Objectives:
- Know that waves can be transverse or longitudinal and that the main difference between them is the direction in which they vibrate compared to the direction in which the wave transfers energy.
- Know that electromagnetic waves are transverse.
- Know that longitudinal waves have compressions and rarefactions.
- Know that sound waves are longitudinal.
- Know that mechanical waves can be transverse or longitudinal.

Specification Reference
P1.5.1

2. Transverse and Longitudinal Waves

Waves can be either transverse or longitudinal. These words sound complicated but they describe something simple — the direction of the vibrations that the wave causes.

Transverse waves

Waves transfer energy in the same direction as they travel.
Transverse waves vibrate sideways to the direction that they travel in.

In transverse waves the vibrations are perpendicular (at 90°) to the direction of energy transfer of the wave.

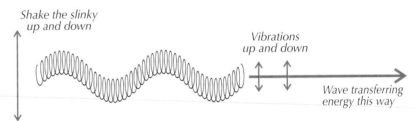

Shake the slinky up and down

Vibrations up and down

Wave transferring energy this way

Figure 1: *A transverse wave on a slinky spring.*

Here are some examples of transverse waves:

- Light and all other electromagnetic waves (p. 291).

- Ripples on water.

- Waves on strings.

- A slinky spring wiggled up and down (see Figure 1).

Longitudinal waves

Longitudinal waves have vibrations along the same line as they travel. They have areas of compression, in which the particles are bunched together, and areas of rarefaction, in which the particles are spread out — see Figure 2.

In longitudinal waves the vibrations are parallel to the direction of energy transfer of the wave.

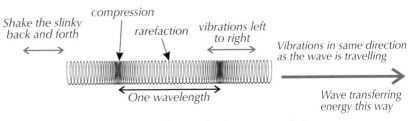

Shake the slinky back and forth

compression

rarefaction

vibrations left to right

Vibrations in same direction as the wave is travelling

One wavelength

Wave transferring energy this way

Figure 2: *A longitudinal wave on a slinky.*

Examples of longitudinal waves are:

- Sound waves (p. 302) and ultrasound.

- Some (not all) earthquake waves called seismic waves.

- A slinky spring when you push the end (see Figure 2).

Figure 3: Damage caused by an earthquake. The energy transferred by earthquake waves can be seen in the damage they cause.

Mechanical waves

Mechanical waves are waves that need a medium to travel in. This means they can't travel in a vacuum.

They can be either transverse or longitudinal. Water waves, sound waves (see page 302), seismic waves and waves in springs and ropes are all examples of mechanical waves.

Tip: A vacuum just means completely empty space — there aren't even any air particles. Light is <u>not</u> a mechanical wave — it can travel through a vacuum.

Practice Questions — Fact Recall

Q1 What is a transverse wave? Give one example.

Q2 What is a longitudinal wave?

Q3 What is meant by areas of compression and rarefaction in a longitudinal wave?

Q4 Which of the following waves is longitudinal?

    A light   **B** ultrasound   **C** water ripples   **D** a wave on a string

Q5 a) What is the name given to waves that need a medium to travel in?

    b) Are these waves longitudinal or transverse, or can they be either?

    c) Give an example of this type of wave.

- Know that waves can change direction at a boundary or obstacle by either reflecting, refracting or diffracting.
- Know that reflection and refraction can happen when waves meet boundaries between media.
- Know that waves are only refracted if they are not travelling along the normal.
- Know that waves can be diffracted when they meet an obstacle or pass through a gap.
- Know that a gap or obstacle the same size as the wavelength of a wave will cause it to diffract most.

Specification Reference P1.5.1

Tip: A medium could be anything — solid, liquid or gas — that a wave is moving through. Water, air, glass, tea... they're all media.

Tip: There's more detail on reflection later — on pages 298-300.

3. Wave Properties

All waves can bounce, bend and spread out... and of course there's a posh sciencey name for each. So here you go — reflection, refraction and diffraction.

Changing a wave's direction

When waves arrive at an obstacle or meet a boundary between two substances, their direction of travel can change. This could happen by reflection, refraction or diffraction.

Waves are often said to be travelling through a '**medium**' — it's just a fancy word for 'substance'. The plural of medium is media (and so unsurprisingly just means substances).

Reflection

When a wave meets a boundary between two media, it can bounce back. This is called **reflection**.

Reflection of light is what allows us to see objects. Light bounces off them into our eyes.

When light travelling in the same direction reflects from an even surface (smooth and shiny like a mirror) then it's all reflected at the same angle and you get a clear reflection.

When light travelling in the same direction reflects from an uneven surface such as a piece of paper, the light reflects off at different angles. (This is why you can't see your reflection in a piece of paper.)

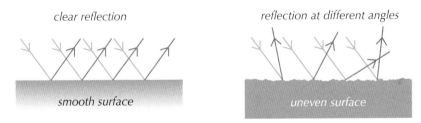

clear reflection *reflection at different angles*

smooth surface *uneven surface*

Figure 1: *A diagram showing reflection from both a smooth surface (left) and an uneven surface (right).*

Reflection's not too bad, but more complicated things can happen when waves meet a boundary between media.

Refraction

A wave can also **refract** at a boundary between two different media.

Tip: Be careful — it's easy to confuse refraction and reflection.

Refraction is when a wave changes direction as it crosses a boundary between media.

The **normal** to the boundary is an imaginary line that's perpendicular (at 90°) to the boundary at the point of incidence (where the wave hits the boundary) — see Figures 2 and 3. Waves are only refracted if they meet the boundary at an angle to the normal. Waves travelling along the normal are not refracted — they don't change direction (see Figure 3).

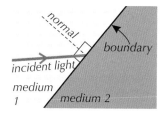

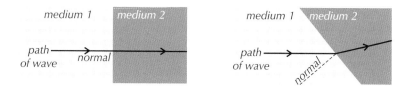

Figure 2: The normal to a boundary between two media.

Figure 3: A diagram showing a wave meeting the boundary between two media both face on (left) and at an angle (right).

Example

When light shines on a glass block, some of the light is reflected, but a lot of it passes through the glass and gets refracted as it does so.

The light is refracted when it enters the glass and again when it leaves the glass.

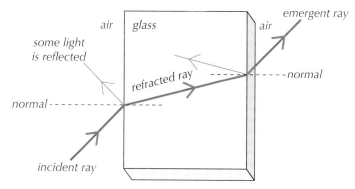

Figure 5: A diagram showing a ray of light being refracted as it passes through a glass block.

Figure 4: Refraction of light waves causes objects to look distorted when they are underwater. The light is bent when it passes through boundaries between media.

Tip: You don't need to know how to work out the amount that waves change direction, just that they do. There's more on refraction on page 303.

Diffraction

All waves **diffract** (spread out) at the edges when they pass through a gap or pass an obstacle.

The amount of diffraction depends on the size of the gap relative to the wavelength of the wave. The narrower the gap, or the longer the wavelength, the more the wave spreads out (see Figure 6).

A narrow gap is one that is the same order of magnitude as the wavelength of the wave — i.e. they're about the same size. So whether a gap counts as narrow or not depends on the wave in question.

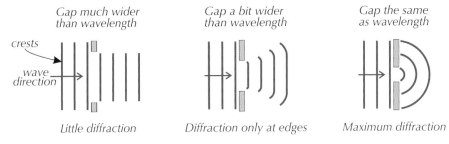

Figure 6: Waves diffracting as they pass through gaps of different sizes.

Gap much wider than wavelength — Little diffraction

Gap a bit wider than wavelength — Diffraction only at edges

Gap the same as wavelength — Maximum diffraction

crests

wave direction

Sound has quite a long wavelength (from several millimetres to several metres), so it diffracts through large gaps and round corners. Light has a very short wavelength (about 0.0005 mm), so it can be diffracted but it needs a really small gap.

Practice Questions — Fact Recall

Q1 What is reflection?

Q2 Why does a mirror produce a clear reflection of an object?

Q3 What is refraction?

Q4 What happens to the path of a wave if it crosses the boundary between two media travelling along the normal?

Q5 What happens to a wave if it crosses the boundary between two media at an angle to the normal?

Q6 What is diffraction?

Q7 A wave passes through a gap. What size gap will cause the wave to spread out the most?

Practice Questions — Application

Q1 A woman looks through a shop window. She sees herself as well as the window display inside the shop. Explain why she can see herself.

Q2 A cat meows in a garden. A dog is standing in the next garden with a solid fence in between as shown below.

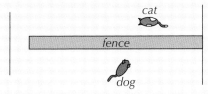

cat

fence

dog

Explain how the dog can hear the cat.

4. Electromagnetic Waves

Electromagnetic waves are a group of waves that all travel at the same speed in a vacuum. All the different wavelengths of EM waves form a spectrum...

The electromagnetic (EM) spectrum

The light that we can see is a type of electromagnetic (EM) wave. Electromagnetic waves are a group of transverse waves. They are sometimes called electromagnetic radiation.

EM waves can have any wavelength (or frequency) within a certain range. They form a spectrum of waves with different wavelengths (and frequencies) which is continuous — meaning there's no gaps in it. Visible light is just one part of this spectrum.

> The **electromagnetic (EM) spectrum** is a continuous spectrum of all the possible wavelengths of electromagnetic waves.

EM waves with different wavelengths (or frequencies) have different properties. We group them into seven basic types, but remember the spectrum is continuous — so the different regions actually merge, see Figure 1.

radio waves	micro-waves	infrared	visible light	ultraviolet	X-rays	gamma rays
10^{-1} m (10 cm) to 10^4 m	10^{-2} m (1 cm)	10^{-5} m (0.01 mm)	10^{-7} m	10^{-8} m	10^{-10} m	10^{-15} m	← wavelength

← Increasing wavelength

Increasing frequency →

Increasing energy →

Figure 1: The electromagnetic spectrum, with increasing frequency and energy and decreasing wavelength from left to right.

There are a few really important things to know about EM waves:

- EM waves vary in wavelength from around 10^{-15} m to more than 10^4 m.

- All the different types of EM wave travel at the same speed (3×10^8 m/s) in a vacuum (e.g. space).

- EM waves with higher frequencies have shorter wavelengths.

Learning Objectives:

- Know that the continuous spectrum of electromagnetic waves is known as the electromagnetic spectrum.

- Know the order of the types of waves in the electromagnetic spectrum.

- Know how wavelength, frequency and energy of the waves change across the electromagnetic spectrum.

- Know that all waves in the electromagnetic spectrum travel at the same speed through a vacuum.

Specification Reference P1.5.1

Exam Tip
You <u>need</u> to know the exact order of the EM spectrum in terms of wavelength, frequency and energy for the exam. Don't forget visible light, it's easily done.

Tip: EM waves can travel in a vacuum, unlike mechanical waves, which need a medium (p. 287).

Exam Tip
You don't need to remember the value for the speed of EM waves, but you <u>absolutely</u> need to remember that they all travel at the same speed in a vacuum. No EM wave is faster than any other — it's another common exam mistake.

Practice Questions — Fact Recall

Q1 Are electromagnetic waves transverse or longitudinal?

Q2 What is the electromagnetic spectrum?

Q3 What range of wavelengths could an electromagnetic wave have?

Q4 Write down the seven types of electromagnetic radiation in order of increasing wavelength.

Q5 Which type of electromagnetic wave has the highest frequency?

Q6 Which type of electromagnetic wave carries the least energy?

Q7 What can you say about the speed of different types of electromagnetic wave travelling in a vacuum?

Practice Question — Application

Q1 An electromagnetic wave source produces microwaves.

a) The wave source is adjusted so that it produces EM waves with a lower frequency. What effect does this have on the wavelength of the waves produced?

b) The wave source is now giving out a different type of electromagnetic radiation. What type of electromagnetic radiation it is now giving out?

Tip: Remember, you might hear electromagnetic waves called electromagnetic radiation — they're the same thing.

5. Communication Using EM Waves

Because of their different properties, different EM waves are used for different purposes... they're especially useful for communicating information.

Radio waves

Radio waves are EM waves with wavelengths longer than about 10 cm (see page 291). Radio waves are used mainly for radio and TV signals.

Different wavelengths of radio wave are used in different ways. Radio waves are sent out by transmitters and received by TV or radio aerials (receivers).

Long-wave radio (wavelengths of 1 – 10 km) can be transmitted and received halfway round the world because long wavelengths diffract (see p. 289) around the curved surface of the Earth (see Figure 2).

Long-wave radio wavelengths can also diffract around hills, into tunnels and all sorts. This diffraction effect makes it possible for radio signals to be received even if the receiver isn't in line of the sight of the transmitter.

Short-wave radio signals (wavelengths of about 10 m – 100 m) don't diffract around the Earth's curve, but they can still be received at large distances from the transmitter. They are reflected (see p. 288) between the Earth and the ionosphere — an electrically charged layer in the Earth's upper atmosphere (see Figure 2).

Medium-wave signals (well, the shorter ones) can also reflect from the ionosphere, depending on atmospheric conditions and the time of day.

The radio waves used for TV and FM radio transmissions have very short wavelengths (10 cm – 10 m). To get reception, you must be in direct sight of the transmitter — the signal doesn't bend around hills or travel far through buildings.

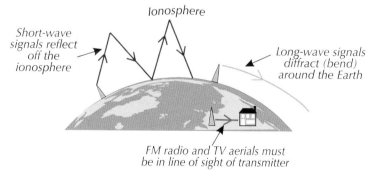

Figure 2: A diagram showing how different wavelength radio waves travel.

Short-wave signals reflect off the ionosphere

Ionosphere

Long-wave signals diffract (bend) around the Earth

FM radio and TV aerials must be in line of sight of transmitter

Microwaves

Communication to and from satellites (including satellite TV signals and satellite phones) uses microwaves. This is because some microwaves can pass easily through the Earth's atmosphere without being reflected, refracted, diffracted or absorbed, which means they can reach satellites.

Learning Objectives:

- Know the uses of waves for communication including radio waves for television and radio, microwaves for mobile phones and satellites and infrared for remote controls.

- Understand the possible health risks that may be linked to mobile phone use.

- Be able to compare the uses in communication of different EM waves.

Specification Reference P1.5.1

Tip: The receiver being in line of sight of the transmitter just means there are no obstacles directly in between them, i.e. light can travel from one to the other.

Figure 1: A television aerial raised high above a house to increase the signal quality. The aerial needs to be in direct sight of the transmitter as the radio waves used for TV signals do not diffract around large obstacles.

Satellite TV

Tip: Satellite TV uses microwaves but terrestrial TV (normal TV) uses radio waves (see previous page) — try not to get them confused in the exam.

For satellite TV, the signal from a transmitter is transmitted into space where it's picked up by the satellite's receiver dish orbiting thousands of kilometres above the Earth. The satellite transmits the signal back to Earth in a different direction where it's received by a satellite dish on the ground.

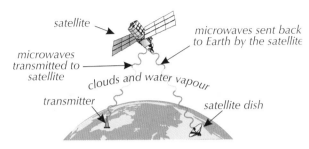

Figure 3: A diagram showing how microwaves are used for satellite communication.

Mobile phones

Mobile phones use microwaves to send signals between your phone and the nearest transmitter.

Remote-sensing satellites

Microwaves are used by remote-sensing satellites that monitor the Earth from space. They can be used to 'see' through the clouds and monitor oil spills, track the movement of icebergs, see how much rainforest has been chopped down and so on.

Figure 4: A remote-sensing satellite that uses microwaves to monitor the Earth.

Health concerns

Some wavelengths of microwaves are absorbed by water molecules and heat them up. This has led to worries about the health risks of using microwaves to transmit signals.

Figure 5: A mobile phone transmitter on top of a block of flats. Placing mobile phone transmitters near homes is controversial due to the possible health risks.

Example

As long as mobile phones are being used to transmit microwaves to and from transmitters, people will be exposed to microwaves. You will get more exposure if you use a mobile phone yourself or live near a mobile phone transmitter.

This is worrying as some microwaves heat up the cells in your body. The temperature rise caused by using a mobile phone is really, really tiny, but it is still unknown whether it could cause cancer. Some people think using your mobile a lot (especially next to your head), or living near a mast, could damage your health.

No conclusive evidence has been found that mobile phones increase the risk of any types of cancer or any other health effects, but the technology hasn't been around long enough to know about their long-term effects.

Infrared

Remote controls

Infrared waves (see p. 291) are used in lots of wireless remote controllers. Remote controls work by emitting different patterns of infrared waves to send different commands to an appliance, e.g. a TV.

Signals in optical fibres

Optical fibres are very thin fibres with a glass or plastic core that can be used to transmit signals of infrared or visible light.

The signal is carried as pulses of light or infrared radiation and is reflected off the sides of a very narrow core from one end of the fibre to the other.

Optical fibres are used in phone lines as they can carry data over long distances very quickly.

Figure 6: *A bundle of optical fibres with visible light being transmitted through them.*

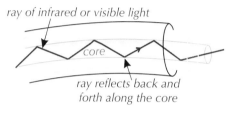

ray of infrared or visible light

core

ray reflects back and forth along the core

Figure 7: *An optical fibre transmitting a pulse of infrared or visible light.*

Practice Questions — Fact Recall

Q1 Explain why long-wave radio wavelengths can be received huge distances from the transmitter.

Q2 What type of electromagnetic waves are used to send terrestrial TV signals?

Q3 Why does your terrestrial TV aerial need to be in direct line of sight of the TV transmitter?

Q4 Why are microwaves ideal for transmitting signals to satellites?

Q5 What type of EM wave is used to transmit mobile phone signals?

Q6 Explain why people think there could be health risks of using mobile phones and the current evidence for these risks.

Q7 Give one use of infrared in communications.

Practice Question — Application

Q1 An Australian broadcasting station wants to broadcast a television signal from Australia that can be received in the UK.

a) Explain why a very short wave radio signal would not be suitable.

b) Explain how a microwave signal could be used for this broadcast.

Learning Objective:
- Know that infrared and visible light can be used for communication, e.g. visible light can be used for photography and infrared can be used for thermograms.

Specification Reference P1.5.1

6. EM Waves and Imaging

Electromagnetic waves aren't only used to communicate information using signals — images can communicate a lot of information too.

Using infrared to detect temperature variations

Infrared (IR) radiation (page 213) is also known as heat radiation. Infrared waves are given out by all hot objects — and the hotter the object, the more infrared waves it gives out.

This means infrared can be used to monitor temperatures. Infrared cameras can create an image showing temperature variations. The images can be colour coded to show different amounts of infrared.

Example 1

The heat loss through a house's uninsulated roof can be detected using an infrared camera and made into an image like Figure 1. You can use them to tell if a house needs insulating more (page 229).

hot

cold

Figure 1: *An infrared image of terraced houses. The image is colour coded by temperature with the reddest parts being the hottest. The roof of the house on the left appears hottest, so it is giving out more heat — it is badly insulated.*

Example 2

Infrared cameras can also be used as night-vision equipment by the military and by the police to spot criminals. Often the image isn't colour coded — the hotter an object is compared to its surroundings, the brighter it appears. It works best at night when the surroundings are colder (see Figures 2 and 3).

person cannot be seen in the dark

night-vision camera senses heat difference between person and surroundings

Figure 3: *A night-vision camera 'seeing' a person in the dark by detecting the infrared that their body gives off and turning it into a picture.*

Figure 2: *Infrared night-vision in use. A man is standing next to a screen showing what the scene looks like through an infrared night-vision camera.*

Photography

It sounds pretty obvious, but photography would be kinda tricky without visible light. Cameras use a lens to focus visible light onto a light-sensitive film or electronic sensor (see Figure 5).

The lens aperture is an opening that controls how much light enters the camera (like the pupil in an eye).

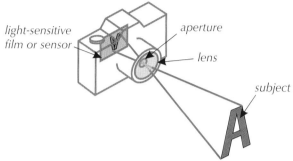

Figure 5: A diagram showing how a camera focuses visible light on to its film or sensor.

Figure 4: Two pictures of moving cars taken with different shutter speeds. The top image has a shorter shutter speed, so less light has been captured. In the bottom photo, the sensor was exposed to light for a longer time so the 'trails' of the car lights are longer.

The shutter speed determines how long the film or sensor is exposed to the light. By varying the aperture and shutter speed (and also the sensitivity of the film or the sensor), a photographer can capture as much or as little light as they want in their photograph.

Practice Questions — Fact Recall

Q1 Why can infrared be used to monitor temperature?

Q2 How does night-vision technology use EM waves to form an image of a person in the dark?

Q3 Give one use of visible light in communication.

Practice Question — Application

Q1 A wildlife documentary team used night-vision equipment to detect a rhino hiding in the bushes. They took two images, A and B, as shown. The temperature scale of the images is also shown.

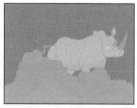

image A

image B

cold

hot

One image was taken during the night and one was taken during the day, but they forgot to label them. Which image was taken during the night, image A or image B? Explain how you know.

Learning Objectives:
- Know that the normal is a line perpendicular to the surface of reflection at the point where the wave is incident on the surface.
- Know the law of reflection: for every reflection, the angle of incidence is equal to the angle of reflection.
- Know what a virtual image is.
- Know that a reflection in a plane mirror produces a virtual image.
- Know that the virtual image produced by a plane mirror is upright and laterally inverted.
- Be able to draw a ray diagram of a reflection from a plane mirror.

Specification Reference P1.5.2

Tip: Note that these two angles are always defined between the ray itself and the normal. Don't ever label them as the angle between the ray and the surface. Definitely uncool.

Tip: The dull side of a mirror is always shown with diagonal lines like in Figure 1.

Tip: It's not just light that follows this rule, it's true for all waves.

7. Reflection

You've seen reflection of waves already on p. 288 — it's just waves bouncing back from a surface. Sadly you need to know a bit more detail for the exam...

The law of reflection

Angles of incidence and reflection

When drawing just a simple reflection from a boundary (see Figure 1) you'll need to draw in a normal (see p. 289). The normal is a construction line that's perpendicular to the boundary at the point the incident wave hits it. It's always drawn as a dashed line and it can help you draw incident and reflected waves.

The **angle of incidence** is the angle between the path of the incident wave and the normal. The **angle of reflection** is the angle between the path of the reflected wave and the normal.

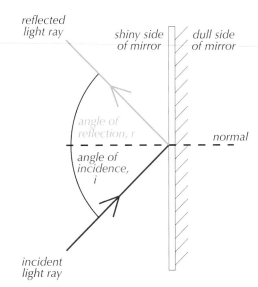

reflected light ray   *shiny side of mirror*   *dull side of mirror*

angle of reflection, r   *normal*

angle of incidence, i

incident light ray

Figure 1: *A diagram showing the normal, angle of incidence and angle of reflection of a light ray reflected by a mirror.*

The law

The **law of reflection** applies to every reflected wave:

$$\text{angle of incidence} = \text{angle of reflection}$$

So, every wave that is reflected will bounce back at exactly the same angle to the normal as the angle that it hit the surface at (but on the other side of the normal).

Images

An image is a picture of an object formed by light from the object. The light rays from the object either pass through its image, or just appear to.

A **virtual image** is an image that is formed when light rays appear to have come from a point that they don't actually pass through. If you put a screen where the image appears to be, the image would not appear on the screen because the light rays forming it aren't actually there.

When light rays are reflected in a plane (flat) mirror, they form a virtual image — the image appears to be 'inside' the mirror, but the light rays that form it don't actually come from there. The image formed is also upright (it's the right way up) and laterally inverted (see Figure 2).

Tip: The other type of image is a real image, where the rays actually pass through the point they appear to have come from. If you put a screen where the image is, the image would be on the screen. But you don't get any of these in reflections.

the knight's sword is in left hand

the laterally inverted knight has been flipped from left to right, so the sword is now in his right hand

the knight stays the same way up

knight   *laterally inverted knight*

Figure 2: *A diagram showing a laterally inverted image of a knight.*

Figure 3: *An ambulance. The writing on the front of an ambulance is laterally inverted, so that when you see it reflected in your car's rear view mirror it is the right way round and you can read it.*

Drawing ray diagrams

A **ray diagram** is a diagram that shows how the rays of light from an object form an image when reflected (or refracted). Here's a step by step guide on how to draw one to show a reflection of an object in a plane mirror.

1. The first thing you want to do is to draw the virtual image, not the rays (see Figure 4). To do that, you need to remember these three things about the image formed by a plane mirror:

    - The image is the same size as the object.

    - It is as far behind the mirror as the object is in front.

    - The image is virtual, upright and laterally inverted (see above.)

Tip: Use a ruler to make sure that the image is the right distance away and to make sure the image and the object are the same size.

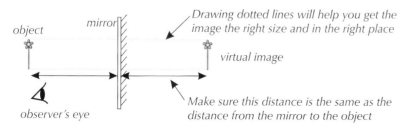

object   mirror   Drawing dotted lines will help you get the image the right size and in the right place

virtual image

observer's eye

Make sure this distance is the same as the distance from the mirror to the object

Figure 4: *A diagram of how draw the virtual image of an object in a plane mirror.*

2. Next, draw a reflected ray by drawing a line going from the top of the virtual image to the top of the eye (see Figure 5). Draw a bold line for the part of the ray between the mirror and eye, this is the reflected ray.

Draw a straight dotted line between the mirror and virtual image. This shows the 'virtual ray' of light — this just marks where the light appears to have come from (rather than the path it's actually travelled).

Draw an arrow on the reflected ray to show it's travelling from the mirror to the eye

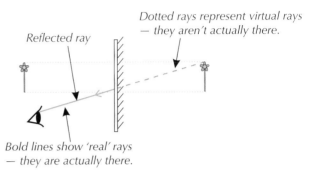

Dotted rays represent virtual rays — they aren't actually there.

Reflected ray

Bold lines show 'real' rays — they are actually there.

Figure 5: *A ray diagram showing how to draw the reflected ray from a mirror to the top of the eye and a virtual ray.*

3. Now draw the incident ray going from the top of the object to the mirror. The incident and reflected rays follow the law of reflection — but you don't actually have to measure any angles. Just draw the ray from the object to the point where the reflected ray meets the mirror.

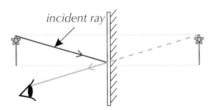

incident ray

Figure 6: *A ray diagram showing how to draw the first incident ray from the top of the object to show the complete reflection of one ray.*

4. Do steps 2 and 3 again for the bottom of the eye, and voilà — there's your ray diagram of a object being reflected in a plane mirror.

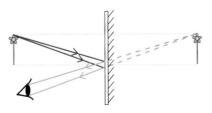

Figure 7: *A diagram showing how to draw the second reflected and incident rays from the top of the image and object to the bottom of the eye.*

Practice Questions — Fact Recall

Q1 What is meant by the normal when a wave reflects at a surface?

Q2 What is the angle of incidence?

Q3 Write down the law of reflection.

Q4 Write down three properties of the image formed when light reflects in a plane mirror.

Q5 What is a ray diagram?

Q6 Draw a ray diagram for a reflection of an object in a plane mirror.

Practice Questions — Application

Q1 Which image shows the reflection of the object shown in a plane mirror, A, B, C or D?

object   *image A*   *image B*   *image C*   *image D*

Q2 Draw a ray of light to show how the person can see the bulb.

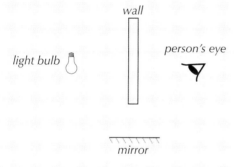

Learning Objectives:
- Know that sound waves are vibrations travelling through a medium and are caused by something vibrating.
- Know that our ear detects the vibrations caused by a sound wave and we hear them as sound.
- Know that sound waves are longitudinal.
- Know that echoes are just sound waves reflecting.
- Know that the pitch of a sound is due to its frequency.
- Know that the loudness of a sound is due to its amplitude.

Specification Reference
P1.5.3

8. Sound Waves

Sound is just another type of wave, and that means it can reflect, refract, diffract... you name a wave property, and sound can do it. It's things like the amplitude and frequency of a sound wave that decide what it sounds like.

What is a sound wave?

Sound waves are caused by vibrating objects. These mechanical vibrations are passed through the surrounding medium as a series of compressions. They're a type of longitudinal wave (see page 286.)

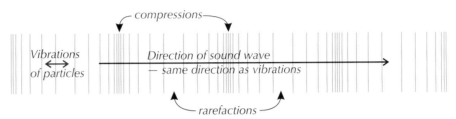

Figure 1: A sound wave made up of compressions and rarefactions of the particles in a medium.

Sometimes the sound will eventually travel through someone's ear and reach their eardrum, at which point the person might hear it.

Sound generally travels faster in solids than in liquids, and faster in liquids than in gases.

Sound can't travel in space, because it's mostly a vacuum (there are no particles to vibrate).

Tip: Sound is a type of mechanical wave (p. 287), because it needs a medium to travel in.

Reflection

Sound waves will be reflected by hard flat surfaces. You hear a delay between the original sound and the reflected sound because the reflected sound waves have to travel further, taking longer to reach your ears. It's known as an **echo**.

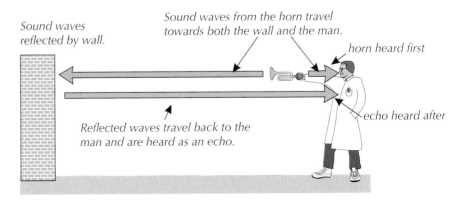

Figure 2: A diagram showing how an echo is heard when sound waves are reflected by a hard flat surface.

Reflection of sound is very noticeable in an empty room. A big empty room sounds completely different once you've put carpet, curtains and a bit of furniture in it. That's because these things absorb the sound and stop it echoing around the room.

Refraction

Sound waves will also refract (change direction) as they enter different media. However, since sound waves are always spreading out (diffracting — see page 289) so much, the change in direction is hard to spot under normal circumstances.

Figure 3: A bat in flight. Some bats use echoes to find their way around by emitting a call and listening for the echo to see how far away an object is from them.

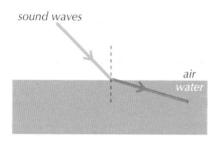

sound waves

air
water

Figure 4: Sound waves refracting as they cross a boundary from air to water.

Pitch and loudness

The pitch of a sound depends on the frequency of the sound wave. High frequency sound waves sound high pitched like a squeaking mouse. Low frequency sound waves sound low pitched like a mooing cow.

Remember, frequency is the number of complete vibrations each second (page 284) — it's measured in Hz. A wave that has a frequency of 100 Hz vibrates 100 times each second. Sound frequencies are also sometimes measured in kHz (1000 Hz) and MHz (1 000 000 Hz).

High frequency (or high pitch) also means shorter wavelength (see p. 284).

Tip: Some sounds are too high or low pitched for humans to hear — for example, we can't hear the sounds that a bat emits (see Figure 3) because they are too high-pitched.

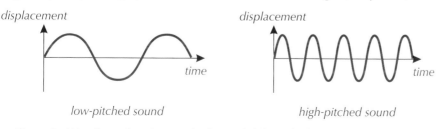

displacement

time

low-pitched sound

displacement

time

high-pitched sound

Figure 5: Waveforms for a low-pitched sound (left) and a high-pitched sound (right). The pitch of a sound depends on its frequency (or wavelength).

The loudness of a sound depends on the amplitude (p. 284) of the sound wave. The bigger the amplitude, the louder the sound.

Tip: A louder sound is caused by a bigger vibration. If you hit a drum harder, it will vibrate more and produce a louder sound.

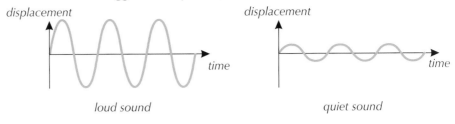

loud sound   *quiet sound*

Figure 6: *Waveforms for a loud sound (left) and a quiet sound (right). The loudness of a sound depends on its amplitude.*

Practice Questions — Fact Recall

Q1   Explain, in terms of particles, why sound cannot travel in a vacuum.

Q2   What causes an echo?

Q3   Why would you not expect to hear an echo in a room with carpets, curtains and furniture?

Q4   What affects the pitch of a sound wave?

Q5   What affects the loudness of a sound wave?

Practice Questions — Application

Q1   The oscilloscope traces of two sound waves, A and B, are shown below. The axis scales are exactly the same on each diagram.

Put the following four words into the sentences below. You may only use each word once.

| low | | high | | quiet | | loud |

Sound A is _____ pitched and _____.

Sound B is _____ pitched and _____.

Q2   A submarine emits sound waves and detects their echoes and allows it to detect objects in its path and work out how far away they are.

Tip: This submarine is using the same technique as the bat on the previous page. This man-made version of navigating using sound is called SONAR (Sound Navigation and Ranging) and it is used a lot to navigate underwater.

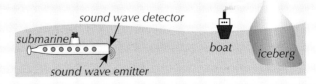

How does the submarine detect that one object is closer?

9. The Doppler Effect and Red-shift

The Doppler effect is what happens to waves when the thing producing them is moving. It's the reason that things sound different when coming towards you, than when they are moving away.

The Doppler effect

When something that emits waves moves towards you or away from you, the wavelengths and frequencies of the waves seem different — compared to when the source of the waves is stationary.

This is because the waves 'bunch up' in front of the moving wave source and 'spread out' behind the moving wave source — this is called the **Doppler effect**.

- The frequency of a wave source moving towards you will seem higher and its wavelength will seem shorter.

- The frequency of a wave source moving away from you will seem lower and its wavelength will seem longer.

The Doppler effect happens to both longitudinal waves (e.g. sound) and transverse waves (e.g. light and microwaves).

Learning Objectives:
- Know that the Doppler effect is where the wavelength and frequency of waves from a moving wave source measured by a stationary observer change.
- Know that the Doppler effect can happen to all waves.
- Know how the change in observed frequency and wavelength depends on the direction of travel of the wave source relative to the stationary observer.
- Know that the Doppler effect of light is called red-shift.

Specification Reference P1.5.4

> ### Example
>
> The Doppler effect is responsible for the vrrroomm from a racing car — the engine sounds lower-pitched when the car's gone past you and is moving away from you.
>
> - The sound waves from a stationary car are equally spaced (see Figure 1).
>
>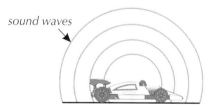
>
> **Figure 1:** *Sound waves from a stationary car.*
>
> - For a moving car, the wavelengths seem longer for a stationary observer behind the car than for a stationary observer in front of the car. So the frequency of sound seems to be lower as the car is moving away from you and higher as it is moving towards you.
>
>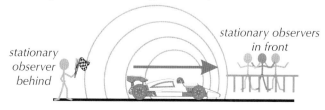
>
> **Figure 2:** *The Doppler effect of sound waves from a moving car.*

Tip: Remember, the higher the frequency of a sound wave, the higher the pitch.

- As the car zooms past you, the sound it makes appears to change — going from high pitched to low pitched.

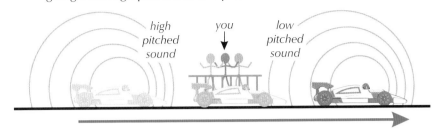

high pitched sound *you* *low pitched sound*

Figure 3: *The sound of a car changing wavelength, frequency and pitch as it moves relative to a stationary observer.*

Red-shift and blue-shift

Tip: See page 291 for the order of the electromagnetic (EM) spectrum.

The Doppler effect of light for a source travelling away from the observer is known as **red-shift**. As a light source moves away from us, the frequency of the light gets lower and shifts towards the red end of the visible light spectrum. This means that the light appears redder than it actually is.

When a light source is moving towards us, the frequency of the light gets higher and shifts towards the blue end of the visible light spectrum, so the light source appears bluer than it actually is. This is called blue-shift.

Stationary observer sees light with a lower frequency and higher wavelength than that actually emitted.

Stationary observer sees light with a higher frequency and lower wavelength than that actually emitted.

stationary observer

Light waves

Light source moving away from observer

Light source moving towards observer

Figure 4: *Light sources moving away from (left) and towards (right) an observer appear to have different frequencies and wavelengths to those emitted.*

Practice Questions — Fact Recall

Q1 What is the Doppler effect? Name two waves that this can happen to.

Q2 What change will a stationary observer see in the wavelength of a wave source that starts to move away from him?

Q3 What is red-shift?

Practice Question — Application

Q1 What direction is the ice cream van moving in the diagram? Explain how you know.

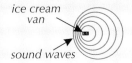

ice cream van

sound waves

10. The Origin of the Universe

Scientists aren't really sure about how the universe began, but there's quite a lot of evidence for something called the Big Bang — it's exciting stuff.

Red-shift of distant galaxies

Absorption spectra

Different chemical elements absorb different frequencies of light. Each element produces a specific pattern of dark lines at the frequencies that it absorbs in the visible light spectrum. A spectrum with dark lines in it is called a line absorption spectrum.

Dark lines in the visible light spectrum show which frequencies of light have been absorbed.

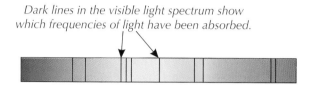

Figure 1: *A line absorption spectrum. The dark lines show the frequencies of light that have been absorbed.*

Red-shift of spectra

When we look at light from distant galaxies we can see the same absorption patterns we see on Earth, but at slightly lower frequencies than they should be — they're shifted towards the red end of the spectrum. The light is red-shifted (see p. 306).

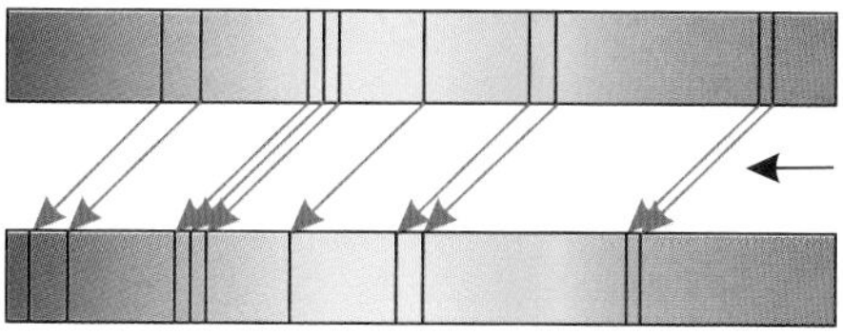

Absorption spectrum measured on Earth.

Absorption spectrum measured from light from a distant galaxy.

← *The whole spectrum has been red-shifted.*

Figure 2: *Two absorption spectra, one measured on Earth (top) and one measured from light from a distant galaxy which has been red-shifted (bottom).*

The light from almost all distant galaxies is red-shifted, which suggests they're moving away from us very quickly (see p. 306). It's the same result whichever direction you look in.

More distant galaxies have greater red-shifts than nearer ones. This means that more distant galaxies are moving away from us faster than nearer ones.

These red-shift observations are evidence that the whole universe is expanding.

Learning Objectives:

- Know that the light from most distant galaxies is red-shifted.

- Understand that the further away a galaxy is, the greater the red-shift of the light from it and the faster is it moving away from us.

- Know that the red-shift of light from distant galaxies provides evidence that the universe is expanding, and supports the Big Bang theory.

- Know that the Big Bang theory says that the universe began at a very small point and then began to expand.

- Know that cosmic microwave background radiation (CMBR) is microwave radiation that fills and comes from all parts of the universe. It comes from radiation emitted shortly after the universe began.

- Know how the Big Bang theory explains the CMBR and that it's the only theory we currently have to explain why it exists.

- Know the limitations of the Big Bang theory.

Specification Reference P1.5.4

Tip: Spectra is just the plural of spectrum.

The Big Bang theory

So red-shift tells us that distant galaxies are moving away from us. But something must have got them going. That 'something' was probably a big explosion — so they called it the Big Bang.

Tip: Our best guess is that the Big Bang happened about 13.8 billion years ago.

According to the **Big Bang theory**, all the matter and energy in the universe was once compressed into a very small space. Then it exploded from that single 'point' and started expanding.

The expansion is still going on. We can use the current rate of expansion of the universe to estimate its age.

The Steady State theory

Tip: You don't need to know about the Steady State theory, but you should appreciate that the Big Bang is not the only theory we've considered.

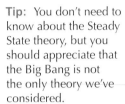

The Big Bang isn't the only game in town. The 'Steady State' theory says that the universe has always existed as it is now, and it always will do. It's based on the idea that the universe appears pretty much the same everywhere. This theory explains the apparent expansion by suggesting that matter is being created in the spaces as the universe expands. But there are some big problems with this theory.

The discovery of the cosmic microwave background radiation (CMBR) was strong evidence that the Big Bang was the more likely explanation of the two.

Figure 3: A whole sky image of cosmic microwave background radiation. The colours show temperature variations, but there's actually not much variation and it is almost all the same temperature.

Cosmic microwave background radiation (CMBR)

What is CMBR?

Scientists have detected low-frequency electromagnetic radiation coming from all parts of the universe.

This radiation is mostly in the microwave part of the EM spectrum (see p. 291). It's known as the **cosmic microwave background radiation (CMBR)**.

The Big Bang theory is the only theory that can explain the CMBR.

Tip: Neither red-shift or CMBR are proof of the Big Bang theory — they just support it.

Tip: Remember, radiation with less energy has a lower frequency.

Explaining CMBR

Just after the Big Bang while the universe was still extremely hot, everything in the universe emitted very high frequency (high energy) radiation.

As the universe expanded it has cooled, and this radiation has dropped in frequency and is now seen as microwave radiation.

Limitations of the Big Bang

Today nearly all astronomers agree there was a Big Bang. However, there are some who still support the Steady State theory. Some of these say the evidence just points that way. Others maybe don't want to change their mind — that would mean admitting they were wrong in the first place.

The Big Bang explains the universe's expansion well, but it isn't perfect. As it stands, it's not the whole explanation of the universe. There are observations that the theory can't yet explain, and it doesn't explain what actually caused the explosion in the first place, or what the conditions were like before the explosion (or if there was a 'before').

It seems most likely the Big Bang theory will be adapted in some way to account for its weaknesses rather than just dumped — it explains so much so well that scientists will need a lot of persuading to drop it altogether.

Practice Questions — Fact Recall

Q1 How is the red-shift of a galaxy related to its distance from us?

Q2 Explain how the red-shift of light from distant galaxies shows the universe is expanding.

Q3 What is the Big Bang theory for how the universe began?

Q4 What is CMBR and when was it formed?

Q5 Why did the discovery of CMBR provide such strong support for the Big Bang theory?

Practice Question — Application

Q1 The diagram below shows two absorption spectra, one measured from light from a distant galaxy and one measured in a laboratory.

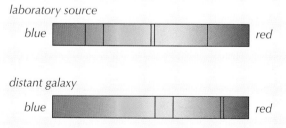

laboratory source

blue   red

distant galaxy

blue   red

What can you say about the movement of the distant galaxy in relation to Earth? Explain your answer.

Section Checklist — Make sure you know...

Wave Basics

☐ That waves are vibrations that transfer energy by causing particles or fields to vibrate.

☐ That the amplitude of a wave is the displacement from its rest position to a crest (or trough).

☐ That the wavelength of a wave is the length of one full cycle, measured from e.g. crest to crest.

☐ That the frequency of a wave is the number of complete waves passing a certain point, or produced by a wave source, per second.

☐ That the wave equation for wave speed is true for all waves and is $v = f \times \lambda$.

Transverse and Longitudinal Waves

☐ That there are two types of wave — transverse or longitudinal.

☐ That the vibrations in transverse waves are perpendicular to the direction of energy transfer.

☐ Some examples of transverse waves, including electromagnetic waves.

☐ That longitudinal waves have regions of compression and rarefraction, and that their vibrations are parallel to the direction of energy transfer.

☐ Some examples of longitudinal waves, including sound.

☐ That mechanical waves, e.g. sound, are waves that need a medium to travel in — they cannot travel in a vacuum. They can be either transverse or longitudinal.

Wave Properties

☐ That reflection is when a wave bounces back when it meets a boundary between two media.

☐ That refraction is where a wave changes direction when it crosses a boundary between two media at an angle to the normal.

☐ That diffraction is when a wave spreads out when it passes through a gap or meets an obstacle.

☐ That waves are diffracted most when the size of the gap or obstacle is of the same size as the wavelength of the wave.

☐ That sound has quite a long wavelength and light has a very short wavelength, and what this means for the diffraction of both sound and light.

Electromagnetic Waves

☐ That electromagnetic (EM) waves are a group of transverse waves that all travel at the same speed in a vacuum.

☐ That the EM spectrum is a continuous spectrum of all the possible wavelengths (or frequencies) of EM waves, split into seven types and varying in wavelength from 10^{-15} m to more than 10^4 m.

☐ The order of waves in the EM spectrum in terms of frequency, energy and wavelength.

cont...

Communication Using EM Waves

☐ How radio waves are used for TV and radio communication and that different wavelengths diffract by different amounts, which affects how they can be used.

☐ How microwaves are used for satellite communications and mobile phones.

☐ That there may be health risks associated with using or living near mobile phone equipment.

☐ How infrared is used for wireless remote controls and transmitting information using optical fibres.

EM Waves and Imaging

☐ How infrared and visible light can be used for photography and imaging (e.g. night-vision).

Reflection

☐ The definition of a normal and that for every reflected wave, the angle of incidence is equal to the angle of reflection.

☐ That a virtual image is formed when light rays appear to have come from a point they don't actually pass through. A plane mirror forms a virtual, upright, laterally inverted image.

☐ How to draw a ray diagram to show how an image is formed of an object reflected in a plane mirror.

Sound Waves

☐ That sound waves travel as vibrations in a medium which can be detected as sound by your ear.

☐ That sound waves are longitudinal and that echoes are reflected sound waves.

☐ That the higher the frequency of a sound wave, the higher the pitch of the sound. The higher the amplitude of the sound wave, the louder the sound.

The Doppler Effect and Red Shift

☐ What the Doppler effect is and that red-shift is the Doppler effect of light — it causes the frequency (and so the colour) of the observed light from a moving source to appear to shift.

The Origin of the Universe

☐ That the light from most distant galaxies is red-shifted. The further away a galaxy is, the larger the red-shift seen and so the faster the galaxy is moving.

☐ That observations of red-shift are evidence for the Big Bang theory.

☐ That the Big Bang theory says the universe began at one very small point and then started to expand.

☐ That CMBR is uniform microwave radiation found everywhere in the universe.

☐ That the Big Bang theory is the only current explanation we have for CMBR and how it explains it.

☐ The limitations of the Big Bang theory.

Exam-style Questions

1   The diagram shows transverse waves on a rope.

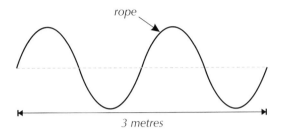

1 (a) (i)   What is the wavelength of each wave on the rope?

(1 mark)

1 (a) (ii)   The frequency of the waves is 2 Hz. Calculate the speed of the waves.
Use the correct equation from the equations listed on page 381.
Clearly show how you work out your answer.
Give your answer in m/s.

(2 marks)

1 (a) (iii)   Complete the sentence by drawing a circle around the correct answer from the box.

Increasing the
| frequency |
| wavelength |
| amplitude |
of the waves on the rope will increase the

number of complete waves passing a point on the rope each second.

(1 mark)

1 (b)   A wave on a rope is a transverse wave. Waves can be transverse or longitudinal.
1 (b) (i)   Give **one** similarity between transverse and longitudinal waves.

(1 mark)

1 (b) (ii)   **List A** gives the names of three waves. **List B** gives two possible wave types.
Draw **one or more** lines from each wave in **List A** to the correct wave type(s) in **List B**.

List A

Sound waves

Mechanical waves

Radio waves

List B

Transverse

Longitudinal

(3 marks)

2   The diagram shows the electromagnetic spectrum.

radio waves	micro-waves	infrared	visible light	ultraviolet	X-rays	gamma rays

2 (a)   Name **two** properties of electromagnetic waves that **increase** across the electromagnetic spectrum in the direction of the arrow shown.

(2 marks)

2 (b)   Which **two** types of electromagnetic wave are used for transmitting TV signals?

(2 marks)

2 (c)   Infrared radiation can be used to monitor temperatures.
Give **one** other use of infrared radiation.

(1 mark)

3   The diagram shows a kite flying above a calm pond with a flat surface.
An observer sees a reflection of the kite on the water.

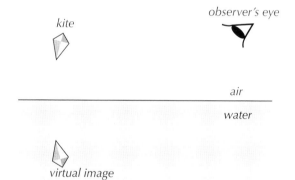

3 (a) (i)   Draw a ray diagram to show how the virtual image of the kite is formed.

(4 marks)

3 (a) (ii)   The image of the kite is virtual and laterally inverted.
Give **one** more property of the image formed.

(1 mark)

3 (b)   Not all of the light from the kite will be reflected by the water.
Some of the light may pass through the surface of the water and bend as it does so.

3 (b) (i)   Name this effect.

(1 mark)

3 (b) (ii)   Explain why the light that travels vertically down from the kite towards the water will not bend when it passes through the surface of the water.

(1 mark)

4   An ambulance is travelling down a street at high speed as shown in the diagram.
It has a loud siren and flashing blue lights to alert nearby drivers.

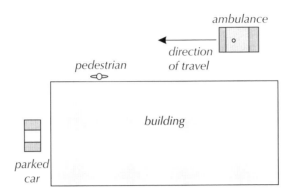

4 (a)   A car and the ambulance are in the positions shown in the diagram.

In terms of wave properties, explain why the driver in the parked car can hear the ambulance siren.

(1 mark)

4 (b)   The pedestrian standing by the street listens to the ambulance siren as it passes him.
He notices that the sound changes as the ambulance goes past.

(b) (i)   Name this effect.

(1 mark)

(b) (ii)   When will the siren sound the most high-pitched to the pedestrian?
Explain your answer.

(3 marks)

5   The CMBR is the name given to low-energy electromagnetic radiation that fills the
universe. The existence of the CMBR supports the 'Big Bang' theory of how the
universe began.

(a)   What does 'CMBR' stand for?

(1 mark)

(b)   Describe **one** other piece of evidence that supports the Big Bang theory.
You should outline the Big Bang theory and how this evidence supports the theory in
your answer.

(4 marks)

1. Controlled Assessment Structure

To get your Science GCSE, you'll need to do a controlled assessment as well as all your exams. This section tells you all about the controlled assessment and what you'll have to do.

What is the controlled assessment?

The controlled assessment is a type of test that you'll sit during your science lessons at school. The assessment is known as an investigative skills assessment (ISA) and it'll involve doing some research and some practical work as well as answering some questions on an exam paper. The controlled assessment is designed to test your How Science Works skills, not your knowledge and understanding of specific topics. So it's a good chance for you to show that you're really good at science and not just good at memorising facts.

> **Tip:** There's loads of information in the How Science Works section that'll help you with your controlled assessment so have a look at pages 1-15 before you get started.

What you'll have to do

There are five things that you'll need to do as part of the controlled assessment:

- First of all, you'll be given the outline of an investigation and a hypothesis and you'll have to go away and plan an experiment.

- Next you'll have to sit an exam paper which will ask you questions about the research that you've done and the method you've chosen.

- Then you'll actually get to carry out the experiment that you've planned (or a similar one) and record some results.

- Once you've done the experiment you'll be given some time to process the data that you've got — you'll get to calculate some averages and draw some pretty graphs.

- Finally, you'll do another exam paper which will ask you questions about your experiment, your results and your conclusions.

***Figure 1**: A student conducting an experiment.*

What is the controlled assessment worth?

The controlled assessment is worth 25% of the total marks for your GCSE, so it's just as important as the other exams you'll do, even though you're doing some (or all) of it in class and not in an exam hall. Don't worry though, there's loads of stuff over the next few pages to help you prepare.

> **Tip:** The controlled assessment might feel more informal, but you should take it just as seriously as all your other exams.

2. Planning and Research

The first step of the controlled assessment is to do some research and plan your experiment. Here's what you need to know...

What you'll be told

At the very beginning of your controlled assessment, your teacher will give you the context of an investigation and a hypothesis. The context will usually be a problem that a scientist might come across out in the real world.

Example

The context for your investigation could be something like:

"An electricity company is developing a new power station that uses a type of wave-powered turbine. The faster the wave speed of a surface water wave reaching a turbine, the faster the turbine will turn.

The company wants to find out if the depth of water affects the speed of a surface water wave. This will tell them where to put their turbines to get them to turn fastest."

The hypothesis that you'll need to investigate might be:

"The speed of a surface water wave depends on the depth of the water it is travelling in."

What you need to do

Tip: When researching your method, make sure you keep a note of any alternative methods too. You might be asked to briefly outline an alternative method that you could use, and explain why your chosen method is better.

Once you've been told the context of your investigation and the hypothesis that you should test, you'll need to do some research and come up with a possible method for an experiment to test the hypothesis. You should also research the context of the experiment a bit, so you understand why your investigation will be useful.

Example

If you were given the context and hypothesis in the example above, you'd need to do a bit of research to find out the following:

- Why would you expect the depth of the water to affect the speed of surface water waves.

- What experiments could you do to investigate the effect of water depth on the speed of surface water waves — this will involve finding a suitable way of creating surface water waves and measuring how fast they travel.

Tip: Although your teacher will give you a context for the experiment, you'll have to do all the research on your own.

When you're researching your method you need to think about what hazards might be associated with the experiment and what you need to do to make sure your experiment is a fair test (there's more on this on page 321). You should also think about what equipment you'll need and what recordings you'll need to make.

Tip: You might be given time to do your planning research in a lesson or you might be given it to do for homework.

Where to find information

There are lots of places where you can find information. Textbooks are an excellent place to start. Your teacher might be able to provide these or you could get some from the library. The internet can also be an excellent source of information.

When you're doing your research, make sure you look at a variety of resources — not just one book or website. Also, make sure you jot down exactly where you've found your information. You will be asked about the research you've done in your first ISA test and just saying you used 'a textbook' or 'the internet' won't be good enough — you'll need to give the names of any textbooks and their authors, and the names of any websites that you used.

Exam Tip
As you're doing your research, think about why you've found a particular source useful. Was the explanation really clear? Or was there a helpful diagram? You could get asked about this in the exam.

Understanding the hypothesis

A hypothesis is a specific statement about the things that you'll be testing and the result you're expecting to get.

Tip: See page 6 for lots more on hypotheses.

Examples

These are all hypotheses:

- There is a link between the rate of evaporation of a liquid and the air flow over the liquid.

- The stability of an emulsion does not depend on the proportion of emulsifier used.

- The number of a species of lichen will increase as the distance from a power station increases.

Tip: A hypothesis isn't a fact so it might not be true — it is just a statement that you are going to test.

A hypothesis will always contain an independent and a dependent variable — you need to identify which is which, so you know what to change and what to measure in your experiment.

Example

If the hypothesis was: **"The speed of a surface water wave depends on the depth of the water it is travelling in."** (see previous page) then the independent variable is the depth of the water and the dependent variable is the surface water wave speed.

Tip: The independent variable is the factor you'll change, the dependent variable is the factor that you'll measure.

Taking notes

As you're doing your research, you need to make some notes. You'll be given a sheet of A4 paper on which to make your notes and you'll be able to take these notes into your ISA tests with you — so it's in your interest to make them top notch. This example shows you what your notes sheet might look like and highlights the kind of notes you might make.

Example

Hypothesis:
The speed of a surface water wave depends on the depth of the water it is travelling in.

Research Sources:
The Sciences of Waves by J. Smith, published by RVN (good diagram of equipment, but no control variables listed) www.physencyclopedia.com/waves (no diagram)

Method(s):
Create a surface water wave in a tray of water by dropping one end of the tray from a small height.

Fair test: Use a wooden block to always drop the tray from the same height so that the wave produced is always the same. Always use the same tray and always use water.

Record the time it takes for the wave produced to travel a certain distance in the tank.

Repeat the experiment for several different depths of water.

Equipment:

Tray	Beaker
Water	Ruler
Wooden block	Stopwatch

Risk Assessment Issues:
Water on the floor — slip hazard.
Make sure spilt water is cleared up and hands are dry before handling equipment, e.g the glass beaker.

Relating the investigation to the context:
What is the best position for a wave turbine to make the turbine turn fastest? If the depth of water affects the surface water wave speed, then the turbine speed will depend on the water depth.

Tip: You shouldn't write a really detailed method at this stage — your notes will be checked to make sure you've not got too much detail. Just jot down the general details of the method(s) you could use to help to remind you when you're in the ISA tests.

Tip: You will need to explain how you are making your experiment a fair test in the ISA test, so you should have researched the variables that will need to be controlled and the ways you will control them — making a <u>brief</u> note of them here.

3. Section 1 of the ISA Test

After you've done your planning, you'll do the first ISA test. This asks you questions about the research that you've done and the method you'll use.

Hypotheses and variables

In section 1 of the ISA test you'll be asked how you'll test the hypothesis. You could be asked to identify the independent and dependent variables, as well as the control variables in your experiment.

Exam Tip
Remember, you're allowed to take one A4 page of your research notes into the ISA test with you.

> **Example**
>
> In the wave speed investigation, the independent variable is the depth of the water, the dependent variable is the surface water wave speed. The control variables are the size of the wave (which is controlled by the height the tray is dropped from), the tray used and the type of liquid used.

Have a look at page 6 to help you work out what the different variables in your experiment are.

Control group

Sometimes you can't control all the variables (e.g. the weather). In experiments like this, you'll need to use a control group or control experiment. A control group is one that is kept in the same conditions as the groups you are testing, but doesn't have anything done to it — see page 7. By comparing your test results to a control group, you can check that what you've done differently to the others compared with the control is really causing the effects seen.

Figure 1: *The plant on the left is a control plant in this experiment. It was kept in the same conditions as the other plants, but no testing was done on it. The other plants were exposed to different amounts of radiation, the control wasn't exposed to any.*

How to write a good method

In this part of the assessment you'll almost certainly be asked to write down a description of the method you're going to use. You need to give a clear and detailed description of how you would carry out your experiment. You must remember to include things like:

- A list of all the equipment you're going to need.

- A logical, step-by-step guide as to what you're going to do.

- What you're going to measure and how you're going to measure it.

- What control variables you're going to regulate and how you're going to regulate them.

- What hazards there are and how you're going to make sure the experiment is safe.

Exam Tip
You need to make sure you use correct spelling, punctuation and grammar too, otherwise you won't get full marks.

The equipment list

Your method should start with a list of the equipment that you'll need.

Example

To do the experiment planned in the previous topic (on surface water wave speed) you'd need the following equipment:

- A water-tight tray that can be filled with water.
- Enough water to fill the tray to the maximum depth that will be used.
- A large glass beaker to add water to the tank.
- A ruler that can measure in mm to measure the depth of the water.
- A 3 cm high wooden block that can be placed under one end of the tank, and removed to create the wave.
- A stopwatch to measure the time taken for the wave to travel a certain distance in the tank.

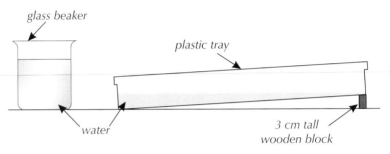

Figure 2: *Diagram showing some of the equipment needed for this investigation.*

Tip: You can include a labelled diagram of the apparatus you're going to use if you want to, but you don't have to.

Describing the method

Once you've written your equipment list, you should then write down exactly what you're going to do, listing the steps in the order that you're going to do them. Here's an example of a method.

Tip: It's OK to give your method as a numbered list — this is an easy way to make sure you cover all the points in the right order.

Tip: Never just say you're going to do something. Always say how you're going to do it. E.g. don't just say you're going to measure the depth — say you're going to measure the depth using a ruler.

Example

1. Lay the tray on a flat surface. Use the beaker and the ruler to add water to the tray until the depth of the water is 0.5 cm.

2. Slowly lift one end of the tray so that it is propped up 3 cm high by the block of wood. Make sure the same block is used in the same position throughout the experiment.

3. Wait a while to allow the water in the tray to settle completely.

4. Simultaneously pull the block of wood from under the end of the tray and start the stopwatch.

5. Count the number of times the surface water wave travels from one end to the other, stopping the stopwatch when the wave has travelled the length of the tray four times.

---

6. Record the time in seconds that it took for the wave to travel the length of the tank four times.

7. Repeat the experiment at this depth twice more. Then do three repeats of the experiment for water depths of 1.0 cm, 1.5 cm, 2.0 cm and 2.5 cm.

Tip: Don't forget to repeat your experiment. This will allow you to spot anomalous results more easily, and let you calculate means, which will make your results more accurate and reduce the impact of errors.

Fair testing

To make your experiment a fair test you need to make sure you control all of the variables. You will probably be asked to explain, as part of your method, what you're going to do to make sure your experiment is a fair test.

Example

In our experiment, we're helping to make it a fair test by dropping the tray from the same height each time so that the wave produced is always the same. Also, by using the same tray each time the experiment is repeated, so that the wave is always travelling the same distance. Water will be used each time we repeat the experiment.

Tip: There's more on fair tests and controlling variables on pages 6-7.

Things that you might need to watch out for completely depend on the experiment — use your common sense to make sure that anything that might affect the result is kept the same.

If you're using a sample in an experiment, e.g. testing a simple reflex response on 30 people, you also need to make sure that your sample size is appropriate for the experiment. It should be large enough to be representative of the population but not too large that you can't sensibly carry out the test — see p.2 for more.

Hazards

There will always be hazards associated with any experiment. In your plan you should identify these hazards and say how you're going to reduce any risk.

Example

In the experiment on surface water wave speed, the main hazard is spilt water becoming a slipping hazard. When doing this experiment the method should make sure that the tray and distance it drops won't cause the water to splash out of the tray. If water is spilt, it should be mopped up straight away and a wet floor hazard sign could also be used to alert people. Hands should be dried before handling any equipment.

Figure 3: *To manage a possible hazard, a wet floor sign can be used to alert people that there might be water on the floor.*

Tip: There are lots of other hazards that you might need to watch out for. See page 8 for more on hazards.

Method selection

You might be asked to explain why you've chosen the method you have. Think about things like equipment choices, whether it is practical to do in class, how long it will take to do and anything else that made you choose it.

Preliminary investigations

In this part of the test, you could be asked how you would use a preliminary investigation (or a trial run) to help you come up with your method. Trial runs are useful for working out what range of values would be best to use for the independent variable and what intervals to have between the values.

Tip: When you write about your preliminary investigations, make sure you describe the tests you would do and how they would help you to make a decision about the method.

Tip: See page 7 for lots more information on trial runs and why they are useful.

> **Example**
>
> In our experiment, a trial run could have been useful for three reasons:
>
> - To work out the height to drop the tray from. It should be high enough to create a surface water wave that you can easily see, but not so high that the water splashes out of the tray.
>
> - To work out the depths of water that are sensible to use in the tray available, and the intervals that you'll increase the depth in.
>
> - To work out how many lengths of the tray you should time the wave for. For example, you could do the experiment several times timing the wave travelling different numbers of lengths. You might find that one length is too fast to measure accurately, but after ten lengths, the wave might have become so small it can't be seen.

Table for results

In this part of the test, you will also need to draw a table for your results that you can fill in when you do the experiment. There are a few things to remember when drawing tables for results:

Tip: You don't have to draw your table for results by hand — you can use a computer instead.

- Make sure you include enough rows and columns to record all of the data you need to. You might also want to include a column for processing your data (e.g. working out an average).

- Make sure you give each column a heading so you know what's going to be recorded where.

- Make sure you include units for all your measurements.

Here's an example of a jolly good table for results.

> **Example**

Tip: Your table for results won't look exactly like this one. You might need more or less rows and columns depending on what kind of data you're collecting.

Water depth (cm)	Time (s)			Average time (s)
	Repeat 1	Repeat 2	Repeat 3	
0.5				
1.0				
1.5				
2.0				
2.5				

4. Doing the Experiment

If your plan isn't too outrageous, you'll then get to actually do the experiment you've planned. So grab your safety goggles and your lab coat...

Good laboratory practice

When it comes to actually doing the investigation, you might be allowed to do the one you planned, or you might be given another method to use by your teacher. When you're doing your experiment it's important that you use good laboratory practice. This means working safely and accurately.
To ensure you get good results, make sure you do the following:

- Measure all your quantities carefully — the more accurately you measure things the more accurate your results will be.

- Try to be consistent — for example, if you need to stir something, stir every sample for the same length of time.

- Don't let yourself get distracted by other people — if you're distracted by what other people are doing you're more likely to make a mistake or miss a reading.

As you're going along, make sure you remember to fill in your table of results — it's no good doing a perfect experiment if you forget to record the data.

Tip: If you're given an alternative method it doesn't necessarily mean your method was bad — it could be that your teacher thinks there are too many different methods in the class or your school doesn't have the right equipment for you.

Processing your results

Once you've got your data you might need to process it. This could involve calculating an average (by adding all your data together and dividing by the number of values) or working out a change in something (by subtracting the start reading from the end reading).

Then you'll need to plot your data on a graph. It's up to you what type of graph you use. See pages 11-13 for more information on how to draw a good graph.

Tip: See pages 11-13 for more on processing your results and calculating averages.

Tip: Your graph will be marked along with your exam papers so make sure it's nice and neat and all your axes are properly labelled.

Things to think about

As you're doing the experiment there are some things you need to think about:

- Is the equipment you're using good enough?
- Is there anything you would have done differently if you could do the experiment again?
- Have you got any anomalous results (see page 325) and if so can you think what might have gone wrong?
- Do the results you've got support the hypothesis?

These are all things that you could get asked about in the second part of your ISA so it's a good idea to think about them now while the experiment is still fresh in your mind.

Figure 1: *A student working in a laboratory.*

5. Section 2 of the ISA Test

Once you've done your experiment and processed the results it's time for the final part of your controlled assessment — the second ISA test.

Making conclusions

Tip: Remember, there's loads of information on processing data and making conclusions in the How Science Works section. Make sure you are really familiar with pages 9-15 before you go into your ISA tests.

In section 2 of the ISA test you will be asked to draw conclusions about your data. You could be asked what your data shows, or whether it supports the hypothesis. When drawing conclusions it's important to back them up with data from your results. You should describe the general trend in the data but also quote specific numerical values.

Example

This would be a good answer to the question: "Do your results support the hypothesis of this investigation?"

Yes, my results do support the hypothesis. The time a wave takes to travel a fixed distance depends on its speed. The time that the surface water wave took to travel four lengths of the tray decreased as the depth of the water in the tray increased. For example, a wave took an average of 5.6 seconds in 1.0 cm deep water and an average of 3.1 seconds in 2.5 cm deep water. So surface water wave speed does depend on water depth because the times decreased, and so the waves got faster as the depth increased.

Tip: It doesn't matter if the answer to this question is yes or no — the important thing is that your results support your conclusion.

Comparing results

In Section 2 of the test you will probably be asked to share your results, or compare them with the results that other people in the class got. This lets you see what similarities or differences there are between sets of results, and allows you to determine if your results are reproducible. If everyone in the class got similar results to you then your experiment is reproducible. If everyone got different results to you, your results aren't reproducible. It's OK to say your results aren't reproducible, though you should try to suggest why they weren't. And as always, back up anything you say by quoting some data.

Tip: Sharing results also gives you more data to calculate means from, which will make them more accurate.

Improving your method

In this part of the assessment, you might be given the opportunity to evaluate how you would improve the experiment if you did it again.

Example

- You could say that it would be better to use a deeper tray with more water to start with, because for the shallower depths the wave got quite small. This made it difficult to see by the time it had completed four lengths of the tank and could have affected the time measured.

- You could say that you'd repeat the results more times to increase the repeatability and accuracy of the results.

- You could say that you'd use a better technique (e.g. using a mechanical system to create a wave that is exactly the same each time) to help make sure your experiment was a fair test.

Tip: When suggesting an improvement to the method, it's really important that you explain how the improvement would give you better data next time.

Anomalous results

You could be asked whether or not there are any anomalous results in your data. Anomalous results are results that don't seem to fit with the rest of the data. If you're asked about anomalous results make sure you quote the result and explain why you think it is anomalous.

Tip: See page 10 for more information on anomalous results.

> **Example**
>
> I think the measurement that the time for 0.5 cm deep water was 8.7 seconds was an anomalous result because it doesn't seem to fit with the rest of the data (it's too high).

If you don't have any anomalous results, that's fine — just make sure you explain why you're sure none of your results are anomalous.

Tip: You could also be asked to suggest a reason for an anomalous result, e.g. in this case the wave could have been quite small and difficult to see by the time it completed the final length, making your timing wrong.

> **Example**
>
> I don't think there were any anomalous results in my data because an anomalous result is one that doesn't seem to fit with the rest of the data and all of my data points were very close to the line of best fit.

Analysing other data sources

In this final part of the controlled assessment you won't only get asked about your own data. You'll also be given some case studies to look at and be asked to analyse that data as well. You could be asked to compare this data to your own data and point out similarities and differences. Or you could be asked whether this data supports or contradicts the hypothesis.

As with making conclusions about your own data, when you're answering questions about these secondary sources it's crucial that you quote specific pieces of data from the source. You also shouldn't blindly trust the data in these sources — you should think as critically about this data as you did about your own data. Don't assume that it's better than yours and be on the look out for mistakes.

Exam Tip
The important thing when analysing other data sources is to read the question carefully and make sure you answer it — don't just describe the data without referring back to the original question.

Applying your results to a context

Another thing you could be asked to do is explain how your results can be applied to a particular context. This means thinking of a practical application of what you've found out. You should have done some research on this in the planning part of the controlled assessment. You can use the notes you made then to help you answer questions like this.

> **Example**
>
> We found out that increasing the depth of the water decreases the time taken for a wave to travel a fixed distance, and so increases surface water wave speed. Applying this to the context of the wave turbines of a power station — if the wave turbines are in deeper water, the wave speed will be faster than if they are in shallower water. The faster the waves, the faster they will make the turbines turn, so the turbines will turn faster in deeper water and so should be placed in as deep water as possible.

1. The Exams

Unfortunately, to get your Science GCSE you'll need to sit some exams. And that's what these pages are about — what to expect in your exams.

Assessment for Core Science (GCSE Science A)

The Core Science qualification for AQA A is called GCSE Science A. To get this qualification you'll have to do some exams that test your knowledge of biology, chemistry, physics and How Science Works. All the content that you need to know is in this book — there's even a dedicated How Science Works section on pages 1-15.

You'll also have to do a Controlled Assessment (also known as an 'ISA'). There's more about this on pages 315-325.

The exams

There are two different ways you can be assessed — Route 1 and Route 2. Remember that, whichever route you're taking, you could be asked questions on How Science Works in any of your exams. Also, you're allowed to use a calculator in all of your GCSE Science exams, so make sure you've got one.

Route 1

If you're following Route 1, you'll sit separate exams for biology, chemistry and physics. Here's how it works...

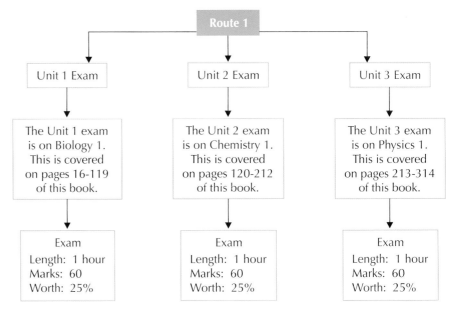

Route 2

If you're doing Route 2, you'll sit two exams that each contain a mixture of biology, chemistry and physics questions.

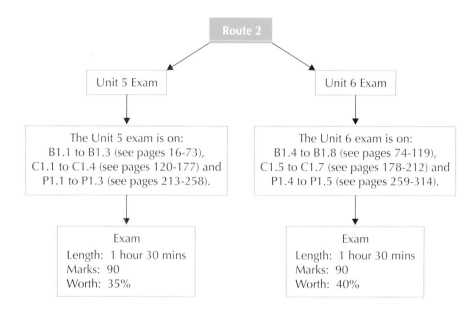

Route 2

Unit 5 Exam

Unit 6 Exam

The Unit 5 exam is on:
B1.1 to B1.3 (see pages 16-73),
C1.1 to C1.4 (see pages 120-177) and
P1.1 to P1.3 (see pages 213-258).

The Unit 6 exam is on:
B1.4 to B1.8 (see pages 74-119),
C1.5 to C1.7 (see pages 178-212) and
P1.4 to P1.5 (see pages 259-314).

Exam
Length: 1 hour 30 mins
Marks: 90
Worth: 35%

Exam
Length: 1 hour 30 mins
Marks: 90
Worth: 40%

Exam Tip
If you don't know which route you're doing ask your teacher, so you can revise the right stuff for the right exam.

Controlled assessment (ISA)

As well as your exams, you'll have to do a controlled assessment.
The controlled assessment involves a test made up of two sections, which will be based on a practical investigation that you've researched, planned and carried out.

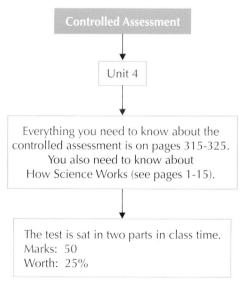

Controlled Assessment

Unit 4

Everything you need to know about the controlled assessment is on pages 315-325.
You also need to know about
How Science Works (see pages 1-15).

The test is sat in two parts in class time.
Marks: 50
Worth: 25%

Exam Tip
It doesn't matter what exam route you're taking for this — everyone has to do a controlled assessment.

Exam Tip
As well as the test, you'll have to do some research and carry out a practical investigation for your controlled assessment.

2. Exam Technique

Knowing the science is vitally important when it comes to passing your exams. But having good exam technique will also help. So here are some handy hints on how to squeeze every mark you possibly can out of those examiners.

Time management

Exam Tip
If a question is only worth 1 mark, don't waste time writing more than you need to.

Good time management is one of the most important exam skills to have — you need to think about how much time to spend on each question. Check out the length of your exams (you'll find them on the previous pages and on the front of your exam papers). These timings give you about 1 minute per mark. Try to stick to this to give yourself the best chance to get as many marks as possible.

Don't spend ages struggling with a question if you're finding it hard to answer — move on. You can come back to it later when you've bagged loads of other marks elsewhere. Also, you might find that some questions need a lot of work for only a few marks, while others are much quicker — so if you're short of time, answer the quick and easy questions first.

> **Example**
>
> The questions below are both worth the same number of marks but require different amounts of work.
>
> **1** **(a)** Give the names of the **two** main elements found in steel.
>
> *(2 marks)*
>
> **2** **(a)** Balance the equation shown below for the reaction between aluminium and hydrochloric acid.
>
> $$......Al \quad + \quad ......HCl \quad \rightarrow \quad ......AlCl_3 \quad + \quad ......H_2$$
>
> *(2 marks)*
>
> Question 1 (a) only asks you to write down the names of two elements — if you can remember them this shouldn't take you too long.
>
> Question 2 (a) asks you to balance an equation — this may take you a lot longer than writing down a couple of names, especially if you have to have a few goes at it before getting it right.
>
> So, if you're running out of time it makes sense to do questions like 1 (a) first and come back to 2 (a) if you've got time at the end.

Exam Tip
Don't forget to go back and do any questions that you left the first time round — you don't want to miss out on marks because you forgot to do the question.

Making educated guesses

Make sure you answer all the questions that you can — don't leave any blank if you can avoid it. If a question asks you to tick a box, circle a word or draw lines between boxes, you should never, ever leave it blank, even if you're short on time. It only takes a second or two to answer these questions, and even if you're not sure what the answer is you can have a good guess.

Look at the question below.

1 (a) Which of the following are illegal drugs? Tick **two** boxes.

Cannabis ☐ Statins ☐

Nicotine ☐ Heroin ☐

(2 marks)

Say you knew that heroin was illegal, and that nicotine was in cigarettes, but weren't sure about the other two drugs.

You can tick heroin — you know it's illegal. If nicotine is in cigarettes then it must be legal, so leave that box blank. That leaves you with cannabis and statins. If you're not absolutely sure which is legal and which isn't, just have a guess. You won't lose any marks if you get it wrong and there's a 50% chance that you'll get it right.

Exam Tip
If you're asked, for example, to tick two boxes, make sure you only tick two. If you tick more than two, you won't get the marks even if some of your answers are correct.

Command Words

Command words are just the bits of a question that tell you what to do. You'll find answering exam questions much easier if you understand exactly what they mean, so here's a brief summary of the most common ones:

Command word:	What to do:
Give / Name / State / Write down	Give a brief one or two word answer, or a short sentence.
Complete	Write your answer in the space given. This could be a gap in a sentence or table, or you might have to finish a diagram.
Describe	Write about what something's like, e.g. describe the trend in a set of results.
Explain	Make something clear, or give the reasons why something happens. The points in your answer need to be linked together, so you should include words like because, so, therefore, due to, etc.
Calculate	Use the numbers in the question to work out an answer.
Suggest	Use your scientific knowledge to work out what the answer might be.
Compare	Give the similarities and differences between two things.
Evaluate	Give the arguments both for and against an issue, or the advantages and disadvantages of something. You may also need to give an overall judgement.

Some questions will also ask you to answer 'using the information provided' (e.g. a graph, table or passage of text) — if so, you must refer to the information you've been given or you won't get the marks.

Exam Tip
When you're reading an exam question, you might find it helpful to underline the command word. It can help you work out what type of answer to give.

Exam Tip
It's easy to get <u>describe</u> and <u>explain</u> mixed up, but they're quite different. For example, if you're asked to describe some data, just state the overall pattern or trend. If you're asked to explain data, you'll need to <u>give reasons</u> for the trend.

3. Question Types

If all questions were the same, exams would be mightily boring. So really, it's quite handy that there are lots of different question types. Here are just a few...

Exam Tip
You'll need to use black ink or a black ball-point pen to write your answers, so make sure that you've got a couple ready for the exam.

Quality of written communication (QWC)

All of the exams you take for GCSE Science A will have at least one 6 mark question that assesses your quality of written communication — this just means that the examiner will assess your ability to write properly. This may seem like a bit of a drag, but you will lose marks if you don't do it. Here are some tips on how to get all the marks you can...

- Make sure your scribble (sorry, writing) is legible.

- Be careful with your spelling, punctuation and grammar — they need to be accurate.

- Make sure your writing style is appropriate for an exam. You need to write in full sentences and use fairly formal language. For example, the sentence "cooking in vegetable oil rather than water improves the flavour of food" is an appropriate style. "Vegetable oil makes food taste dead good" isn't — it's too informal.

- Organise your answer clearly. The points you make need to be in a logical order.

- Use specialist scientific vocabulary whenever you can. For example, if you're describing a reflex you'd need to use scientific terms like sensory neurone and motor neurone. You also need to use these terms correctly — it's no good knowing the words if you don't know what they mean.

Exam Tip
Make sure you write enough to get all the marks that are available. QWC questions are worth six marks, so a one sentence answer isn't likely to be enough — you'll need to write at least a paragraph or two.

Exam Tip
You should really be doing these things all the way through your exam — but they're particularly important in the QWC questions, so it's worth taking special care with them there.

You'll be told which questions will be used to assess the quality of your written communication. On the front of your exam paper it will say something like 'Question 2 should be answered in continuous prose' — and that's the question where your writing will be assessed. There'll also be a reminder when you get to the question itself. It'll say something like:

In this question you will be assessed on the quality of your English, the organisation of your ideas and your use of appropriate specialist vocabulary.

Evaluating information

In the exam, you may be given some information to read and then be asked to evaluate it.

> **Example**
>
> Drug X and drug Y are both weight loss drugs. You may be given some information on how drug X and drug Y work, how effective they are and what side effects they have. You could then be asked to evaluate the use of drug X and drug Y in aiding weight loss.

In the previous example, you're basically being asked to compare the use of the two types of drug — including the advantages and disadvantages of each. This means you need to do more than just pick out relevant information from the question and repeat it in your answer — you need to make clear comparisons between the two.

Example

If the information tells you that people taking drug X lose 1 kilogram per week on average and that people taking drug Y lose 1.5 kilograms per week on average, you need to say in your answer that "people taking drug Y lose **more** weight per week on average than people taking drug X". It's even better to say that "people taking drug Y lose **0.5 kilograms more** weight per week on average than people taking drug X".

The question may ask you to write a conclusion too, e.g. make an overall judgement about which drug is best. If so, you must include a conclusion in your answer and you must back it up with evidence from the question.

Calculations

Questions that involve a calculation can seem a bit scary. But they're really not that bad. Here are some tips to help you out...

Showing working

The most important thing to remember is to show your working. You've probably heard it a million times before but it makes perfect sense. It only takes a few seconds more to write down what's in your head and it might stop you from making silly errors and losing out on easy marks. You won't get a mark for a wrong answer but you could get marks for the method you used to work out the answer.

Units

Make sure you always give units for your answer when you're asked for them. You could get a mark for getting the units right even if you haven't managed to do the calculation.

Significant figures

The first significant figure (s.f.) of a number is the first digit that isn't a zero. The second, third and fourth significant figures follow on immediately after the first (even if they're zeros). If you need to round an answer to a calculation, give it to the lowest number of significant figures given in the question data. You should write down the number of significant figures you've rounded to after your answer.

Figure 1: *A calculator. Under the pressure of an exam it's easy to make mistakes in calculations, even if they're really simple ones. So don't be afraid to put every calculation into the calculator.*

Example

Say you need to round 0.1793 m to two significant figures. The first digit that isn't a zero is 1, so that's the first significant figure, and the second is 7. The third significant figure is a 9, so round the second significant figure up from 7 to 8. Bob's your uncle, you've got 0.1793 m = 0.18 m (to 2 s.f.).

Standard form Higher

You need to be able to work with numbers that are written in standard form. Standard form is used for writing very big or very small numbers in a more convenient way. Standard form must always look like this:

This number must always ⟶ $A \times 10^n$ *This number is the number of places the decimal point moves.*
be between 1 and 10.

You can write numbers out in full rather than in standard form by moving the decimal point. Which direction to move the decimal point, and how many places to move it depends on the value of 'n'. If 'n' is positive, the decimal point needs to move to the right. If 'n' is negative the decimal point needs to move to the left.

Examples

Here's how to write out 9.3×10^4 in full.

- Work out which way the decimal point needs to move, by looking at the 'n' number. Here it's a positive number (4) so the decimal point needs to move to the right.

- Then count the number of places the decimal point has to move to the right. In this example it's four:

$$9.3 \times 10^4 = 9\,3\,0\,0\,0.$$

- So 9.3×10^4 is the same as 93 000.

Here's how to write out 5.6×10^{-5} in full.

- 'n' is a negative number (–5) so the decimal point needs to move to the left.

- Count five places to the left.

$$5.6 \times 10^{-5} = .0\,0\,0\,0\,5\,6$$

- So 5.6×10^{-5} is the same as 0.000056.

The key things to remember with numbers in standard form are...

- When 'n' is positive the number is big. The bigger 'n' is, the bigger the number is.

- When 'n' is negative the number is small. The smaller 'n' is (the more negative), the smaller the number is.

- When 'n' is the same for two or more numbers, you need to look at the start of each number to work out which is bigger. For example, 4.5 is bigger than 3.0, so 4.5×10^5 is bigger than 3.0×10^5.

Answers

Biology 1

Biology 1.1 Keeping Healthy

1. Diet and Metabolic Rate

Page 18 — Fact Recall Questions

Q1 To release energy.

Q2 To keep your skin, bones, blood and everything else generally healthy.

Q3 Metabolic rate is the speed at which the chemical reactions in your body occur.

Q4 false

There are slight variations in the resting metabolic rate of different people.

Q5 The more active you are, the more energy you use.

Page 18 — Application Questions

Q1 Because the body needs protein for growth, cell repair and cell replacement.

Q2 a) Joe because he does a lot more exercise than Paula, so he's likely to have a lot more muscle / he's a man and Paula's a woman, so he's likely to have a lot more muscle.

b) Joe because he is more active than Paula.

Q3 a) E.g. because he is more active than the man in the research station, so he will use more energy.

b) E.g. carbohydrates and fats because they both release energy (and because fats help to keep you warm).

2. Factors Affecting Health

Page 20 — Fact Recall Questions

Q1 That their diet is badly out of balance.

Q2 Excess fat or carbohydrate in the diet can lead to obesity.

Q3 E.g. arthritis / type 2 diabetes / high blood pressure / heart disease.

Q4 true

Q5 Exercise increases the amount of energy used by the body and decreases the amount stored as fat. It also builds muscle so it helps to boost metabolic rate. Therefore people who exercise are less likely to suffer from health problems such as obesity.

Q6 E.g. some people may inherit factors that affect their metabolic rate. Some people may inherit factors that affect their blood cholesterol level.

3. Evaluating Food, Lifestyle and Diet

Page 23 — Application Questions

Q1 a) i) Food A

ii) Too much high energy food in the diet could lead to obesity.

b) $1.44 \div 6 \times 100 = \textbf{24\%}$

c) Food B because it is lower in fat, saturated fat, salt and calories / because it has more green and orange labels than Food A and no red labels.

Q2 No because, any two from: e.g. the trial was carried out by the manufacturers. / Not enough people were tested in the trial/the sample size wasn't big enough. / Only women were tested in the trial — the milkshake may not be as effective for men. / The manufacturers are relying on the women saying they've lost weight rather than actually measuring their weight loss. / No controls were used, so there was no comparison made between people drinking the slimming milkshake and people trying to lose weight using diet and exercise alone. / The results haven't been reproduced.

4. Fighting Disease

Page 26 — Fact Recall Questions

Q1 E.g. bacteria — cell damage, producing toxins. Viruses — cell damage.

Q2 By engulfing and digesting foreign cells/pathogens. By producing antitoxins. By producing antibodies to lock onto and kill invading cells.

Q3 That if they are infected with that particular pathogen again, their white blood cells will rapidly produce the antibodies to kill it and they won't get ill.

Page 26 — Application Questions

Q1 a) John should now be immune to measles. If he is infected with the measles virus again, his white blood cells should rapidly produce the antibodies against it — meaning he won't get ill.

b) Antibodies are specific to a particular type of antigen. John has never had German measles before, so he won't have made antibodies against the antigens on the German measles virus. This means it will take his white blood cells time to produce antibodies against the virus, during which he could get ill.

Q2 a) E.g. by releasing toxins. Through cell damage.

Clostridium tetani actually releases a powerful toxin that causes severe muscle spasms — but you don't need to know that to answer the question. You just need to be able to apply what you already know about how bacteria make you feel ill.

b) E.g. it uses platelets to help blood clot quickly and seal wounds before *Clostridium tetani* can enter.

5. Fighting Disease — Vaccination
Page 28 — Application Question
Q1 a) A big outbreak of whooping cough.
 b) E.g. the vaccination will involve injecting a small amount of the dead or inactive whooping cough pathogen. The pathogen will carry antigens, which will trigger the white blood cells to produce antibodies to attack the pathogen. If the vaccinated person is infected with the whooping cough pathogen at a later date, their white blood cells should be able to rapidly mass produce antibodies to kill off the pathogen.
 c) If a large percentage of the population are vaccinated it means that the people who aren't vaccinated (i.e. very young babies) are less likely to catch the disease because there are fewer people to pass it on.

6. Fighting Disease — Drugs
Page 30 — Fact Recall Questions
Q1 false
Q2 A drug used to kill or prevent the growth of bacteria. E.g. penicillin / methicillin.
Q3 Different antibiotics kill different types of bacteria, so it's important to be treated with the right one.
Q4 Viruses reproduce using your own body cells, so it's difficult to develop drugs that destroy the virus without killing the body's cells.
Q5 a) E.g. MRSA/methicillin-resistant *Staphylococcus aureus*
 You could get asked about MRSA in your exam, so make sure you know what it is.
 b) natural selection
Q6 It helps to prevent antibiotic resistance from spreading.

Page 30 — Application Questions
Q1 a) Because antibiotics don't destroy viruses.
 b) E.g. because it won't tackle the underlying cause of Chloe's flu (it will only help to relieve her symptoms).
Q2 E.g. because it's important for doctors to avoid over-prescribing antibiotics in order to slow down the development of antibiotic resistance. James' infection is only mild.
Q3 E.g. people with a *Streptococcus pneumoniae* infection may have been treated with penicillin. A mutation may have caused some of these bacteria to be resistant to the penicillin, meaning that only the non-resistant bacteria would have been killed. The individual resistant bacteria would have survived and reproduced, increasing the population of penicillin-resistant *Streptococcus pneumoniae* bacteria.

7. Fighting Disease — Investigating Antibiotic Action
Page 32 — Application Questions
Q1 a) i) E.g. by passing it through a flame.
 ii) To avoid contaminating his culture with unwanted microorganisms.
 b) i) 1, 2, 3 and 5. The bacteria were able to grow around these discs.
 ii) Disc 4. This had the largest clear zone around it, so it must have killed the most bacteria.
 iii) E.g. the size of the paper discs. / The concentration of the antibiotics.
 c) To prevent unwanted microorganisms from the air getting into the culture and contaminating it.
 d) Because harmful pathogens aren't likely to grow at this temperature.

8. Fighting Disease — Past & Future
Page 34 — Fact Recall Questions
Q1 That if doctors washed their hands in an antiseptic solution, it cut the death rate of women from puerperal fever in his hospital.
Q2 They have decreased them dramatically.
Q3 They're trying to develop new antibiotics that will be effective against antibiotic-resistant strains of bacteria.

Page 34 — Application Question
Q1 E.g. we'd never encountered the mutated version of the H1N1 virus before, so no one was immune to it. There were also no effective vaccinations/antiviral drugs against it. It may have also been hard to stop it spreading between countries as so many people now travel by plane.

Pages 37-38 — Biology 1.1
Exam-style Questions
1 a) i) $64 \div (1.56^2) = $ **26.3** *(1 mark)*
 ii) overweight *(1 mark)*
 If you got Kate's BMI wrong and this meant you ended up getting her weight description wrong too, don't panic. Providing the weight description you wrote down matches the BMI you gave for part a) i), you can still get the mark here.
 b) releasing energy *(1 mark)*
 c) To lose weight, you need to take in less energy than you use up *(1 mark)*. Exercise helps you to lose weight because it increases the amount of energy you use up *(1 mark)*.
2 a) by damaging your cells *(1 mark)*
 b) i) Robin will be injected with a small amount of dead or inactive hepatitis A virus *(1 mark)*. The virus will carry antigens, which will cause Robin's white blood cells *(1 mark)* to produce antibodies to attack the virus *(1 mark)*. If Robin is infected with the live hepatitis A virus at a later date, his white blood cells should be able to rapidly mass produce antibodies to kill off the virus *(1 mark)*.

ii) Antibodies are specific to a particular type of pathogen *(1 mark)*. This means that the hepatitis A vaccination will not cause Robin to produce antibodies that will be effective against the hepatitis B virus *(1 mark)*.

c) As a virus, hepatitis A will reproduce using the body cells of the person it infects *(1 mark)*. This makes it difficult to develop a drug against the virus without killing the body cells *(1 mark)*.

3 a) A microorganism that causes disease *(1 mark)*.

   b) In 1980, there were just over 4 million reported measles cases *(1 mark)*. Between 1980 and 2010 the number of reported measles cases dropped to around 0.4 million (after rising to a peak of 4.5 million in around 1982) *(1 mark)*. The estimated vaccine coverage was around 12% of the population in 1980 *(1 mark)*. Between 1980 and 2010 it increased to around 85% *(1 mark)*.

   The question asks you to use data from the graph to support your answer — so you must include some figures to get the marks. The graph has three different axes, which can make things a bit tricky. Take your time and work out what each one shows before answering the question.

   c) E.g. the data suggests that as the estimated percentage vaccination coverage increased, the number of reported measles cases decreased — this supports the case for vaccinating people against measles *(1 mark)*. However it doesn't prove that the increase in vaccination coverage definitely caused the decrease in measles cases, since other factors may have been at work *(1 mark)*. It also doesn't tell us anything about the side effects of the vaccine *(1 mark)*.

4 a) Any two from, e.g. heat/sterilise the agar jelly *(1 mark)* / sterilise the inoculating loop before using it, e.g. by passing it through a flame *(1 mark)* / sterilise the Petri dish before using it *(1 mark)*.

   b) Antibiotic 5 because this disc has the biggest clear zone around it *(1 mark)*. This means that more bacteria were killed/unable to grow around antibiotic 5 than around any of the other antibiotics / the bacteria were least resistant to antibiotic 5 *(1 mark)*.

   It stands to reason that the best antibiotic for getting rid of the infection is the one that kills the most bacteria.

   c) E.g. people infected with this bacteria may have been treated with these antibiotics *(1 mark)*. Mutations may have caused some of these bacteria to be resistant to these antibiotics *(1 mark)*, meaning that only the non-resistant bacteria were killed *(1 mark)*. The individual resistant bacteria would have survived and reproduced *(1 mark)*, increasing the population of the resistant strain *(1 mark)*.

Biology 1.2 Nerves and Hormones

1. The Nervous System

Page 41 — Fact Recall Questions

Q1 A change in your environment that you might need to respond to.

Q2 receptors

Q3 the nucleus

Q4 nose and tongue

Q5 glands

Q6 E.g. motor neurones, relay neurones

Page 41 — Application Questions

Q1 a) i) The sound of the cat moving.
      ii) Receptors in the dog's ears that are sensitive to sound.
      iii) sensory neurone
   b) i) motor neurone
      ii) They will contract.

Q2 A loud bang — ears — receptors sensitive to sound
A moving object — eyes — receptors sensitive to light
Walking on a slanted floor — ears — receptors sensitive to changes in position
Touching a hot object — skin — receptors sensitive to changes in temperature
An unpleasant smell — nose — receptors sensitive to chemical stimuli
Standing on a pin — skin — receptors sensitive to pain

2. Synapses and Reflexes

Page 44 — Fact Recall Questions

Q1 a) a synapse
   b) Chemicals diffuse across the gap between the two neurones, which sets off an electrical impulse in the next neurone.

Q2 A reflex is a fast, automatic response to a stimulus.

Q3 No
   Reflexes are automatic — you don't have to think about them, so they don't pass through conscious parts of the brain.

Q4 a relay neurone

Q5 The secretion of a hormone from the gland.

Page 44 — Application Question

Q1 a) pain
   b) A muscle in the leg. It contracts, moving the foot away from the source of the pain (the pin).
   c) Stimulus → Receptor → Sensory neurone → Relay neurone → Motor neurone → Effector → Response

3. Homeostasis

Page 46 — Fact Recall Questions

Q1 The maintenance of a constant internal environment.

Q2 To keep it the temperature at which the enzymes in the body work best.

Q3 Through the skin as sweat. Via the kidneys as urine.

Q4 Any three from, e.g. through the skin as sweat / via the lungs in the breath / via the kidneys as urine / via faeces.

Q5 E.g. insulin

Q6 To ensure that the cells get a constant supply of energy.

4. Hormones

Page 48 — Fact Recall Questions

Q1 by the blood (plasma)

Q2 false

They only affect particular cells, called target cells, in particular places.

Q3 E.g. FSH/follicle stimulating hormone / LH/luteinising hormone

Q4 E.g. oestrogen

Q5 nerves

5. The Menstrual Cycle

Page 51 — Fact Recall Questions

Q1 Causing an egg to mature in one of the ovaries and stimulating the ovaries to produce oestrogen

Q2 oestrogen

Q3 It stimulates the release of an egg at around the middle (day 14) of the menstrual cycle.

Q4 the pituitary gland and the ovaries

Page 51 — Application Question

Q1 a) LH (luteinising hormone). LH is the hormone responsible for stimulating the release of an egg. The concentration of the hormone on the graph increases just before the middle of the cycle (day 14) — the time at which an egg is normally released.

b) the pituitary gland

c) LH is needed to stimulate the release of an egg. This woman's LH level peaks at a much lower level than the other woman's, suggesting that she may not be releasing an egg during her menstrual cycle. This could be the reason why she's struggling to have children.

6. Controlling Fertility

Page 54 — Fact Recall Questions

Q1 It inhibits FSH production, which prevents egg maturation and therefore release.

Q2 progesterone

Q3 Large doses of oestrogen were thought to cause a lot more side effects.

Q4 E.g. they don't always work so they may have to used many times, which can be expensive. / They can result in unexpected multiple pregnancies.

Q5 The eggs are fertilised in the lab using the male's sperm.

Q6 When they are tiny balls of cells.

Page 54 — Application Question

Q1 a) FSH stimulates egg maturation in the ovaries. Jenny's low FSH level may mean that her eggs are not maturing (and therefore not being released), decreasing her fertility and chances of getting pregnant.

b) $(6695 \div 16652) \times 100 = \textbf{40.2\%}$

c) IVF often involves the transfer of more than one embryo into the uterus, which results in an increased chance of multiple pregnancies, and therefore more multiple pregnancies in those undergoing IVF.

7. Plant Hormones

Page 58 — Fact Recall Questions

Q1 The growth response of a plant to gravity.

Q2 Auxin inhibits cell elongation in a root.

Q3 An uneven amount of water either side of a root produces more auxin on the side with more water. This inhibits growth on that side, causing the root to bend in that direction.

Page 58 — Application Questions

Q1 a) In Petri dish A, there will be an even distribution of auxin across the shoot of each cress seedling. In Petri dish B, auxin will accumulate on the shaded side of the cress seedling shoots.

This causes the cress seedlings in Petri dish A to grow straight up and the cress seedlings in Petri dish B to bend towards the light.

b) i) To make sure that any difference in growth between shoots in Petri dish A and those in Petri dish B was due to the difference in light position only and not due to any other variables.

ii) Any two from, e.g. the number of cress seeds planted in each Petri dish / the temperature the Petri dishes were kept at / the type of cress seed used / the amount of water available in each dish /the light intensity.

Q2 a) For this type of plant, rooting powder B is the best type of rooting powder to use for the first three weeks of growth. This is because it's more effective at increasing root length each week for the first three weeks after planting, than rooting powder A.

It's important to remember that the results only apply to this particular type of plant. You also can't say what will happen after the three week period Dan recorded his results for.

b) It was a control. / To show that the results were likely to be due to the presence of the rooting powder and nothing else.

Pages 61-62 — Biology 1.2
Exam-style Questions

1 a) i) the muscle in the upper arm *(1 mark)*
   ii) sensory neurone *(1 mark)*
 b) It would get faster *(1 mark)*. The presence of the drug increases the amount of chemical released at the synapses, so it would take less time for an impulse to be triggered in the next neurone *(1 mark)*.
 c) E.g. reflexes are fast *(1 mark)*, so we quickly respond to danger, decreasing our chances of injury *(1 mark)*. Reflexes are automatic *(1 mark)*, so we don't have to waste time thinking about our response, which reduces our chance of injury *(1 mark)*.

2 a) i) C, because the plant is growing towards it *(1 mark)*.
   ii) Sample X because it has been taken from the side that has grown more/the side in the shade *(1 mark)*. Auxin makes the cells in plant shoots elongate faster *(1 mark)*, so that must be the sample containing the most auxin *(1 mark)*.
 b) Rooting powders contain plant hormones (such as auxin) *(1 mark)*. These promote root development, helping the new plant to grow *(1 mark)*.

3 How to grade your answer:
 0 marks:
 There is no relevant information.
 1-2 marks:
 A comparison is made between the two types of pill.
 3-4 marks:
 Two clear comparisons are made between the two types of pill. The answer has a logical structure and spelling, punctuation and grammar are mostly correct.
 5-6 marks:
 At least three clear, detailed comparisons are made between the two types of pill. The answer has a logical structure and uses correct spelling, grammar and punctuation.
 Here are some points your answer may include:
 The combined oral contraceptive pill has a lower failure rate than the progesterone-only pill, so it is a more effective form of contraception.
 Both pills should be taken at the same time everyday, but the combined oral contraceptive pill is still effective if taken up to 12 hours late, whereas the progesterone-only pill may only be taken up to 3 hours late. This means that the combined pill offers more flexibility over when it is taken.
 Women taking the combined oral contraceptive pill have a higher risk of blood clots than those taking the progesterone-only pill (which can be taken by some women who have a history of blood clots).
 The progesterone-only pill is useful for women who are breast feeding, whereas the combined oral contraceptive pill cannot be taken by these women.

This question asked you to <u>evaluate</u> the use of the two types of oral contraceptive pill written about in the passage. In this case, 'evaluate' basically means compare, so it's not enough to just pick bits of information out of the text and say whether it's a good or bad point about that particular type of pill — you need to make clear comparisons between the two types to get the marks. E.g. 'The combined oral pill has a <u>lower</u> failure rate than the progesterone only pill, so it is a <u>more effective</u> form of contraception.' You could also get a mark here for making a sensible conclusion about which type of pill is best.

Biology 1.3 The Use and Abuse of Drugs

1. Drugs and Drug Claims
Page 65 — Fact Recall Questions
Q1 Because some of the chemical changes caused by drugs can lead to the body becoming dependent on the drug.
Q2 Any two from: e.g. heroin / cocaine / nicotine / caffeine.
 You need to know that heroin and cocaine are examples of addictive drugs for the exam — make sure you learn them.
Q3 a) E.g. stimulants / anabolic steroids
 b) E.g. stimulants increase heart rate. / Anabolic steroids increase muscle size.
Q4 Lower the risk of heart and/or circulatory diseases.

Page 65 — Application Question
Q1 a) i) performance-enhancing drugs / stimulants.
   ii) Amphetamines increase heart rate, so glucose and oxygen will be transported to Beth's muscles faster (giving her more energy).
 b) E.g. because the use of performance-enhancing drugs in sport is banned by all sporting bodies.
 c) E.g. it's unfair if people gain an advantage by taking drugs, not just through training.
 d) E.g. drug-free sport isn't really fair anyway — different athletes have access to different training facilities, coaches, equipment, etc. / It would mean that athletes who take a banned substance without knowing are not penalised (punished).

2. Testing Medicinal Drugs
Page 68 — Fact Recall Questions
Q1   laboratory testing

Q2   human cells, tissues and animals

Q3   Any two from: e.g. to find out whether the drug works. / To find out about the drug's toxicity. / To find out the best dosage of the drug.

Q4   a) healthy volunteers
      b) It is very low.

Q5   A placebo is a substance that's like the drug being tested but doesn't do anything.

Q6   A double-blind trial is a clinical trial where neither the doctor nor the patients know who has been given the drug and who has been given the placebo, until the results of the trial have been gathered.

It's helpful to remember that 'double' means 'two' — so in a double-blind trial, there are two groups of people (doctors and patients) who don't know who receives the drug or who receives the placebo.

Page 68 — Application Questions
Q1   a) E.g. a capsule without paracetamol
      b) E.g. an inhaler without steroids
      c) E.g. an injection without cortisone

Q2   a) i)   No, because it was a double-blind trial.
          ii) E.g. a pill without any weight-loss drug.
      b) E.g. Group 2 was included in the trial to make sure that the new drug, Drug X, worked as well as/ better than other, similar weight-loss drugs already available on the market (like Drug Y). / To see how Drug X compared to Drug Y.
      c) That, on average, people taking Drug X in this trial lost 4 lbs more than those taking the placebo, but 3 lbs less than those taking Drug Y.

3. Recreational Drugs
Page 70 — Fact Recall Questions
Q1   Illegal drugs, any two from: e.g. heroin / ecstasy / cannabis.
Legal drugs, e.g. nicotine and alcohol.

Q2   Any two from: e.g. cannabis is a "stepping stone" — the effects of cannabis create a desire to try harder drugs. / Cannabis is a "gateway drug" — cannabis use brings people into contact with drug dealers. / It's all down to genetics — certain people are more likely to take drugs generally, so cannabis users will also try other drugs.

Q3   Legal drugs because so many people take them.

Pages 72-73 — Biology 1.3
Exam-style Questions
1   a) Cannabis *(1 mark)*, Ecstasy *(1 mark)*
    b) i)   These are withdrawal symptoms *(1 mark)*. They occur when a drug addict stops taking a drug *(1 mark)*.
        ii) E.g. it may cost the NHS a lot of money to treat these diseases *(1 mark)*. / These diseases can cause a lot of sorrow/anguish to the people affected by them *(1 mark)*. / There may be a cost to economy in lost working days due to illness *(1 mark)*.

2   a) A sleeping pill *(1 mark)*.
    b) i)   When thalidomide was given to pregnant women it caused abnormal limb development in many babies *(1 mark)*. This happened because the drug had not been tested as a drug for morning sickness *(1 mark)*.
        ii) Thalidomide was banned *(1 mark)*. Drug testing became much more thorough from then on *(1 mark)*.

3   How to grade your answer:
0 marks:
No relevant information is given.
1-2 marks:
There is a brief description of drug testing in either the laboratory or in a clinical trial.
3-4 marks:
There is a description of drug testing in both the laboratory and in a clinical trial. The answer mentions the need to discover the drug's effectiveness, toxicity or dosage. The answer has a logical structure and spelling, grammar and punctuation are mostly correct.
5-6 marks:
There is a detailed description of drug testing in both the laboratory and in clinical trials. The answer clearly explains the need to discover the drug's effectiveness, toxicity and dosage. The answer has a logical structure and uses correct spelling, grammar and punctuation.
Here are some points your answer may include:
The drug will usually be tested first on human cells and tissues in the laboratory.
The drug will then tested on live animals to see if it works and to find out about toxicity and dosage.
If the drug passes animal trials, it will then be tested on human volunteers in a clinical trial.
In a clinical trial, the drug will be given to healthy volunteers first in low doses. This is to make sure it has no harmful side effects.
If the results from healthy volunteers are good, the drug will be tested on sick volunteers. This is to find the optimum dose of the drug.

4   a) i)   Tablets without any aspirin in them *(1 mark)*.
        ii) To make sure that the aspirin was the only thing responsible for any results obtained *(1 mark)*.

b) Up to around 6 years after joining the study, there was little difference in the proportion of participants diagnosed with colorectal cancer in the control group and in the treatment group *(1 mark)*. But between 6-10 years after joining the study, the proportion diagnosed in the control group increased compared to the treatment group *(1 mark)*. After 10 years, the proportion diagnosed with colorectal cancer was much higher in the control group than in the treatment group — 0.6 compared to 0.1 at 11 years *(1 mark)*.

c) Any three from, e.g. the study only looked at colorectal cancer, not all cancers *(1 mark)*. / The study only used participants who already had an increased risk of developing colorectal cancer due to genetic factors *(1 mark)*. / The results only show that taking aspirin for 2 years or more reduced the risk by around a half (0.14 for placebo and 0.06 for aspirin) *(1 mark)*. / The participants took 600 mg a day, and there's no indication of what 'an aspirin' contains *(1 mark)*.

Biology 1.4 Adaptations and the Environment

1. Adaptations and Competition
Page 77 — Fact Recall Questions
Q1 A characteristic which increases an organism's chance of survival in the environment in which it lives.

Q2 It enables the plant to store water for use during very dry periods.

Q3 Any two from: e.g. having thorns/sharp spines / the ability to produce poison / warning colours.

Q4 a) An organism that is adapted to survive in extreme conditions.

b) Any two from: e.g. very hot conditions / very salty conditions / high pressure conditions.

Q5 light, space, water and minerals/nutrients

Q6 space/territory, food, water and mates

Page 77 — Application Question
Q1 *Equus assinus* lives in desert conditions. This is because its long ears help to give it a large surface area compared to its volume. This helps it to lose more body heat, which stops it from overheating in the hot desert. It has short fur so it has little insulation, which is good for losing body heat. It is a grey or brown colour which helps it to be camouflaged in its desert environment. This could help it to avoid predators or sneak up on prey. *Alopex lagopus* lives in arctic conditions. This is because its short ears and muzzle help to reduce its surface area compared to its volume, which reduces heat loss. Its thick coat gives it good insulation, which helps to keep it warm. Its white coat gives it camouflage in its snowy environment, which helps it to avoid predators or sneak up on prey.

2. Environmental Change
Page 79 — Fact Recall Questions
Q1 Any three from: e.g. a change in the occurrence of infectious diseases / a change in the number of predators / a change in the number of prey/the availability of food sources / a change in the number or types of competitors.

Q2 Any three from: e.g. a change in average temperature / a change in average rainfall / a change in the level of air pollution / a change in the level of water pollution.

Page 79 — Application Questions
Q1 a) i) It decreased.
   ii) a non-living factor
   Here the environmental change of acid rain was caused by a non-living factor.

b) The population size of the frogs is likely to have decreased because there were fewer mayfly to eat.
   Here the environmental change was caused by a living factor — the mayfly.

Q2 a)
$$\frac{12.2 - 13}{13} \times 100 = \mathbf{-6.2\%}$$

b) E.g. a rise in global temperature, which is a non-living factor.

c) E.g. it has caused a decrease in the polar bear population size.

3. Measuring Environmental Change
Page 81 — Fact Recall Questions
Q1 An organism that is very sensitive to changes in its environment and so can be used to study environmental change.

Q2 sulfur dioxide

Q3 invertebrate animals

Q4 Any three from: e.g. temperature of the sea surface / amount of snow/ice cover / temperature of the atmosphere / amount of rainfall / dissolved oxygen concentration of water.

Page 81 — Application Questions
Q1 56 km, because at this distance there is the least percentage cover of lichen. Lichen are sensitive to the amount of sulfur dioxide in the atmosphere, so there will be fewer of them around sources of sulfur dioxide, such as power stations.

Q2 a) Polluted water has a low concentration of dissolved oxygen, so stonefly larvae can't tolerate polluted water. This means that area A is the cleanest as this is the only area of the river where there are lots of stonefly larvae.
   Remember, clean water will have a higher concentration of dissolved oxygen than polluted water.

b) Areas B and C must be polluted because there are no stonefly larvae there. There is only a moderate level of water louse in Area C, whereas there is a high level of sludgeworms in both Area B and C. This suggests that sludgeworms are most well adapted to survive in polluted water.

Biology 1.5 Energy and Biomass in Food Chains

1. Pyramids of Biomass
Page 85 — Fact Recall Questions
Q1 Biomass is the mass of living material.
Q2 Each bar of a pyramid of biomass represents the biomass of one trophic level. Biomass nearly always decreases as you move up a food chain, so the bars of the pyramid will get smaller nearer the top.

Page 85 — Application Questions
Q1

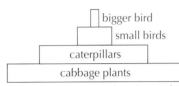

Remember the producer (e.g. the plant) always goes at the bottom of the pyramid.
Q2 a) phytoplankton
    b) bass
    c) Because biomass has been lost between the krill trophic level and the herring trophic level in the food chain.

2. Energy Transfer in Food Chains
Page 87 — Fact Recall Questions
Q1 light energy
Q2 chemical energy
Q3 Green plants and algae absorb light energy from the Sun and use it to convert carbon dioxide and water to chemical energy during photosynthesis. The energy's stored in the cells of the plants and algae and then it gets passed along the food chain when animals eat the plants or algae.
Q4 False.
    Energy is lost at every stage of a food chain.

Page 87 — Application Question
Q1 This is because the ducks respire and energy is released from respiration. Some of this energy is used to fuel life processes, such as movement, but much of the energy is lost to the environment as heat. Energy is also lost in the ducks' waste materials, as well as in ducks that die before the fox can eat them (these ducks are broken down by microorganisms and the energy is passed to them).

Biology 1.6 Waste Materials and The Carbon Cycle

1. Decay
Page 89 — Fact Recall Questions
Q1 To use them for growth and other life processes.
Q2 a) The material in dead organisms is broken down/ digested/decayed by microorganisms. This process releases the elements back into the soil.
    Don't write that microorganisms 'eat' the dead material — you won't get a mark for that in the exam.
    b) In waste products.
Q3 Warm, moist and oxygenated.
    'Oxygenated' or 'aerated' means plenty of oxygen is present.
Q4 A stable community is one in which the materials taken out of the soil are balanced by those that are put back in — there's a constant cycle happening.
Q5 It recycles elements/nutrients back into the soil which plants can use for growth.

Page 89 — Application Question
Q1 To let oxygen in — microorganisms which break down waste material need oxygen for respiration.
Q2 Sunny areas of the garden will have higher temperatures. Microorganisms work best in warm conditions, so compost is made faster.
Q3 The presence of water vapour would increase the moisture inside the compost bin and, as microorganisms work best in moist conditions, it would help compost to be made more quickly.
    To answer these questions you just need to remember the conditions that microorganisms need to work best and apply that knowledge to the question.

2. The Carbon Cycle
Page 91 — Fact Recall Questions
Q1 photosynthesis
    If you're asked to name a process in the carbon cycle, make sure you give the actual name of the process, don't just describe it. For example, put 'feeding/eating' and not 'food'.
Q2 To make carbon compounds / carbohydrates, fats and proteins.
Q3 It becomes part of the fats and proteins in the animals.
Q4 They release carbon dioxide when they respire.
Q5 It is released as carbon dioxide when the fossil fuels are burnt/combusted.

Exam-style Questions

1   How to grade your answer:

0 marks:
No relevant information is given.

1-2 marks:
There is a brief description of one or two steps in the carbon cycle, but no names of any processes are given.

3-4 marks:
There is a description of three or four steps in the carbon cycle, but not all of the processes are named. The answer has a logical structure and spelling, grammar and punctuation are mostly correct.

5-6 marks:
There is a detailed description of five or six steps in the carbon cycle with named processes. The answer has a logical structure and uses correct spelling, grammar and punctuation.

Here are some points your answer may include:
The grass absorbs carbon dioxide from the air in photosynthesis.
The grass uses this carbon to make carbon compounds.
This carbon is passed onto the cows when the cows eat the grass, and onto humans when the humans eat the cows, so it moves through the food chain.
Dead organisms/waste materials are broken down/ decayed by detritus feeders/microorganisms.
All the organisms/the grass/cows/humans/ microorganisms respire and release carbon dioxide into the atmosphere.
Burning fossil fuels/wood also releases carbon dioxide into the air.

2   a) It provides the light energy *(1 mark)* needed for producers/green plants and algae to photosynthesise *(1 mark)* and produce chemical energy *(1 mark)*, which is passed on throughout the food chain by organisms eating each other *(1 mark)*.
     b) C, because algae are at the start of the food chain/ are producers *(1 mark)*.
     c) i) Width of bar A = 12 squares.
            Width of bar B = 30 squares.
            So ratio of bar B to bar A = 30:12 = **2.5:1**
            (2 marks for correct answer, otherwise 1 mark for correctly finding the widths of bar A and bar B).
        ii) Biomass is lost in waste products/faeces/urine *(1 mark)*, in the parts of organisms which are inedible *(1 mark)* and in organisms that die before they're eaten *(1 mark)*.

    This question is about how biomass is lost between trophic levels of a food chain, so be careful not to waste time writing about how energy is lost as well.

3   a) i) A characteristic that helps an organism to survive in its environment *(1 mark)*.

        ii) It has a thick bushy tail to help it keep warm at night when temperatures drop very low *(1 mark)*. It has a long, pointed muzzle so it can catch prey through the narrow entrance of a burrow *(1 mark)*. It has thick pads on the bottom of its feet to protect them as it's moving over rocky ground *(1 mark)*.

    You might not have come across any of these adaptations before, but just use the information you're given about the rocky mountains and think sensibly about how the features would help the wolf survive there.
     b) i) It is decreasing *(1 mark)*.
        ii) The outbreak of rabies is responsible for the trend *(1 mark)*. In the years when there were rabies outbreaks the population size fell *(1 mark)*. For example, the numbers fell from 401 to 327 in 2008 / 341 to 265 in 2011 when there was also a rabies outbreak*(1 mark)*.

    There's a lot of data to look at in the table, so think carefully about what you're looking for. The numbers of prey don't really change much throughout the study, so that's unlikely to have caused the change in the number of wolves. This means it's sensible to look at the outbreaks of rabies.
        iii) It has made the wolf population move to higher ground *(1 mark)* from an average height of 3.4 km above sea level in 2007 to an average height of 4 km above sea level in 2012 *(1 mark)*.

Biology 1.7 Genetic Variation and its Control

1. Variation
Page 95 — Application Questions
Q1   E.g. how often you train / how hard you train / how well you are coached / how good the facilities you train at are / how good your diet is.
     You're not expected to know the answer to this question, just to make sensible suggestions.
Q2   The results from Study 1 suggest that genes must influence IQ because identical twins have the same genes and non-identical twins have different genes. The results from Study 2 suggest that environment also influences IQ. This is because identical twins have exactly the same genes, which means that differences in their IQs must be down to differences in their environment/the way they were brought up.

2. Genes, Chromosomes and DNA
Page 97 — Fact Recall Questions
Q1   in the nucleus
Q2   a) short sections of DNA/a chromosome (that control our characteristics)
     b) controlling the development of different characteristics

Page 97 — Application Questions
Q1 a) X
    b) Z
    c) Y
Q2 Because genes are too small.

3. Reproduction
Page 99 — Application Question
Q1 a) Asexual reproduction. There is only a single parent cell and no fusion of gametes. The offspring are genetically identical/clones.
    b) Sexual reproduction. There are two parents, gametes have fused together and offspring show genetic variation.

Remember, sexual reproduction doesn't always involve sexual intercourse — it's the fusion of gametes that's important. Both animals and plants can reproduce sexually.

    c) Sexual reproduction. There are two parents and the offspring has characteristics of both parents, suggesting that it has a mixture of genes from both parents.
    d) Asexual reproduction. There is only one parent and no fusion of gametes. The offspring are genetically identical to the mother snake.

4. Cloning
Page 103 — Fact Recall Questions
Q1 a) Any two from: e.g. they can be produced quickly. / They can be produced cheaply. / Lots of ideal offspring/offspring with known characteristics can be produced.
    b) tissue culture
Q2 Embryo transplant. Adult cell cloning.

Page 103 — Application Questions
Q1 By giving it an electric shock.
Q2 No. The egg cell from the domestic cat will have had its nucleus/genetic material removed before the black-footed cat nucleus was inserted. So the embryo will only contain genetic material from the black-footed cat.
Q3 a) E.g. there are more domestic cats around than black-footed cats, so using domestic cats to carry the embryos may mean more black footed kittens can be produced.
    b) E.g. using skin cells from adults that have died as well as those that are still alive may increase the number of possible 'parents', so more black-footed cats can be produced.

The idea behind using adult cell cloning to help save endangered species is that it's a way of producing lots of offspring relatively rapidly — you need to apply this idea to the question to make sensible suggestions here.

Q4 E.g. the cloned animals may also not be as healthy as normal ones. Cloning could also give the animals a reduced gene pool, meaning that if a new disease appears, they could all be wiped out.

5. Genetic Engineering
Page 106 — Fact Recall Questions
Q1 So that the animal or plant develops useful characteristics.
Q2 a) genetically modified
    b) E.g. insects, herbicides

Page 106 — Application Questions
Q1 Enzymes would be used to cut out the *Bt* crystal protein gene from the *B. thuringiensis* chromosome. Enzymes would then be used to cut a chromosome from the cotton plant and then to insert the crystal protein gene.
Q2 E.g. if insects ate the crop, they'd be poisoned by the protein. If less of the crop was eaten by insects, this could improve crop yield.
Q3 E.g. it could affect the number of weeds/flowers/ insects that live in and around the crop. / People might develop allergies to the crop. / The gene for the *Bt* protein might get into the natural environment affecting, e.g., weeds.

Pages 108-109 Biology 1.7
Exam-style Questions
1 a) chromosomes, characteristics, gametes, variation **(1 mark for each correct answer)**
   b) (i) genes **(1 mark)**
      (ii) It is caused by differences in their environment **(1 mark)**. / A named environmental factor, e.g. diet **(1 mark)**.
   c) Sexual reproduction is the fusion of male and female gametes **(1 mark)** from two parents **(1 mark)**, which results in the offspring having a mixture of their parents' genes **(1 mark)**, so they are genetically different to their parents **(1 mark)**.

Even though these twins are genetically identical to each other (i.e. clones), they are not clones of their parents because they have been produced by sexual reproduction.

2 a) i) The embryo will be split (many times) **(1 mark)** before any cells become specialised **(1 mark)**. The cloned embryos will then be implanted into host mothers to continue developing **(1 mark)**.
       ii) Asexual reproduction because: any two from, e.g. there was only one parent **(1 mark)**. / There was no fusion of gametes **(1 mark)**. / There was no mixing of genes **(1 mark)**.
   b) Because gametes were taken from the male and female pig and then fused **(1 mark)**. This will have created an embryo with a mixture of genes from both parents **(1 mark)**.

c) How to grade your answer:

0 marks:
No relevant information is given.

1-2 marks:
There is a brief description of one possible benefit and one possible concern of cloning pigs.

3-4 marks:
There is a description of at least two possible benefits and two possible concerns of cloning pigs. The answer has a logical structure and spelling, grammar and punctuation are mostly correct.

5-6 marks:
There is a detailed description of at least three possible benefits and three possible concerns of cloning pigs. The answer has a logical structure and uses correct spelling, grammar and punctuation.

Here are some points your answer may include:
Cloning could produce lots of 'ideal' pigs quickly, which could benefit farmers (who want to quickly increase the size of their herds/quality of their stock).
Studying cloned pigs could help scientists to understand the development of the embryo/ageing/age-related disorders.
Cloning pigs could help to save rare/endangered types/breeds of pig.
Cloning pigs will result in a reduced gene pool.
If a new disease appears, the cloned pigs could all be wiped out.
It's possible that cloned pigs may not be as healthy as normal pigs.
Cloning pigs could lead to the cloning of humans.

Biology 1.8 Evolution

1. Evolution and Natural Selection
Page 111 — Fact Recall Questions
Q1 over 3 billion years ago
Q2 They evolved from simple organisms.
Q3 a) The process by which species evolve.
   b) (Charles) Darwin
Q4 a) A change in an organism's DNA.
   b) A mutation in a gene can result in a useful characteristic. This characteristic may give the organism a better chance of surviving and reproducing and therefore passing on the mutation to future generations by natural selection. Over time the beneficial mutation will accumulate in the population, which may lead to changes in the species.

Page 112 — Application Questions
Q1 E.g. the original rats showed variation — some were resistant to warfarin, others weren't / a mutation appeared which made some rats resistant to warfarin. The warfarin-resistant rats were better adapted to the environment (because they weren't killed by the warfarin), so they were more likely to survive and breed successfully. This meant that the gene for warfarin-resistance was more likely to be passed on to the next generation.
You could get asked to explain the selection of pretty much any characteristic in the exam — make sure you can apply the key points of Darwin's theory to any context.

Q2 a) By around $3.5 - 2.1 = $ **1.4 cm** (accept any answer between 1.3 and 1.5 cm).
   b) E.g. the reindeer population in 1810 would have shown variation — some would have had shorter fur and some longer fur. The reindeer with shorter fur would have been better adapted to the new, warmer environment they found themselves in (as they would have been less likely to overheat), so they would have been more likely to survive and breed successfully. This meant that the gene for short fur was more likely to be passed on to the next generation. This gene became more common in the population, eventually reducing the average fur length.

2. Ideas About Evolution
Page 114 — Application Questions
Q1 E.g. because of the different work they do/their different backgrounds / because Kyra is a geneticist and Neil is a psychologist.
Q2 It shows that the acquired characteristic of clipped flight feathers is not passed on from the parent birds to their offspring.
Q3 a) E.g. Lamarck may have argued that if an anteater used its tongue a lot to reach into ant nests, then its tongue would get longer. This acquired characteristic would then be passed on to the next generation and the anteater's offspring would have been born with long tongues.
   b) E.g. tongue lengths in anteaters used to vary — some were long and some were short / a mutation occasionally caused some anteaters to be born with a long tongue. Long-tongued anteaters were better adapted to their environment/could get more food with their long tongues, so were more likely to survive and reproduce. So the gene(s) for a long tongue were more likely to be passed on to the next generation and eventually all anteaters were born with long tongues.

3. Classification

Page 117 — Fact Recall Questions

Q1 By studying their similarities and differences.
Q2 E.g. that they are in competition with each other.

Page 117 — Application Questions

Q1 An animal because it is able to move about (which plants can't do) and because it is unable to make its own food (which plants can do).
Q2 a) i) the lion
   ii) the snow leopard
   b) the jaguar
   c) yes
   The lion and the snow leopard are two of the most distantly related organisms on this tree, but they still share a common ancestor:

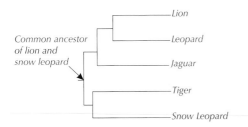

Common ancestor of lion and snow leopard

Lion
Leopard
Jaguar
Tiger
Snow Leopard

Page 119 — Biology 1.8
Exam-style Questions

1 a) crocodiles and birds *(1 mark)*
   b) turtles *(1 mark)*
   c) The original milk snake population showed variation — some had similar colouring to the coral snake, others didn't / A mutation appeared which caused some milk snakes to have similar colouring to the coral snake *(1 mark)*. Milk snakes that looked like the coral snake were less likely to be eaten *(1 mark)* and so more likely to reproduce and pass on the gene(s) for coral snake colouring to the next generation *(1 mark)*.
   d) It went against common religious beliefs at the time *(1 mark)*. Darwin couldn't explain how useful characteristics appeared or were passed on (as he didn't know about genes) *(1 mark)*. There wasn't enough evidence to convince many scientists *(1 mark)*.

Chemistry 1.1 The Fundamental Ideas in Chemistry

1. Atoms and Elements
Page 122 — Fact Recall Questions

Q1 E.g. atoms have a small nucleus surrounded by electrons. The nucleus is in the middle of the atom and contains protons and neutrons. The electrons occupy shells around the nucleus.
Q2 a) +1
   b) 0
   c) −1
Q3 The number of protons in its nucleus.
Q4 An element is a substance that only contains one type of atom.
Q5 There are about 100 elements.

Page 122 — Application Questions

Q1 One type of atom.
Q2 47
Q3 34
Q4 The atoms contain different numbers of protons so they are atoms of different elements.
Q5 a) +17
   b) −1
   c) The particle has an overall charge so it is not an atom.

2. The Periodic Table
Page 125 — Fact Recall Questions

Q1 The number of protons in an atom.
Q2 The total number of protons and neutrons in an atom.
Q3 They have the same number of electrons in their outer shell.
Q4 They each have one electron in their outer shell.
Q5 The noble gases.
Q6 They have a stable arrangement of electrons. / They have a full outer shell.

Page 125 — Application Questions

Q1 Metals — any three elements from the left side of the purple line on the periodic table on page 123.
   Non-metals — any three elements from the right side of the purple line on the periodic table on page 123.
Q2 Beryllium, magnesium, calcium, strontium, barium, radium.
Q3 a) S
   b) Cl
   c) K
Q4 a) 20
   b) 29
   c) 5
Q5 a) 80
   b) 39
   c) 4

Q6 a) 11
b) 11
c) 23 – 11 = **12**
Q7 a) 26
b) 26
c) 56 – 26 = **30**
Q8 5
Nitrogen and arsenic are in the same group (Group 5) so must have the same number of electrons in their outer shells.

3. Electron Shells
Page 127 — Fact Recall Questions
Q1 An energy level.
Q2 2 electrons
Q3 8 electrons
Q4 8 electrons
Q5 The one closest to the nucleus. / The one with lowest energy level.

Page 127 — Application Questions
Q1 Neon
Q2 Carbon
Q3 Sulfur
Q4

Q5

Q6 2, 8, 5
Q7 2, 8, 2

4. Compounds
Page 131 — Fact Recall Questions
Q1 An ion is a charged particle.
Q2 Positive ions.
Q3 Negative ions.
Q4 Ionic bonding.
Q5 Covalent bonding.

Page 131 — Application Questions
Q1 One carbon atom and one oxygen atom.
Q2 One hydrogen atom, one nitrogen atom and three oxygen atoms.
Q3 D
D is a compound because it contains atoms of different elements chemically joined together. A and C only contain atoms of one element, so can't be compounds. B contains atoms of different elements, but there are no bonds between the atoms.
Q4 Negative ions.

Q5 Lose electrons.
Q6 Positive ions.
Q7 Gain electrons.
Q8 Ionic bonding.
Magnesium is a metal and oxygen is a non-metal, so the bonding in magnesium oxide is ionic bonding.
Q9 Covalent bonding.
Sulfur and oxygen are both non-metals, so the bonding in sulfur dioxide is covalent bonding.

5. Equations
Page 135 — Application Questions
Q1 a) Iron sulfate and copper.
b) Copper sulfate and iron.
c) copper sulfate + iron $\rightarrow$ iron sulfate + copper
Q2 a) copper + oxygen $\rightarrow$ copper oxide
b) 127 + 32 = **159 g**
No atoms are lost or made during a chemical reaction, so the total mass at the end of a reaction is the same as the total mass at the start of the reaction.
Q3 68 – 56 = **12 g**
The total mass of nitrogen and hydrogen must equal the mass of ammonia produced.
Q4 a) sodium hydroxide + hydrochloric acid $\rightarrow$ sodium chloride + water
b) Total mass of reactants = 80 + 73 = 153 g. 153 – 36 = 117 g. So **117 g** of sodium chloride are formed.
Q5 a) $Cl_2 + \mathbf{2}KBr \rightarrow Br_2 + \mathbf{2}KCl$
b) $\mathbf{2}HCl + Mg \rightarrow MgCl_2 + H_2$
c) $C_3H_8 + \mathbf{5}O_2 \rightarrow \mathbf{3}CO_2 + \mathbf{4}H_2O$
d) $Fe_2O_3 + \mathbf{3}CO \rightarrow \mathbf{2}Fe + \mathbf{3}CO_2$
Q6 $H_2SO_4 + \mathbf{2}LiOH \rightarrow Li_2SO_4 + \mathbf{2}H_2O$

Pages 137-138 — Chemistry 1.1
Exam-style Questions
1 a) i) non-metals *(1 mark)*
ii) compounds *(1 mark)*
b) i) carbon monoxide + oxygen $\rightarrow$ carbon dioxide *(1 mark)*
ii) Two molecules of carbon monoxide *(1 mark)* react with one molecule of oxygen *(1 mark)* to form two molecules of carbon dioxide *(1 mark)*.
c)

(1 mark for drawing six electrons, 1 mark for placing two in the first shell and four in the second shell.)

2 a)

Atomic number	13
Mass number	27
Number of protons	13
Number of electrons	13
Number of neutrons	14

(1 mark for each correct answer.)

b) i) $2Al + 6HCl \rightarrow 2AlCl_3 + 3H_2$
(1 mark for correctly balancing the left hand side of the equation. 1 mark for correctly balancing the right hand side of the equation.)

ii) Mass of reactants: 135 + 547.5 = 682.5 g
(1 mark)
Mass of hydrogen: 682.5 – 667.5 = **15 g**
(1 mark)

Remember — the total mass of the products is the same as the total mass of the reactants.

iii) covalent bonding *(1 mark)*

c) i) Group 7 *(1 mark)*

ii) Chlorine and bromine both have the same number of electrons in their outer shell / both have 7 electrons in their outer shell *(1 mark)* so react in a similar way *(1 mark)*.

iii) Argon is a noble gas / is in Group 0 *(1 mark)*. This means it has a full outer shell of electrons / a stable arrangement of electrons so it is unreactive *(1 mark)*.

Chemistry 1.2 Limestone and Building Materials

1. Limestone and Other Carbonates

Page 141 — Fact Recall Questions

Q1 Calcium carbonate/$CaCO_3$.

Q2 calcium carbonate → calcium oxide + carbon dioxide
$CaCO_3 \rightarrow CaO + CO_2$

Q3 A metal salt, carbon dioxide and water.

Q4 calcium sulphate/$CaSO_4$.

Q5 Calcium oxide

Q6 If you make a solution of calcium hydroxide in water (called limewater) and bubble gas through it, the solution will turn cloudy if there's carbon dioxide in the gas. The symbol equation is as follows:
$Ca(OH)_2 + CO_2 \rightarrow CaCO_3 + H_2O$

Page 141 — Application Questions

Q1 zinc carbonate → zinc oxide + carbon dioxide

Q2 a) Magnesium chloride
b) $MgCO_3 + 2HCl \rightarrow MgCl_2 + CO_2 + H_2O$

2. Using Limestone

Page 143 — Fact Recall Questions

Q1 a) To make cement, powdered limestone is heated in a kiln with clay.
b) To make mortar you add water and sand to cement.
c) To make concrete you add sand and aggregate to cement.

Q2 Any two from: e.g. Concrete can be poured into moulds to make blocks or panels that can be joined together. / Using concrete is a cheap and easy way of constructing buildings. / Concrete doesn't rot when it gets wet. / Concrete is fire-resistant. / Concrete is resistant to corrosion.

Q3 Any two from: e.g. Limestone is used to make dyes, paints and medicines. / Limestone products can be used to neutralise acidic soils (e.g. by farmers). / Acidity in lakes and rivers caused by acid rain can be neutralised by limestone products. / Limestone can be used in power station chimneys to neutralise sulfur dioxide (a cause of acid rain).

Q4 a) Any three from: e.g. Quarrying makes big, ugly holes in the landscape. / Quarrying processes make lots of noise and dust in quiet, scenic areas. / Quarrying destroys the habitats of animals and birds. / Quarries cause increased traffic (usually lorries), which causes more noise and pollution. / Waste materials produce unsightly tips.
b) E.g. Limestone quarries and associated businesses provide jobs for people and bring more money into the local economy. This can lead to local improvements in transport, roads, recreation facilities and health, which local people can benefit from.

Q5 E.g. Concrete is quite unattractive as a building material. / Concrete has low tensile strength and can crack.

Page 144 — Application Question

Q1 a) E.g. Richard should use concrete in his garage. It is hard-wearing and cheap. A more attractive floor that was as hard-wearing (marble) would be very expensive. Wood wouldn't be a good choice as it's not as hard-wearing as the other materials.
b) E.g. Richard could use wood flooring in his conservatory. It is attractive but not as expensive as marble. Concrete, although cheaper, would be an unattractive choice. Wood is less hard-wearing than concrete or marble but will be suitable for use indoors.

For this question the reasons that you use to support your floor choices might be a bit different from the ones shown above, or you might have picked different materials than the ones shown above. That's fine as long as you've supported your answers with good reasons.

Chemistry 1.3 Metals and Their Uses

1. Metal Ores

Page 145 — Fact Recall Questions
Q1 A metal ore is a rock which contains enough metal to make it profitable to extract the metal from it.
Q2 If the market price of a metal falls, it might cost more to extract the metal than would be gained from selling it. So the amount of metal extracted would fall. If the market price of the metal increased then more of the metal might be extracted from its ore, as more money could be made from it.
Q3 Any two from: reduction / electrolysis / displacement reactions.

2. Extracting Metals from Rocks

Page 147 — Fact Recall Questions
Q1 a) Electrolysis
   b) Reduction
Q2 More reactive.
Q3 Oxygen
Q4 They have many stages and use a lot of energy.
Q5 Any two from: e.g. aluminium, magnesium, calcium, sodium, potassium.

Page 147 — Application Question
Q1 a) Reduction with carbon.
   b) Electrolysis
   c) Reduction with carbon.
   d) Electrolysis

3. Extracting Copper

Page 150 — Fact Recall Questions
Q1 Smelting
Q2 a) The positive electrode.
   b) Electrons are pulled off copper atoms at the positive electrode.
   c) The negative electrode.
Q3 a) Bioleaching and phytomining.
   b) E.g. The methods are less damaging to the environment. / The methods are cheaper.
Q4 a) A displacement reaction.
   b) E.g. Scrap iron is very cheap.
   c) Iron sulfate and copper.

4. Impacts of Extracting Metals

Page 152 — Fact Recall Questions
Q1 E.g. Mining metal provides materials to make useful products. / Mining provides local people with jobs. / Mining brings money into the area which means services such as transport and health can be improved.

Q2 E.g. Mining causes noise / scarring of the landscape / loss of habitats / release of gases such as CO_2 and SO_2 / contribution to acid rain, global dimming and climate change.
Q3 E.g. Mining requires energy, which usually comes from burning fossil fuels. This releases carbon dioxide and sulfur dioxide, which contribute to acid rain and climate change.
Q4 a) Recycling metal saves energy because it only uses a small fraction of the energy needed to mine and extract new metal.
   b) Any three from: e.g. conserves fossil fuels / saves money (on energy costs) / conserves metal resources / reduces the amount of rubbish being sent to landfill.

Page 152 — Application Question
Q1 a) i)

	Tonnes of waste metal to landfill	Cost (£)
Year 1	15 000	1 725 000
Year 2	12 000	1 380 000

   ii) The council would save £1 725 000 – £1 380 000 = **£345 000**.
   b) E.g. by recycling more metal.

5. Properties and Uses of Metals

Page 155 — Fact Recall Questions
Q1 B
Q2 a) E.g. electrical wiring.
   b) Any two from: e.g. They are strong/hard to break. / They can be bent into different shapes. / They are good conductors of heat.
Q3 They are strong and have low density/are lightweight.
Q4 It can be bent into different shapes (like pipes) and doesn't react with water.
Q5 It's not too bendy, it's light and it doesn't react with water.
Q6 Metals can corrode when exposed to air and water. Metals can also suffer from metal fatigue which can cause them to break.

Page 155 — Application Question
Q1 E.g. Rachel should buy an aluminium frame. Aluminium has a very low relative density so it's very lightweight. It's also highly resistant to corrosion so won't corrode when it gets wet, and it's quite strong. It isn't the cheapest type (steel) but it isn't the most expensive either (titanium). Titanium shares similar properties to aluminium but it's more expensive.
For this question you might have chosen a different type of frame that Rachel should buy. That's fine as long as you've backed up your choice with good reasons.

6. Alloys
Page 158 — Fact Recall Questions
Q1 About 96%
Q2 It contains impurities that make it brittle.
Q3 In pure iron atoms are arranged regularly in layers that can slide over each other. This makes pure iron soft and bendy.
Q4 Carbon
Q5 Stainless steel
Q6 As a pure metal it is too soft for many uses.
Q7 a) Copper and tin.
b) Copper and nickel.
Q8 It's too soft.

Page 158 — Application Questions
Q1 High-carbon steel could be used (as it's a very hard, inflexible type of steel).
Q2 Stainless steel could be used (as it is resistant to corrosion).

Pages 160-163 — Chemistry 1.2-1.3
Exam-style Questions
Q1 a) i) E.g. alloys are mixtures of two or more metals *(1 mark)*, or a mixture of a metal and a non-metal *(1 mark)*.
ii) Iron *(1 mark)*
iii) Harder *(1 mark)*
b) E.g. It is easily shaped *(1 mark)*.
c) i) E.g. aluminium is resistant to corrosion *(1 mark)*.
ii) E.g. aluminium has a low density, which means that it is lightweight *(1 mark)*.
iii) E.g. pure aluminium is too soft *(1 mark)*.
iv) Aluminium is extracted by electrolysis *(1 mark)* which requires lots of energy *(1 mark)*.
Q2 a) i) E.g. calcium oxide and water *(1 mark)*.
ii) $CaO + H_2O \rightarrow Ca(OH)_2$ *(1 mark for correct left-hand side of equation. 1 mark for correct right-hand side.)*
b) i) Limewater *(1 mark)*.
ii) The solution of calcium hydroxide would go cloudy *(1 mark)*.
iii) $Ca(OH)_2 + CO_2 \rightarrow CaCO_3$ *(1 mark)* $+ H_2O$ *(1 mark)*.
c) i) Calcium hydroxide increases soil pH *(1 mark)*.
ii) A neutralisation reaction *(1 mark)*.
iii) The liming took place in May/June *(1 mark)* as after this month the soil pH increased steadily *(1 mark)*.
Q3 a) $CuCO_3$ *(1 mark)*
b) i) Thermal decomposition *(1 mark)*
ii) Carbon dioxide/CO_2 *(1 mark)*
c) Electrolysis *(1 mark)*

d) i) E.g. chalcopyrite is a low-grade copper ore *(1 mark)*. To extract copper from a low-grade ore is very expensive using the method outlined in the diagram *(1 mark)*.
ii) E.g. bioleaching could be used to extract copper from chalcopyrite *(1 mark)*. Bioleaching is less damaging to the environment *(1 mark)* and is also cheaper *(1 mark)* than the method outlined above.
e) i) E.g. copper is a good conductor of electricity *(1 mark)* and can be drawn out into wires *(1 mark)*.
ii) E.g. Plumbing/pipes *(1 mark)*.
Q4 a) clay *(1 mark)*, sand *(1 mark)*, aggregate *(1 mark)*, concrete *(1 mark)*.
b) i) Iron oxide is heated in the blast furnace *(1 mark)* with carbon *(1 mark)*. The iron oxide is reduced to iron *(1 mark)*.
ii) It contains impurities *(1 mark)*.
iii) E.g. gold *(1 mark)*. Gold is unreactive *(1 mark)*.
c) i)

Statement	Env. Impact Tick (✓)
Jobs are created in the local area.	
Traffic to and from the mine/ quarry causes pollution.	✓
Habitats are destroyed.	✓
Dust from the site can cause health problems for local people.	

(1 mark for each correct tick.)
ii) E.g. mining and quarrying requires lots of energy that comes from burning fossil fuels *(1 mark)*. This releases the greenhouse gas carbon dioxide into the atmosphere *(1 mark)*.

Chemistry 1.4 Crude Oil and Fuels

1. Fractional Distillation of Crude Oil
Page 166 — Fact Recall Questions
Q1 A substance made from two or more elements or compounds that aren't chemically bonded to each other.
Q2 A hydrocarbon is a molecule that only contains hydrogen and carbon.
Q3 Fractional distillation
Q4 Near the top.
Compounds with a small number of carbon atoms have low boiling points so they condense near the top of the fractionating column where it is cooler.

Page 166 — Application Questions

Q1 a) Butane

Butane condenses at the lowest temperature because it has the smallest number of carbon atoms.

b) Tetracontane

Tetracontane has the largest number of carbon atoms so it will condense at a high temperature near the bottom of the fractionating column.

Q2 a) Petrol

The fractionating column is hottest at the bottom and coolest at the top, so the fraction with the lowest boiling temperature range will be removed at the top. This is petrol.

b) i) 125 °C
ii) Naphtha

The boiling point of octane is within the boiling temperature range of naphtha, so octane will be found in naphtha.

2. Properties and Uses of Crude Oil

Page 168 — Fact Recall Questions

Q1

Q2 Propane

Q3 Because all of the atoms in alkanes have formed bonds with as many other atoms as they possibly can. / Because alkanes don't contain any carbon-carbon double bonds. / Because alkanes only contain single carbon-carbon bonds.

Q4 The shorter the molecules (the shorter the carbon chains) the more flammable the alkane is. / The longer the molecules (the longer the carbon chains) the less flammable the alkane is.

Page 168 — Application Questions

Q1 The general formula of an alkane is $C_nH_{2n + 2}$, so if octane has 8 carbon atoms, it must have $(2 \times 8) + 2$ = 18 hydrogen atoms. So the chemical formula of octane is C_8H_{18}.

Q2 As hexadecane has long carbon chains, it will be very viscous. Its viscosity makes it suitable for use as a lubricant.

3. Environmental Problems

Page 172 — Fact Recall Questions

Q1 a) Carbon dioxide and water (vapour).
b) E.g. carbon monoxide, carbon particulates, unburnt fuel.

Q2 Sulfur dioxide

Q3 When the fuel burns at a high temperature.

Q4 a) Sulfur dioxide and oxides of nitrogen.
b) Any two from: e.g. It can cause lakes to become acidic and many plants and animal may die as a result. / It can kill trees. / It can damage limestone buildings or stone statues.
c) E.g. The sulfur impurities can be removed from fuel before it is burnt. / Harmful gases can be removed from fumes before they are released into the atmosphere. / The use of fossil fuels could be reduced.

Q5 a) Global warming is the increase in the average temperature of the Earth.
b) E.g. It could cause other types of climate change such as changing rainfall patterns. / It could cause severe flooding due to melting of the polar ice caps.

Page 172 — Application Questions

Q1 a) Yes — burning hexadecane as a fuel will contribute to climate change because one of the products is carbon dioxide which causes global warming.
b) Yes — if the hexadecane contains sulfur impurities, sulfur dioxide may be produced which could cause acid rain / if the hexadecane is burnt at high temperatures, nitrogen oxides could be produced which could cause acid rain.

Q2 This is global dimming — it could be caused by particles of soot and ash that are released into the atmosphere when fossil fuels are burned. These particles could reflect sunlight back into space or could help produce more clouds that reflect the sunlight back into space.

Q3 $C_5H_{12} + 8O_2 \rightarrow 5CO_2 + 6H_2O$

Q4 $2C_6H_{14} + 13O_2 \rightarrow 12CO + 14H_2O$

4. Alternative Fuels

Page 174 — Fact Recall Questions

Q1 A renewable fuel made from plant material. Examples include ethanol and biodiesel.

Q2 Advantages: e.g. Ethanol is carbon neutral. / The only products produced when ethanol burns are carbon dioxide and water. / Ethanol is a renewable fuel. / Growing crops for ethanol provides jobs. Disadvantages: e.g. Engines need to be converted before they can use ethanol fuels. / Ethanol fuel isn't widely available. / If demand for ethanol increases, farmers may switch to growing crops for ethanol instead of crops for food and food prices could increase.

Q3 Vegetable oils (e.g. rapeseed oil and soy bean oil).

Page 174 — Application Questions

Q1 The company could use biodiesel to run their vans, rather than diesel.

You couldn't give using ethanol or hydrogen gas as an answer to this question because the company would have to replace their vans with vans that are adapted to use ethanol or hydrogen gas as fuel.

Q2 a) The energy to make the hydrogen comes from burning fossil fuels and burning fossil fuels releases carbon dioxide and other pollutants.
b) They could use electricity from a renewable energy source (e.g. solar power) to make their hydrogen.

Pages 176-177 — Chemistry 1.4
Exam-style Questions

1 a) i) The crude oil is heated so that it evaporates
           (1 mark). The vaporised gases rise up the
           fractionating column and cool gradually
           (1 mark). As they cool they condense
           (1 mark). Different compounds condense
           at different temperatures and so they are
           separated *(1 mark)*.
       ii) They have short carbon chains. / They have low
            boiling points. *(1 mark)*
   b) How to grade your answer:
       0 marks:
       No environmental impacts are given.
       1-2 marks:
       Brief description of one or two environmental
       impacts.
       3-4 marks:
       Several environmental impacts are clearly
       described. The answer has some structure and
       spelling, grammar and punctuation are mostly
       correct. Some specialist terms are used.
       5-6 marks:
       Several environmental impacts are described in
       detail. The answer has a logical structure and
       uses correct spelling, grammar and punctuation.
       Relevant specialist terms are used correctly.

       Here are some points your answer may include:

       Burning petrol releases carbon dioxide which
       contributes to global warming.

       If the petrol has sulfur impurities in it, sulfur
       dioxide might form when the petrol burns and this
       contributes to acid rain.

       If the fuel is burnt at very high temperatures,
       oxides of nitrogen may be formed and this
       contributes to acid rain.

       If there is not enough oxygen available when
       the fuel is burnt carbon particulates may be
       produced and released into the atmosphere.
       These contribute to global dimming.

2 a) Any two from: e.g. Fossil fuels are non-renewable
       so they will eventually run out. / Burning fossil
       fuels contributes to global warming. / Burning
       fossil fuels contributes to global dimming. /
       Burning fossil fuels can lead to the production
       of acid rain. / Burning fossil fuels damages the
       environment. *(1 mark for each correct answer,
       maximum 2 marks)*
   b) i) Because the CO_2 released when ethanol is
           burnt was taken up by the plants as they grew
           (1 mark).
       ii) Any two from: e.g. ethanol is not widely
            available. / Engines need to be converted
            before they will work with ethanol fuels. /
            People have concerns that using ethanol as
            a fuel may lead to increased food prices.
            *(1 mark for each correct answer, maximum
            2 marks)*

   c) i) Sulfur dioxide can cause acid rain *(1 mark)* so
           a fuel that produces less sulfur dioxide will be
           better for the environment *(1 mark)*.
       ii) Positive: e.g. Growing crops for biodiesel is
            labour intensive *(1 mark)*, so provides jobs for
            local people *(1 mark)*.
            Negative: e.g. If there is increased demand for
            biodiesel, farmers may switch to growing crops
            for biodiesel and fewer crops will be grown
            for food *(1 mark)*, so food will become more
            expensive *(1 mark)*.

3 a) C_nH_{2n+2}
       *If you're asked to give the general formula of the alkanes
       in the exam make sure you use upper case letters for the
       C and the H and lower case letters for the n and 2n + 2 —
       you could lose marks if you don't.*
   b) i) Decane because it has the longest carbon
           chains *(1 mark)*.
       ii) Propane because it has the shortest carbon
            chains *(1 mark)* so has the lowest boiling point
            (1 mark).
   c) i) $C_7H_{16} + 11O_2 \rightarrow 7CO_2 + 8H_2O$
           *(3 marks for correct answer, otherwise 1 mark
           for correct formulae on the left-hand side,
           1 mark for correct formulae on the right-hand
           side, 1 mark for balancing the equation)*.
       ii) If there is not enough oxygen *(1 mark)*.
       iii) If the heptane is burned at a very high
            temperature *(1 mark)* nitrogen in the air will
            react with oxygen in the air to form nitrogen
            oxides *(1 mark)*.

4 a) E.g. because the only product when hydrogen is
       burnt is water. / Because burning hydrogen does
       not produce carbon dioxide. *(1 mark for any
       correct answer)*.
   b) i) E.g. the hydrogen is difficult to store. / You still
           need to use energy from other sources to make
           the hydrogen. / Hydrogen is highly flammable
           so could cause explosions. *(1 mark for each
           correct answer, maximum 2 marks)*
       ii) E.g. They could use biodiesel *(1 mark)*.
            Biodiesel is carbon neutral / produces
            less sulfur dioxide / produces less carbon
            particulates / is a renewable resource so is
            better for the environment *(1 mark)*.
            Biodiesel can be mixed with ordinary diesel
            fuel/doesn't require engines to be converted
            so it would be cheaper than hydrogen gas
            (1 mark).

Chemistry 1.5 Other Useful Substances from Oil

1. Cracking Crude Oil
Page 179 — Fact Recall Questions
Q1 a) Cracking is the process used to break long-chain hydrocarbons down into smaller ones. It is useful because shorter-chain hydrocarbons are usually more useful than longer-chain hydrocarbons.
b) E.g. fuel and making plastics.
Q2 A thermal decomposition reaction.
Q3 a) The long-chain hydrocarbon is heated so that it vaporises. The vapour is then passed over a powdered aluminium oxide catalyst at a temperature of about 400-700 °C. The long-chain molecules will crack on the surface of the catalyst.
b) By mixing the vaporised hydrocarbon with steam at a very high temperature.
Q4 E.g. alkanes and alkenes.

2. Using Crude Oil
Page 181 — Fact Recall Questions
Q1 E.g. lots of energy is released when they burn / they burn cleanly / they are a reliable source of energy.
Q2 a) E.g solar power / wind power / nuclear power / tidal power / biofuels.
b) E.g. everything is already set up for using crude oil. / Crude oil fractions are often more reliable. / It will take time to adapt things so that renewable energy sources can be used on a large scale.
Q3 E.g. oil spills can happen when the oil is being transported. / Burning oil releases gases that contribute to global warming/global dimming/acid rain.
Q4 E.g. new oil reserves have been discovered in the last 40 years. / Technology has improved which means we can now extract oil that was too difficult or too expensive to extract 40 years ago.
Q5 E.g. crude oil is non-renewable and alternative fuels for transport are available, so stopping using crude oil for transport would mean we could keep the crude oil for things that it's essential for, like making chemicals and medicines.

3. Alkenes and Ethanol
Page 183 — Fact Recall Questions
Q1
$$\begin{array}{c} \quad\quad\; H \;\; H \\ H \quad\quad\; | \;\;\; | \\ \backslash C = C - C - H \\ H / \quad\quad\quad | \\ \quad\quad\quad\quad\; H \end{array}$$
Q2 Because more atoms can be added to them — they contain a double bond that can open up, allowing the two carbon atoms to bond with other atoms.
Q3 a) Technique 1: By hydrating ethene with steam in the presence of a catalyst.
Technique 2: By fermenting sugars.
b) E.g. making ethanol from ethene is cheap at the moment, but ethene comes from crude oil which is a non-renewable resource so when the crude oil starts to run out it will become very expensive. Ethanol made by hydration also occurs at a high temperature
Making ethanol by fermentation requires lower temperatures and simpler equipment and uses less energy than making ethanol from ethene. Sugars are also a renewable resource that won't run out so the production of ethanol by fermentation should remain cheap. But the ethanol produced by fermentation isn't very concentrated and it needs to be purified. Plus, growing more crops to make sugars for ethanol could lead to more deforestation.

Page 183 — Application Questions
Q1 Bottle A contains propene because the solution turned bromine water colourless.
Bottle B must therefore contain propane.
Q2 C
You can tell that C is the alkene because it's the only one that contains just carbon and hydrogen atoms AND has twice as many hydrogen atoms as carbon atoms.

4. Using Alkenes to Make Polymers
Page 186 — Fact Recall Questions
Q1 Many small alkene monomers are joined together to form long-chain polymers.
Q2 E.g. the monomers that the polymer is made from and the conditions (temperature and pressure) of the polymerisation reaction.
Q3 It gets softer as it gets warmer, so a memory foam mattress will mould to your body shape when you lie on it.
Q4 a) Biodegradable means the material can be broken down by microorganisms.
b) Non-biodegradable
Q5 Polymers are made from crude oil. Crude oil is non-renewable so the price of crude oil, and therefore the price of polymers, will increase when the crude oil reserves start to run out.

Page 186 — Application Questions
Q1 Poly(chloroethene)
Q2 a)
$$\begin{array}{c} F \backslash \quad\quad / H \\ \quad C = C \\ H / \quad\quad \backslash H \end{array}$$
b)
$$\begin{array}{c} F \backslash \quad\quad / F \\ \quad C = C \\ F / \quad\quad \backslash F \end{array}$$
Q3 a)
$$\left(\begin{array}{c} H \;\; H \\ | \;\;\; | \\ -C - C - \\ | \;\;\; | \\ H \;\; Br \end{array} \right)_n$$
b)
$$\left(\begin{array}{c} H \;\; H \\ | \;\;\; | \\ -C - C - \\ | \;\;\; | \\ H \;\; OH \end{array} \right)_n$$

Page 188 — Chemistry 1.5
Exam-style Questions

1 a)

$$\underset{H}{\overset{H}{\diagdown}}C=C\underset{H}{\overset{Cl}{\diagup}}$$

(1 mark for drawing the carbon-carbon double bond correctly, 1 mark for drawing the four single bonds correctly)

b) i) Ethene is an alkene *(1 mark)*.

ii) Long chain hydrocarbons are vaporised *(1 mark)* and passed over a catalyst *(1 mark)* at a high temperature *(1 mark)* so that thermal decomposition takes place *(1 mark)*. / Long chain hydrocarbons are vaporised *(1 mark)*, mixed with steam *(1 mark)* and heated to a very high temperature *(1 mark)* so that thermal decomposition takes place *(1 mark)*.

iii) Ethanol *(1 mark)*.

2 a) i) C_nH_{2n} *(1 mark)*

You can only have the mark for this question if the C and the H are capital letters and the n and the 2n are written as subscript. cnh2n and CNH2N are not correct answers.

ii) Alkenes are unsaturated *(1 mark)* because they contain a double bond that can open up allowing the two carbon atoms to bond with other molecules *(1 mark)*.

iii) Add some of the solution to bromine water *(1 mark)*. If the bromine water turns from orange to colourless, alkenes are present *(1 mark)*.

b) i) Poly(propene) / polypropene *(1 mark)*

ii) Lots of propene molecules *(1 mark)* join together to form long chains *(1 mark)*.

c) Polymers are non-biodegradable / aren't broken down by micro-organisms *(1 mark)*, so if they are put into a landfill site they'll still be there years later *(1 mark)*.

Chemistry 1.6 Plant Oils and Their uses

1. Plant Oils
Page 191 — Fact Recall Questions

Q1 a) The olives are crushed. The crushed plant material is then pressed between metal plates to squash the oil out.

b) E.g. using a centrifuge / using distillation.

Q2 E.g. (steam) distillation.

Q3 Vegetable oils contain useful nutrients.

Q4 a) Food cooks quicker in vegetable oil than in water because vegetable oils have higher boiling points than water, so they can cook food at a higher temperature.

b) E.g. cooking with vegetable oil gives food a different flavour/makes the flavour more intense.

c) E.g. using oil to cook food increases the energy we get from eating it/makes the food more fattening/makes us more likely to put on weight.

We all need energy, and vegetable oils are really energy rich. But that's the reason that you have to be careful not to eat too much of them — they can be really fattening.

Q5 a) Vegetable oils are suitable for use as fuels because they can provide a lot of energy.

b) E.g. biodiesel

2. Unsaturated Oils
Page 193 — Fact Recall Questions

Q1 An unsaturated oil contains double bonds between some of the carbon atoms in its carbon chain. A saturated oil doesn't contain any carbon-carbon double bonds.

Q2 Add some bromine water to the oil. If the mixture turns colourless then the oil is unsaturated.

Q3 a) nickel, 60 °C

b) E.g. spreads/margarines / baking cakes and pastries

Q4 Saturated fats increase the amount of cholesterol in the blood, which can block up the arteries and increase the risk of heart disease. Unsaturated fats reduce blood cholesterol.

Remember, unsaturated fats are the good ones and saturated fats are the bad ones. Don't get them mixed up.

Page 193 — Application Question

Q1 a) Sample X, because hydrogenated oils have higher melting points than unsaturated oils.

b) Sample Y

Hydrogenating oils gets rid of double bonds. The natural oil will have more double bonds than the hydrogenated oil, so it will also have a higher degree of unsaturation.

c) The bromine water would be decolourised because sample Y contains unsaturated fats.

3. Emulsions
Page 196 — Fact Recall Questions

Q1 No — oils will not dissolve in water.

Q2 a) E.g.

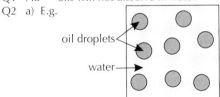

oil droplets

water

b) E.g. the oil-in-water emulsion will be thicker.

Q3 a) Any two from: E.g. salad dressing / mayonnaise / ice cream / whipped cream / milk.

b) E.g. moisturising cream / cosmetics / paints

Q4 a) An emulsifier is a substance that stops an emulsion from separating out.

b) Advantage — e.g. emulsifiers stop emulsions from separating out and this gives them a longer shelf-life. / Emulsifiers allow food companies to produce food that's lower in fat but that still has a good texture.

Disadvantage — e.g some people are allergic to certain emulsifiers.

Q5 a) Hydrophilic head ——→ ⚬〜〜 ←—— Hydrophobic tail

b) E.g. emulsifier molecules have a hydrophilic end that's attracted to water and a hydrophobic end that's attracted to oil. When you shake oil and water together with an emulsifier, the oil forms droplets, surrounded by a coating of emulsifier with the hydrophilic bit facing outwards. Other oil droplets are repelled by the hydrophilic bit of the emulsifier, while water molecules surround it. So the emulsion won't separate out.

Page 196 — Application Questions
Q1 a) Put the oil and the water in a flask/bottle, seal it and shake well.

b) Kevin's method. An emulsion of oil and water will be thicker than either oil or water. So an emulsion will coat the salad leaves better.

Q2 To act as an emulsifier, molecules of Polysorbate 80 must have a hydrophilic end and a hydrophobic end.

Page 198 — Chemistry 1.6
Exam-style Questions
1 a) E.g. to stop it separating out / to make it more stable *(1 mark)*.

b) i) Washing-up liquid and mustard *(1 mark)*.
   You need both things here to get the mark.

ii) The emulsions in tubes B and E took much longer to separate out than the other tubes *(1 mark)*. This means that the test substances in tubes B and E must be making the emulsion more stable *(1 mark)*.

2 a) E.g. the seeds could be crushed and the oil pressed out of them *(1 mark)*.
   Any sensible method would get you a mark here.

b) E.g. saturated fats increase the amount of cholesterol in the blood, which can lead to heart disease *(1 mark)*. Cottonseed oil contains more saturated fat than olive oil, so it is less healthy *(1 mark)*.

c) E.g. food will cook faster in oil than in water. / Cooking with vegetable oil gives food a different flavour. / Cooking in oil makes flavours seem more intense. / Using oil to cook food increases the energy you get from eating it *(1 mark)*.

d) React the oil with hydrogen/hydrogenate the oil *(1 mark)* in the presence of a nickel catalyst *(1 mark)* at about 60 °C *(1 mark)*.

Chemistry 1.7 Changes in the Earth and its Atmosphere

1. Plate Tectonics
Page 201 — Fact Recall Questions
Q1 a) Scientists thought that the mountains formed due to the surface of the Earth shrinking as the Earth cooled down after it was formed.

b) Scientists now think that the Earth's crust is made up of tectonic plates and that mountains are formed when these tectonic plates collide.

Q2 Wegener's theory of continental drift says that there used to be just one supercontinent (called Pangaea) and that this supercontinent broke apart into smaller chunks which gradually drifted apart to form the continents we know today.

Q3 E.g. there may have been land bridges between the continents that allowed animals to walk from one continent to another.

2. The Earth's Structure
Page 204 — Fact Recall Questions
Q1 The crust.
Q2 The mantle has all the properties of a solid except that it can flow very slowly.
Q3 Iron and nickel.
Q4 Convection currents in the mantle.
Q5 Very slowly — speeds of a few cm per year.
Q6 At the boundaries between tectonic plates.
Q7 E.g. exactly when the earthquake will happen, exactly where the earthquake will happen and how strong the earthquake will be.

Page 204 — Application Questions
Q1 a) The mini-earthquakes could be a sign that the volcano is about to erupt.

b) E.g. The mini-earthquakes could be a false alarm and evacuating is very expensive/inconvenient.

Q2 Earthquakes occur when tectonic plates suddenly move, so they often occur at boundaries between tectonic plates. Palmdale is located on the boundary between two tectonic plates and so it will get lots of earthquakes.

3. The Evolution of the Atmosphere
Page 207 — Fact Recall Questions
Q1 Nitrogen and oxygen
Q2 The early atmosphere was probably mostly carbon dioxide with virtually no oxygen. There may also have been water vapour and small amounts of methane and ammonia.
Q3 When the Earth began to cool, the water vapour in the air condensed to form the Earth's oceans.
Q4 Green plants and algae absorb carbon dioxide and use it in photosynthesis.
Q5 It has been locked away in sedimentary rocks and fossil fuels or it has dissolved in the oceans.
Q6 a) Carbon dioxide (CO_2)
   b) The oceans are absorbing more carbon dioxide which is causing them to become more acidic.
Q7 Fractional distillation

Page 208 — Application Questions

Q1 a) The concentration of water vapour in the atmosphere decreased from about 25% 4.5 billion years ago to virtually 0% 4 billion years ago. This is because 4.5 billion years ago the Earth began to cool and the water vapour in the atmosphere condensed to form the Earth's oceans.

b) E.g. the concentration of carbon dioxide in the early atmosphere was initially high but decreased due to it dissolving in the oceans and being absorbed by plants and green algae. So the red/dotted line, which starts high and then decreases must represent carbon dioxide.
The concentration of oxygen in the early atmosphere was initially low but increased due to plants and green algae producing oxygen during photosynthesis. So the green/dashed line, which starts low and then increases must represent oxygen.

Q2 a) The pH of the oceans has decreased. The rate at which the pH of the oceans was decreasing got faster.

b) E.g. humans are burning more fossil fuels which is leading to an increase in the concentration of CO_2 in the atmosphere. As a result, the oceans are absorbing more CO_2 from the atmosphere and this is causing them to become more acidic/decrease in pH.

c) E.g. the increase in the acidity of the oceans could be harmful to wildlife. / Eventually the oceans won't be able to absorb any more CO_2, so there will be even more CO_2 in the atmosphere, which could result in more global warming.

4. Life on Earth
Page 209 — Fact Recall Questions

Q1 According to the primordial soup theory, life first began when lightning struck, causing a chemical reaction between the gases in the Earth's atmosphere (nitrogen, hydrogen, ammonia and methane). This reaction resulted in the formation of amino acids that later combined to produce organic matter, which eventually evolved into living organisms.

Q2 E.g. because life began a very long time ago and there is no evidence left today of the earliest forms of life. / Because we can't be certain under what conditions life began. / Because we don't have the capabilities to test many of the theories of how life began.

Pages 211-212 — Chemistry 1.7
Exam-style Questions

1 a)

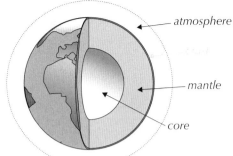

(1 mark for each correct label)

b) i) Any two from: e.g. similar fossils were found on the opposite sides of oceans. / The coastlines of Africa and South America seem to match, as if they once fitted together. / Matching layers have been found in rocks in different continents. / Fossils have been found in places where the current climate would have killed them off. *(1 mark for each correct answer, maximum 2 marks)*

ii) E.g. Wegener's explanation of how the continents moved was not very convincing and other scientists had shown that it couldn't be correct. / A lot of Wegener's evidence could be explained by the existence of land bridges between the continents, which was the accepted theory at the time.
(1 mark for any correct explanation)

c) i) Radioactive decay *(1 mark)*
ii) Most tectonic plates move very <u>slowly</u> *(1 mark)*, at a rate of a few <u>centimetres</u> *(1 mark)* per year.

d) X drawn anywhere along the plate boundary *(1 mark)*. X drawn somewhere opposite the area affected by the tsunami *(1 mark)*.

2 a) Nitrogen *(1 mark)*

b) i) Volcanoes *(1 mark)*
ii) Any two from: e.g. lots of the carbon dioxide was absorbed by the oceans. / Some carbon dioxide was absorbed by plants and algae when they evolved. / The carbon dioxide was locked away in sedimentary rocks/fossil fuels.
(1 mark for each correct answer, maximum 2 marks)

c) E.g. the increased concentrations of carbon dioxide is causing global warming *(1 mark)*. Increased concentrations of carbon dioxide mean the oceans are absorbing more carbon dioxide and becoming more acidic *(1 mark)*.

d) E.g. one theory is that lightning *(1 mark)* caused a chemical reaction between nitrogen, hydrogen, ammonia and methane in the atmosphere *(1 mark)* leading to the formation of amino acids which came together to form organic matter *(1 mark)*.

Physics 1.1 Energy Transfer by Heating Processes

1. Infrared Radiation

Page 214 — Fact Recall Questions

Q1 Heat radiation is the transfer of heat energy by infrared radiation.

Q2 It will emit more radiation than it absorbs.
It can help to think of whether an object will cool down or heat up. A hot object in cool surroundings will cool down, so overall it must be losing energy — it must be emitting more than it absorbs.

Q3 Its rate will increase.

Q4 A dark, matt surface.

Q5 A light, shiny surface.

Q6 A light, shiny surface.

Page 214 — Application Question

Q1 E.g. The ball bearing on the plate with the matt black surface will drop first. Matt, black surfaces are better absorbers of infrared radiation, so this plate will absorb infrared radiation from the Bunsen burner at a higher rate than the silvered plate. This means it will heat up and melt the wax more quickly, causing the ball bearing to fall from it first.

2. Kinetic Theory

Page 216 — Fact Recall Questions

Q1 Solid, liquid and gas.

Q2 The particles in a solid are held close together by strong forces in a fixed, regular arrangement. The particles don't have much energy and so can't move around — they can only vibrate about fixed positions.

Q3 The particles in a liquid have more energy than in a solid. They are still close to each other, but unlike in a solid, they're able to move past each other and form irregular arrangements.

Q4 Gas

Q5 a) As a solid is heated, its particles gain energy and vibrate more. Eventually the particles have enough energy to be able to move past each other — at which point the solid becomes a liquid.
   b) The particles of a liquid can move past each other, which means liquids are able to flow. The particles in a solid are unable to move past each other, and so solids are unable to flow.

Page 217 — Application Questions

Q1 E.g. The balls represent the particles of a solid — they don't swap positions, they're close together and are arranged in a (fairly) fixed pattern.

Q2 a) A gas.
   b) E.g. their average kinetic energy.
   You could also say their speed or velocity.

3. Conduction and Convection

Page 221 — Fact Recall Questions

Q1 E.g. The transfer of energy through a substance due to particle collisions. The particles of a heated substance gain extra kinetic energy and vibrate more. The particles collide with their neighbouring particles and pass on some of this energy, causing energy eventually to be passed through the substance.

Q2 A material with smaller spaces between its particles — the particles are closer and so will collide and pass energy to each other more often.

Q3 Metals contain free electrons which are able to move through the metal. Unlike the particles in most solids, they can travel and collide and pass their energy on to particles further into the metal, rather than just the particles surrounding their fixed position. This means energy is transferred much more quickly through metals than in most other solids.

Q4 Convection is the transfer of heat by the movement of more energetic particles in a gas or liquid from a hotter to a cooler region.

Q5 Solids
   The particles in a solid can only vibrate about their fixed positions — they can't move from one place to another and take their energy with them.

Q6 Energy is transferred from heater coils at the bottom of the tank to nearby water by conduction. This increases the energy of the water particles. This causes the particles to move around faster and have larger distances between them — the density of the water decreases. Because the warm water by the coils is less dense than the cooler water above it, the warmer water rises and the cooler water sinks. The cooler water sinks towards the heater coils and gets heated, causing the process to continue.

Page 221 — Application Question

Q1 The air near the window becomes cool — the energy of the air particles decreases, causing them to be closer together and the density of the air to increase. This causes the cooler air to sink and the warmer less dense air to rise up. The warmer air is then cooled by being near the window and the process continues. Over time this will gradually cool all of the air in the room.

4. Condensation and Evaporation

Page 224 — Fact Recall

Q1 When a gas cools, the particles in the gas slow down — lose kinetic energy and are closer to each other. When the temperature of the gas gets cool enough, the particles will be close enough to clump together and the gas will become a liquid.

Q2 Condensation
   Visible steam is formed when water vapour, an invisible gas, cools and forms droplets of liquid water.

Q3 Evaporation is where a liquid becomes a gas.

Q4 E.g. To be travelling in the correct direction, to be travelling fast enough/have enough kinetic energy to overcome the attractive forces of the other particles in the liquid.

Q5 As only particles with the highest kinetic energies evaporate from the liquid, the average kinetic energy of the particles in the remaining liquid decreases. This causes a cooling effect, so the temperature of the liquid drops.

Q6 E.g. Increase the temperature of the liquid, decrease the density of the liquid (e.g. by heating it), increase the surface area of the liquid, increase the airflow over the liquid (e.g. put the liquid in a draught).

Q7 E.g. Decrease the temperature of the gas, increase the concentration of gas in the air, allow the gas to come into contact with a colder surface.

Page 224 — Application Question

Q1 E.g. Blowing air across a hot drink reduces the concentration of water molecules above the drink's surface, which causes the drink to evaporate more quickly. Evaporation causes a cooling effect on the liquid that remains behind, as only the highest energy particles evaporate, so the average energy of the particles in the remaining liquid decreases. So by increasing the rate of evaporation, you increase the rate at which the drink cools.

5. Rate of Energy Transfer
Page 227 — Fact Recall Question

Q1 a) It would decrease the rate of energy transfer between the object and its surroundings.
    b) It would increase the rate of energy transfer between the object and its surroundings.
    c) It would increase the rate of energy transfer between the object and its surroundings.
    d) It would decrease the rate of energy transfer between the object and its surroundings.
    e) This would have no effect.
    The temperature difference between the object and surroundings has stayed the same, so the rate of energy transfer will also be the same.

Page 228 — Application Questions

Q1 Antelope squirrels are small and so have a high surface area to volume ratio. This will give a relatively high rate of heat transfer between the squirrel and its surroundings, which will help the squirrel keep cool in the hot environment it lives in.

Q2 E.g. Any two from: The radiator is made from metal which is a good conductor, and so will give a high rate of energy transfer from the radiator. / The radiator has a large surface area to radiate heat from, causing it to have a high rate of energy transfer to its surroundings. / The radiator has a large surface area to volume ratio to ensure a high rate of energy transfer to its surroundings.

6. Saving Energy in the Home
Page 231 — Fact Recall Questions

Q1 a) Foam squirted into the gap between the bricks of a cavity wall stops convection currents being set up in the gap and reduces the amount of radiation across the gap.
    b) An insulating material laid on a loft floor helps reduce heat loss by conduction (as it's an insulator) and radiation (as it covers the surface of the loft floor).
    c) Instead of just having a pane of glass, double-glazed windows have a double layer of glass separated by an air gap. Because air is a gas, it conducts poorly and will reduce energy loss by conduction through the window.

Q2 $$\text{payback time} = \frac{\text{inital cost}}{\text{annual saving}}$$

Q3 You can judge the effectiveness of insulation from how much money installing the insulation will save you annually — the more money it saves you, the more effective it is. Cost-effectiveness is measured by how short the payback time for the insulation is — the shorter the payback time, the quicker you'll make your money back and so the more cost-effective the insulation is.

Q4 U-value is a measure of how insulating a material is.

Q5 E.g. to heat buildings and for washing.

Page 232 — Application Question

Q1 a) i) Cavity wall insulation saves the most money annually and so would be the most effective insulation to install.
        ii) The most cost-effective insulation to install will be the insulation with the shortest payback time.
            $$\text{payback time} = \frac{\text{inital cost}}{\text{annual saving}}$$
            Hot water tank jacket:
            Payback time = 15 ÷ 30 = 0.5 years
            Cavity wall insulation:
            Payback time = 432 ÷ 72 = 6 years
            So the **hot water tank jacket** is more cost-effective to install.
    b) They should choose **material 2** because it has a lower U-value. The lower the U-value of a material, the better at insulating it is.

7. Specific Heat Capacity
Page 234 — Fact Recall Questions

Q1 The amount of energy needed to change the temperature of 1 kg of a material by 1 °C.

Q2 Materials with a high specific heat capacity are used so they can store large amounts of energy.

Q3 E.g. any three of: water, concrete, brick, oil.

Page 235 — Application Questions

Q1 $\theta = 100\ °C - 20\ °C = 80\ °C$

$E = m \times c \times \theta$
$= 0.3 \times 4200 \times 80$
$= \mathbf{100\ 800\ J}$

Q2 a) Steel — it has the lowest specific heat capacity and so will cool down quicker than the other materials shown in the table.
b) Water — it has the highest specific heat capacity and so will be able to store the most energy.
c) Glass — it has the highest specific heat capacity of the solid materials, and so will be able to absorb the most energy for a given change in temperature. The limited change in temperature will protect the surface beneath it.

Q3 $m = 400\ g = 0.4\ kg$
$\theta = 113\ °C - 25\ °C = 88\ °C$
$E = m \times c \times \theta$

$c = \dfrac{E}{m \times \theta}$

$= \dfrac{70\ 400}{(0.4 \times 88)}$
$= \mathbf{2000\ J/kg°C}$

Pages 238-239 — Physics 1.1
Exam-style Questions

Q1 a) i) radiation *(1 mark)*
ii) The foil is shiny, so it will reflect infrared radiation back and stop it from being lost from the house *(1 mark)*.
b) E.g. The fibreglass is an insulator and so will reduce energy transfer by conduction *(1 mark)*. It will also cover the surface of the loft floor and so reduce energy transfer by radiation *(1 mark)*.
c) E.g. The lower the U-value, the better at insulating it is and so the better the material will be at reducing energy loss *(1 mark)*.
d) payback time $= \dfrac{\text{inital cost}}{\text{annual saving}} = \dfrac{54}{30}$
$= \mathbf{1.8\ years}$

(2 marks for the correct answer, otherwise 1 mark for showing '54 ÷ 30'.)

Q2 a) E.g. The heat sink is made of a metal which is a good conductor of heat *(1 mark)*. This means the heat sink will be able to transfer heat energy away from the component quickly *(1 mark)*. The heat sink has many fins to give it a very large surface area / large surface area to volume ratio *(1 mark)*. This means it will transfer energy to its surroundings at a high rate *(1 mark)*.

When you're explaining how a device is designed to minimise or maximise heat transfer, don't just say what features it has — make sure you explain how those features affect its rate of energy transfer and why that's useful.

b) E.g. The cooler the air around the heat sink, the larger the temperature difference will be between the heat sink and its surroundings *(1 mark)*. This will increase the rate of heat transfer between the heat sink and its surroundings, so will improve the rate it transfers energy away from the component that it is cooling *(1 mark)*.

Q3 a) **B** *(1 mark)*
b) The particles in a gas have more energy on average than those in a liquid *(1 mark)*.
c) How to grade your answer:
0 marks:
There is no relevant information.
1-2 marks:
There is a brief description of how particles in the liquid sweat evaporate and cause cooling. No explanation for this cooling effect is given.
3-4 marks:
There is some explanation of how the evaporation of sweat particles causes a cooling effect, and how the fan increases the rate of evaporation.
5-6 marks:
There is a clear and detailed explanation of how the evaporation of the sweat particles decreases the average kinetic energy of the remaining sweat left behind and causes a cooling effect and why the fan increases this rate of evaporation. The answer has a logical structure and uses correct spelling, grammar and punctuation.

Here are some points your answer may include:
The particles that evaporate from the sweat will have the highest energies.
This leads to a decrease in the average particle energy of the sweat left behind, and causes a cooling effect.
Using a fan increases the airflow, and so the concentration of sweat in the air near the person's skin will be reduced.
This will increase the rate of evaporation of the sweat, and so increase the rate of cooling.

Q4 a) E.g. Energy is transferred to the water particles close to the heating coil. This causes the particles to move at higher speeds and move apart *(1 mark)*. The distance between the particles increases, so the density of the warm water decreases *(1 mark)*. The warm water is less dense than the cold water above it, so it rises *(1 mark)*. Colder water sinks to the bottom of the kettle, where it will then be heated. This cycle creates a convection current *(1 mark)* that gradually heats the water inside the kettle.
b) $\theta = 100\ °C - 10\ °C = 90\ °C$
$E = m \times c \times \theta$
$= 1.2 \times 4200 \times 90$
$= \mathbf{453\ 600\ J}$

(3 marks for the correct answer, otherwise 1 mark for showing the temperature difference is 90 °C and 1 mark for the correct substitution of values into $E = m \times c \times \theta$.)

c) i) Condensation *(1 mark)*
   ii) E.g. The particles meet much cooler air when they leave the kettle *(1 mark)*. They will lose energy (due to the lower temperature / collisions with air particles) *(1 mark)*. Eventually, the particles will have low enough energies that they clump together and form liquid droplets that are visible *(1 mark)*.

Physics 1.2 Energy and Efficiency

1. Energy Transfer
Page 241 — Fact Recall Questions
Q1 Electrical, light, sound, kinetic (or movement), nuclear, thermal (or heat), gravitational potential, elastic potential, chemical.
Q2 Energy can be transferred usefully from one form to another, stored or dissipated — but it can never be created or destroyed.

Page 241 — Application Questions
Q1 a) E.g. a burglar alarm
   b) E.g. a catapult
   c) E.g. a loudspeaker
Q2 a) Elastic potential energy to kinetic energy (plus a small amount of sound and heat energy).
   You could also consider the energy transfers in the muscles of the archer.
   b) Electrical energy to light, sound and heat energy.
   c) Chemical energy to electrical energy. Then electrical energy to light and heat energy.

2. Efficiency of Machines
Page 246 — Fact Recall Questions
Q1 E.g. it means that it wastes very little of the energy or power it's supplied with.
Q2 E.g. some of the energy that's supplied to any device is always lost or wasted, often as heat.
Q3 a) It will be spread out, usually as heat.
   b) It causes them to become warmer.
   c) The energy becomes increasingly spread out, so it can't be easily used or collected back in again.
   d) E.g. by using a heat exchanger. Cool fluid is pumped through escaping heat so that the fluid gains heat energy. This heat energy can then be converted into a form of energy that's useful again.

Page 246 — Application Questions
Q1 a) $\text{efficiency} = \dfrac{\text{useful power out}}{\text{total power in}}$
   $= \dfrac{54}{90}$
   $= \mathbf{0.6}$
   b) Useful energy out = 800 – 277 = 523 J
   $\text{efficiency} = \dfrac{\text{useful energy out}}{\text{total energy in}}$
   $= \dfrac{523}{800}$
   $= \mathbf{0.654}$ (to 3 s.f.)

Q2 a) $\text{efficiency} = \dfrac{\text{useful power out}}{\text{total power in}}$
   $= \dfrac{12.6}{36}$
   $= \mathbf{0.35}$
   percentage efficiency = 0.35 × 100 = **35%**

   b) $\text{efficiency} = \dfrac{\text{useful energy out}}{\text{total energy in}}$
   $= \dfrac{4.5}{7.5}$
   $= 0.6$
   percentage efficiency = 0.6 × 100 = **60%**
   The heat and sound produced by the lamp aren't useful — only the light is.
Q3 a) useful energy out = 275 + 190 = **465 kJ**
   b) wasted energy = 650 – 465 = **185 kJ**
   c) $\text{efficiency} = \dfrac{\text{useful energy out}}{\text{total energy in}}$
   $= \dfrac{465}{650}$
   $= \mathbf{0.715}$ (to 3 s.f.)
Q4 a) Low-energy bulb:
   payback time = 3.50 ÷ 5.60 = 0.625 years
   LED bulb:
   payback time = 16 ÷ 10 = 1.6 years
   b) The LED bulb.
   The LED bulb has a slightly longer payback time, but it also has a much longer lifetime and larger annual saving.
   c) The LED bulb.
   You don't need to do a calculation to tell this. Both bulbs have the same output power, so whichever has the least input power transfers the largest proportion of its input energy into useful energy and is the most efficient.
   d) E.g. it costs less to buy / he plans to use it for less than the payback time of the LED bulb.

Q5 Rearrange $\text{efficiency} = \dfrac{\text{useful energy out}}{\text{total energy in}}$
   $\text{total energy in} = \dfrac{\text{useful energy out}}{\text{efficiency}} \times 100\%$
   $= \dfrac{816}{68} \times 100\%$
   $= \mathbf{1200\ J}$

3. Sankey Diagrams

Pages 248-249 — Application Questions

Q1 Machine B — both machines have the same energy in, but machine B has a much thinner arrow for wasted heat and sound energy. This means more of the energy in is turned into useful heat and kinetic energy.
You can also see that the arrows for useful heat and kinetic energy are larger for machine B.

Q2 a) 400 J is 20 squares wide, so each square represents $400 \div 20 = $ **20 J**.

b) Heat and sound are both forms of wasted energy. Total width of the heat and sound arrows is $10 + 3 = 13$. So the total energy wasted is $13 \times 20 = $ **260 J**.

c) useful energy out = energy in – wasted energy out
= 400 J – 260 J = 140 J

$$\text{efficiency} = \frac{\text{useful energy out}}{\text{total energy in}}$$
$$= \frac{140}{400}$$
$$= \textbf{0.35 (or 35\%)}$$

Page 250 — Physics 1.2

Exam-style Questions

1 a) Light energy *(1 mark)* and sound energy *(1 mark)*.

b) i) 1600 J is 20 squares wide, so each square represents $1600 \div 20 = $ **80 J** *(1 mark)*.
Heat energy arrow is 4 squares wide, so heat energy wasted = $4 \times 80 = $ **320 J** *(1 mark)*.

ii) Useful energy out = 1600 – 320 = **1280 J**.

$$\text{efficiency} = \frac{\text{useful energy out}}{\text{total energy in}}$$
$$= \frac{1280}{1600}$$
$$= \textbf{0.8}$$

(3 marks for correct answer, otherwise 1 mark for finding the correct value for energy out and 1 mark for attempting to calculate efficiency with the correct formula.)
You could also work out the total useful energy by working out how much each useful energy arrow represents. Each square represents 80 J (from part (i)), so total useful energy = 10 squares + 6 squares = $(10 \times 80) + (6 \times 80) = 1280$ J.

c) (i)

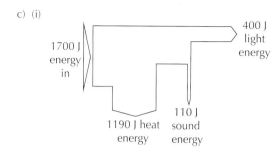

(1 mark for one wasted heat energy arrow and two useful energy arrows labelled sound and light. 1 mark for a thick wasted energy arrow that is much thicker than either useful energy arrows, but thinner than the input energy arrow. 1 mark for the arrow for sound being thinner than the arrow for light energy. All arrows should be clearly labelled with the type of energy they represent.)

(ii) E.g. any three of: it costs less to buy than television B *(1 mark)* / it has a shorter payback time (4 years rather than 7.5) *(1 mark)* / it is more cost-effective over a short period of time than B *(1 mark)* / it requires less energy to work/it has a lower input energy per second *(1 mark)*.

Physics 1.3 The Usefulness of Electrical Appliances

1. The Cost of Electricity

Page 254 — Fact Recall Questions

Q1 It depends on the power of the appliance and the amount of time the appliance is switched on.

Q2 $E = P \times t$. E is energy transferred in joules or kilowatt-hours, P is power measured in watts or kilowatts and t is time in seconds or hours.

Q3 Cost = number of kWh used $\times$ price per kWh

Q4 kilowatt-hours

Page 254 — Application Questions

Q1 a) $E = P \times t = 60 \times 60 = $ **3600 J**

b) 24 hours = $(24 \times 60 \times 60)$ s = 86 400 s
$E = P \times t = 0.1 \times 86\,400 = $ **8640 J**

Q2 a) $E = P \times t = 2 \times 0.5 = $ **1 kWh**

b) 2800 W = 2.8 kW
$E = P \times t = 2.8 \times 0.25 = $ **0.7 kWh**

Q3 a) cost = number of units $\times$ price per unit
= $17 \times 15 = $ **255p (or £2.55)**

b) $E = P \times t = 3 \times 1 = 3$ kWh
cost = number of units $\times$ price per unit
= $3 \times 15 = $ **45p**

c) 6 minutes = 0.1 hours
$E = P \times t = 2.4 \times 0.1 = 0.24$ kWh
cost = number of units $\times$ price per unit
= $0.24 \times 15 = $ **3.6p**

Q4 $E = 480$ kJ = 480 000 J, $P = 1.1$ kW = 1100 W
$E = P \times t$, so $t = E \div P = 480\,000 \div 1100$
= **440 s** (to 2 s.f.)

2. Choosing Electrical Appliances

Page 257 — Fact Recall Question

Q1 Any three from: e.g. it can affect their convenience and safety because they don't have electric lighting or devices / it can mean they're not as healthy because they can't refrigerate items such as food and vaccines / it can affect access to hospital care because modern medical machines won't work / it can affect communication because of a lack of internet or phones.

Page 257 — Application Questions

Q1 a) 300 W = 0.3 kW

$E = P \times t = 0.3 \times 168 = $ **50.4 kWh**

b) cost = number of units × price per unit

= 50.4 × 10 = 504p = **£5.04**

c) 550 W = 0.55 kW

$E = P \times t = 0.55 \times 168 = 92.4$ kWh

cost = number of units × price per unit

= 92.4 × 10 = 924p = **£9.24**

d) saving = £9.24 – £5.04 = **£4.20**

e) Advantage: Freezer A costs less to run every week than Freezer B.

Disadvantage: Freezer A is more expensive to buy than Freezer B.

Q2 Advantage: e.g. the phone can be charged where there's no access to mains electricity. Disadvantage: e.g. the battery charger only works when there's enough sunlight to charge it.

Page 258 — Physics 1.3

Exam-style Questions

1 a) cost = number of kWh × price per kWh

So, number of kWh = cost ÷ price per kWh

= 16 759 ÷ 9 = 1862.11 kWh

meter reading = 6048.09 + 1862.11 = **7910.2**

(3 marks for correct answer, otherwise 1 mark for correct working to calculate the number of kWh used, and 1 mark for calculating 1862.11 kWh)

b) i) 2.5 hours = 150 minutes = 9000 s

P = 2.5 kW = 2500 W

$E = P \times t = 2500 \times 9000 = $ **22 500 000 J**

(2 marks for correct answer, or 1 mark for correct working if answer incorrect)

ii) $E = P \times t = 2.5 \times 2.5 = 6.25$ kWh

cost = number of units × price per unit

= 6.25 × 9 = 56.25p = **56p (to nearest penny)**

(3 marks for correct answer, otherwise 1 mark for showing '2.5 × 2.5' and 1 mark for calculating 6.25 kWh correctly)

iii) 20p = £0.20

payback time = initial cost ÷ saving per wash cycle = 400 ÷ 0.20 = **2000 wash cycles**

(2 marks for correct answer, or 1 mark for correct working if answer incorrect)

iv) Advantage: e.g. it has the shortest cycle time / it is the most efficient machine *(1 mark)*

Disadvantage: e.g. it's the most expensive machine *(1 mark)*

Physics 1.4 Methods We Use to Generate Electricity

1. Energy Sources and Power Stations

Page 260 — Fact Recall Questions

Q1 Coal, oil and natural gas.

Q2 a) Any four from: wind, solar, waves, geothermal, tides, food, hydroelectric, biofuels.

b) E.g. they often produce much less energy than non-renewable resources / a lot of them are less reliable because they depend on the weather.

Q3 a) uranium and plutonium

b) nuclear fission

Q4 a) Fossil fuels are burned to heat the water in a boiler.

b) Water is heated to produce steam, which drives a turbine. This turbine is coupled to an electrical generator, which turns and generates electricity.

2. Wind and Solar Power

Page 262 — Fact Recall Questions

Q1 The wind turns the blades of the turbine, which are connected to an electrical generator inside the turbine. This generates electricity as it turns.

Q2 Generating electricity using wind causes no atmospheric pollution.

Q3 E.g. any two from: wind turbines can be very noisy, disturbing local residents / they generate no electricity when there's no wind / wind turbines are considered by some to be unsightly.

Q4 the Sun's radiation

Q5 E.g. supplying a device in a remote location with another source of energy, e.g. connecting it to the National Grid or having to access the device to replace a battery, would be very difficult and expensive.

Q6 Solar cells generate a relatively small amount of electricity compared to other energy sources, so connecting them to the National Grid is generally impractical and more costly than the value of the electricity they provide.

3. Hydroelectricity and Tides

Page 265 — Fact Recall Questions

Q1 Rainwater is caught (behind a dam) and allowed out through turbines. These turbines are connected to generators, which generate electricity.

Q2 E.g. any two from: flooding of a valley can result in rotting vegetation which releases methane and CO_2 / hydroelectric power stations can have a large impact on local wildlife and habitats / they can cause noise and visual pollution.

Q3 Remote areas can be difficult to supply with fuel or connect to the National Grid. Having a hydroelectric power station in a remote location to provide electricity avoids these problems, as it can be more easily connected to homes and needs no fuel to run.

Q4 a) At times when there is low demand and surplus electricity, pumped-storage power stations pump water from a lower reservoir into a higher reservoir. This water is then ready to be released back down into the lower reservoir and generate electricity as it passes through turbines connected to generators.

b) Pumped-storage hydroelectric power stations only use electricity to pump water at times of low demand when electricity is cheap. The energy stored is used to generate electricity at times of high demand when it's expensive — making the value of the electricity generated much higher than that used to store the energy.

Q5 Tidal barrages are dams with turbines in them. They stop the tide flowing in a river estuary (or similar), so that a height difference of water builds up on both sides. The tide water is then allowed to flow through turbines from the higher side to the lower side. The motion of the turbines turns a generator, which produces electricity.

4. Other Renewable Resources
Page 268 — Fact Recall Questions

Q1 When a wave hits the structure, the motion of the wave forces air up through a turbine which drives a generator and generates electricity. When the wave retreats, the air is forced back out through the same turbine, generating more electricity.

Q2 E.g. generating electricity from waves causes no atmospheric pollution.

Q3 E.g. any one of: the electricity supply is not very reliable, as no electricity can be generated when the sea is calm / they can only be built by water / they can spoil the view (visual pollution) / they can be a hazard to passing boats.

Q4 Steam and hot water rise from underground to the surface and are used to drive a turbine, which is connected to a generator that generates electricity.

Q5 Geothermal power stations can only be built in volcanic areas.

Q6 Biofuels are burned just like fossil fuels to heat water. This produces steam which passes through a turbine and drives a generator to generate electricity.

5. Energy Sources and the Environment
Page 271 — Fact Recall Questions

Q1 E.g. carbon dioxide and sulfur dioxide.

Q2 a) nuclear fuel

b) Any two from e.g. highly radioactive waste is produced, which is difficult to dispose of / transportation and mining of nuclear fuel causes a small amount of atmospheric pollution / nuclear disasters (e.g. Chernobyl) can dramatically harm people/the environment.

Q3 a) If a process is carbon neutral, it removes as much CO_2 from the atmosphere as it releases.

b) The plants used to make biofuels absorb the same amount of CO_2 from the atmosphere as they release when they're burnt to generate electricity. The process is only carbon neutral if we keep growing biofuels at the same rate as they are burned.

Q4 a) Carbon dioxide contributes to the greenhouse effect and an excess of it causes global warming, so it's important that we limit the amount released into the atmosphere.

b) Carbon capture and storage is where carbon dioxide produced in fuel burning power stations is caught and stored instead of being released into the atmosphere.

c) E.g. any two of: storing it in empty oil and gas fields / dissolving it in seawater at the bottom of the ocean / capturing it with algae used to make oils.

6. Choosing Energy Sources
Page 274 — Fact Recall Questions

Q1 a) gas-fired power stations
b) nuclear power stations

Q2 E.g. any two from: Wind — wind farms need to be placed in exposed, windy places like moors and coasts or out at sea. / Geothermal — geothermal power stations can only be built in volcanic areas. / Hydroelectric — hydroelectric power stations can only be built in remote locations, e.g. where valleys can be flooded. / Waves — wave power stations have to be on a coast. / Tides — tidal barrages can only be located where there's an estuary.

Q3 Increasing supply (e.g. building more power stations) or decreasing demand (e.g. encouraging people to use less electricity by turning off lights when they leave the room, buying more efficient appliances, etc.)

Page 275 — Application Questions

Q1 E.g. a gas-fired station should be built as these have the fastest start-up time and so can provide for a rapid increase in energy needs.

Q2 a) i) E.g. hydroelectric. The data from the table shows this is a reliable energy source that provides a moderate amount of power which should be able to meet the increased energy demands of the town. The long start-up time for building this type of power station is not an issue as more electricity isn't immediately needed. The town is between two river estuaries, which makes building a hydroelectric power station plausible. This method of generating electricity is good for keeping atmospheric pollution low — unlike fossil fuel power stations it doesn't release harmful gas emissions into the atmosphere.

ii) Advantage — e.g. any one from: tidal barrages cause no atmospheric pollution once they're built / tides are reliable / there are no fuel costs and low running costs / tidal barrages can store energy for use at times of peak demand. Disadvantage — e.g. any one from: tidal barrages prevent free access to boats / wildlife habitats can be destroyed / barrages can spoil the view / smaller amounts of energy are provided during small tides or when the water level is identical on both sides of the barrage.

b) E.g. solar. There will be plenty of sunshine in the desert, so solar radiation should be able to generate sufficient electricity to power the research station. Solar panels are quick to set up (and take down), which is great as the research station is only temporary. Because it's in a remote location, getting to the site to top up alternative fuel supplies would be difficult and costly. Connecting the station to a mains electricity supply would also be difficult and costly, and wasteful given that the station is only there temporarily.

7. Electricity and the National Grid
Page 278 — Fact Recall Questions
Q1 a) A transformer changes the voltage of a current supply.
   b) When electricity is transmitted, energy is lost through heating in the cables. This energy loss is proportional to the current. Transmitting electricity at a high voltage reduces the current for the same amount of power, so transformers are used to increase the voltage and reduce the energy loss.
Q2 *A* — power station
   B — step-up transformer
   C — pylons / electricity cables
   D — step-down transformer
   E — consumers
Q3 a) overhead
   b) overhead
   c) overhead
   d) underground
   e) overhead
   f) overhead
   g) underground
   h) underground
   i) overhead

Pages 281-282 — Physics 1.4
Exam-style Questions
1   cells, remote, small
    (1 mark for each correct answer)
2   (a) non-renewable energy sources:
       Coal (49.9%), Oil (2.4%), Gas (20.3%) and Nuclear (19.6%).
       Total percentage = 49.9 + 2.4 + 20.3 + 19.6
                        = **92.2%**
       (2 marks for correct answer, otherwise 1 mark for correctly identifying all of the non-renewable energy sources in the table)

(b) E.g. coal, oil and gas are the energy sources listed that emit the most harmful gases (e.g. CO_2, methane, sulfur dioxide) when used to generate electricity *(1 mark)*. A far greater percentage of Country 1's electricity comes from using these sources, so this country will produce more atmospheric pollution *(1 mark)*.
The reservoirs in hydroelectric power stations release a small amount of methane. This is nothing in comparison to the amount of harmful gases released by burning fossil fuels.
(c) (i) E.g. any one from: biofuels are carbon neutral / biofuels are renewable / biofuels don't release sulfur dioxide (the cause of acid rain) when burned *(1 mark)*.
    (ii) E.g. any one from: producing biofuels can release methane, an atmospheric pollutant / growing biofuels can cause deforestation and the destruction of wildlife habitats *(1 mark)*.
3   (a) wind *(1 mark)*
    (b) Coal is burned to heat water *(1 mark)*. This water turns into steam, which drives a turbine *(1 mark)*. The turbine is connected to an electrical generator, which generates electricity *(1 mark)*.
    (c) E.g. any one from: it's a reliable source of energy / it can produce large amounts of electricity / it is relatively cheap and readily available (for now) *(1 mark)*.
    (d) (i) carbon dioxide *(1 mark)*
        (ii) E.g. global warming *(1 mark)*
4   (a)   E.g. any two from: underground cables would be less exposed to the weather and so would be less likely to be damaged or need repair / there is a lower risk of getting an electric shock from underground cables / underground don't cause visual pollution / underground cables aren't a hazard to low flying aircraft. *(2 marks — 1 mark for each correct answer.)*
    (b) (i) (step-down) transformer *(1 mark)*
        (ii) To transmit the same amount of power at a lower voltage requires a higher current *(1 mark)*. This increases the energy losses in the cables and makes transmitting electricity at lower voltages more wasteful than at high voltages *(1 mark)*.
5   (a) E.g. any two from: carbon dioxide / sulfur dioxide / methane *(2 marks — 1 mark for each correct gas)*
    (b) E.g. any one of: they are an unreliable energy source / they only produce a small amount of electricity *(1 mark)*.
Don't just list the disadvantages of using waves to generate electricity — look at the information you're given in the question and pick out the disadvantages that show this type of energy source won't suit what the government have said they want.

(c) How to grade your answer:

0 marks:
There is no relevant information.

1-2 marks:
There is a brief explanation of one or two advantages/disadvantages of hydroelectricity.

3-4 marks:
There is an explanation of three or four advantages/disadvantages. At least one link is made between the advantages and disadvantages of hydroelectricity and the requirements of the government. The answer has a logical structure and spelling, punctuation and grammar are mostly correct.

5-6 marks:
There is a clear and detailed evaluation of the advantages and disadvantages of hydroelectricity and how well it meets the needs of the government. The answer has a logical structure and uses correct spelling, grammar and punctuation.

Here are some points your answer may include:
Generating electricity using hydroelectricity is a reliable method of generating electricity, which is one of the governments requirements.
The government also wants the power stations built to produce large amounts of electricity, which is possible with a large hydroelectric power station.
Hydroelectric power stations only release a small amount of methane into the atmosphere. They release a much smaller amount of harmful gases into the atmosphere than other methods of generating a large, reliable supply of electricity, e.g. burning fossil fuels. Keeping down emissions is one of the government's requirements.
Hydroelectric power stations are expensive and take a long time to build, which does not match the government's requirements.

Physics 1.5 Waves

1. Wave Basics
Page 285 — Fact Recall Questions
Q1 Energy
Q2 a) The displacement from the rest position to a crest (or trough).
    b) The length of a full cycle of a wave (e.g. the distance from one crest to the next).
Q3 Frequency
Q4 $v = f \times \lambda$, where v is speed in m/s, f is frequency in Hz and λ is wavelength in m.

Page 285 — Application Questions
Q1 The wavelength is the length of one full cycle. The distance shown on the diagram is only half a cycle, so it is twice the distance shown on the diagram, **4.0 m**.
Q2 Using the wave equation:
    $v = f \times \lambda = 15 \times 0.45 = $ **6.75 m/s**
Q3 a) E.g.

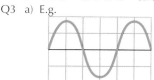

The wave must still be centred around the rest position, but the crest (and troughs) should be higher (and lower) than in the original trace.

b) E.g.

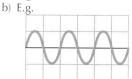

The wave must still be centred around the rest position, but there should be more complete waves than in the original oscilloscope trace.
Q4 $v = f \times \lambda$
    So rearranging gives $f = v \div \lambda$
    $= (3.0 \times 10^8) \div (7.5 \times 10^{-7})$
    $= $ **4 × 10¹⁴ Hz**

2. Transverse and Longitudinal Waves
Page 287 — Fact Recall Questions
Q1 A transverse wave is a wave in which the vibrations are perpendicular to the direction of energy transfer of the wave. Example: e.g. any one of: light / an electromagnetic wave / a water ripple / a slinky spring moved up and down at the end (perpendicular to the direction of travel of the wave through the spring).
Q2 A longitudinal wave is a wave in which the vibrations are parallel to the direction of energy transfer of the wave.
Q3 An area of compression is an area of a longitudinal wave where the particles are bunched together. An area of rarefaction is an area of a longitudinal wave where the particles are spread out.
Q4 B ultrasound.
    The rest of the waves are transverse.
Q5 a) Mechanical waves.
    b) They can be either transverse or longitudinal.
    c) E.g. sound waves, water waves, seismic waves / waves in springs.

3. Wave Properties
Page 290 — Fact Recall Questions
Q1 Where waves bounce back when they hit a boundary between two materials.

Q2 The surface of a mirror is smooth and shiny, so the light waves that hit it all get reflected at the same angle and produce a clear reflection.

Q3 When a wave changes speed and direction as it crosses the boundary between two different media.

Q4 Nothing, the light doesn't refract.

Q5 It refracts.

Q6 When a wave spreads out as it passes through a gap or passes an obstacle.

Q7 A gap that is the same size as the wavelength of the wave.

Page 290 — Application Questions
Q1 Reflection of light allows her to see herself.

Q2 Sound has a long wavelength so it diffracts around and through the gap in the fence and reaches the dog.

4. Electromagnetic Waves
Page 292 — Fact Recall Questions
Q1 Transverse

Q2 A continuous spectrum of all the possible wavelengths of electromagnetic waves.

Q3 From 10^{-15} m to more than 10^4 m.

Q4 Gamma rays, X-rays, ultraviolet, visible light, infrared, microwaves, radio waves.

Q5 Gamma rays

Q6 Radio waves

Q7 The speed of any electromagnetic wave in a vacuum is the same.

Page 292 — Application Question
Q1 a) The wavelength increases.
   b) Radio waves

5. Communication Using EM Waves
Page 295 — Fact Recall Questions
Q1 Their wavelength is so large, that they are diffracted by the Earth's curved surface, so they can travel large distances.

Q2 (Short-wave) radio waves.

Q3 Because the radio waves used to transmit TV signals have a very short wavelength, so they do not diffract (bend) around large obstacles like mountains and buildings so the signal will be blocked and won't reach the transmitter.
   Remember — a shorter wavelength means less diffraction around large obstacles because the most diffraction occurs when the wavelength is a similar size to the gap or obstacle.

Q4 Microwaves can pass through the Earth's atmosphere and reach the satellites.

Q5 Microwaves.

Q6 Mobile phones use microwaves to transmit phone calls. When mobile phones are being used, people are exposed to microwaves. Microwaves can be absorbed by the water in the cells in the body, causing them to heat up a small amount. The risks of this temperature rise are unknown, but it could cause types of cancer. There is no conclusive evidence that mobile phone use is a health risk, but they have not been in use long enough for us to know about their long-term effects.

Q7 E.g. optical fibres / remote controls.

Page 295 — Application Question
Q1 a) Very short wave radio signals do not diffract very much at all. The receiver has to be in line of sight of the transmitter, and the UK is not in line of sight of Australia.
   b) Microwaves can pass through the Earth's atmosphere, which means they can be transmitted to a satellite in orbit and then sent back down to Earth to be received. This allows a signal to be broadcast from Australia and received in the UK via a satellite TV signal.

6. EM Waves and Imaging
Page 297 — Fact Recall Questions
Q1 Because it is given out by hot objects, and the hotter an object is, the more it will give out.

Q2 It detects the temperature variation between the person, and the surroundings by detecting the infrared radiation given out. It forms an image where hottest parts of the image are brightest. A person is (usually) hotter than their surroundings, so the person will shown up brighter on the image so that they can be seen.

Q3 Photography

Page 297 — Application Question
Q1 Image B was taken at night.
   In image B, the temperature difference between the rhino and its surroundings is much greater. At night, the temperature of the surroundings is lower, so the surroundings show up darker and the hotter rhino can be seen more easily.

7. Reflection

Page 301 — Fact Recall Questions

Q1 The normal is an imaginary line that is perpendicular (at right angles) to the surface of reflection at the point where the wave is incident on it.

Q2 The angle between the path of the incident wave and the normal.

Q3 For any reflection, the angle of incidence is equal to the angle of reflection.

Q4 Any three from: virtual / upright / same size / laterally inverted.

Q5 A diagram that shows how the rays of light from an object form an image.

Q6

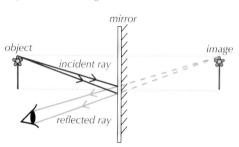

Page 301 — Application Questions

Q1 Image C is the correct image — it is upright, the same size and laterally inverted (flipped left to right).

Q2

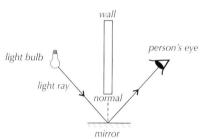

(The angle of incidence and angle of reflection should be exactly the same.)

8. Sound Waves

Page 304 — Fact Recall Questions

Q1 Sound travels by making particles vibrate, so it can't travel in a vacuum, where there are no particles.

Q2 The reflection of the sound waves reaching you. The sound has to travel further than the original sound to get to you, so you hear the echo shortly after the original sound.

Q3 Carpets, curtains and furniture all absorb sound waves, so they do not reflect enough sound for an echo to be heard.

Q4 Frequency

Q5 Amplitude

Page 304 — Application Questions

Q1 Sound A is low pitched and quiet. Sound B is high pitched and loud.

Q2 The emitted sound waves reflect when they meet an object and bounce back. The sound waves reach the submarine and are detected as an echo. The sound waves have to travel further to the iceberg and back than to the boat and back, so the echo caused by the boat will be heard earlier than the echo caused by the iceberg. The submarine will hear two echoes and know that one object is closer than the other.

9. The Doppler Effect and Red-shift

Page 306 — Fact Recall Questions

Q1 The change in the observed frequency and wavelength of a wave for a source moving towards or away from a stationary observer. E.g. any two from: sound waves, visible light, microwaves.

Q2 The wavelength will increase.

Q3 Red shift is the result of the Doppler effect for a source of light moving away from the observer. The wavelength of the light increases, making it appear more red than its true colour.

Page 306 — Application Question

Q1 To the left — the sound waves will spread out behind the moving van and bunch up in front of it. The waves are bunched up on the left hand side of the diagram, so it must be moving that way.

10. The Origin of the Universe

Page 309 — Fact Recall Questions

Q1 The further away a galaxy is, the more red-shift we see.

Q2 We see red-shift in almost all galaxies, suggesting that almost all galaxies are moving away from us very quickly.

Q3 All the matter and energy in the universe was once compressed into a very small space. Then it exploded from that single 'point' and started expanding.

Q4 CMBR is cosmic microwave background radiation — uniform microwave radiation coming from all parts of the universe. It was formed from radiation given out just after the big bang.

Q5 The Big Bang theory is the only theory that we have that can explain CMBR.

Page 309 — Application Question

Q1 The galaxy is moving away from us because the dark lines in the spectrum have moved towards the red end of the visible spectrum.

Pages 312-314 — Physics 1.5
Exam-style Questions

1 (a) (i) $3.0 \div 2 = $ **1.5 m** *(1 mark)*
     (ii) $v = f \times \lambda = 2 \times 1.5 = $ **3 m/s.**
        (2 marks for correct answer, otherwise 1 mark for substituting in the correct values.)
        You'd still get full marks for a) ii) if you calculate a) i) wrong, but then used that value correctly to calculate a speed.
     (iii) frequency *(1 mark)*
   (b) (i) E.g. they transfer energy / can be reflected / can be refracted / can be diffracted *(1 mark)*.
     (ii)

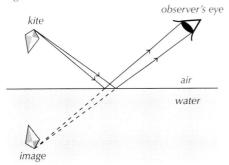

List A	List B
Sound waves	Transverse
Mechanical waves	Longitudinal
Radio waves	

        (3 marks available — 1 mark for connecting each wave in List A correctly.)

2 (a) Frequency *(1 mark)* and energy *(1 mark)*.
   (b) Radio waves *(1 mark)* and microwaves *(1 mark)*.
   (c) E.g. remote controls / sending information down optical fibres *(1 mark)*.

3 (a) (i) E.g.

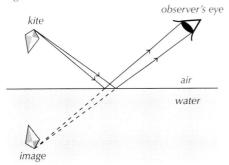

        (4 marks available — 1 mark for a ray drawn correctly from the top of the object and being reflected by the air-water boundary and reaching the observer's eye. 1 mark drawing a dotted line to show a virtual ray in the correct position for the first ray drawn. 1 mark for at least one arrow drawn in the correct direction. 1 mark for showing two sets of real/virtual rays with the virtual rays coming from the same point on the kite image)
     (ii) E.g. The image is the same size as the object / same distance from the surface as the object *(1 mark)*.
   (b) (i) Refraction *(1 mark)*
     (ii) The light is travelling along the normal to the water, so it will not refract *(1 mark)*.

4 (a) The sound waves from the siren diffract around the corner *(1 mark)*.
   (b) (i) The Doppler effect *(1 mark)*.

   (ii) Before the ambulance passes the pedestrian *(1 mark)*. This is because the sound waves in front of the moving ambulance will seem to the pedestrian to have a higher frequency *(1 mark)*, and so the sound heard will have a higher pitch *(1 mark)*.

5 (a) Cosmic microwave background radiation *(1 mark)*.
   (b) E.g. The red-shift of light from distant galaxies *(1 mark)*. The further away a galaxy is, the more the light from it is red-shifted *(1 mark)*. This means the more distant the galaxy, the faster it is travelling away from us, which shows that the universe is expanding *(1 mark)*. This is evidence for the Big Bang theory, which states that in the past the universe was smaller and may have started from a small initial point before expanding *(1 mark)*.

Glossary

A

Accurate result
A result that is very close to the true answer.

Adaptation
A characteristic that helps an organism to survive.

Addiction (drugs)
Being dependant on a particular substance.

Adult cell cloning
A method of cloning animals, which involves taking the nucleus from an adult body cell and inserting it into an unfertilised egg cell which has had its nucleus removed.

Alkane
A saturated hydrocarbon with the general formula C_nH_{2n+2}. E.g. methane, ethane, propane etc.

Alkene
An unsaturated hydrocarbon that contains a carbon-carbon double bond and has the general formula C_nH_{2n}. E.g. ethene, propene etc.

Allele
An alternative form of a gene.

Alloy
A metal that is a mixture of two or more metals, or a mixture involving metals and non-metals.

Amplitude
The displacement from the rest position to the crest (or trough) of a wave.

Anabolic steroid
A type of performance-enhancing drug that increases muscle growth.

Anomalous result
A result that doesn't seem to fit with the rest of the data.

Antibiotic
A drug used to kill or prevent the growth of bacteria.

Antibiotic resistance
When bacteria aren't killed by an antibiotic.

Antibody
A protein produced by white blood cells in response to the presence of an antigen (e.g. on the surface of a pathogen).

Antigen
A molecule on the surface of a cell. A foreign antigen triggers white blood cells to produce antibodies.

Antitoxin
A protein produced by white blood cells which counteracts the toxins produced by invading bacteria.

Asexual reproduction
A type of reproduction involving only one parent and no fusion of gametes (and so no mixture of genes). The offspring produced are genetically identical to the parent — they're clones.

Atmosphere
The layer of air that surrounds the Earth.

Atmospheric pollution
Pollution caused by releasing harmful gases into the atmosphere, such as carbon dioxide, sulfur dioxide and methane.

Atom
A neutral particle made up of protons and neutrons in the nucleus, with electrons surrounding the nucleus.

Atomic number
The number of protons in the nucleus of an atom. It's also known as proton number.

Auxin
A plant hormone that controls the growth of a plant in response to different stimuli.

B

Bacterium
A single-celled microorganism without a nucleus. Some bacteria are able to cause disease.

Balanced diet
A diet that contains the right amounts of the different nutrients needed by the body.

Bias
Prejudice towards or against something.

Big Bang theory
All the matter and energy in the universe was once compressed into a very small space. It started expanding rapidly from that single 'point'.

Biodegradable
Can be broken down by microorganisms.

Biodiesel
A type of biofuel produced from vegetable oils.

Biofuel
A type of renewable fuel that is produced from plants and waste. E.g. ethanol or biodiesel.

Bioleaching
The process by which copper is separated from copper sulfide using bacteria.

Biomass
The mass of living material.

Blood cholesterol level
The level of cholesterol (a fatty substance) in the blood.

C

Carbon capture and storage (CCS)
The process of capturing carbon dioxide emitted (from power stations) and storing it so that it's not released into the atmosphere.

Carbon cycle
The continuous cycle of carbon from the air, through food chains and back into the air.

Carbon neutral fuel
A fuel is carbon neutral if it absorbs as much CO_2 from the atmosphere (when it's grown) as it releases when it's burned.

Categoric data
Data that comes in distinct categories (e.g. type of fuel or metals).

Cavity wall insulation
Insulation in the gap between the bricks in a cavity wall to help reduce energy transfer — usually in the form of an insulating foam which can be squirted into the gap.

Cell elongation
The enlargement of a cell. Plant cells grow by cell elongation.

Cell membrane
A membrane which surrounds a cell.

Central Nervous System (CNS)
The brain and spinal cord. It's where reflexes and actions are coordinated.

Chromosome
A long length of coiled up DNA, which carries genes.

Classification (of organisms)
The process of sorting organisms into groups based on their similarities and differences.

Climate change
Any change in the Earth's climate. E.g. global warming, changing rainfall patterns etc.

Clinical trial
A set of drug tests on human volunteers.

Clone
An organism that is genetically identical to another organism.

Cloning
Making a genetically identical copy of another organism.

Complete combustion
When a fuel burns in plenty of oxygen. The only products are carbon dioxide and water.

Compound
A substance made up of atoms of at least two different elements, chemically joined together.

Condensation
The process where a gas changes into a liquid.

Conduction
A method of energy transfer through a solid. The particles in a heated part of the solid gain kinetic energy and so vibrate more. They collide with neighbouring particles and pass some of their kinetic energy to them. In this way, energy is transferred through the solid.

Conservation of energy principle
Energy can be transferred usefully from one form to another, stored or dissipated — but it can never be created or destroyed.

Continental drift
The movement of the Earth's continents.

Continuous data
Numerical data that can have any value within a range (e.g. length, volume or temperature).

Control experiment
An experiment that's kept under the same conditions as the rest of the investigation, but doesn't have anything done to it.

Control group
A group that matches the one being studied, but the independent variable isn't altered. It's kept under the same conditions as the group in the experiment.

Control variable
A variable in an experiment that is kept the same.

Convection
A method of energy transfer through liquids and gases. The particles of a heated region of a gas or liquid gain energy and move apart, decreasing the density of the gas or liquid in that region. The warm gas/liquid rises above denser cooler liquid, and the denser cooler liquid sinks. The cooler gas or liquid then gets heated, and the process continues. This flow of liquid/gas due to changes in density is called a convection current.

Core
The innermost layer of the Earth, thought to be made of iron and nickel.

Correlation
A relationship between two variables.

Cosmic microwave background radiation (CMBR)
Uniform microwave radiation coming from all parts of the universe.

Cost-effective (types of insulation)
The shorter the payback time, the more cost-effective a method of insulation is.

Covalent bond
A chemical bond formed when atoms share a pair of electrons to form molecules.

Cracking
The process that is used to break long-chain hydrocarbons down into shorter, more useful hydrocarbons.

Crust
The thin, outer layer of the Earth (the bit that we live on).

Culture (of microorganisms)
A population of one type of microorganism that's been grown under controlled conditions.

Cutting (plants)
A small piece of a plant (usually with a new bud on) that can be taken and grown into a new plant.

Cytoplasm
A jelly-like substance found inside cells.

D

Decommissioning
The process of shutting down a power station so that it's completely safe and poses no risk to people or the environment.

Deficiency disease
A disease caused by a lack of a certain nutrient in the diet, e.g. a vitamin or a mineral.

Dependent variable
The variable in an experiment that is measured.

Detritus feeder
An animal that feeds on dead material and breaks down animal waste products.

Diffraction
When waves spread out as they pass through a narrow gap or go round obstacles.

Direct proportionality
When a graph of two variables is plotted and the variables increase or decrease in the same ratio.

Discrete data
Numerical data that can be counted in chunks with no in-between value (e.g. number of people).

Displacement (in waves)
The distance that a particle in a wave has moved from its rest position.

Displacement reaction
A reaction where a more reactive metal replaces a less reactive metal in a compound.

Distillation
A way of separating a liquid out from a mixture. You heat the mixture until the bit you want evaporates, then cool the vapour to turn it back into a liquid.

Distribution (of organisms)
Where organisms are found in a particular area.

DNA
The molecule in cells that stores genetic information.

Doppler effect
The change in the observed frequency and wavelength of a wave emitted by a source moving towards or away from an observer.

Double glazing
Windows made up of two layers of glass or plastic, separated by a layer of air. This helps reduce energy transfer by conduction through the windows.

Double-blind trial
A clinical trial where neither the doctors nor the patients know who has received the drug and who has received the placebo until all the results have been gathered.

Drug
A substance that alters the chemical reactions in your body.

E

Ecological relationship
The interaction between organisms in the same environment.

Effective (types of insulation)
The more money a type of insulation saves you annually on energy bills, the more effective the insulation is.

Effector
Either a muscle or gland which responds to nervous impulses.

Efficiency
The proportion of input energy (or power) transferred into useful output energy (or power).

Electrolysis
The process of breaking down a substance using electricity.

Electrolyte
A liquid used in electrolysis to conduct electricity between the two electrodes.

Electromagnetic spectrum
A continuous spectrum of all the possible wavelengths of electromagnetic waves.

Electron
A subatomic particle with a relative charge of –1. Electrons are located in shells around the nucleus.

Electron shell
A region of an atom that contains electrons. It's also known as an energy level.

Electronic structure
The number of electrons in an atom (or ion) of an element and how they are arranged.

Element
A substance that is made up of only one type of atom.

Embryo transfer (cloning)
A method of cloning animals, where an embryo is created and then split, before any cells become specialised, to produce clones. The clones are then transferred in the uteruses of host mothers.

Emulsifier
A substance that can be added to an emulsion to make it more stable and stop it from separating out.

Emulsion
A mixture made up of lots of tiny droplets of one liquid suspended in another liquid.

Energy level
A region of an atom that contains electrons. It's also known as an electron shell.

Epidemic
A big outbreak of disease.

Evaporation
The process where a liquid changes into a gas.

Evolution (of a species)
The gradual change in a species over time.

Evolutionary relationship
How organisms are related to other organisms through evolution.

Extremophile
An organism that's adapted to live in seriously extreme conditions.

Fair test
A controlled experiment where the only thing that changes is the independent variable.

Fermentation
The process of using yeast to convert sugars into ethanol.

Fertilisation
The fusion of male and female gametes during sexual reproduction.

Fertility
The ability to conceive a child.

Flammability
How easy it is to ignite a substance.

Follicle Stimulating Hormone (FSH)
A hormone produced by the pituitary gland involved in the menstrual cycle. It causes eggs to mature in the ovaries and stimulates the ovaries to produce oestrogen.

Fossil fuel
A fuel that is produced over millions of years from the buried remains of plants and animals. The fossil fuels are coal, oil and natural gas. They're non-renewable resources that we burn to generate electricity.

Fraction
A group of hydrocarbons that condense together when crude oil is separated using fractional distillation. E.g. petrol, naphtha, kerosene etc.

Fractional distillation
A process that can be used to separate the substances in a mixture according to their boiling points.

Frequency
The number of complete waves passing a certain point per second or the number of waves produced by a source each second. Measured in hertz, Hz.

Gamete
A sex cell, e.g. an egg cell or a sperm cell in animals.

Gene
A short section of DNA, found on a chromosome, which controls the development of a characteristic.

Genetic engineering
The process of cutting out a useful gene from one organism's chromosome and inserting it into another organism's chromosome.

Genetically modified (GM) crop
A crop which has had its genes modified through genetic engineering.

Geothermal energy
Heat energy from hot rocks underground. Hot steam and water that rise up to the Earth's surface in volcanic areas are used to generate electricity.

Geotropism
See gravitropism.

Gland
The place where hormones are produced and secreted from.

Global dimming
The decrease in the amount of sunlight reaching the Earth's surface due to an increase in the amount of particulate carbon in the atmosphere.

Global warming
The increase in the average temperature of the Earth.

Gravitropism
The growth of a plant in response to gravity. Also known as geotropism.

Greenhouse effect
The process by which thermal radiation from the Sun is absorbed by 'greenhouse gases' in the Earth's atmosphere, so that the amount of heat absorbed is larger than the amount of heat radiated back into space.

Group
A column in the periodic table that contains elements with similar properties.

Hard drug
A drug that is believed to cause serious addiction and be more harmful to a person's health than a soft drug.

Hazard
Something that has the potential to cause harm (e.g. fire, electricity, etc).

Heat radiation
The transfer of heat energy by infrared radiation.

Homoeostasis
The maintenance of a constant internal environment.

Hormone
A chemical messenger which travels in the blood to activate target cells.

Hot water tank jacket
Insulation (usually fibreglass) wrapped around a hot water tank to limit heat loss by conduction and radiation.

Hydrocarbon
A compound that is made from only hydrogen and carbon.

Hydrogenation
The addition of hydrogen to a compound.

Hydrophilic
Attracted to water (water loving).

Hydrophobic
Attracted to oil or repelled by water (water hating).

Hypothesis
A possible explanation for a scientific observation.

Immunity
The ability of the white blood cells to respond quickly to a pathogen.

Incomplete combustion
When a fuel burns but there isn't enough oxygen for it to burn completely. Products can include carbon monoxide and carbon particulates. Also known as partial combustion.

Independent variable
The variable in an experiment that is changed.

Infectious disease
A disease caused by a pathogen.

Infrared (IR) radiation
A type of electromagnetic wave continually emitted and absorbed by all objects.

In Vitro Fertilisation (IVF)
The artificial fertilisation of eggs in the lab.

Ion
A charged particle formed when one or more electrons are lost or gained from an atom or molecule.

Ionic bonding
A strong attraction between oppositely charged ions.

Kilowatt-hour
The amount of electrical energy used by a 1 kW appliance left on for 1 hour.

Kinetic theory
The theory that explains the different states of matter (solid, liquid and gas) by the arrangement and energies of their particles.

L

Limewater
A solution of calcium hydroxide in water. When carbon dioxide is bubbled through it the solution turns cloudy.

Linear relationship
When a graph of two variables is plotted and the points lie on a straight line.

Living indicator
An organism that is sensitive to changes in its environment, so can be used to study environmental change.

Loft insulation
Insulation (usually fibreglass wool) laid on loft floors to reduce heat transfer by conduction and radiation.

Longitudinal wave
A wave in which the vibrations are parallel to the direction of energy transfer.

Luteinising Hormone (LH)
A hormone produced by the pituitary gland, which stimulates egg release around the middle of the menstrual cycle.

M

Malnourishment
A condition in which you don't have the right balance of foods to stay healthy.

Mantle
The layer of the Earth between the crust and the core. It has all the properties of a solid but can flow very slowly.

Mass number
The total number of protons and neutrons in an atom.

Mean (average)
A measure of average found by adding up all the data and dividing by the number of values there are.

Mechanical wave
A wave that needs a medium to travel in.

Medium
A substance that a wave can travel through.

Menstrual cycle
The monthly sequence of events in which the female body releases an egg and prepares the uterus (womb) in case it receives a fertilised egg.

Metabolic rate
The speed at which the chemical reactions in the body occur.

Metabolism
The chemical reactions in the body that keep you alive.

Mixture
A substance made from two or more elements or compounds that aren't chemically bonded to each other.

MMR vaccine
A vaccination against the diseases measles, mumps and rubella.

Molecule
A particle made up of at least two atoms held together by covalent bonds.

Monomer
A small molecule that can be joined together with other small molecules to form a polymer.

Monounsaturated fat
A fat that contains just one carbon-carbon double bond.

Motor neurone
A nerve cell that carries electrical impulses from the CNS to effectors.

MRSA (methicillin-resistant *Staphylococcus aureus*)
A strain of bacteria that is resistant to the powerful antibiotic methicillin.

Mutation
A change in an organism's DNA.

N

National Grid
The network that distributes electricity from power stations to consumers.

Natural selection
The process by which species evolve.

Negative correlation
When one variable decreases as another variable increases.

Negative ion
A particle with a negative charge, formed when one or more electrons are gained.

Nervous system
The organ system in animals that allows them to respond to changes in their environment.

Neurone
A nerve cell. Neurones transmit information around the body, including to and from the CNS.

Neutron
A subatomic particle with a relative charge of 0 and a relative mass of 1. Neutrons are located in the nucleus of an atom.

Noble gases
The elements in Group 0 of the periodic table.

Non-living indicator
Something that is not alive, but can be measured or monitored to give information about environmental change, e.g. temperature.

Non-renewable energy resource
An energy resource that is non-renewable will run out one day. It will run out more quickly the more we use it to generate electricity.

Normal
An imaginary line that's perpendicular (at 90°) to a surface at the point of incidence of a wave (i.e. where the wave hits the surface).

Nucleus (of an atom)
The central part of an atom or ion, made up of protons and neutrons.

Nucleus (of a cell)
A structure in a body cell which contains genetic material in the form of chromosomes.

Nutrient
A substance needed by the body in order to survive and grow, e.g. protein.

O

Obesity
A condition defined as being 20% or more over the maximum recommended body mass.

Oestrogen
A hormone produced by the ovaries which inhibits the release of FSH during the menstrual cycle. It's found in some oral contraceptives.

Optimum dose (in drug testing)
The dose of a drug that is most effective and has few side effects.

Oral contraceptive
A hormone-containing pill taken by mouth in order to reduce fertility and therefore decrease the chance of pregnancy.

Ore
A rock that contains enough metal to make it profitable to extract.

Ovary
An organ in the female body which stores and releases eggs. It is also a gland and secretes the hormone oestrogen.

P

Pandemic
A worldwide outbreak of a disease.

Partial combustion
When a fuel burns but there isn't enough oxygen for it to burn completely. Products can include carbon monoxide and carbon particulates. Also known as incomplete combustion.

Pathogen
A microorganism that causes disease, e.g. a bacterium or virus.

Payback time
The time it takes for the amount of money saved to equal the cost of an appliance or energy-saving measure (e.g. installing loft insulation).

Peak demand
Times at which the demand for electricity is highest — usually around meal times.

Penicillin
A type of antibiotic.

Performance-enhancing drug
A drug that can improve a person's performance in sport.

Periodic table
A table of all the known elements, arranged so that elements with similar properties are in groups.

Photosynthesis
The process that plants use to capture light energy from the Sun.

Phototropism
The growth of a plant in response to light.

Phytomining
The process by which copper can be extracted from plants that have been grown in copper-rich soils.

Pituitary gland
A gland located in the brain that is responsible for secreting various hormones, including FSH and LH.

Placebo (in drug testing)
A substance that's like the drug being tested but doesn't do anything.

Polymer
A long chain molecule that is formed by joining lots of smaller molecules (monomers) together.

Polymerisation
The process of joining lots of small molecules (monomers) together to form a much longer molecule (a polymer).

Polyunsaturated fat
A fat that contains more than one carbon-carbon double bond.

Positive correlation
When one variable increases as another variable increases.

Positive ion
A particle with a positive charge, formed when one or more electrons are lost.

Power
The rate energy is transferred.

Precise result
When all the data is close to the mean.

Prediction
A statement based on a hypothesis that can be tested.

Primordial soup theory
A theory that suggests life started when lightning caused gases in the atmosphere to react and form amino acids, which then formed organic matter.

Product
A substance that is formed in a chemical reaction.

Progesterone
A hormone produced by the ovaries, which is involved in the menstrual cycle. It's found in some oral contraceptives.

Proton
A subatomic particle with a relative charge of +1 and a relative mass of 1. Protons are located in the nucleus of an atom.

Proton number
The number of protons in the nucleus of an atom. It's also known as atomic number.

Pumped storage
A way of storing surplus energy by using 'spare' electricity to pump water into a higher reservoir. The water can then be passed through turbines, connected to generators, to turn the stored energy back into electricity.

Pyramid of biomass
A diagram to represent the biomass at each stage of a food chain.

R

Random error
A small difference in the results of an experiment caused by things like human error in measuring.

Range
The difference between the smallest and largest values in a set of data.

Ray diagram
A diagram that shows how the rays of light from an object form an image.

Reactant
A substance that reacts in a chemical reaction.

Reactivity series
A list of elements arranged in order of their reactivity. The most reactive elements are at the top and the least reactive at the bottom.

Receptor
A group of cells which are sensitive to a stimulus. E.g. light receptor cells in the eye are sensitive to light.

Recreational drug
A drug used for fun, e.g. alcohol, cannabis.

Red-shift
The shift in the observed wavelength and frequency of a light source moving away from a stationary observer towards the red end of the electromagnetic spectrum.

Reflection
When a wave bounces back as it meets a boundary between two media.

Reflex
A fast, automatic response to a stimulus.

Reflex arc
The passage of information in a reflex from receptor to effector.

Refraction
When a wave changes direction as it crosses a boundary between two media.

Relay neurone
A nerve cell that carries electrical impulses from sensory neurones to motor neurones.

Reliable result
A result that is repeatable and reproducible.

Renewable energy resource
An energy resource that is renewable won't run out, no matter how much we use it.

Repeatable result
A result that will come out the same if the experiment is repeated by the same person using the same method and equipment.

Reproducible result
A result that will come out the same if someone different does the experiment, or a slightly different method or piece of equipment is used.

Resolution
The smallest change a measuring instrument can detect.

Rooting powder
A powder containing plant hormones, which can be applied to plant cuttings to assist root development.

Sankey diagram
A diagram that uses arrows of different thicknesses to show the energy transfers that occur in a device.

Saturated
A molecule that contains only single bonds and so can't have any more atoms added to it.

Selective weedkiller
A weedkiller that contains plant hormones. It kills weeds (unwanted plants), without affecting the growth of crops.

Sense organ
An organ which contains receptors that detect stimuli, e.g. the eye.

Sensory neurone
A nerve cell that carries electrical impulses from the receptors in the sense organs to the CNS.

Sexual reproduction
A type of reproduction involving the fusion of male and female gametes from two parents. The offspring contain a mixture of their parents' genes and so are genetically different to their parents.

Smart material
A material that has properties that change in response to external stimuli, like heat or pressure.

Soft drug
A drug that is believed to be less addictive and less harmful to a person's health than a hard drug.

Solar cell
A device that generates electricity directly from the Sun's radiation.

Specific heat capacity
The amount of energy (in joules) needed to raise the temperature of 1 kg of a material by 1 °C.

Stable community
A community in which the materials taken out of the soil and used are balanced by those that are put back in — the materials are constantly cycled.

Start-up time
The time it takes to get a power station up and running from scratch.

Statins
A group of medicinal drugs that are used to decrease the risk of heart and circulatory disease.

Sterilisation (avoiding contamination)
The process of destroying microorganisms (such as bacteria) on an object.

Stimulant
A type of performance-enhancing drug that increases heart rate.

Stimulus
A change in the environment.

Subatomic particle
A particle that is smaller than an atom. Protons, neutrons and electrons are all subatomic particles.

Surface area to volume ratio
The ratio of the surface area and volume of an object. The higher the surface area to volume ratio of an object, the higher the rate of energy transfer between the object and its surroundings.

Synapse
The connection between two neurones.

Systematic error
An error that is consistently made every time throughout an experiment.

Target cell
A particular cell in a particular place, which is affected by a hormone.

Tectonic plates
The huge chunks of crust and upper part of the mantle that float on the mantle below.

Temperature
A measure of how hot an object is.

Thalidomide
A drug that was developed as a sleeping pill in the 1950s, but that harmed babies when used untested on pregnant women to relieve morning sickness.

Theory
A hypothesis which has been accepted by the scientific community because there is good evidence to back it up.

Thermal decomposition
A reaction where one substance chemically changes into at least two new substances when it's heated.

Tidal barrage
A dam built across a river estuary with turbines connected to generators inside. When there's a difference in water height on either side, water flows through the dam, turning the turbines and generating electricity.

Tissue culture (plants)
A method of cloning plants in which a few plant cells are put on a growth medium containing hormones and allowed to grow into new plants.

Toxicity
How harmful something is, e.g. a drug.

Toxin
A poison. Toxins are often produced by bacteria.

Transformer
A device that changes the voltage of an electricity supply. Step-up transformers increase the voltage and step-down transformers decrease the voltage.

Transition metals
The metal elements found in the central block of the periodic table.

Transverse wave
A wave in which the vibrations are perpendicular (at 90°) to the direction of energy transfer.

Trial run
A quick version of an experiment that can be used to work out the range of variables and the interval between the variables that will be used in the proper experiment.

Trophic level
A stage in a food chain.

Type 2 diabetes
A condition in which the body is unable to control blood sugar level.

U-value
A measure of how effective a material is at insulating. The lower the U-value, the better the insulator.

Unsaturated
A molecule that contains at least one double bond and so can have more atoms added to it.

Uterus
The main female reproductive organ and where the embryo develops during pregnancy. (Another word for the womb.)

Vaccination
The injection of dead or inactive microorganisms to provide immunity against a particular pathogen.

Valid result
A result that answers the original question.

Variable
A factor in an investigation that can change or be changed (e.g. temperature or concentration).

Variation
The differences that exist between individuals.

Virtual image
An image that is formed when light rays appear to have come from one point, but have actually come from another.

Virus
A disease-causing agent about 1/100th of the size of a bacterial cell. Can only replicate within host body cells.

Viscosity
How runny or gloopy a substance is.

Volatility
How easily a substance turns into a gas.

Wasted energy
Energy that is dissipated (lost to the surroundings), often as heat.

Wave
A vibration that transfers energy without transferring any matter.

Wavelength
The length of a full cycle of a wave, e.g. from crest to crest.

White blood cell
A blood cell that is part of the immune system (and so helps to defend the body against infection).

Withdrawal symptom
A symptom, e.g. a headache, vomiting, which is caused by not taking an addictive drug.

Zero error
A type of systematic error caused by using a piece of equipment that isn't zeroed properly.

Acknowledgements

Data acknowledgements

Data used to construct the measles graph on page 38 from http://www.who.int/immunization_monitoring/diseases/big_Measles_global_coverage.JPG accessed March 2013.

Data used to produce the IVF table on page 54 from the Human Fertilisation and Embryology Authority (HFEA).

Data on pregnancy rates used in question on page 54 from the Human Fertilisation and Embryology Authority (HFEA).

Data used to create the aspirin study graph and table on page 73 reprinted from The Lancet, Vol 378, Prof John Burn et al. Long-term effect of aspirin on cancer risk in carriers of hereditary colorectal cancer: an analysis from the CAPP2 randomised controlled trial. Pages 2081-2087, © 2011, with permission from Elsevier.

Data used to construct the arctic sea ice graph on page 79 courtesy of the National Snow and Ice Data Center, University of Colorado, Boulder.

Data used to construct the big cat evolutionary tree on page 117 reprinted from Molecular Phylogenetics and Evolution, Vol 56. Brian W. Davis, Gang Li, William J. Murphy. Supermatrix and species tree methods resolve phylogenetic relationships within the big cats, Panthera (Carnivora: Felidae). Pages 64-76. © 2010, with permission from Elsevier.

Graph to show trend in atmospheric CO_2 concentration and global temperature on page 171 based on data by EPICA Community Members 2004 and Siegenthaler et al 2005.

Graph showing changing ocean acidity on page 208 from Feely, R.A., C.L. Sabine, and V.J. Fabry (2006): Carbon dioxide and our ocean legacy: Clear the air and conserve our ocean legacy. Brochure, National Environmental Trust, Washington, D.C., 4pp.

Photograph acknowledgements

Cover Photo **Nigel Cattlin**/Science Photo Library, p 2 **Gustoimages**/Science Photo Library, p 3 **Philippe Plailly**/Science Photo Library, p 4 **Philippe Plailly**/Science Photo Library, p 5 **Frank Zullo**/Science Photo Library, p 6 **Andrew Lambert Photography**/Science Photo Library, p 7 **Robert Brook**/Science Photo Library, p 8 **Tony McConnell**/Science Photo Library, p 9 **Rosenfeld Images Ltd**/Science Photo Library, p 10 **Martyn F. Chillmaid**/Science Photo Library, p 15 **Pr. M. Brauner**/Science Photo Library, p 16 **Maximilian Stock Ltd**/Science Photo Library, p 17 **Ria Novosti**/Science Photo Library, p 19 **Biophoto Associates**/Science Photo Library, p 21 **Paul Rapson**/Science Photo Library, p 23 (left) **Paul Rapson**/Science Photo Library, p 23 (right) **Paul Rapson**/Science Photo Library, p 24 (top) **Eye of Science**/Science Photo Library, p 24 (bottom) **Ami Images**/Science Photo Library, p 25 (Fig. 3) **Juergen Berger**/Science Photo Library, p 25 (Fig. 5) **Biology Media**/Science Photo Library, p 28 **Saturn Stills**/Science Photo Library, p 30 **Scott Camazine**/Science Photo Library, p 31 **Michael Gabridge/Visuals Unlimited, Inc.**/Science Photo Library, p 33 Science Photo Library, p 39 **Kate Jacobs**/Science Photo Library, p 40 **Sovereign, ISM**/Science Photo Library, p 42 **Thomas Deerinck, NCMIR**/Science Photo Library, p 43 **PH. Gerbier**/Science Photo Library, p 46 **Mark Turnball**/Science Photo Library, p 47 **Scott Camazine**/Science Photo Library, p 49 **Professors P. M. Motta & J. Van Blerkom**/ Science Photo Library, p 52 **Cordelia Molloy**/Science Photo Library, p 53 (Fig. 3) **Mauro Fermariello**/Science Photo Library, p 53 (Fig. 4) **Zephyr**/Science Photo Library, p 55 **Martin Shields**/Science Photo Library, p 56 **Martin Shields**/Science Photo Library, p 57 **Martin Shields**/Science Photo Library, p 58 **Geoff Kidd**/Science Photo Library, p 67 **St. Bartholomew's Hospital**/Science Photo Library, p 70 (Fig. 1) **James Stevenson**/Science Photo Library, p 70 (Fig. 2) **Alex Bartel**/Science Photo Library, p 74 (Fig. 1) **Mark Phillips**/Science Photo Library, p 74 (bottom) **Leonard Rue Enterprises**/Science Photo Library, p 75 (Fig. 2) **Stephen J. Krasemann**/Science Photo Library, p 75 (Fig. 3) **Bjanka Kadic**/Science Photo Library, p 76 **Nature's Images**/Science Photo Library, p 77 **John Devries**/Science Photo Library, p 78 **Dr. John Brackenbury**/Science Photo Library, p 80 **Paul Rapson**/Science Photo Library, p 81 **Vaughan Fleming**/Science Photo Library, p 89 **Gustoimages**/Science Photo Library, p 90 **Dr Jeremy Burgess**/Science Photo Library, p 94 (Fig. 1) **Kate Jacobs**/Science Photo Library, p 94 (bottom) **Coneyl Jay**/Science Photo Library, p 96 (Fig. 2) **Dr Gopal Murti**/Science Photo Library, p 96 (Fig. 3) **Power and Syred**/Science Photo Library, p 97 **Manfred Kage**/Science Photo Library, p 98 **Eye of Science**/Science Photo Library, p 99 **Wim van Egmond/Visuals Unlimited, Inc.**/Science Photo Library, p 100 (top) **Sinclair Stammers**/Science Photo Library, p 100 (bottom) **Nigel Cattlin/Holt Studios**/Science Photo Library, p 101 **Gerard Peaucellier, ISM**/Science Photo Library, p 102 (Fig. 6) **James King-Holmes**/Science Photo Library, p 102 (Fig. 8) **Gustoimages**/Science Photo Library, p 103 **Tony Camacho**/Science Photo Library, p 106 (top) **Pasieka**/Science Photo Library, p 106 (bottom) **Bill Barksdale/Agstockusa**/Science Photo Library, p 108 **Gary Parker**/Science Photo Library, p 110 Science Photo Library, p 113 **Sheila Terry**/Science Photo Library, p 115 (top) **Tom & Pat Leeson**/Science Photo Library, p 115 (bottom) **Richard Herrmann/Visuals Unlimited, Inc.**/Science Photo Library, p 117 (Fig. 2) **Christopher Swann**/Science Photo Library, p 117 (middle) **Matthew Oldfield**/Science Photo Library, p 119 **Ken M. Highfill**/Science Photo Library, p 121 Science Photo Library, p 124 **Andrew Lambert Photography**/Science Photo Library, p 125 (top) **Aaron Haupt**/Science Photo Library, p 125 (bottom) **Chris Martin-Bahr**/Science Photo Library, p 128 (top) Science Photo Library, p 128 (middle) **Andrew Lambert Photography**/Science Photo Library, p 128 (bottom) **Martyn F. Chillmaid**/Science Photo Library, p 138 **Andrew Lambert Photography**/Science Photo Library, p 141 **Andrew Lambert Photography**/Science Photo Library, p 142 **Ria Novosti**/Science Photo Library, p 143 (top) **Martin Bond**/Science Photo Library, p 143 (bottom) **Martin Bond**/Science Photo Library, p 145 **Ben Johnson**/Science Photo Library, p 149 **Dirk Wiersma**/Science Photo Library, p 151 **Patrick Dumas/Eurelios**/Science Photo Library, p 153 **Philippe Psaila**/Science Photo Library, p 154 **Custom Medical Stock Photo**/Science Photo Library, p 156 **David Guyon**/Science Photo Library, p 157 **Martin Bond**/Science Photo Library, p 160 **Christophe Vander Eecken/Reporters**/Science Photo Library, p 164 **Paul Rapson**/Science Photo Library, p 168 **Martyn F. Chillmaid**/Science Photo Library, p 170 (top) **Simon Fraser**/Science Photo Library, p 170 (bottom) **Adam Hart-Davis**/Science Photo Library, p 171 **Bjorn Svensson**/Science Photo Library, p 173 **Ashley Cooper, Visuals Unlimited**/Science Photo Library, p 174 **Martin Bond**/Science Photo Library, p 178 **Paul Rapson**/Science Photo Library, p 179 **Paul Rapson**/Science Photo Library, p 180 (top) **Richard Folwell**/Science Photo Library, p 180 (bottom) **Andy Levin**/Science Photo Library, p 182 **Jerry Mason**/Science Photo Library, p 186 **Victor de Schwanberg**/Science Photo Library, p 189 **Sheila Terry**/Science Photo Library, p 190 **David Munns**/Science Photo Library, p 193 **Paul Rapson**/Science Photo Library, p 194 (left) **Martyn F. Chillmaid**/Science Photo Library, p 194 (right) **Martyn F. Chillmaid**/Science Photo Library, p 195 **Martyn F. Chillmaid**/Science Photo Library, p 200 **Sinclair Stammers**/Science Photo Library, p 202 **Theodore Clutter**/Science Photo Library, p 203 **Ria Novosti**/Science Photo Library, p 204 **Bernhard Edmaier**/Science Photo Library, p 206 **Andrew Lambert Photography**/Science Photo Library, p 207 **Steve Allen**/Science Photo Library, p 214 **Mark Sykes**/Science Photo Library, p 215 **Mehau Kulyk**/Science Photo Library, p 216 **Charles D. Winters**/Science Photo Library, p 220 **Martyn F. Chillmaid**/Science Photo Library, p 222 **Tek Image**/Science Photo Library, p 224 **Scimat**/Science Photo Library, p 225 **Tony Craddock**/Science Photo Library, p 226 **Norman Chan**/iStockphoto, p 227 (left) **John Beatty**/Science Photo Library, p 227 (right) **Mark Phillips**/Science Photo Library, p 228 **Carlos Dominguez**/Science Photo Library, p 229 **Mark Sykes**/Science Photo Library, p 230 **Tony McConnell**/Science Photo Library, p 234 **Martyn F. Chillmaid**/Science Photo Library, p 238 **Paul Rapson**/Science Photo Library, p 239 **Trevor Clifford Photography**/Science Photo Library, p 241 **Victor De Schwanberg**/Science Photo Library, p 242 (left) **Victor De Schwanberg**/Science Photo Library, p 242 (right) **Murat Giray Kaya**/iStockphoto, p 243 **Cynoclub**/iStockphoto, p 244 **PagaDesign**/iStockphoto, p 253 **Sheila Terry**/Science Photo Library, p 255 **Cordelia Molloy**/Science Photo Library, p 256 (Fig. 2) **Brian Bell**/Science Photo Library, p 256 (Fig. 3) **GustoImages**/Science Photo Library, p 260 **Martin Bond**/Science Photo Library, p 261 **Chris Hellier**/Science Photo Library, p 262 (Fig. 4) **Paul Rapson**/Science Photo Library, p 262 (Fig. 5) **Martin Bond**/Science Photo Library, p 263 **David Parker**/Science Photo Library, p 264 **Jerry Mason**/Science Photo Library, p 265 **Martin Bond**/Science Photo Library, p 266 **Martin Bond**/Science Photo Library, p 267 **Martin Bond**/Science Photo Library, p 268 **Ashley Cooper, Visuals Unlimited**/Science Photo Library, p 269 **U.S. Coast Guard**/Science Photo Library, p 270 **Matteis/Look at Sciences**/Science Photo Library, p 273 **David Woodfall Images**/Science Photo Library, p 276 **Ria Novosti**/Science Photo Library, p 277 (Fig. 3) **Ictor**/iStockphoto, p 277 (Fig. 4) **Richard R. Hansen**/Science Photo Library, p 277 (Fig. 5) **David Nunuk**/Science Photo Library, p 284 **Tek Image**/Science Photo Library, p 287 **David Weintraub**/Science Photo Library, p 289 **Alistair Cotton**/iStockphoto, p 293 **Alex Bartel**/Science Photo Library, p 294 (Fig. 4) **European Space Agency**/Science Photo Library, p 294 (Fig 5) **Cordelia Molloy**/Science Photo Library, p 295 **Kevin Curtis**/Science Photo Library, p 296 (Fig. 1) **Tony McConnell**/Science Photo Library, p 296 (Fig. 2) **George Steinmetz**/Science Photo Library, p 297 (top) **Spirit of America**/Shutterstock, p 297 (bottom) **Spirit of America**/Shutterstock, p 299 **LTH NHS Trust**/Science Photo Library, p 303 **Merlin D. Tuttle**/Science Photo Library, p 308 **NASA**/Science Photo Library, p 315 **Martyn F. Chillmaid**/Science Photo Library, p 319 Science Photo Library, p 321 **Visual7**/iStockphoto, p 323 Science Photo Library, p 331 **Photostock-Israel**/Science Photo Library.

Every effort has been made to locate copyright holders and obtain permission to reproduce sources. For those sources where it has been difficult to trace the originator of the work, we would be grateful for information. If any copyright holder would like us to make an amendment to the acknowledgements, please notify us and we will gladly update the book at the next reprint. Thank you.

Index

Equations Page

If you're going to be tested on physics in an exam, you'll be given an equations sheet listing some of the equations you might need to use. That means you don't have to learn them (hurrah), but you still need to be able to pick out the correct equations to use and be really confident using them. The equations sheet won't give you any units for the equation quantities — so make sure you know them inside out.

The equations you'll be given in the exam are all on this page, along with a few handy tips on how to use formula triangles. You can use this sheet as a reference sheet when you're doing the exam-style questions at the end of each physics section.

Equations

E = energy transferred $\longrightarrow$ $E = m \times c \times \theta$ $\longleftarrow$ θ = temperature change

m = mass $\qquad$ c = specific heat capacity

$$\text{efficiency} = \frac{\text{useful energy out}}{\text{total energy in}} \qquad \text{efficiency} = \frac{\text{useful power out}}{\text{total power in}}$$

Efficiencies can be converted from a decimal into a percentage by multiplying by 100.

E = energy transferred $\longrightarrow$ $E = P \times t$ $\longleftarrow$ t = time

P = power

v = speed $\longrightarrow$ $v = f \times \lambda$ $\longleftarrow$ λ = wavelength

f = frequency

Formula triangles **Higher**

If you're sitting the higher exams, it's dead important to learn how to rearrange equations. You can put most equations into a triangle to help you rearrange them. There are two easy rules:

- If the formula is "$A = B \times C$" then A goes on the top and $B \times C$ goes on the bottom.
- If the formula is "$A = B \div C$" then B must go on the top (because that's the only way it'll give "B divided by something") — and so pretty obviously A and C must go on the bottom.

Example Higher

The equation $v = f \times \lambda$ will make this formula triangle:

To use a formula triangle, cover up the thing you want to find and write down what's left showing. To find λ in the example formula triangle, cover up λ and you get v/f left showing, so "$\lambda = v/f$" (or "$\lambda = v \div f$" if you prefer).

The Periodic Table

Relative atomic mass (A$_r$)

Atomic (proton) number

1 H Hydrogen 1		

Group 1	Group 2												Group 3	Group 4	Group 5	Group 6	Group 7	Group 0
																		4 He Helium 2
7 Li Lithium 3	9 Be Beryllium 4												11 B Boron 5	12 C Carbon 6	14 N Nitrogen 7	16 O Oxygen 8	19 F Fluorine 9	20 Ne Neon 10
23 Na Sodium 11	24 Mg Magnesium 12												27 Al Aluminium 13	28 Si Silicon 14	31 P Phosphorus 15	32 S Sulfur 16	35.5 Cl Chlorine 17	40 Ar Argon 18
39 K Potassium 19	40 Ca Calcium 20	45 Sc Scandium 21	48 Ti Titanium 22	51 V Vanadium 23	52 Cr Chromium 24	55 Mn Manganese 25	56 Fe Iron 26	59 Co Cobalt 27	59 Ni Nickel 28	63.5 Cu Copper 29	65 Zn Zinc 30		70 Ga Gallium 31	73 Ge Germanium 32	75 As Arsenic 33	79 Se Selenium 34	80 Br Bromine 35	84 Kr Krypton 36
85 Rb Rubidium 37	88 Sr Strontium 38	89 Y Yttrium 39	91 Zr Zirconium 40	93 Nb Niobium 41	96 Mo Molybdenum 42	98 Tc Technetium 43	101 Ru Ruthenium 44	103 Rh Rhodium 45	106 Pd Palladium 46	108 Ag Silver 47	112 Cd Cadmium 48		115 In Indium 49	119 Sn Tin 50	122 Sb Antimony 51	128 Te Tellurium 52	127 I Iodine 53	131 Xe Xenon 54
133 Cs Caesium 55	137 Ba Barium 56	139 La Lanthanum 57	178 Hf Hafnium 72	181 Ta Tantalum 73	184 W Tungsten 74	186 Re Rhenium 75	190 Os Osmium 76	192 Ir Iridium 77	195 Pt Platinum 78	197 Au Gold 79	201 Hg Mercury 80		204 Tl Thallium 81	207 Pb Lead 82	209 Bi Bismuth 83	209 Po Polonium 84	210 At Astatine 85	222 Rn Radon 86
223 Fr Francium 87	226 Ra Radium 88	227 Ac Actinium 89	261 Rf Rutherfordium 104	262 Db Dubnium 105	266 Sg Seaborgium 106	264 Bh Bohrium 107	277 Hs Hassium 108	268 Mt Meitnerium 109	271 Ds Darmstadtium 110	272 Rg Roentgenium 111								

Periods 1 2 3 4 5 6 7